Compton Mackenzie

24. FEB 95	M Hutch
24. MAR. 1995	SIMPSON RW
31. 05. 95	Luran 06
3RD COPY	Barraclaugl
	6 anderson
	Silver K w
	M Robertso 06
	Noble
	Noble
	Cameron AC

This book is due for return on or before the last date indicated on label. Renewals may be obtained on application.

PERTH AND KINROSS DISTRICT LIBRARY

Compton Mackenzie
A Life

ANDRO LINKLATER

The Hogarth Press
LONDON

Published in 1992 by
The Hogarth Press
20 Vauxhall Bridge Road
London SW1V 2SA

First published by
Chatto & Windus Ltd 1987

A CIP catalogue record for this book is
available from the British Library.

ISBN 0 7012 0984 4

Printed and bound in Great Britain by
Mackays of Chatham PLC, Chatham, Kent

Cover design and illustration by Jeff Fisher

FOR MARTIN AND MARIE LOUISE

Contents

List of illustrations

Acknowledgements

Lady Mackenzie has had to wait much longer than she should have to see the completion of this biography of her husband. I should like to acknowledge with gratitude her patience and the kindness and encouragement she has shown me at every stage of research and writing.

I am also indebted for their generosity with letters, reminiscences and observations to Sir Compton's many friends and acquaintances, and especially to: the late Lord Boothby, Dr J. L. Campbell, Nicholas Crocker, Monica Dickens, Joan Forman, Hamish Hamilton, Sir Rupert Hart-Davis, Alan Howard, T. E. B. Howarth, Robin MacEwen, Ruairidh MacKay, E. M. C. Mackenzie, L. Mackenzie Miall, Diana Pym, Adrian and Anthea Secker, Sylvia Secker, the late Norah Smallwood, Janet Stone, Colin Summerford, the late Frank Swinnerton, Fred Urquhart, the late Joyce Weiner, Terence de Vere White.

My debt is particularly great to Janet Dunbar, who let me read her unpublished biography of Sir Compton, and to Fred Urquhart, who allowed me to make use of the notes and material he had assembled for a projected biography.

I am also grateful for help from: Verily Anderson, Rodney Bennett, Alan Bold, Mrs Lorna Byrne, Francis Bywater, Joan Cope, Noel Dinwiddie, Barbara Guest, David Horne, Angus Macdougall, Mrs Raggett, Sir Brooks Richards, Miss C. B. Stewart, Nicholas Wright.

The Humanities Research Center of the University of Texas in Austin houses the library and papers of Sir Compton Mackenzie among its unrivalled collection of manuscripts, books and personal papers pertaining to twentieth-century writers in English. I should like to add my tribute to those of many other biographers who have benefited from the efficiency and kindness of its staff. I must also acknowledge the help given by the staff of the British Library, the London Library, the National Portrait Gallery, the St Paul's School archives, and the BBC Written Archives at Caversham.

I would like to thank the Scottish Arts Council for their travel and research grant which enabled me to return to Texas for further research.

Finally, I must record my heartfelt appreciation of Jeremy Lewis's saint-like patience and editorial prodding.

I gratefully acknowledge permission to use quotations from the following works: from Macdonald & Co. for *The Passionate Elopement, Carnival, Sinister Street, Guy and Pauline, The Adventures of Sylvia Scarlett*; from Chatto & Windus for *Vestal Fire, Extraordinary Women, The East Wind of Love, The South Wind of Love, The West Wind of Love, The North Wind of Love, Gallipoli Memories, Athenian Memories, My Life and Times* Octaves One to Ten; from William Collins *As Much as I Dare* by Faith Compton Mackenzie; from Heinemann for *The Georgian Literary Scene* by Frank Swinnerton and *Francis Brett-Young* by Jessica Brett-Young; from Hutchinson for *Figures in the Foreground* by Frank Swinnerton; from Routledge and Kegan Paul for *A Fretful Midge* by Terence de Vere White; from Constable for *Ellen Terry and Bernard Shaw; a correspondence* edited by Christopher St John; from the Estate of Eric Linklater for *The Man on My Back*; and from Valda Grieve and Martin Brian and O'Keeffe for *The Complete Poems of Hugh MacDiarmid* edited by Michael Grieve and W. R. Aitken.

The author and publisher would like to thank the following for illustrations reproduced here:
BBC Hulton Picture Library: 1, 14, 20; Cannon Films and the National Film Archive: 22; *The Glasgow Herald*: 18, 19, 25; The John Hillelson Agency Ltd (photo: Eve Arnold – Magnum): 30; Keystone Press: 24; Manders and Mitchenson Theatre Collection: 5; National Portrait Gallery: 4; Kenneth Robertson: 31; *The Scotsman*: 26, 27; Topham Picture Library: 28, 29.

Foreword

The life of Compton Mackenzie is not shrouded in mystery. Among the sources of information available to a biographer are ten volumes of autobiography, four of war memoirs, and seven of miscellaneous memories; in all a total of over three million words of self-description beside which the eight tomes of Casanova's *Memoirs* seem modest. In addition to this overtly autobiographical writing, Mackenzie wrote a dozen works of non-fiction on subjects as various as the Duke of Windsor, the tobacco industry and the National Trust, in which he was drawn to dwell at some length upon the events of his own life.

It must be said that in his place few could have resisted the temptation to mine so rich a seam. By the age of forty he had been successively poet, preacher, novelist and spy, and to such effect that Arthur Quiller-Couch anthologised his verse, at least one of his congregation could remember the theme of a sermon half a century later, Henry James designated him 'by far the most promising novelist of his generation', and Mansfield Cumming, founder of the Secret Intelligence Service (later MI6), wanted to appoint him his successor. In the last forty years of his life he was a record enthusiast who founded the *Gramophone* magazine, a political idealist who helped to bring the Scottish nationalist movement into being, an early radio personality and one of television's first big names, as well as continuing to be a full-time author who produced over one hundred books before he died in 1972.

Since he was blessed with a memory which retained vividly the images of faces, places and events from as far back as an observation made at the age of seven months, this dizzying succession of achievements is recorded in some detail. By blood and background, however, Mackenzie was an actor. Adept though he was at taking on a role, he rarely betrayed the man behind the mask in his autobiographical writings.

His personal papers, which are housed with efficiency and care by the Humanities Resources Center at the University of Texas in Austin, are scarcely more revealing. This is not because they are few in number. No doubt some correspondence and newspaper clippings were lost in his frequent moves from house to house, but what survives appears to include the entire contents of his postbag from about the age of thirty onwards, together with copies of many of his own letters, typescripts of novels, tax returns, visiting cards, bills and press notices. There are also some of his mother's and first wife's personal papers, among them the latter's diary covering the entire period of their marriage. I once estimated that a researcher working all the hours that the Center remains open would take almost two years to read and note all their contents. I should admit now that it was not possible to devote so much time.

Despite their abundance, the personal papers offer little more than the published works in the realm of self-revelation. His letters in particular tended to be dashed off in a hurry – and in the execrable hand of a natural left-hander trained to hold the pen in his right – which allowed little scope for rumination or confession.

With great kindness, his widow and friends have also helped with their memories. Although one close friend thought that he might not have wanted a biography written, I eventually met four different people whom he had encouraged to undertake the project. Two of them did devote much time to it, and with the utmost generosity let me profit from their labour.

In the face of such a bountiful supply of information it seems almost wilful to have concluded that it did not adequately explain the variety of his career and the waywardness of his writing. The real key to these mysteries seemed to lie in his fiction, and especially the early novels, *Carnival*, *Sinister Street* and *Guy and Pauline*, and the great work of his middle age, *The Four Winds of Love*. All are built closely upon events in his own life and upon emotions connected with those events so that their male protagonists, Maurice Avery, Michael Fane, Guy Hazlewood and John Ogilvie often appear as shadows of their author rather than simply creations of his imagination. This is especially true of Michael Fane in *Sinister Street* and John Ogilvie in *The Four Winds of Love*, and in certain instances I have felt it legitimate to infer directly Mackenzie's emotional reaction from that of his characters. For example, where both Mackenzie and Fane share the same house as children, suffer the same nightmares and the same drunken nanny to whose repressive regime each is left by their adored but absent mother, I have assumed that the effect upon the author's state of mind was the same as upon his creation's. Equally when the middle-aged Ogilvie first discovers a Scots heritage behind his English upbringing and education, and then commits himself to Scottish nationalism, I have allowed his enthusiasm to amplify Mackenzie's in the same circumstances for the same cause.

Apart from the circumstantial evidence pointing to this direct connection, there is another more immediate link. Mackenzie's ability to relive his past was the essential source from which his fiction was constructed, and critics repeatedly accused him of relying more on this faculty than on imagination. His reply was not so much a rebuttal as a deflection. 'Such critics forgot (if most of them ever knew) that Mnemosyne was by Zeus the mother of the Nine Muses,' he wrote in his autobiography. 'The mythopoeia of Hellas had no doubt of the importance of memory to art.'

Everyone who checked his memory while he was still alive was eventually convinced that although he might embellish, he did not invent. Despite my own scepticism, I came to the same conclusion. In addition, when I came to check the letters and reports quoted in his autobiography I found they were quoted accurately and in context with little of any moment being omitted in the editing. In consequence the main facts of his biography accord closely with those of his autobiography – a comparatively rare coincidence. The difference lies in the perspective provided by the personal papers of his mother and his first wife, and by his own fiction. Although these sometimes throw a darker light on events treated lightly in his reminiscences, they also help to explain the extraordinary and probably unique nature of his writing.

ANDRO LINKLATER

The first stage

On a dark winter's evening in the reign of William IV, a party of wandering actors persuaded a farmer to ferry them across the Humber. The boat he used for transporting cows was the only one available, but they all crowded aboard, among them the company's 'First Low Comedian', a good-looking young man whose stage name was Henry Compton. As the boat approached the far shore, a voice called out from the jetty to ask what cargo she was carrying. 'Nowt but lakers and dung,' the ferryman shouted back.

This accurately conveyed the social standing of lakers or actors or, as the profession had it, theatricals. Outside London, only the larger towns had theatres; elsewhere the company would play in the open or a temporary booth. As wandering players they ranked a little above gypsies, and the resident companies were only a degree more respectable.

Although he would later tell the story as a joke, Henry Compton must have felt the implied slur more than most. He had begun life as Charles Mackenzie, the son of a prosperous family with an interest in the London docks, and as a youth was apprenticed to his uncle's respectable clothing business. His father John Mackenzie had taken to preaching in Nonconformist chapels, but this had been the only sign of a theatrical streak in the blood. For three generations, ever since the first of the family came south from Cromarty in the Highlands of Scotland, they had been unremarkable but prosperous wharfingers on the Thames.

When John Mackenzie married Elizabeth Symonds, he chose his wife from a family whose vigorous Puritanism merely reflected his own, and it was to save both Mackenzies and Symondses the shame of having a relation on the stage that their son changed his name. Where the Henry came from is a mystery, but Compton was his grandmother's maiden name. The disguise should have been impenetrable, but his background was too unusual in the theatre not to attract attention.

'I am told that you have considerable humour and that you are a gentleman,' a playwright wrote to him when he was beginning to make his name and appearing in the theatres at Leeds and Manchester. 'We have low comedians in London who possess the first quality, but are minus in the latter. A gentleman will always make his way.'

With the accession of Queen Victoria in 1837, the fortunes of both the stage and Henry Compton took a step upwards. In that year the thirty-two-year-old actor received his first London engagement, and writing to him the manager of the Theatre Royal Lyceum prophesied, 'Theatricals must turn for the better, as they are now at their worst. The young Queen must be fêted. She will encourage the stage; all young persons love it.'

Curiously enough she did. Over the next forty years the stage and Henry Compton in particular advanced in public esteem to such an extent that he was commanded to perform at Windsor Castle and, after his death in 1877, the Queen took two boxes at a benefit performance for his widow and children.

Of the three categories of comedian – broad, low and light – the low comedian approximates to the actor who today would be known as 'specialising in comic roles'; the broad was more or less farce and clowning, while the light could take Restoration comedy parts and was often indistinguishable from the romantic lead. Throughout his career, Henry Compton restricted himself to the low comedian's range. His Lancelot Gobbo and Tony Lumpkin became such favourites that in Leeds the audience took up a collection to present him with a silver snuff-box, and from Manchester he received a watch and chain. In his last years, when he played the First Gravedigger to Henry Irving's Hamlet, a London critic wrote, 'In every scene but one, [Irving] was the centre of attention, but in that one scene in which he came to dialogue with the Grave-digger, Mr Compton, he fell immediately and naturally into second place.'

A man of great vigour, Compton used to exercise by sparring with the prizefighter Jem Ward, or by rowing with the Thames watermen, activities more in keeping with the Regency era of his youth. Despite the success of his own career, he also kept the prejudice of the early nineteenth century against the stage, and when he married an actress, Elizabeth Montague, in 1847, he immediately insisted that she give up her career, only permitting her to take part in the amateur productions put on by his friend, Charles Dickens.

Such attitudes were becoming outdated, and he himself had done much to transform them. After his death an anonymous 'Clergyman of the Church of England' wrote in appreciation of 'an actor who, more than any other comedian, has helped me and thousands of others to understand certain sides of Shakespearean comedy, and who is further-more one of the truest, most self-respecting, most artistic actors the stage in our time has seen'.

Nevertheless his death in 1877 left his family in such poverty that two huge benefits were given for them in London and Manchester. Even at the height of his fame he did not earn more than twenty pounds a week, and for much of the time had to bring up a family of seven children on an income of much less. He warned them individually and collectively against adopting a career which offered such high risks for so little financial reward. 'I've worked hard, played hard and travelled hard,' he would say, 'but I've brought home little hard cash.'

When Henry Compton died, a great theatrical boom was just begin-ning. Theatres were being built at such speed that by the end of the century the smallest towns had at least one, and larger cities like Leicester or Northampton had three or four. For probably the only time in its history there was something close to full employment on the stage. In contrast to Henry Compton's youth, newcomers were attracted to it in such numbers that in 1900 three-quarters of London's actors and actresses came from a non-theatrical background.

'Five and twenty years ago a gentleman was rare on the stage,' remarked the actor-manager, Seymour Hicks, in 1910. 'Nowadays gentlemen hover round it thick as May flies on a Hampshire stream.'

The offspring of lawyers, soldiers, parsons and colonial servants, these newcomers brought with them the standards of their parents, and a consequent concern for the respectability of 'the dramatic profession'.

Although it had risen far in social terms since the beginning of the reign, the late Victorians were never quite sure exactly where the stage did rank in a socially sensitive world. They certainly never accorded it the status of a profession like the law. They were doubtful of actresses' morals, and they knew, or suspected, that many theatres, especially those featuring the ballet, became the haunt of prostitutes, who were attracted by the men in the audience who in turn were attracted by the girls on stage. Yet when Henry Irving was knighted in 1898, the accolade recognised not only his dramatic genius but the acceptability of his career. In different ways that ambivalence profoundly affected the lives of both Compton's son Edward and his grandson Compton Mackenzie.

Despite Henry Compton's warning against it as a career, six of his seven children went on the stage, and his second son Edward quickly showed that he had the looks, voice and talent to leap out of the comedian class and play romantic leads. In 1879 he toured the United States playing opposite Adelaide Neilson, who rivalled and some thought surpassed Ellen Terry as the leading actress of the day. When they fell in love and became engaged to be married, Edward Compton could count himself exceptionally blessed – he was astonishingly handsome, a leading man at twenty-five, and about to marry one of the outstanding actresses of her generation.

In August 1880 they went to Paris to buy her trousseau, but just before leaving a premonition made Adelaide suggest that she should change her will in order to leave everything to her fiancé. Edward dismissed her fears, unwisely as it turned out. Soon after they arrived in Paris she drank a glass of iced milk and a little later collapsed in his arms. That same evening she died. With Adelaide Neilson's death went not only his marriage but his professional and financial future as well. So profound was the shock that most of his hair fell out, and when her will was published it showed that she had left just £2000 to him, but £25,000 to 'my old and steadfast friend, Admiral Henry Glyn'.

If in later life Edward became a little tedious in his desire for the safety which wealth confers, it can be argued that he knew from experience how far down the ladder an impecunious actor could fall. Certainly the memory of his father's grinding struggle against poverty was never far from his mind.

To play romantic leads in a toupee was impossible, and with a commendable lack of self-pity he became a light comedian, specialising in roles where a wig or some other headgear could be worn.

Adelaide Neilson's bequest was large enough for him to form his own touring company, the Compton Comedy Company, or CCC. By February 1881 his players were hired, rehearsed and costumed (scenery and props were provided by the theatres), and he had secured a sufficient number of bookings from theatres outside London to take the company out on its first tour. The core of their repertory was eighteenth-century comedy, such as *She Stoops to Conquer* and *The Rivals*, which conveniently required an actor to wear a becoming wig whatever the state of his scalp. The freak resemblance of Compton to one of his actors, William Calvert, allowed them to play *The Comedy of Errors*, and his own favourite role came in an eighteenth-century pastiche called *Davy Garrick*. A policy of giving the public what they wanted – in Cork, for instance, he allowed the plays to be selected by public vote – combined with rigorous economy, made the CCC a financial success from the start. At the end of only his second season, in June 1882, a trade paper quoted him as saying, 'I've worked hard, played hard and travelled hard, and notwithstanding the hard times I've netted sufficient hard cash to prevent my being hard up.' The shade of Henry Compton must have nodded approvingly.

In that same month Edward married his leading lady, Virginia Bateman. He had always been susceptible to a pretty face, and when she became engaged to another actor in the company, Fred Wyndham, his competitive instincts were aroused. Amidst scenes of jealousy and upbraiding, one engagement was broken off and another entered into, to be followed swiftly by a wedding.

His new wife came, like him, from a theatrical family, her two elder sisters being child prodigies on the stage in the United States and Britain, while her younger sister had appeared frequently as Irving's leading lady at the Lyceum. She was the daughter of the American theatrical impresario, Hezekiah Linthicum Bateman, who had launched Irving to stardom and indeed employed Edward's father as the Gravedigger in that memorable *Hamlet*.

When he came to examine the influence of inheritance upon his character, Compton Mackenzie could find little to thank his father's family for other than 'my sense of responsibility', which he thought came from the Comptons, and 'my amiable temperament', which was inherited from Emmeline Montague, his grandmother. The Batemans, on the other hand, seemed much more promising as the breeding-ground of genius.

Named after an obscure prophet and in childhood stuffed full of Methodism until he ran away from home, Hezekiah spent the rest of his life cursing, drinking and publicising himself, his family and his theatres. To spread the fame of the then unknown Henry Irving, he persuaded the authorities in 1872 to let him decorate the Strand with cardboard bells, ostensibly to celebrate Queen Victoria's thirty-five years on the throne, but when she drove by to a thanksgiving service in St Paul's he added billboards announcing Irving's appearance in the melodrama, *The Bells*, at Bateman's theatre, the Lyceum. Years before, in the early 1850s, he had also made stars out of his two elder daughters, Kate and Ellen, by putting them on stage at the ages of six and four respectively, and skilfully playing on the nineteenth-century public's fascination with infant prodigies. He launched them first in his native country, and their performance of scenes from Shakespeare drew huge audiences wherever they played from California to New York. Having paid Hezekiah's drink bills and gambling debts and helped to rescue their family from financial ruin, the girls were brought to London where they enjoyed the same immense popularity. Over the next decade the Batemans crossed the Atlantic regularly until at the outbreak of the American Civil War – Hezekiah was a Southerner – they made London their home.

Bateman's explosive temper had earned him the nickname 'Chain-Lightning' and, as his daughter, Virginia might have been thought to have inherited something of his temperament. It is, however, unlikely that Edward saw anything of that side of her, for in the course of an unhappy and unstable childhood she had learned to exert an ironclad control over her emotions. Dominated by a brilliant and ruthless mother, she was on the surface no more than a competent, biddable actress with an excellent memory for lines. It is possible that Edward married her for these qualities alone – she certainly never aroused in him the passion that he felt for Adelaide Neilson, whose portrait he kept hanging in the front hall throughout their married life – but it is also possible that Virginia was pregnant. They were married on 12 June 1882, just seven months before the birth of their eldest son, Edward Montague Compton Mackenzie.

The CCC had reached West Hartlepool on their touring schedule when the labour pains began. They were so protracted – for three nights and two days – that the doctor considered killing the baby in order to save the mother's life, but special forceps for which he had telegraphed to London arrived in time and on 17 January 1883 the child was delivered safely. Four weeks later he was christened with the names of his father, paternal grandmother and the family stage name, and in the parish register his surname was entered as Mackenzie. This entry was Virginia's decision – her husband had travelled on with the company – and its significance was to be made clear in the life that followed. For practical purposes, however, Edward Montague Compton Mackenzie was reduced to Monty.

As the child of touring actors, Monty led a gypsy existence in the first two and a half years of his life. Each week produced a different town and a different home. Edward always stayed in lodgings rather than a hotel, and since he was a man of strictly regular habits his landladies soon knew them as well as his wife. The company was only in its third season when his son was born, and its schedule was already taking on a rhythm which was to become as immutable as the months of the year. From August it slowly progressed northward to Christmas in Newcastle or Carlisle, and a New Year's loop through Edinburgh, Aberdeen and Glasgow. With the spring they were in Ireland, moving southward from Belfast to Cork. There was a break for Holy Week, and by May they had crossed over to Wales and the West of England towards a final holiday in June and July.

It was the railways which made the touring companies possible. They would play six nights and two matinees in a town, and on the Sunday take the train to the next booking. Until the 1860s, the provincial theatres had usually had their own stock companies, each with a repertory of farces, classics and pantomimes, for which star names would be imported to take the leading roles. With the advantage of playing together month after month, the touring companies offered a more unified and polished performance, but the acting belonged closely to the declamatory style of the stock company in which, as Bernard Shaw put it,

The actress learnt, not how to interpret plays, but how to appear sweet and gentle, or jealous and wicked, or funny and matronly, or deaf and palsied, and how to make up her face and wear wigs. The actor learnt how to appear sprightly, or romantic, or murderous, or bucolic, or doddering, and how to make funny faces. . . . The stock actor, with his conscientiously articulated elocution which reached the back row of the pit effectively (it is really more satisfactory to hear an actor say meechee-yah-eeld and know that he means my child than to hear him say msha and wonder what on earth he is mumbling), his pompous entrance which invited and seized the attention of the audience, his momentous exit on the last word of his last speech . . . could plead that he knew the routine of his business . . . But only those who have . . . lived to witness the effect of entrusting to his skilled hands a part in a play by Ibsen, can imagine how completely he could kill the dramatic idiom of a modern play.

Taught well, Shaw concluded, the technique gave an actor an immediate level of competence which only the very great could transcend, but only the very inept could fail to attain. His early exposure to this rhetorical style left its mark on Monty. It was the style he recognized as real acting – the restrained manner of Ibsen and Shaw never appealed – but he always looked on acting as a knack easily acquired. In his writing, too, it was the sweep of emotion which interested him, not the psychological structure of a character.

His acquaintanceship with the theatre began early. His mother rejoined the company two months after his birth, and at first kept him with her as much as possible. Among his earliest memories was the sight of his

7

father rehearsing the players in a new piece and of the actresses waving to him from the stage while he sat on his mother's lap. He was breast-fed in the dressing room, and when she was on stage the other women in the company became surrogate mothers. Two in particular he became so attached to he could soon attempt their names – 'Aiky' for the matronly Eleanor Aickin, and 'Newwiarp' for the young and buxom Nellie Harper – and it was one of the company's jokes that as he was being carried into a Llandudno hotel, whose entrance was guarded by two well-endowed caryatids, he had caressed one pair of stone breasts, saying 'Aiky', and then stretched out to pat the other and say 'Newwiarp'.

That he should have begun to talk when scarcely nine months old was only the outward sign of a preternatural development of consciousness. Two months earlier he had registered on his conscious memory a scene of being lifted from his pram by his nurse to see some black and white rabbits playing in a field.

'I can remember feeling surprised,' he once remarked in a broadcast, 'which shows that I must already have been watching ordinary rabbits with some interest.'

With the possible exception of Dr Johnson's friend Samuel Parr, who claimed that he could remember sucking at his mother's breast, this retention of a memory from seven months seems to be unparalleled. The schedule of the company allowed him to place the incident accurately during the July holiday, and the scene could not have been suggested to him later for the nurse left soon afterwards and when he asked his mother about the occasion she knew nothing of it. He could recall a growing number of incidents from the next eighteen months, and after the age of two his memory was almost continuous.

Any baby would have touched the hearts of the company's actresses, but one so alert and responsive must have enslaved them with little difficulty. The character of the Compton Comedy Company in fact provided an unusually secure background for a young child. Despite the strain of constant travelling and performing, it always had a reputation within the profession of being, in the words of Sydney Paxton, one of its members, 'a most comfortable engagement'. There were no real stars, and its repertory, consisting as it did mostly of eighteenth-century comedy, demanded skill and good timing rather than great presence. The atmosphere was in consequence surprisingly free of intrigue and temperament, and the fact that its best actor, Lewis Ball, stayed with it for twenty years, and others for almost as long, suggests that the majority of Edward Compton's troupe enjoyed working for him. They certainly did not stay for the money. Virginia Compton, his leading lady, was paid only five pounds a week, and she complained that the CCC was the only company she had been in which travelled third class. Paxton, too, observed that 'Mr Compton was not exactly a philanthropist with regard to salaries', but qualified the criticism by adding that he was 'a very just, level-headed manager who certainly appreciated his artistes and their work'.

Careful though he was over money, Edward Compton showed himself to be a jolly, clowning father, the reverse of the Victorian paterfamilias of legend. He had no inhibition about getting onto the ground to play with his child, and he would accommodate himself to whatever game was suggested. When his twelve-month-old 'Montyboy' began to walk a Guinness bottle across the carpet of their Glasgow lodgings, Edward gripped a Bass bottle and walked it back until they met with a satisfying clink. To Monty's demand for 'keek it' he compliantly began to kick the furniture until he realised from the boy's outrage that he was meant to fetch a cricket bat. If anything he was too exuberant. The bottle game ended in broken glass; a chase resulted in Monty's falling into a sunken water-butt, and no sooner had he been put into dry clothes than Edward engaged him in a mock battle on the edge of the bath and tumbled him into the water again. Another amusement of his father was to teach him bloodthirsty lines from Shakespeare, in Colley Cibber's version, so that given the cue, 'My lord, the Duke of Buckingham is taken,' the two-year-old Monty would thrust out his hand with the command, 'Off with his head,' and then sternly folding his pudgy arms declare, 'So much for Buckingham.' As the company made its way through the country, there were always new audiences for his performance, and fresh admirers to be charmed.

Much of this he could recall in later life, together with the oil lamp swinging above his cot in the railway compartment, the smell inside an old-fashioned pram and the sensation of being bumped over a pavement in it, and shortly after his second birthday the sight of children walking barefoot through the streets of Cork. With the exception of this last memory, which upset him, none of the early sensations was particularly distressing. There was no fixed point in his existence, or rather, the shifting world of the CCC with his mother at the centre was his entire existence. So long as she was with him all was well, and Virginia, delighted by his precocity, could always be persuaded to let him stay and amuse her.

Every Garden of Eden has its snake, and in the childhood of Compton

Mackenzie the reptile was his nanny, Annie Curry. He was almost two when she arrived to take charge not only of him but of the new baby which Virginia was expecting. She was about fifty-five at the time, but to her new charge she was 'the oldest and ugliest woman in the world'. Her hair was grey; her face small and puckered like a monkey's, and she breathed heavily through a pug nose which she used to rub with the back of her hand when annoyed.

By Victorian standards he had been shamelessly spoiled and pampered, and hopelessly over-indulged in his precocity, and Nanny made it her duty to instill the opposite virtues of self-restraint and obedience. Anything that sounded like a demand, whether for information or pleasure, was either fobbed off with non-responsive answers like 'Because' or 'Curiosity killed the cat,' or was deemed a treat which had to be earned. He had learned to read before he was two, but his books became hostages against bad behaviour and were liable to be removed as a punishment. A favourite toy, a walk on the grass, staying up later than six o'clock, and above all the chance to see his mother, all became treats which had to be merited.

From their first encounter, when he was punished for knocking a plate to the floor by being sent to bed without seeing his mother, he was 'sharply aware of the old woman's intrusion between me and my adored mother'. That was the ultimate sanction and he was powerless against it. His early resistance faded quickly and outwardly at least he surrendered to her rule.

Yet in itself, Annie Curry's behaviour, however oppressive, hardly accounts for the blight which spread so pervasively across his childhood that the fictional account of those years which appeared in *Sinister Street* was entitled 'The Prison House'. Indeed it became a cliché of his serious novels that their protagonists should suffer from an unhappy, haunted childhood – Jenny Pearl in *Carnival*, Michael Fane in *Sinister Street*, Sylvia Scarlett in the novel of the same name, and Mark Lidderdale in *The Altar Steps*. It was almost as though he could not imagine a sensitive person whose mind was not initially marked by neglect or bullying. 'I can echo the words of Seneca,' he wrote in his autobiography. '*Tenacissimi sumus eorum quae pueri percipimus*: we cling most closely to what we observed in boyhood.'

The break with his early happiness was caused by more than the arrival of a narrow-minded nanny. In the spring of 1885 his brother Frank was born, and he no longer had his mother's undivided attention even when he was with her. A year later, in June 1886, his father bought a house in London and gradually Monty ceased to live in the expansive, theatrical world of the Compton Comedy Company.

His introduction to 54 Avonmore Road, West Kensington, was gentle, and even enjoyable. For the first few nights he slept in a double bed with Nellie, a young housemaid, and catching a glimpse of her naked as she undressed by gaslight he enjoyed an infantile erection. Later in the summer he and Frank were allowed to join the CCC in Portsmouth, and significantly the sight of manacled convicts working at the harbour struck an inexpressible chord of sympathy in him. The summer holiday ended with a visit to his mother's elder sister, Kate, who was married to a tall, affable doctor called George Crowe; at their house he made his first acquaintance with a missioner-priest, the Reverend Robert Dolling, whose saintliness was later to inspire him with an ambition to become a priest himself.

When the children returned to London their parents came with them. Instead of going on tour Edward had taken the Strand Theatre for the autumn in an attempt, the first of many, to establish himself in the capital. It ought to have given Monty the chance to see more of his mother, but in November she gave birth to a daughter, Viola, who was barely weaned before the failure of Edward's season doomed the CCC to go back on the road, or rather the rails, once more. To soften the blow, his grandmother, Henry Compton's widow, came to stay and for his fourth birthday Monty was given a lancer's uniform, but nothing could blot out the catastrophe of his mother's impending departure. In February 1887, they went away on tour – his adored mother, his playful father and his coterie of loving ladies – leaving him behind at 54 Avonmore Road, an address which came to be imbued with all the mean and dispiriting qualities of his nanny.

Avonmore Road was part of the surge of speculative building in the last two decades of the nineteenth century which pushed the western boundary of London beyond Hammersmith and into Chiswick. Red brick was the material, profit the motive, and like the houses built for first-time buyers today, they offered urban respectability on the cheap. They attracted retired colonial and military officers as well as a sprinkling of theatrical and artistic families, but the majority were bought by the growing class of civil and municipal servants. Further out in Chiswick where the land was less expensive, the buildings became quite substantial, but the houses in Avonmore Road were as tall and thin and uniform as a speculative builder could make them.

Each had three storeys, an attic and a large basement which contained a kitchen and morning room. It was here that the children and servants ate. On the ground floor, a tiled hall led to the formal dining room and a drawing room. Both this and the next floor up, which consisted of the main bedroom and bathroom, were adult territory. The top floor and attic, where the nursery and servants' bedrooms were situated, again became children's ground. When his parents were at home the distinction became less important, but while they were away the two intermediate floors were closed off and the long staircase climbing past locked and silent rooms became alive with terrors.

At the back of each house, a narrow garden ran down to a railway cutting, beyond which lay coalyards and the blank backs of warehouses. Although the busy Hammersmith Road went past barely a hundred yards away, 54 Avonmore Road, set as it was between the railway line on one side and waste ground on the other, could easily seem cut off from the rest of the world, especially to a nervous child.

In *Sinister Street*, the description of the nightmare world he now entered opens with two-year-old Michael Fane examining the iron bars of his cot:

for Michael each bar possessed a personality. Minute scratches lent variety of expression: slight irregularities infused certain groups with an air of deliberate consultation. From the four corners royal bars, crowned with brass, dominated their subjects. Passions, intrigues, rumours, ambitions, revenges were perceived by Michael to be seething below the rigid exterior . . . one bar in particular, set very much askew, seemed sly and malignant.

Adult though the language is, the microscopic vision and anthropomorphic fancy have the authentic ring of a small child's experience. Seen with this acute attention, in which eye and imagination overlapped, the jerry-built structure of number 54 came alarmingly to life. The attic which served as the day nursery was a friendly room with a sloping roof and wallpaper patterned in green leaves; on the floor below there was a spare bedroom and the night nursery where the children's two little cots flanked the enormous bed belonging to Nanny. There the floor was covered with cold oilcloth – forerunner of linoleum – and a small cupboard stood stocked with every variety of liquid and powder which might loosen the bowels; the only safe place was the narrow cot guarded by iron bars. Even this had its dangers, for when he first looked out of the window at the coalyards beyond the railway line, Nanny warned him that the coalmen might carry him away if he misbehaved.

'Can they climb?' he asked anxiously.

'Climb like kittens,' she assured him, and the cry of the coalmen in the streets outside became as menacing as a leopard's in the jungle.

Nanny's influence was equally strong downstairs, and especially in the morning room with its rituals of breakfast porridge and dinner of mutton and suet pudding, eaten under threat of Dr Gregory's powder or some other patent laxative from the well-stocked cupboard. Through the muddy windows he could see the yellow gaze of cats on the sill and the inquisitive stare of pedlars and tramps coming down the steps to the tradesmen's entrance. The one comfortable room was the kitchen, well guarded by an iron railing outside the window, and warm with the smell of cooking.

There were two servants, a cook and a housemaid, but in his parents' absence it was Nanny who ran the household. Every morning he was taken for a walk in Kensington Gardens, his brother Frank in the pram and Monty tagging along at Nanny's side under orders not to stray and certainly not to talk or play with other children. In the afternoon he was usually left to read. He devoured books obsessively, everything from nursery rhymes to *Don Quixote*, which he read at the age of five.

Throughout this time, and until he was four and a half years old, he referred to himself not as 'I' but in the third person as 'Monty'. This habit usually disappears once a reasonable command of language has been achieved. In his case the command of language was attained so early and the failure to use 'I' so delayed that one can only assume that it did reflect an understanding that he existed for other people rather than for himself. All his mother's comments on his behaviour in these earliest years were of his responsiveness to others – 'You were always ready to be interested,' or 'How anxious you were to be good' – and he himself had no memories of self-assertive rebellion against Nanny's rule.

It is easy to imagine that Annie Curry, with her rigid idea of how a child ought to behave, must have been further irritated by his long continuation with a form which would have sounded self-important. When he brought home a bunch of speedwell flowers and told her they were the same shade of blue as 'Monty's eyes', she told him sharply that he had mousy-brown hair and had no call to be conceited. His opinions were dismissed as 'old-fashioned' and his attitude towards his younger brother as 'dictatorial'. Compared to the emotional surfeit of the Compton Comedy Company, he was now on starvation rations, and the manner in which his imagination played obsessively with the unseen dangers around the house was not the only symptom of a lack of stimulus. Increasingly he fell into abstracted trances, he bit his fingernails and even in photographs his look appears sad and withdrawn.

His nervousness reached outside the house as well. He was terrified by the appearance of the catsmeat man in the street wearing a bloody apron, by the sweep with his blackened face and the sinister gypsies who, as Nanny told him, used to steal children. And so when she lost him one June morning in 1887 during a walk in Kensington Gardens he was ready to panic. He had always been taught his full name, but it was this emergency that brought home its importance. He ran as fast as he could to the nearest police station and gasped, 'My name is Edward Montague Compton Mackenzie. I live at 54 Avonmore Road, and I am lost.' A tall policeman was deputed to take him home and the emergency passed, but it left its mark in that he ceased to speak of himself in the third person. It was as though an existence other than 'Monty' had been independently confirmed. Nevertheless his first use of 'I' was hesitant, and his self-consciousness extended to his father's games and jokes which now began to embarrass rather than entertain him.

The barren routine was broken by occasional visits from relations, such as his grandmother or uncle George Crowe, but he had no friends of his own age, and when he was taken to the Christmas pantomime it was by himself. The impact of the pantomime's lights and noise and gaiety upon his inturned imagination was profound, and it is a reasonable assumption that nothing struck him more forcibly than the exhilarating end of the Transformation scene – a spectacular set-piece of costume and staging – when the clowns, Harlequin, Pantaloon and Columbine came tumbling on stage.

Descended from the *commedia dell'arte* and French traditions of mime and dance, Harlequin appeared initially as a mischievous servant and later as the spirit of mischief. 'Is he good?' asks the young Jenny Pearl in *Carnival*, the second of Compton Mackenzie's novels.

'Good – in a manner of speaking,' answers Vergoe the old clown, 'but an awkward sort of a laddie, with his sabre and all. But no malice at bottom, I'm sure of that.'

Paired with Columbine, sometimes his daughter and sometimes an impossible love, he had entered the British theatre in the seventeenth century, reached a peak of popularity in the eighteenth century and, now reduced to this last foothold in the pantomime, was about to leave the stage. Before he did, his shameless, subversive high spirits imprinted themselves so deeply on Monty's mind that his red and gold chequered figure ran like a motif through many of his novels and the first half of his life.

The pattern of touring allowed his mother and father to make only two visits home a year, during Holy Week when the provincial theatres were closed, and in July after the season ended. At Christmas the children would usually be taken to join the company in whatever town they were playing, but otherwise the year was composed of those long periods of empty waiting which added up to 'the endless purgatory of childhood'.

By contrast, the arrival of his parents in their four-wheeled cab piled high with luggage marked the beginning of paradise. The front door of the house, locked in their absence, was thrown open and the house was filled with the drama of their presence. Rooms long closed were stripped of dust sheets and came alive with the bustle of people. Voices spoke, not with the repressed tones of a nanny, but with the open extravagance of the theatre. And lips kissed, not from duty but out of love and pleasure. For a time the shadows and fantasies were driven away.

Starved emotionally by his mother's absence, it is clear that Monty desired an impossible abundance of affection, enough to fill the long, blank days before she came and the long, blank period after she left. He took his books and toys to whatever room she was in, so that he could be with her whenever possible; he told her stories, asked her questions, invented excuses to hold her undivided attention, and when she came to kiss him good-night he could scarcely bear to let her go, pleading for another, longer embrace.

It was a losing battle. He had to compete with his brother Frank whose appetite for adventure and happy temperament was apparently immune to Nanny's discipline, and later with his sister Viola who was growing up vivacious and strong-willed. Most of all there was the relentless demand of the touring schedule which took her away time after time. 'Monty would not like to be an actor,' he said determinedly at three years old, and nothing ever made him alter his distaste for the profession.

In June 1887 the family went on holiday to Cromer in Norfolk, and it remained in memory as a golden summer because for much of the time Nanny was occupied with Frank and Viola, so that his mother could be alone with him. When she went to the beach in the morning, he conquered his fear of the sea and went paddling because 'my chief object in life then was to please my mother'. In the afternoon when she stayed inside to embroider the coat her husband wore as Charles Surface, he remained with her to catch her attention with a Punch and Judy show. And when bedtime came at six o'clock, according to Nanny's inexorable timetable, 'I had a device for one more kiss, but much, much the longest kiss in the world.' Long after she had gone, he would lie awake yearning to be grown up and free of 'the perpetual threat of being left with my old nurse to spend with her an endless time of unreasonableness ahead'.

Neither then nor later could he admit that the real source of his unhappiness was not his old nurse but his mother. It was she who employed Annie Curry and implicitly supported her regimen despite the evident deterioration in the child's appearance and behaviour. It was she who actually inflicted the ultimate sanction of refusing to see him when he misbehaved. And at the end of those summer holidays, it was she who insisted that he be left behind with an old friend rather than be allowed to accompany them on the first part of the tour. Even when his father had succumbed to the boy's frenzied sobbing and brought him along to the station, his mother did not soften. 'I can still hear the coldness in my mother's voice,' he wrote almost seventy-five years later, 'and feel the longing to be kissed and forgiven as I sit beside her in the railway-carriage.'

Her coldness, like her acceptance of Annie Curry's unthinking discipline, arose, he decided later, from her fear of being accused of spoiling him. 'My mother was always convinced,' he wrote, 'that anything she herself very much wanted to do was the wrong thing to do.' And so, instead of giving way to her real wish to lavish affection on him, she deliberately made herself remote, and refused to replace Annie Curry long after she knew her to be a liar and a drunkard.

Virginia Compton's character, however, was more complex and more powerful than this simple explanation might suggest. Even when he was in his fifties, Monty still sought her approval and her displeasure still made him as uncomfortable as in his childhood. For her he would be precocious, pious, extravagant and captivating, to which she would respond adoringly, freezingly, admiringly or neglectfully. She was at war with herself and her children were caught up in the battle. Since all were subjected to the same upbringing at the hands of Annie Curry, it was evident that she was the agent rather than the thwarter of Virginia's wishes. But as the oldest and most sensitive of them, Monty caught the full brunt of the repressed and ambivalent personality which had been nurtured by the Bateman family.

2

Suffering is good
for the soul

Where genius was concerned, Hezekiah Bateman was no more than a flamboyant consort to the blood royal. His wife, Sydney Frances, was the daughter of a cashiered naval officer called Joseph Cowell, who took to the stage when his life at sea was ended by a court martial for striking a senior officer He made his name and his home in the United States where he numbered among his friends General Lafayette and William Henry Harrison, the ninth president. To his children he passed on a precocious ability which saw the elder, Sam, perform on stage at the age of nine, but it was Sydney Frances who betrayed the greater and longer-lasting quality.

At the age of two and a half she taught herself to read, and by the time she was four her favourite book was Sterne's *A Sentimental Journey*. At fifteen she was an accomplished actress; as a wife she wrote successful plays and fostered the wayward, motherless Irving, and in widowhood she restored Sadler's Wells, both as a building and a theatre. All who met her, and her friends included James Whistler, Sir Frederick Pollock and Henry Irving, were immediately struck by her intelligence and energy. Much of this her children inherited, but she also passed on another, less acceptable characteristic.

Although she was only sixteen when she married Hezekiah, that short-tempered man expected her to be both a perfect wife and, in hard times, the family breadwinner. Since she was by far the more richly talented of the pair, she acted both parts successfully – Bateman never looked at another woman, and she dramatised popular novels with great effect culminating in *Leah*, a melodrama which played to huge audiences in New York and had a record-breaking run in London. However, the effort of sustaining both roles while bringing up six children twisted her character to extraordinary malevolence.

The two eldest children were the prodigies Kate and Ellen; then came a pair of boys, Richmond and Harry, and finally Virginia and the youngest child Isabel. The boys seem to have suffered most because their parents despised them for lacking the precocity of their elder sisters. Even as a teenager Richmond was thrashed by both parents, his mother being in the habit of hitting him round the head with a wooden-backed hairbrush. Harry, who was a cripple, escaped his father's blows, but was nagged so mercilessly by his mother about his dog, Gyp, that in desperation he shot it. Both left home as soon as they could, at which their mother cut them off from the rest of the family. No one was allowed to visit them or even mention their names, and when Richmond was burned to death while rescuing passengers from a ship's fire, her only comment on his heroism was, 'I wouldn't have expected anything else.'

Yet the boys' mistreatment had less severe consequences than her manipulation of the girls. The most fortunate was Ellen, married off at fifteen to Claude Greppo, a French silk merchant almost twice her age. As the family's only reliable source of income, Kate was driven back to the stage after a break as a teenager. She grew to hate it and vented her anger on her younger sisters. Her mother, however, managed her with ruthless efficiency, fending off admirers and, when one slipped through the net, forcibly breaking off the engagement. When she did allow Kate to marry it was on the understanding that she would continue to act. It was a marriage violently opposed by the rest of the family because her intended husband, Dr George Crowe, though charming and handsome, had an unsavoury reputation. He turned out to be infected with syphilis and eventually died in an asylum. By the end of her life, beautiful Kate, of whom Fanny Kemble had once written to Robert Browning, 'I went home and thanked God for making anything so beautiful,' had lost part of her face and most of her mind to the disease.

'I expect if she would have let us all do what we wanted ourselves,' Virginia observed fifty years later, 'instead of always knowing the one and only way for everybody – it might have been so much easier for her and for everyone else – but she was *really* clever and none of us was.'

Dictatorial interference combined with periods of neglect provided the pattern of Virginia's upbringing. The neglect was in part forced upon the family by the need to earn money. After the great financial success of the early 1850s, when Kate and Ellen were appearing as infant prodigies, the Batemans gradually found themselves struggling once more. In 1859 Kate was put back on the stage, and thereafter her mother acted as her manager, following her on tours across the United States and Britain. The other children were left with minders until a long run allowed them to be brought together again . From such occasions Virginia remembered in general an atmosphere of quarrels and bad temper, and in particular her mother finding her diary and reading it aloud to amuse the rest of the family. 'I was supposed to be very sullen,' she commented, 'and I daresay I was. I was certainly always keeping in the things I most wanted to say.'

Disliking her own appearance, Sydney Frances was merciless towards any vanity in her daughters, and physical blemishes she felt to be good for them. While the family were in England following the success of *Leah*, Virginia's eye became infected and was left untreated until an abscess had formed. This too was neglected. Another sore grew over her face and, according to Virginia's recollection, her mother merely expressed surprise that 'I wasn't a mass of infection.' A form of erysipelas developed so that she lost all her hair. She was given a wig to wear which had been used by Kate in her child prodigy days and which was too small to stay on. Despite this handicap, at fourteen she was put on stage with the Bateman company which took *Leah* on tour, and for two years she acted unpaid on both sides of the Atlantic, covering her disfigurement with make-up. Only when an eminent London eye surgeon saw her and absolutely insisted on the necessity for treatment did Mrs Bateman allow her daughter to go into hospital.

'I'm afraid Mother let this happen on purpose,' Virginia wrote. 'I can't imagine anything else. I was very pretty and always having nice things said to me and of me, and I suppose she thought to be disfigured would be good for me. I daresay it was, for I never grumbled or reproached her.'

Instead she blamed herself, thinking that she must really be an orphan whom her mother had been obliged to adopt, or wondering fearfully whether she had picked up a venereal disease from one of the minders who had looked after her in childhood. During this period her single ally was Isabel, the youngest child, but by the time Virginia was cured, Isabel had to undergo her own ordeal.

In 1870, Hezekiah Bateman bought the lease of the rundown Lyceum Theatre with the intention of making it the headquarters for his own company in which the leading female roles would be played by Kate and the inexperienced but lovely Isabel, then fifteen years old. A few months later he heard Irving recite Hood's tragic poem *The Dream of Eugene*

Aram, and promptly offered the thirty-three-year-old actor, then hardly known to London audiences, a three-year contract as leading man. From then on the Lyceum was his showcase. Initially the hard-working Kate had to remain on tour to subsidise the theatre's takings with the money she earned, but in September 1871 Irving had his first big success in *The Bells*, a melodrama of an Alsatian burgomaster consumed by guilt for the murder of a French Jew.

During rehearsals Irving had been accustomed to stay with the Batemans rather than his wife Florence, and following the triumph of his first night, he left her for good. For the next four years Mrs Bateman mothered him with a devotion she had never shown to her own children. It is possible that she saw in him something of her eldest son, Frank, who died as a baby but who would have been approximately Irving's age.

To keep him from drinking she provided cups of beef tea and every night brought him back home from the theatre. To that extent her behaviour was irreproachable, but she also apparently believed that her youngest daughter should become his mistress. Isabel was expected to sit up with him late at night after her parents had gone to bed, and to entertain him alone when they took him on holiday. Her mother's intentions were so obvious that they became the subject of comment in the theatre papers of the day. Convention understood her to have in mind no more than 'a strict alliance of friendship', but gossip took a broader view and so, understandably enough, did Irving.

A few years later Isabel was to form a Celibate Society with a spinster friend, and eventually she joined an Anglican order of nuns. Some of Irving's biographers suggested that it was out of disappointment, but Virginia remembered being enlisted to sit up with Isabel to protect her against Irving's advances, and even Kate's husband, who was hardly a model of propriety himself, protested after discovering Isabel struggling in Irving's arms. In search of help, she and Virginia took to religion, provoking their mother to jeer at them as Sister Angelica and Sister Serafina. With the encouragement of a friendly vicar Isabel held out and when she was eighteen finally summoned up the courage to tell her mother that she would no longer see Irving alone.

By then Irving too had begun to feel himself caught within a web, and following the death of Hezekiah Bateman in 1875 during the first overwhelming success of *Hamlet*, he began to dream of being in sole charge of the theatre. When a second production of the play was planned in 1877, he requested a new leading lady. Even the loyal Virginia had noted Isabel's inability to lose herself in a role, and the critic of the *Hornet* observed of the Bateman daughters in general that 'They may be very charming ladies, but they are not altogether suited to the parts with which they have been entrusted.' Mrs Bateman, however, reacted angrily to Irving's request, writing that if Isabel did not play Ophelia, 'it would be an endoresement, signed by you – the friend of her family – and by me, her mother, of her entire incompetency.'

It is worth noting that she did not actually deny the incompetency, merely the public endorsement of it, for her opinion of her children's abilities was never high. Rather than fight Irving over Isabel's casting, however, she responded with a quixotic generosity for which there is no rational explanation other than the tangled emotion of seeing her proto-son about to leave the family. She had bought Sadler's Wells, then a derelict theatre, and now she handed over to Irving the lease of the Lyceum, together with its scenery, props and costumes. She could ill afford such a lavish gift on top of the costs of rebuilding Sadler's Wells, but in a letter to Irving she declared that 'with some luck and a great deal of economy we may be able to make a living, and,' she added in a characteristic afterthought, 'as no special gifts are required for the conduct of such a place, the girls can make a living out of it after I am gone.'

It was necessary that the girls should devote themselves to this new project heart and soul. Kate, faithful as always, was joined by Isabel, conscience-stricken at having defied her mother in one matter and determined to make amends in every other, but Virginia received an invitation to join a touring company. The invitation carried the more weight for being issued by Walter Clayton, an actor with whom she had long been in love. Since it explains so much about her character and subsequent actions, it is worth quoting her account of the occasion.

The opening had occurred because the company's leading lady had taken to drink, and a replacement was required at once. When Virginia, then aged twenty-four, told her mother, the response was a categorical, 'You can't possibly do it. I won't allow you.' Her daughter asked for time to make up her own mind, promising to give an answer by the following morning.

I knew what it meant giving up Clayton with whom I was deeply in love – not at all a passionate love, but he was the only person I really loved, and I was more in love with him than he was with me. I sat stunned, overwhelmed, trying to think, trying to know what to do. My whole idea was simple, to say, I shall play the part, I shall take the engagement – not to do so was to give up the only chance I had ever had of working on my own. I sat by my window and wondered, and with the dawn I saw in ordinary printed letters, slanting, rose-red – I can see them now – 'Honor thy father and thy mother.' That decided the whole question instantly and for always.

In that choice the fundamental pattern of Virginia Bateman's character can be found. Brought up without affection or attention, her emotions were wild and fanciful, but she imposed upon them a rigid discipline which was constantly at war with her desires. 'I think my temper is very like [my mother's],' she observed, 'only I trust that by the grace of God I have a certain command over myself that she lacked.' It was an inadequate command. Her mood would switch in an instant from affection to a coldness which froze the offender. Her tongue was as sharp as her mother's, and she neglected and manipulated her children no less wilfully. Nevertheless, if there was one virtue she expected above any other from her children it was self-control.

Having come to her decision, Virginia stayed with her mother until the latter died in 1881. Then she joined the newly formed Compton Comedy Company, and in 1882 married the manager, Edward Compton. She did not love him, either then or later, but she did at first respect him for his careful, disciplined habits. It was only later, after his flirtations with other actresses became too open, that she began to despise him. By then her eldest child was old enough to become her ally against her husband.

With no other model but her own upbringing, it is perhaps not surprising that her attitude towards her children, and especially her daughters, should have been a repetition of her mother's. At the smallest sign of vanity, even at a friend's compliment upon their appearance, she would send the girls up to their room. Viola was put on the stage at six years, and later aged eighteen was given all the lover's roles to play opposite her father so that he should not be tempted into off-stage affairs. And when her youngest daughter, Fay, showed some sign of sexual awareness at the age of sixteen, Virginia preferred to see her married off to a thirty-eight-year-old alcoholic rather than remain single.

It is possible that she guessed at Monty's suffering, but accustomed as she was to subject her own emotions to discipline, she could not help believing that suffering, whether accidental or self-inflicted, was good for the soul. In retrospect she decided that her baldness in adolescence 'was very good for me', Kate's syphilis 'developed her wonderful character', and although 'the Irving episode practically ruined Isabel's life . . . she was forming a wonderfully fine character through all these trials'.

Whatever her innermost feelings, her actual behaviour towards her children reflected that Spartan outlook, and it is fair to say that Annie Curry was rather the instrument than the thwarter of her wishes.

She was not unusual in her outlook. Central to the theory of upbringing was the idea of combating original sin, and in its most extreme form it could give rise to advice such as John Wesley's famous admonition: 'Break their wills betimes, begin this great work before they can run alone, before they can speak plain or perhaps speak at all. Let him have nothing he cries for, absolutely nothing, great or small. Make him do as he is bid, if you whip him ten times running to effect it. Break his will now and his soul will live, and he will probably bless you to all eternity.'

Even if few parents actually followed this draconian rule – and the 'probably' must have aroused some well-founded doubts – fewer still would have questioned the principle behind it, that a rod spared was a child spoiled. By these standards Virginia Compton's remoteness was not remarkable, and Annie Curry's regime may be regarded as stiff rather than severe. What did make Monty's upbringing unusual was its pattern – the long period of waiting followed by the impossible joy at his mother's presence, the bitter desolation of her departure and the bleak suspense until June or Christmas or Palm Sunday brought her back again. In the year following that golden summer of 1888, the emotional emptiness dropped him into a nightmare such as only children know, and his recovery marked him for the rest of his life.

The first blow came in the days after his father had carried him sobbing and ashamed to the railway carriage. A few mornings later he was alarmed to find his parents quarrelling over the breakfast table. Whatever else was fantasy his parents' marriage had always seemed solid, and struggling to establish what was real, he interrupted their argument by saying anxiously, 'I thought people are married because they love each other.' 'I can see,' he recalled, 'the expression on my mother's face as she turned to my father and said: "You're perfectly right, Edward."' It sheds a small light on Virginia's cast of mind that out of the variety of responses open to her – from telling him to mind his own business to explaining that quarrels in a marriage do not preclude love – she should have chosen one which was emotionally untrue.

When he returned to Annie Curry's charge that autumn, his nervousness developed into paralysing terror. The small protection which the house had offered against the menace of the outside world almost vanished. As the hours of darkness lengthened, the phantoms of child-stealing coalmen penetrated the walls as easily as the raucous cries of the street pedlars. To these existing threats was now added another. In the autumn of 1888 Jack the Ripper began his psychopathic attacks on prostitutes in the East End of London. The news of each fresh killing was broadcast by the newsboys who came running through the dusky streets with the evening paper shouting, 'Horrible murder in White-chapel! Woman cut to pieces! Murder in Whitechapel!' Monty used to hide until the hoarse cries and running steps had passed by, but when he emerged the evidence was there inside the house in the form of a blazoned headline above columns of grey print. He would stare at the paper, caught between dread and fascination, but could never resist reading of the mutilations inflicted on the Ripper's latest victim. As though they were not bad enough, he overheard Nanny telling the cook that Charles Peace, a notorious criminal of her younger days, had committed murders far more terrible, using the hook which he wore in place of a hand.

The word 'Whitechapel' came to be imbued with such dread that even in daylight on a crowded street the sight of it on the front of a bus was enough to make the boy pull his nanny away in fright. As the daylight faded and the November fogs, thickened by the smoke from a million coal fires, began to shroud the gardens and waste ground about Avonmore Road, there was nothing to protect him from the perils of the night.

'I recall the gathering dread as the lamplighter came round in the dusk with his glimmering rod to light the street lamps,' he wrote. 'Night was coming and those gas lamps of long ago with their feeble rays only made the darkness between them more terrifying.'

He no longer slept in the company of his brother and Nanny, but had been put into a room by himself in an adult bed which seemed intolerably wide. There was a single gas-jet in the room which was turned low so that the flame burned 'like a very small crocus from a blue base'. The door was left ajar so that he could hear the reassuring rumble of an occasional train on the other side of the house. Sometimes a hansom cab passed with a comforting jingle and creak of leather beneath his window, but otherwise the vast silence of the night was peopled entirely by fears and sounds which were inhuman and could not be kept out.

'My protective fantasy was to build myself an impenetrable room,' he wrote, 'which began with a covering of thin wood to which was added a covering of steel to which was added a covering of thick wood to which was added a covering of bricks to which was added a covering of stone.'

Inside this shelter he tried to imagine himself safe, but at five years old the terrors were more powerful than the defences. They came at him waking and sleeping. In the first half of the night, his imagination, over-fed with tales of violence, heard death in the street cries outside and the strange creaks and slitherings inside. He imagined mice running into his open mouth as he slept so that he choked to death, or one of the cats which wailed in the street jumping onto his face and clawing it before he could awake to defend himself. When, exhausted by terror, he fell asleep, it was to be tormented by nightmares, and by one in particular which never altered.

He found himself walking down a long, glistening wet street, lit by gas lamps. The houses on either side were dark and malignant, and though he knew them to be evil, he felt an overwhelming urge to enter one. He would knock on the door, but when his knocking produced no answer, he would move on. At length one house, more frightening than the others, would draw him to its door. Again he knocked, but this time very slowly the door opened. Struggling convulsively to escape the horror lying within, he forced himself awake, but the nightmare's terrors had invaded the room. There were faces in the wardrobe, a body in the laundry basket, mice scuttling in the fireplace, and spiders hanging down from the ceiling. The gas-jet itself had become a thin corpse's finger, and its shifting shadows brought the furniture and carpet to slow, pulsating life. If he closed his eyes tight shut he could distract himself with the circles of coloured light, but eventually the dread of being burned alive forced him to look round the room for flames. If he buried his head beneath the pillow, the threat of being smothered by the murderer beneath the bed soon drove him out again. There was no escape possible until at last grey streaks of dawn appeared behind the Venetian blinds and the sparrows began to chirp. 'Those London sparrows of long ago!' he wrote in old age. 'No nightingale nor lark nor thrush ever won such gratitude from my heart as the twittering of those London sparrows.'

The anxiety of these years is not immediately apparent in his autobiography where the record of pantomimes, visits to relations and summer holidays bulks larger than the emptiness of his parents' absence. 'I have written of these nightly fears and fantasies in *Sinister Street*,' he argued, 'and there is no point in writing about them again . . . There was often much unhappiness in my childhood, but I am temperamentally incapable of dwelling upon unhappiness; I sympathise with the sundial's preference for sunny hours.' Nevertheless it was the experience of the night which made the sunlight precious.

In the spring of 1889 the battle to secure his mother's undivided attention reached its culmination. On the last evening of his parents' Easter visit, when as a special treat the children were to be allowed to stay up till eight o'clock, a wealthy friend called Coward came to the house and invited Compton and his wife out to dinner. Monty overheard their discussions, his father arguing for acceptance, his mother pointing out that it was their last night at home.

I can recall as if it were yesterday the agony of apprehension in which I listened to this conversation and heard my mother at last surrender . . . As they were going out of the front door Coward turned to me to put it right by pressing into my hand half a sovereign.

The door closed. The jingle of the hansom-cabs and trot of the horses' hooves grew less and less audible until silence fell. Then I went up to my bedroom and as I climbed the stairs I thought, not in so many words exactly of course, but with the equivalent surge of emotion:

'You can never again in life afford to depend on the love of somebody, you must always be prepared henceforth to be disappointed, and then if you are disappointed you will be able to bear it because you knew that it might happen.'

The emotion ran deeper than a passing sense of betrayal. The incident had not been isolated but part of a consistent pattern in which he had always taken second place to the other demands upon his mother's attention. His reaction must have had predecessors on the many previous occasions when she had left him behind to go on tour, but it was on this particular evening that the feeling crystallised.

What had been the centre of his existence – his mother's affection – was now treated as he himself had been treated, by being relegated to minor significance. In the experience of his *alter ego*, he described a similar change after an identical experience: 'Michael began to feel that his love for his mother, or her love for him, did not matter. He began to feel that only what he himself thought and wanted did matter, and when she went away again he was sorry, but not so sorry as before.' In his autobiography, however, he was chiefly at pains to fend off any Freudian interpretation: 'I can assert with a completely clear knowledge of my reaction and an equally clear memory of it that jealousy of my father did not enter into it. I was never jealous of my father. I had no possessive love for my mother.' In the 1920s, he pointed out, he had read everything then published by Freud and Jung and found that it provided little food for thought. 'So I am not prepared to be told by some devotee of psychoanalysis that the Oedipus-complex entered into the failure of my mother to resist my father's wish for her to do what somebody presumably of importance to his career wanted him to do.'

His protest was so forceful that it is worth examining what he was defending himself against. Apart from his epistemological objection to Freudian analysis, it was of crucial importance to him to be in absolute control of himself and his desires. Whatever he could not do or have was discarded as though the wish had never existed. Since even conscious regrets or frustrations were given no place, it was utterly impossible for him to accept a theory which held that he was subject to the unconscious desires of the libido.

However, it is not necessary to invoke the resources of psychoanalysis to suspect that the incident had a more profound significance than he was prepared to admit. His desire for maternal affection which was never satisfied in childhood never abated in maturity, and it marked all his most important relationships with women. Yet he always exercised over it an unyielding control which only rarely broke, and then with catastrophic consequences. It was not simply disappointment he feared from giving way and letting himself trust someone else's love completely. Both *Sinister Street* and his behaviour as an adolescent and an adult indicate that beyond the limits of conscious control he sensed a chaos of profoundly destructive emotions. It is not too fanciful to suggest that behind the last door in his nightmare street the horrifying power which threatened to engulf him was his anger and terror at being abandoned by his mother. To lose control was to unlock the door and let loose these atavistic passions.

That evening represented the nadir of his misery and thereafter his fortunes slowly improved. His fears gradually began to subside so that the possibility of being stolen by gypsies and coalmen no longer appeared so real. While he still had no friends of his own age, he and his brother Frank made common cause against their sister Viola, whose virtuosity in reciting nursery rhymes seemed too much like showing off. Reading, however, remained his chief means of creating a tolerable world to live in.

The first real book to make an impression on him was Cervantes' *Don Quixote*. Like the old knight, he too mistook the windmills for wicked giants and was left with the impression that those who jeered at Quixote were the ones deceived. Although the book was confiscated by his nanny after he fell asleep while reading, his copy with its pages creased by the weight of his five-year-old head remained with him till his death, and in the hero athwart the conventions of his time he found one of the lodestars of his life.

If *Don Quixote* suggested living in a time remote from modern thought – especially Nanny's thought – it was Scott's *Tales of a Grandfather*, which his aunt and godmother Isabel Bateman gave him for Christmas in 1890, that pinpointed the time and place he should have lived in. The most thumb-marked pages of his copy concerned the triumphs of Prince Charles Edward Stuart in 1745; from the prince's decision to turn back at Derby the pages were almost unmarked. As the experience of being lost had proved, he was a Mackenzie, and though the clan was equivocal in its support for the Jacobite cause he could still feel closer to the Highlanders who gave all for a dream and an ideal than to the Redcoats with their disciplined uniformity and relentless imposition of reality. He lived the events of the Forty-Five with such intensity that almost half a century later he could trace the pattern of his life back to the emotion of reading Scott's words.

When he was five he was sent to a kindergarten run by two spinsters, the Misses Allen, who taught him to write with his right hand although he was naturally left-handed, and to play the piano, but again no more than the right-hand part. They also laid great stress upon the accomplishments of a little gentleman, and in so doing handed him a weapon against his nurse. Her uncouth sniffing and dowdy dress showed that she was no lady, and thus allowed him to perceive the limits of her power. On walks, he and his brother Frank began to dawdle behind for fear that a stranger might really take her for their mother, and one day when she insisted on obedience because she represented his mother, he retorted with the deadly exactitude of a child, 'Why you're not a lady, so how could you be my mother?'

Another, though short-lived, challenge to her authority came from the vast, bawdy-tongued figure of Mrs Frith the cook, who appeared in the kitchen for a few glorious months. Mrs Frith could tell stories of drunks and women's drawers and bellies and bottoms as though nannies had never forbidden such things to be mentioned. To Monty she was the incarnation of liberty. He so loved her that when he came to write of her in *Sinister Street* he could not even bear to disguise her by another name. Mrs Frith she remained in fact and fiction, and in both forms Nanny eventually had her dismissed for being drunk and disorderly in the kitchen. She left with Monty an abiding affection for women who could tell bawdy stories.

It was only in imagination that his emotions were allowed full rein – he could hate the Redcoats or identify himself with the chivalrous indignation of Don Quixote – but his feelings for real people, his parents, his nanny or the succession of ineffective governesses who came after he was withdrawn from kindergarten were tempered by the rules which he set himself. If he could not afford to love his mother too much, nor could he let himself hate his nanny. He could tell lies in order to avoid punishment, but he must not want anything he could not have.

At a comparable stage of Michael Fane's childhood, the secret world he was beginning to construct for himself exerted a perverse attraction:

Michael had for so long been familiar with ugliness that he was dangerously near to an eternal imprisonment in a maze of black fancies. He had come to take pleasure in the grotesque and the macabre, and even on the sunniest morning his imagination would turn to twilight and foggy eves, to basements and empty houses and loneliness and dust.

From this gloomy maze he was rescued by the arrival of a new governess with the suitable name of Miss Champion. She was young and sympathetic, the daughter of a colonel who had retired to Falmouth, and her stories of Cornwall and its seafaring past offered a glimpse of another world. But her two outstanding qualities in Monty's eyes were her ability to override the more absurd demands made by his nanny and her willingness to answer questions as though he were a reasonable being. Within a few months of her arrival the nightmares at last ceased, and the shades of the prison-house began to lift.

There was a summer holiday at Great Yarmouth with pierrots, nigger minstrels and donkey rides along the beach, and the following year in 1890 he was allowed to go with the company to the Isle of Man where he kissed a little girl of his own age and never forgot it. There were the *Boy's Own Paper* and the *Magnet* to read. And for the whole of one winter his mother stayed at home.

This break with routine arose from Edward Compton's attempt to put on Henry James's play *The American*. The experiment was a sign not only of his financial confidence but of his unquenchable desire to conquer London. Henry James referred to his play as 'my tribute to the vulgarest of the muses', and the muse was clearly not disposed to forgive the insult, for *The American* was a failure. However, Monty remembered the fascination of visiting the great man and exploring his study where he kept three desks of different sizes so that he could write standing, sitting or lying.

The company was in London for much of 1890 and 1891, and the redecoration of 54 Avonmore Road which his mother undertook during this period symbolised the change that took place in Monty's spirits. The walls were distempered in light colours – ivory, *café au lait* and Wedgwood blue – bright furniture came from Maples, and upstairs in the children's quarters Monty was given a bedroom to share with his five-year-old brother.

The newly painted walls were hung with prints of Wellington at Waterloo and Nelson's death at Trafalgar, and a mezzotint entitled *Not Worth Powder and Shot*, which represented a highwayman gazing disappointedly at a ragged old fiddler tramping across a desolate moorland. They were the pictures and furnishings of a thoroughly conventional late Victorian family, and the installation of a whistle to attract the attention of the servants in the basement showed that it was a family whose fortunes were improving.

Edward Compton was an actor-manager, and in the theatre that was the position of the aristocrat, but he wished his son to be something more – a gentleman. There were several ways to qualify, but for those who lacked either estates or lineage or reserves of capital, the only sure route was through the public schools.

3
The sinister streets
of adolescence

In the famous list of public school virtues which Thomas Arnold commended to the scholars of Rugby in 1837, intelligence ranked low. 'What we must look for here,' he said, 'is first, religious and moral principle; secondly gentlemanly conduct; thirdly intellectual ability.' It was a programme designed to reform the corrupt practices of eighteenth-century education, and in the early years of Victoria's reign a headmaster had no more pressing task. Over the next half century the ranking gradually changed; evangelical zeal waned, a civil and imperial service selected by examination came into being and the new salaried classes wished to learn habits proper to the station they aspired to. Gentlemanly conduct assumed in consequence the highest priority.

In *A French Eton*, written a generation after his father's remarks, Matthew Arnold criticised the tendency of the public schools to give the middle class an education 'more suited to an aristocracy than to a clerisy', but by then the trend was established. A grounding in the classics, a prefectorial system and team games inculcated the aristocratic virtues of using power justly and valuing style above achievement. In the wake of the 1863 Royal Commission on the Public Schools which led to the introduction of standard text books, a recommended syllabus and more open university examinations, intellectual ability leapfrogged into second place above religious and moral principle, which came to be represented by the hollow routine of morning chapel. It was possible, therefore, for an academically minded headmaster to make his school not only a breeding-ground for gentlemen but a forcing-ground for scholarship winners.

It was to this category that Frederick William Walker, High Master of St Paul's School, belonged. His regime was 'Spartan in its intellectual toughness and severity', according to Leonard Woolf, one of his star pupils. 'His vision of the school and education was narrow and fanatical. The object of a public school was to give the boys the severest and most classical of classical educations.' There was a history and modern languages side for the idle, and a science side for the odd, but the classics – translation, composition and commentary – made up the high road to Oxford and Cambridge, and a gentleman would look askance at any other university. The school had recently been relocated to West Kensington and Walker's ability to transform a plodder into a scholarship chance rapidly attracted the children of the salaried classes who lived round about.

The junior school of St Paul's, Colet Court, had only been opened in 1884, but by the time the eight-year-old Compton Mackenzie arrived in the autumn of 1891, its rituals and curriculum were as fixed as little boys and teachers could make them. Outside the classroom the unwritten rules were legion, from the vital need to use one's surname only and to carry schoolbooks in a bag to the desirability of supporting Oxford or Cambridge and one or other of the independent bus companies running along the Hammersmith Road. To each season there was a game, in autumn conkers, or conquerors as it was in Monty's day, snowball fights in winter, spinning tops in spring and marbles for the summer, and to each game there were laws, a slang and a hierarchy. Nothing could ever be changed any more than the curriculum which led from the first line of Cook's *Latin Primer*, 'Cornelia Juliam amat', to Virgil's *Georgics*.

On his first day in this intimidating world, the impossibility of explaining how his parents came to have a different name from himself led to his being entered as 'Compton' rather than 'Mackenzie'. He bore the name until he went to St Paul's itself, by which time he had mastered the intricacies of living in a rule-infested masculine society.

His chief asset was his intelligence. At Colet Court it was customary to ask whether eight-year-old boys – the age of admittance – could read, and Virginia Compton's response that her son had been reading since he was two was greeted with some scepticism. Nevertheless, in the space of two and a half years he had raced through the system from the lowest class to the top, gathering school prizes almost as a matter of course.

In similar fashion he satisfied the most searching demands of the examiners who inhabited school corridors and playgrounds, and here too speed of wit was his great strength. He discovered the weapon in his first term when he successfully made fun of an older boy at the cost of a mere slap in the face. 'I was conscious of something akin to jubilation over the lesson I had received about the power of the tongue,' he wrote. 'All he had was a hand with which to avenge his wounded dignity, and provided I could keep the tears from my eyes I was the victor.'

Compared to the amorphous menace of his imagination and the unpredictability of his parents' affection, the rewards and dangers of schoolboy life were blessedly concrete. The bullying was only sporadic, and as a day pupil he escaped the servitude of fagging. He played football bravely if not skilfully, and he found to his relief that, despite the dire picture of himself created by Nanny, other boys liked him. They were all neighbours living like him in low-rent, high-sounding West Kensington. They rode on the same buses, bought in the same shops and often enough shared the same journey home, walking as boys did arm in arm. To be like everyone else became the height of his ambition.

Out of this company there developed one friendship which he valued above the rest and whose memory came to hold a sweetness unequalled by any later intimacy.

There was little obvious reason why Alan Mitchell should have become so close a friend. A good-looking, freckle-faced boy with fair, curly hair, he was no match for Monty academically, nor was there the smallest resemblance between the Mitchell family's military background and the theatrical atmosphere of 54 Avonmore Road. His father was an army captain serving overseas, and like his two brothers Alan was destined for a career in the colonial service. It was not to be a particularly distinguished career, for while his brothers received knighthoods for their service in India and Africa, he himself died unhonoured as the commissioner in Lahore. Yet his character endeared him to Monty and his portrait appeared at least twice in the novels, as Alan Merivale in *Sinister Street* and Jock Airedale in *Sylvia Scarlett*. Not brilliant or imaginative, but reasonable, conscientious and touchingly given to self-sacrifice, he represents in each case the kind of person who is at home in his surroundings, untouched by doubt or self-questioning. In the years of their friendship Monty shared his happy state.

At home, Nanny's rule was finally overthrown by the arrival of the last of a long line of governesses, Miss Mabel Stanwell, 'a small, thin young woman with a somewhat florid complexion and a most determined chin'. The chin was not deceptive. Nanny had been a tyrant, but it took a thoroughgoing disciplinarian to return her to the menial task of looking after Katie, the fourth Compton child, born in November 1891. There were cold baths in the morning, followed by half an hour of piano practice, and no waywardness of appetite or defecation was tolerated.

Leftover scraps of food were served up at the next meal, and if the visit to the lavatory after breakfast was not successful another was prescribed after lunch, a discipline, Monty averred, 'for which I am profoundly grateful'.

Regularity had at last been introduced into every aspect of his life, and he thrived on it. During term-time the network of unyielding rules at home and at school offered security and, as he mastered them, a sense of superiority. Even holidays had a different flavour once they ceased to be oases in a desert of waiting, and they were made the more enjoyable by Frank's development into a suitable companion.

Although the younger brother, Frank possessed an insouciant streak which was missing in Monty. It was Monty who suffered agonies about being sent to school in combinations rather than vest and pants, or about wearing a jacket of Donegal tweed rather than blue serge, or when Frank joined him at Colet Court about hearing his brother blurt out his Christian names, 'because chaps mustn't tell chaps their Christian names in school'. He tasted the dregs of humiliation on the day he won the Consolation Race for under-tens and heard his father shout in that rich voice which could reach the back of the pit, 'Bravo Montyboy!'

Frank on the other hand dressed scruffily and did not mind what he was called, although at Monty's insistence he usually added Mackenzie to the Compton. His cheerful character was what Nanny expected in a boy and he had in consequence always been her favourite. Despite this, he and Monty now became friends. They laughed at the same jokes, scrounged stubs of their father's cigars to smoke in a pipe, and at the seaside raced donkeys and compared the merits of the pierrot shows.

After his disastrous experiment with *The American*, Edward Compton took his company back on tour with the familiar repertory of eighteenth-century comedies. Whatever disappointment he may have felt was masked by the habitual curtain speech in which he assured the audience of his particular pleasure in returning once more to Northampton, Newcastle, Dublin or whatever town he happened to be in, and the appreciation of a provincial audience may have compensated for the indifference of London. 'His dash and spirit were infectious,' judged the *Oxford Magazine* of his performance in *The School for Scandal*, 'and it is easy to see why his company is so good as a whole. Altogether we cannot thank Mr Compton too much for giving us this play so well.' This was unmistakably his niche, but to his dying day he never abandoned his hope of establishing a reputation as something more than a touring actor-manager.

The pinnacle of Monty's triumphant boyhood came in the summer of 1893 when he was ten years old. Such was his confidence in his little world that with a gang of small boys he patrolled the formerly terrifying patches of derelict ground around Avonmore Road, and broke into an abandoned house. At school he and Alan Mitchell strutted the corridors like godlings before the admiring new boys, and without effort he arrived in the second most senior class.

Despite an inclination to show off and to mock slower-witted boys, he was too quick and responsive not to be popular with his teachers. In the schoolboys' lore of swops and slang and tall stories, he was supreme. It was Compton who witnessed the front door of a house blown out by a gas explosion, and had the luck to bow to Queen Victoria when her carriage was halted in the Hammersmith Road so that a groom could extract a stone from the horse's hoof. It was he who led a gang of ten-year-olds with pea-shooters onto the top deck of a blue and chocolate bus of the London Road Car Company in order to pepper the passengers on the red bus of the rival London General Company.

'How well I remember that sun-blessed summer of 1893,' he wrote in his autobiography, and the warmth was the more blessed for being so brief. Success had come too easily in the opinion of his teachers, and it was decided that he would benefit from a more rigorous curriculum than prep school could offer. The golden summer was almost the last of untroubled boyhood, for the following May, at the age of eleven, he was sent to St Paul's itself.

The final echo of its happiness occurred in the holidays following that first term at St Paul's, when he went to Brittany with two teachers and a group of Colet Court boys. He was there to be coached in Greek for his scholarship exam, but there was also time to bathe, to eat pâtisseries in the Breton cafés, and to collect butterflies. This last was the beginning of a hobby which absorbed him for several years, and he opened his collection with two Camberwell beauties and two swallowtails.

There was, however, one troubling note. On the voyage over, he saw a cabin boy being driven below deck by a rope-wielding mate and shortly afterwards heard his screams. Later he found the rope's end stiff with blood, and felt his horror mixed with another emotion. A year earlier he had witnessed a girl being teased to tears for inadvertently revealing a rip in her drawers when she swung too high on a swing. In his reaction to both incidents he recognised a prurient thrill in another's misfortune and felt bitterly ashamed. In Michael Fane the emotion aroused by two identical incidents was to erupt again in adolescence, and it seems probable that for Monty too they were precursors of the crisis that was to come.

Although his new school stood just across the street from the old, the difference between them was more than the width of the Hammersmith Road. There were over six hundred boys at St Paul's, the youngest more than a year older than him, and the eldest, resplendent in bowler hat, tweed suit and neat moustache, might already have been a junior subaltern home on leave, or at least a government clerk with the first superannuation payments made towards his pension. It was a mark, therefore, of the confidence he had gained that he now gave his name as Compton-Mackenzie, the hyphen finally being dropped when he went to Oxford.

In accordance with Walker's policy of picking winners, he was swiftly promoted to a class of thirteen- and fourteen-year-olds. Many years later, Professor Norman Bentwich recalled his first day as a new boy at St Paul's when Walker had shown him round the school and pointed out a childish figure in a class of adolescents saying, 'That is Compton-Mackenzie. He is the cleverest boy in the school and will be head of the school in the year 1900.' St Paul's had just won more open scholarships to Oxford and Cambridge than any other two schools together, so there is no reason to doubt his eye for form.

Monty was soon removed to be given special coaching, and the high spirits which had emerged at Colet Court were briefly doused by the awful presence of the High Master, who kept a personal eye on his favoured few. Leonard Woolf, who had been in this high-flyers' class a year earlier, particularly recalled Walker's red face, bloodshot eyes and blackened teeth, but Monty was struck most forcibly by his thunderous voice and long grey beard 'to which adhered stale morsels of food and the acrid stench of strong cigars'. The twice daily arrival of this monstrous being sliding onto the seat beside him kept his attention fully stretched.

Having survived that ordeal, he found little to fear in other teachers. Their portraits, exact in phrase and gesture, were to appear in *Sinister Street*, and they remained fresh in his mind almost seventy years later: Horace Elam of the Remove, who had a feeling for the poetry in Virgil's *Eclogues*, an ungovernable temper and a rich line in opprobrium – 'You miserable pockpuddings, moonfaced calves and stupid stockfish'; Tommy Gould of the Upper Fifth, who with suave caprice would sometimes forget to ask for the 200 lines of the *Aeneid* set as a punishment and sometimes double it to 400 of Euripides; and, in the Sixth A, the willowy, elegant Digby La Motte, who concealed his homosexuality in his harshness to good-looking boys.

None inspired in him any enthusiasm for learning, and their reports reflected their failure. In his first year Elam noted that the eleven-year-old Monty was one of only five boys in his class 'who can do anything out of the mechanical routine of sentence-writing'. By his second year the praise was qualified – 'Good, but slovenly in his ways' – and thereafter this theme was repeated with variations: 'Works too fast to be accurate,' wrote a master in his third year; 'Clever, but shirks all the time,' judged La Motte in his fourth. Work was something that had to be done, and with a small degree of application he could do it well. His memory served him admirably. He could learn fifteen lines of the *Georgics* during morning prayers, and absorb in a snatched half hour in the evening whatever was necessary to satisfy the minimum requirements in the way of irregular French verbs and Euclid's theorems. In his first years at St Paul's he was always the youngest in his class and often enough at the top of it. He found it too easy, and his high spirits soon turned to the schoolboy distraction of ink pellets, drawing pins and paper darts.

For those who could stand the tedium, Walker's training methods were clearly effective, but it was not a regimen which encouraged independent thought. Those who did not conform were either ground down or discarded. Initially Monty did conform, not only to the headmaster's academic treadmill, but to the social expectations of his fellow Paulines.

In the entrance hall opposite the High Master's study a large plaster-cast statue of the Laocoön stood like a convoluted policeman at a crossroads of corridors and staircases leading to the classrooms. There were radiators along the corridors where the 'bloods' of the school lounged, watching the surge of the boys round the statue. It was a position Monty coveted. At first he was merely part of the throng, dressed like them in Eton jacket and cap or straw hat according to season, his bag crammed like theirs with Liddell and Scott's *Greek Lexicon*, Carey's *Gradus ad Parnassum* and Kennedy's *Revised Latin Primer*. But his popularity and swift progress through the school soon qualified him to join his seniors against the radiators. As had been the case at Colet Court, he happily adapted himself to the rules and conventions of schoolboy society, but it was a narrow and intolerant mould he was being forced into.

Just ahead of Monty, Leonard Woolf was beginning to rebel against

Walker's regimen and the school's oppressive conformity. 'The atmosphere of philistinism at a public school in the last decade of last century,' he wrote in his memoir *Sowing*, 'was pretty heavy, hostile and menacing to any boy who neither in his beliefs nor in his desires accepted the philistine's standards.' As a Jew, Woolf could never forget that he stood outside the narrow ethos of the salaried class. Petty anti-Semitism was as normal as class-consciousness, and the children of those soldiers, lawyers, colonial and civil servants betrayed in cruder form the prejudices of their parents. Uncertain of their own status they clung to the idea of the gentleman which once had been defined by birth but was now to be defined by conduct. A Jew could never be a gentleman, not just because he was different but because he tried too hard.

In a remarkable apology for his participation in these schoolboy attacks upon Jews, Monty looked back with horror from the 1930s at his young self at St Paul's:

It was my delight to put drawing-pins with the sharp end up on the seats of Semitic school-desks. It was my delight to stick the lids of those desks with gelatine lozenges and watch the way the lid would come up with unexpected force and strike a Semitic chin. It was my delight to be a unit in two lines of exuberant young Nordic companions lined up on either side of a corridor in St Paul's school, and when some timid, book-laden young Jew passed along on the way up to his class-room to push him from side to side all the length of those grinning rows until his books were scattered on the floor ... I thought it extremely funny when some much admired athletic seniors plunged a young Jew head foremost into a keg of butter rashly left outside the school tuckshop. I derived a warm feeling of patriotism from seeing a young Jew bounced up and down on one of the drums of the Cadet Corps until the parchment burst and he was left to explain, without sneaking, to the authorities what had happened. And when he did sneak I decided with my young Nordic companions that such vile behaviour was typical of a Jew. Looking back at that silly anti-Semitism manifested with all the crudity of savage boyhood, I recognise that the fundamental cause of it was resentment at the way our Jewish schoolfellows used to sacrifice everything to reaching the top of the class.

The Jews might be the most obvious outcasts, but, as he recalled in his autobiography, there were others.

Believe it or not, when I was at Colet Court the election of a Liberal government was a mystery because a 'gentleman' could not vote for a Liberal candidate without committing an ungentlemanly action. It was doubtful whether a Dissenter could be considered a gentleman: I remember a boy's saying to me with surprise that he had always thought actors were not gentlemen.

There lay the rub. Fundamentally he too was an outsider. Irving had been knighted, the Prince of Wales was seen in the company of actresses, but the gentility to which the children of West Kensington aspired allowed for no such tolerance. In later years he wished that he had rebelled against the system, but at the time the need to be inside the group was stronger than the sense that he did not belong. He found it easy to be popular and, as John Ogilvie in *The Four Winds of Love* observed, 'nothing is so deadening to the display of temperament as popularity.' His disruptive behaviour in class sprang from mischief and high spirits; it was diversion not rebellion, a game within rules rather than resentment against the system. The untormented majority in his class enjoyed his antics, and even his teachers, though they found him a trial, succumbed to his charm. 'He was a source of disruption throughout the School,' Walker observed of him some years later. 'There was no mischief in which he was not involved. The object of his existence seemed to be to bring discipline into disrepute. And yet with all his faults he was a very winning boy.'

He had, at the second attempt, won a scholarship, but any suspicion of being a swot was allayed by his enthusiasm for the central pillar of gentlemanly conduct, games. It was during that May of 1895 that W. G. Grace made his thousand runs for Gloucestershire, and like any other schoolboy Monty had enough cricket statistics stored in his head to appreciate the world-shaking importance of his feat. In the spring he played lacrosse and in the winter rugby, where his position on the wing put him next to the slim, fair figure of Alan Mitchell.

The climax of their friendship came when they were both fourteen, and for the first time since prep school found themselves reunited in the same class. Their elderly teacher, the Reverend J. W. Shepard, was not only deaf but too short-sighted to detect any source of mischief with fewer than three pairs of spectacles. That at least was how Monty remembered the mild cleric, although Shepard's photograph reveals only a single pair of owlish glasses. Nevertheless in memory it was a term of flying ink pellets, gliding darts, carved desks and undetected cheating, of humiliations heaped upon poor Cohen and practical jokes played on 'dear old Shepard', of thundering desk lids, hysterical laughter, and a sudden silence when the High Master himself came to investigate the cause of the pandemonium. 'He might do very well,' Shepard wrote of Monty, 'if he could only be got to take part in the form's work.'

Amongst boys whose voices had not broken, Monty and Alan swaggered supreme, devils in the classroom, heroes on the rugger field. In

Avonmore Road they practised kicking and catching, occasionally varying the fun by drop-kicking the ball at an errand boy's back and daring
the cad to take his revenge. Even at home Monty's supremacy was
unassailable: Nanny had been sacked for drunkenness, and his mother,
retired from acting, was beginning to find in her newly handsome son
an object of affection.

In 1896 Virginia Compton bought a cottage near Alton in Hampshire
which had been advertised as having an orchard and vegetable garden
attached, all for sale at a price of £125. Its name was 'Canadian Cottage',
and although little more than a bright blue shed roofed with corrugated
iron, and surrounded by muddy soil and limp saplings, the seller confidently referred to it as 'your little garden of paradise . . . a pocket-sized
Eden'.

It had once been part of a derelict farm called Beech Farm which a
speculator had bought and put up for sale with the enticing line, 'Back
to the Simple Life. Land for the People in plots of a quarter of an acre
upwards.' The prospect of living off the land with a little extra earned
from market gardening or keeping hens had an irresistible appeal for
dreamers. A community of wooden huts with corrugated iron roofs had
quickly sprung up on an unforgiving soil of chalk and clay from which
only the most callow optimist would have hoped to make a living.
Among the Comptons' neighbours were a former cobbler, a failed
butcher, an alcoholic bassoonist and the minister of the New Jerusalem
Church in Kensington. There was Major Diamond whose career had
been spent in tropical marshland and who built his tin shack on stilts to
remind himself of the 'dear old days'. And there was Commander Anstiss
who so distrusted his neighbours that he planted his plot of land
with discouraging notices saying 'Beware of the Dog' and 'Danger!
Explosives!'

The feuds at Beech had the quality of soap opera and were no less
addictive. It was possible to go birds'-nesting in the beechwoods nearby
and butterfly-collecting in the meadows, but for both boys the prime
attraction was the unending source of comedy in their neighbours. 'I am
beholden to these men and women who went back to the land to lead
the simple life,' Monty admitted. They provided him with his first glimpse
of the comedy in life and the raw material for the most infectiously
high-spirited of his farces, *Buttercups and Daisies*.

His delight in their absurdity had a flavour of the schoolboy's laughter
at anything different from the norm, but it was accompanied by genuine
affection. With Beech thinly disguised as Oak and Alton as Galton, that

part of Hampshire appeared frequently in both serious and comic novels, and it was always presented as a safe haven, the polar opposite of the menace lurking in slum streets.

It was the cottage which gave him his first experience of gardening. The addition of two rooms and a verandah transformed it into a bungalow, which his father, to Monty's acute and lasting embarrassment, insisted on naming 'Holiday Haunt'. To shield it from the road and their neighbours, Virginia decided to buy some shrubs and trees, and Monty was enlisted to help her make the selection.

'I seem to remember I was even more lavish in my ideas than my mother,' he observed, 'and that is claiming a good deal. We . . . ordered trees and shrubs and roses with a prodigality of reckless optimism.'

That shared delight in extravagance created a bond between them, standing as it did in such contrast to Edward's caution. When the wagon arrived, piled ten feet high with their order, both his parents were absent, but St Paul's had enabled the thirteen-year-old Monty to develop a fine confidence in his own judgement. He summoned the failed butcher to assist the nurserymen, and set them all to work digging and planting. 'I was here, there and everywhere in spite of my heavily clay-weighted boots,' he remembered, 'pointing out where the trees and shrubs were to go, and helping to stamp down the soil round them when they were planted.' The love of gardening, and especially of its strategy, never left him, and at one point in his life even seemed to offer a career more attractive than writing.

By then his boyhood was coming to an end, and in the physical sense adolescence had already arrived. He was just five days past his twelfth birthday when one of the older boys in his class asked him whether he ever masturbated, or 'rubbed up' in the Pauline slang, and, when Monty confessed his ignorance, provided the necessary information.

'In bed that night I tried the experiment,' he wrote, 'and when the crisis occurred I was convinced that I had killed myself. In the darkness of my room I looked up, expecting to see angels waiting to welcome me to heaven; it was quite a minute or two before I realised I was not dead, indeed so far from being dead that I was on the contrary feeling more alive than I had ever felt.'

For some time puberty made no difference to his unreflecting enjoyment of schoolboy life. He was 'Monty' to an ever-widening circle of friends. Effortless success and buoyant wit made him as popular with the seniors amongst whom he worked as with his own age group. At the heart of this enjoyment was his friendship with Alan Mitchell, and their conversations about cricket averages and marriage partners and bicycles and rugger prospects flowed with the intimacy of kindred souls. Compounded as they were of childish innocence and adolescent intensity, their feelings for each other had a quality which no subsequent relationship could possess, and its flavour was caught unforgettably in *Sinister Street*:

Michael and Alan were not yet troubled with the fever of adolescence. They were cool and clear and joyous as the mountain torrent: for them life was a crystal of laughter, many faceted to adventure. Theirs was now that sexless interlude before the Eton collar gave way to the 'stick-up', and before the Eton jacket, trim and jaunty, was discarded for an ill-fitting suit that imitated the dull garb of a man. No longer were Michael and Alan grubby and inky . . . no longer did their hair sprout in *bistre* sparseness, for now Michael and Alan were vain of the golden lights and chestnut shadows, not because girls mattered, but because like Narcissus they perceived themselves in the mirror of popular admiration.

The friendship did not survive adolescence. In March 1897 they were co-editors of the Sixth A's paper *Hectoma*, the only issue of which was written entirely by Monty, and some time during the summer term Alan gradually faded out of his life. No reason is suggested in the autobiography, but the circumstances may be surmised from the two works of fiction most closely shaped around Monty's life, *Sinister Street* and *The Four Winds of Love*. In both, the central figure's schoolboy love ends in the same place, in the dusk of a summer's evening as the boys lie side by side on a grassy bank beside the Thames, and with the same realisation of dawning sexual desire. John Ogilvie recognises in his friend an answering passion, but the boy is drowned before it can be given effect; in *Sinister Street* the outcome is more complex: Michael puts his arm affectionately round Alan's neck and 'only profound convention kept him from kissing his friend, and by not doing so he felt vaguely that something was absent from this perfection of dusk'.

From that dangerous moment Alan veers off to become the model of untroubled normality, while Michael plunges into a maelstrom of sexual and spiritual confusion. For both him and Monty the relationship was the first breach of the resolution made eight years earlier never to become emotionally dependent on anyone else.

The high-minded Michael Fane found the heaviness of mourning expressed by some words from *Paradise Lost*:

> Thick as autumnal leaves strewn upon the brook ·
> In Vallombrosa.

It may be noted as an indication of one difference between him and his creator that Monty, in the same state, was consoled by Longfellow's *Psalm of Life*, whose lines he would declaim in a luxury of emotion during his five-minute sessions on the lavatory:

> Tell me not in mournful numbers
> Life is but an empty dream!
> For the soul is dead that slumbers
> And things are not what they seem.

However expressed, the weight of adolescent unhappiness was much the same. His thoughts were so charged with feeling that even in class – usually a mortuary to emotion – he had to fight to hold back the tears when construing Sophocles' *Antigone*. It was in this fraught state of mind that he was prepared for confirmation during the summer.

The ceremony itself had less impact than his first confession when the burden of guilt for what he felt were sexual sins was miraculously lifted. In his jubilation he confided to his mother his intention of becoming a parson when he grew up. This ambition was certainly influenced by the admiration of his mother and Aunt Kate for Robert Dolling, the Portsmouth missioner-priest whom Monty had met as a child and had since learned to call Uncle Robert. Though corpulent and no ascetic, his faith was the natural expression of his personality and the church he had built for seamen was always crowded. Monty now took him as his hero, adopting as his own Dolling's enthusiasm for ritualism.

'Truly he was a great man,' he wrote in 1902 in an obituary for the *Oxford Point of View*. 'His power of organisation was marvellous: added to this he had a boundless compassion for the sick in body or soul. He seemed to have stepped from the ranks of the early Franciscans, for like them his first thought was for the poor and unhappy . . . '

Disapproving of Dolling's High Anglicanism, the Bishop of Winchester eventually closed down his church in Portsmouth, an injustice which Monty resented as though he were the victim. The story appeared in his novel *The Parson's Progress*, where he made the bishop's bigotry the counterpoint to all that true Christianity stood for.

The spiritual mood was still with him when he went to spend his summer holidays with an aunt, Edward Compton's younger sister Emily, near Bournemouth. He had returned to the solitary habits of childhood, brooding by himself and taking long walks alone. On one of these walks, in the hills above Swanage in Dorset, he experienced the first of what he called 'the three great momentary revelations', that of conversion.

As I sat there looking out to sea I suddenly seemed to become more alive than I had ever been, and in this awareness of life in myself to feel what might be described as a new and tremendous responsibility towards life . . . I was equally aware that this life of myself had been bestowed upon me by a force immeasurably greater than any force in me. I knew that God must be and that therefore God must have a purpose for my being. I felt impelled to find the right way to express myself.

His description, as he frequently admitted, was inadequate to convey an experience whose intensity he sometimes compared to that of the disciples seeing the resurrected Christ. Nevertheless it remained always the touchstone of his deepest feelings; whatever else was a pose, the certainty that he had been picked for some special purpose never left him.

The following Sunday he was taken to the High Anglican church of St Clement's in Bournemouth, where he was intoxicated by the beauty of the service, conducted with processions, banners and incense. It fired him with an enthusiasm for Anglo-Catholicism, and the right way to express his sense of special purpose now seemed to be as an Anglo-Catholic priest.

When he returned to school in the autumn of 1897 he formed a society called *De Rebus Ecclesiasticis* with a similarly minded friend called George Chambers, and two other boys. Its purpose was to discuss the canonical justification for retaining Catholic forms of worship in the Anglican service and there were earnest deliberations on the proper colour of a chasuble, the authenticity of the Old Sarum rite and the correct form of a devotion for the Blessed Virgin. Monty's particular interest lay in the legal argument that, while papal authority had been repudiated by the Submission of the Clergy Act of 1533, canon law governing Catholic liturgy and doctrine was expressly left intact. Thus the offices of the pre-Reformation church, its Latin Mass and its calendar of saints, might be observed with at least as much justification as the services of the Church of England Prayer Book.

In the last years of the nineteenth century, this case had gathered sufficient support to precipitate what the newspapers called 'The Crisis in the Church of England', when any alteration in vestments or the order of service was taken to mean a swing High or Low, and a direct provocation to some part of the congregation. Monty launched himself into the battle with the intemperance of a teenager. With the other members of *De Rebus Ecclesiasticis*, he heckled Low Church speakers at public debates and cheered the High. When John Kensit, a fundamentalist

Protestant, was removed after interrupting a High Church service in St Cuthbert's, Monty angrily kicked his top hat down the aisle.

Near Beech he discovered a corrugated iron abbey, founded as a mission to sailors by a one-time Massachusetts sea-captain, where he and Chambers could go on retreat and attend all the offices of the Benedictine rule. It was there that he met a visiting deacon called Sandys Wason who combined an enthusiasm for Anglo-Catholicism with eccentricity in a manner Monty found enchanting. When he was at Oxford, Wason had founded a magazine called the *Spirit Lamp* specialising in parodies of French symbolist verse, one of which began:

> Many a mad magenta moment
> Lights the lavender of Life:
> Keran-happach at her spinet
> Psalms the scarlet song of strife,
> Keran-happach is my wife.
>
> Spinet carving olive stanzas,
> Orange fricassees of sound,
> Nicotine extravaganzas,
> Like a cheese at evening found
> Sitting primrose on the ground.

He was now engaged in 'spiking up', or encouraging to be more Catholic, parsons who were tending towards High Churchness. So far as Monty had a spiritual guide at the time, it was Wason. Although something of a pastoral lightweight compared to Dolling, Wason in his extremeness appealed more strongly to Monty, and until he left St Paul's it was to Wason that he turned for spiritual guidance. He introduced Monty to the vicar of Wield, a village nearby, in whose church he began to serve at Mass, and the following year when Wason was appointed curate at St Michael's, Shoreditch, his church became Monty's refuge from the problems threatening to engulf him.

Religion took him like a fever. He collected icons, crucifixes and rosaries, and his bedroom acquired an oriental perfume from the nightly burning of incense. His devotions were not discouraged. His mother was delighted that he intended to go into the Church, and Ellen Terry promised to come and hear his first sermon. His father, deep in negotiations to acquire a chain of provincial theatres with a businessman called Milton Bode, extended the same toleration as he did to all Monty's youthful excesses. Only his Aunt Isabel, who was about to take her vows as a postulant of the Order of St Mary, Wantage, the next year, reminded him that 'these things are merely adjuncts, helps to religion and that only the love of God filling the heart can fire a man for the priesthood'.

His fierce advocacy of the old, authentic religion soon led him to the fringes of Anglo-Catholicism where the Legitimist societies maintained the old authentic claim of the Stuarts to the crown against the Hanoverian interlopers. Given his attachment to the Mackenzie name and the romantic visions conjured up by *Tales of a Grandfather*, the attraction was obvious. In quick succession he became a member of the Thames Valley Legitimist League, the Society of the White Carnation and the White Rose Association, and beside the crucifixes and rosaries in his bedroom there appeared an amulet worn by MacDonald of Keppoch at Culloden, and a gold locket containing a hair from the head of Prince Charles Edward Stuart.

Unfortunately, as his alter ego, John Ogilvie, discovered, Legitimist sympathisers did not measure up to an idealist's requirements:

To the majority of young men present [at a meeting] there clung an air rather of thwarted femininity than thwarted political hopes. Nothing could have been less like the grave and gallant Jacobites than these wiggling, giggling epicenes. These young men made swan's necks of their arms and they chattered to one another in the too utterly style.

As the first flush of his enthusiasm faded, he became uneasily aware that a full-blooded Legitimist might be considered as ridiculous as the Simple Lifers of Beech. When Don Pedro the Infant, heir to the rightful king of Spain, turned out to be an overweight Cockney living in a semi-detached villa in Edgbaston, or supporters of the Empress of Constantinople queued to kiss her hand in a London flat before partaking of light refreshments served at a shilling a head to the skirl of the pipes, even the most earnest schoolboy could sense that the elements were too disparate to be comfortably united.

However, he had not cut himself off from the normality of St Paul's. In the mood of good intentions after his confirmation, Monty had resolved to give up idleness, and the next term he duly came top of his form. It was his last academic success. He had worked equally hard for a set of preliminary university exams, all of which he passed with the exception of arithmetic, and the one failure meant that he had to take the entire set again the next year. In his indignation he determined never again to waste time on school work, and when the exams came round again, he contemptuously left half the papers blank.

It was not a gesture which Walker would have tolerated from any of his pupils, least of all from one of his highest flyers. The fifteen-year-old Mackenzie was summoned to the High Master's study to provide an explanation. Instead of apologising, Monty announced his intention of giving up classics altogether, and with them all hopes of a university scholarship. Walker's anger exploded in a memorable denunciation:

'You have been the greatest disappointment to me of any boy who has passed through my hands. You came to St Paul's a year younger than any boy in the school, already writing Greek iambics many a boy much higher up in the school might have envied. You could have been as great a Greek scholar as Jebb or Porson, and you have flung it all away to swagger up and down the corridors of this school with the manners and appearance of a deboshed clerk.'

It was 'a nice strafe', as the head of the Secret Service observed some years later when a Foreign Office memo complained of Mackenzie's behaviour in similar terms, and Monty treasured it as such. Nevertheless, apart from indicating the extent of Walker's disappointment, the phrase about 'a deboshed clerk' suggests how far the year of religion and Jacobitism had taken him from public school standards. Refusal to be a scholar was one thing, failure to be a gentleman was altogether more serious.

In the person of John Ogilvie, Monty asserted that 'he had hated the abstract idea of school from the first moment to the last of that penal servitude. A convict could hardly hate his prison more thoroughly.' In fact his attitude was more ambiguous. He resisted authority, but not the conformity of his friends. He admired and envied the ease and self-assurance personified by Jim Torrens, captain of the rugby XV, and 'Fluffy' Hunt, captain of the cricket XI. As a fifteen-year-old, he was proud to be accepted as a friend by these paladins of seventeen and eighteen; it pleased him to be known throughout the school as 'Monty', and he took as his due the respect which small boys accorded to the 'bloods'. Yet here too he did not quite belong.

'I remember listening to a group of my class-mates discussing the comparative advantages of the Home and the Indian Civil Service,' he wrote, 'and being horrified to hear it argued that the Indian Civil Service enjoyed the advantage of providing higher pensions. "Pensions!" I gasped to myself. "Pensions! With the world before them they're thinking of their pensions!"'

At his age such contradictions are not unusual, but in Monty they were the surface expression of a more serious clash of incompatibilities. As his photographs reveal, he had grown into a dangerously good-looking youth. The waves of chestnut hair, carefully combed and centre-parted, the challenging glance of his blue eyes, and the complexion described by its admirers, including Monty, as 'rose-petal', were features liable to excite members of either sex, and evidently did so.

In the same year that W. G. Grace set prep school hearts alight by scoring a thousand runs in May, the Marquess of Queensberry had mystified them by his allegation that Oscar Wilde was 'posing as a sodomite'. At the time Monty had seen the newspaper sellers at Piccadilly Circus with the pink, green and yellow papers draped over their arms and the posters beside them saying 'Well-known Dramatist and Sporting Peer – Result'.

The result had led to Wilde's imprisonment and the social condemnation of any behaviour suggestive of homosexuality. Since homosexuals themselves continued to flourish, their gatherings automatically acquired a subversive character, and offered a haven to anyone athwart society. The network was so diverse and interconnected with other unorthodox movements that Monty might have found his way into it at several different points, through his encounters with the giggling epicenes of Jacobitism, homosexual priests in Anglo-Catholicism, bisexual actors, and misfit monks.

Although it is unclear how he actually did meet Collingwood Gee, a wealthy young homosexual who lived near the school, it was certainly through Gee that he was introduced to Lord Alfred Douglas, the cause of Wilde's downfall. Douglas bought him dinner and presented him with a copy of *The City of the Soul*, his anonymously published poems, and soon afterwards Monty's contacts included the rest of Wilde's circle, Robbie Ross and Reggie Turner, the 'bloods', it could be said, of homosexuality. This was dangerous company for a schoolboy; Douglas's taste might run more to French jockeys, but there was ample justification for Reggie Turner's nickname of 'the Boy Snatcher of Clement's Inn'.

Yet Monty was apparently immune to the dangers, succumbing neither to unwanted advances nor bothered by feelings of desire. 'Although I was not at all physically interested in homosexuals,' he recalled, 'I found their company amusing and was fascinated by the way they were able to believe that they were superior to normal people.'

He used to dine with an ecclesiastical lawyer named Richards, whose sexual taste ran to sadism and who, after dinner and champagne in his chambers, tried to interest him in the experience of scourging. With a public schoolboy's air of self-possession he fended off the invitation, and Richards did not persist. But Monty's apparent savoir-faire was only a pose, and like any sixteen-year-old he was in truth the prey of deep self-consciousness.

'This annoyed me,' he recalled, 'and I made up my mind to cure myself of supposing that when I entered a room everybody in it was criticising the way I had tied my tie.'

His cure was to get onto a crowded bus, wait till it started to move off, then ask the conductor to stop because it was the wrong bus.

I did this with seven buses one after another until I found I could make my apparent mistake, get up and move along over people's toes toward the conductor, stop the bus, and alight without the slightest embarrassment. Indeed, the seventh exit was something in the nature of a triumph for my self-assurance, because I noticed that the drawers of a woman sitting half way along the bus were round her ankles, and I stopped to lean down and murmur to her the information, for which, let me add, I received no thanks but only a glare of indignation.

His exploration of the homosexual world seems to have been conducted in much the same spirit. He had no intention of going beyond the first stop, but he enjoyed testing his ability to remain self-assured in a challenging situation. His guide to many of the homosexual networks was Dick Hewlett, brother of the novelist Maurice.

A raffish part-time actor, Dick Hewlett was bisexual and ready to expore either tendency. He belonged to the bohemian world of experimental painters and poets where the conventions, especially the sexual conventions, of the late nineteenth century were studiously flouted. Although five years apart in age, they became close friends, bound together by a common enjoyment of the bizarre, and until he went to Oxford, Monty had no more intimate companion. It was in Hewlett's company that he frequented the Knightsbridge studio of Adolf Birkenruth, a recognised haunt of homosexuals, and met there Philip Sergeant, a journalist and later a literary agent, who introduced him to the excitement of *fin de siècle* decadent literature. Douglas had already presented Monty with copies of the *Spirit Lamp* which under his own editorship had become the light of the Yellow Age of Oxford decadence, and now Sergeant lent him J. K. Huysmans' necrophiliac poem *A Rebours* and Catulle Mendes' lesbian composition *Mephistophelia*.

'I am grateful to the opportunity I was given to observe homosexuality with a detached curiosity when I was sixteen,' he wrote in his autobiography, 'because now at eighty I recognise that it is quite possible to play with fire and yet avoid getting burnt.'

There is good reason for believing the substance of this assertion. Not only was he essentially truthful in such matters; none of the many homosexuals he knew later recognised in him any responsive feeling. Furthermore, at the very time he was being taken up by Douglas, the family cook at Avonmore Road, a woman in her early twenties, was initiating him into the pleasure of heterosexuality, and at Beech his experience was soon broadened by a girl called Ethel, the inmate of a nearby home for unmarried mothers. In addition to these physical affairs, he was suffering pangs of calf-love for a young actress named Violet Stephenson who was studying at the drama school run by his aunt Kate.

Nevertheless his interest in homosexuality was not quite as disinterested as he later implied. In the aftermath of his brief passion for Alan Mitchell, it would not have been surprising if there had been the usual schoolboy affairs, and in the guise of John Ogilvie he was famous for them, taking them as 'the normal Homeric conquests of the public school hero'. In the aftermath of the Wilde case, however, such passions held an added attraction. 'When the bad behaviour of schoolboys became a criminal offence for which they could be sent to gaol, as they thought,' he remarked in *Literature in My Time*, 'then bad behaviour at school became a magnificent fashion. The result was that indulgence in it became a mark of intellectual pre-eminence.'

Thus the superiority affected by Wilde's friends had its counterpart in his own attitude to schoolboy flirtations, and he flaunted his rebellion against the norms of society by adopting homosexual fashions in dress such as a purple bow-tie and a high double-breasted waistcoat.

It is at this point that a marked pattern emerges from the tale of his adolescent adventures. Whether as schoolboy, Jacobite, innocent in the homosexual world or would-be decadent, he is always half participant and half spectator. However much Reggie Turner or Philip Sergeant might try to attract him, it was impossible for him to become a participant because it would have meant ceasing to be a spectator. Even with Mary the cook and Ethel the unmarried mother there is a suggestion of the same division, since he was attracted as much by their ability to tell uninhibited stories as by their physical appeal. Mary's capacity as an entertainer he compared to that of 'a sophisticated barmaid', but it was Ethel, 'endowed with a gift of telling stories that reminded me of my beloved Mrs Frith', who most captivated him with her accounts of the other girls in the unmarried mothers' home, 'of the way they behaved and talked, each of them evoked with perfect clarity'.

Over the next twenty years a succession of actresses, barmaids and cabaret girls who had the Frith touch were to beguile him with tales of their adventures. That fascination with the underside of society marked two other habits of his seventeenth year, his observation of prostitutes plying for trade at the Earl's Court Exhibition and his appalled study of the freaks who also appeared there, such as the Skeleton Man, the Bearded Lady and the man with the body of a child growing out of his abdomen.

Without *Sinister Street*, it would be reasonable to subsume these interests within an adolescent's natural curiosity in all social and sexual oddities, but the story of Michael Fane, so closely based on the author's life, also links them to the effect of upbringing.

Implicitly in the atmosphere of blind compulsion and explicitly in the book's title, Michael's search through the sleazy side of society recalls the terrified exploration of the sinister street in his childhood nightmares. But in place of the fear of becoming a victim of cruelty there is now a fear, mingled with desire, of being cruel. It begins when he listens to a group of schoolgirls reduce another to tears for the crime of showing her drawers on a swing: 'For the first time he apprehended something of human cruelty and the lust to humiliate ... At the same time he himself experienced in retrospect a certain excitement and did not know afterwards whether he had not taken pleasure in the little girl's shame.' Then, on a school trip to Brittany, when he hears the cabin boy being flogged and finds the rope's end clotted with blood, 'he could not keep back a certain exultation and excitement similar to that which he had felt at the girls' school'. It finally emerges in full force as a teenager when, on retreat at a monastery, he is half-assaulted, half-propositioned by a sexually starved monk and discovers that 'he actually enjoyed in retrospect the humiliation of the man, and his heart beat with the excitement of hearing more'.

So far as Michael Fane is concerned, the association of childhood nightmare with adolescent exploration makes it plain that the fear of evil behind the last door in the sinister street is the fear of this sadistic streak within himself. Part of the book's immense power is the psychological understanding that the repeated partings from his mother and the harsh treatment of his nanny have made punishment, paradoxical though it may seem, the expression of authentic emotion.

The confused feelings of adolescence rendered in fictional form need not be taken as an accurate view of reality. Michael Fane does not have many of the author's qualities, especially not his enjoyment of life, nor curiously his instinctive identification with victims. Nevertheless the subsequent course of his life makes it clear that in the turmoil of these years Monty did feel something within himself which he recognised to be evil. In the light of *Sinister Street* it would not be strange if it were a fear that his fascination with social and sexual oddities was composed of pleasure as well as horror, and that he could inflict pain as well as sympathise with its victims. How far this fear was the product simply of an overstretched adolescent imagination it is impossible to say: in the crisis that eventually broke, only the passive, identifying aspect survived, and the active, inflicting urge, if it ever existed, was obliterated.

'A boy who has lived within himself too much and too long,' was the description applied to Michael, and even the breezy tone of the autobiography cannot conceal the solitary brooding and self-critical censoriousness of the adolescent Monty. And, like Michael, he turned to the church as the only refuge. On the other side of London in St Michael's, Shoreditch, Sandys Wason had introduced him to a stronghold of Anglo-Catholicism. While he was exploring the world of homosexuality, the lesbian and necrophiliac fantasies of *fin de siècle* literature, the experiences of fallen women and what it was to make love to them, he was also continually driven to cross London in order to confess and receive absolution.

It was not a conflict which could be long endured. When the winter term of 1899 began at St Paul's he made a final attempt to fit back into schoolboy society. He was prepared to forego weekends at Beech with the beguiling Ethel in order to write rugger reports for *The Pauline* magazine, and to overlook the patriotic absurdity which brought his friends to school in Union Jack ties and waistcoats when the Boer War broke out. But the norms of school behaviour demanded still more of him. In class, the casual manners of a 'blood' allied to his fastidious style of dress were obviously too much for his teacher, a clean-living athletics enthusiast called Cholmeley, who responded by ostentatiously treating him as a mere schoolboy. On one occasion he saw Monty smoking in a theatre and made him write out *The Bacchae* of Euripides, a pun and a punishment he despised in equal measure. Finally at half-term he arranged a splendid outing to Beech in the company of Jim Torrens and Fluffy Hunt with a couple of juniors to act as fags, and Ethel to amuse himself. Unfortunately Cholmeley learned of the plans, and the inclusion of two small boys gave him the wrong idea. Only Monty's furious demand to plead his innocence before the High Master persuaded him to withdraw the imputation of homosexuality, but the injustice rankled, turning boredom with school to outright anger.

When he went back to St Paul's after Christmas, he realised that he could not stand another year of it. He attempted to feign a nervous breakdown by going without sleep for a fortnight, and although the symptoms failed to convince his doctor the real strain he was suffering evidently did. Instead of school he was prescribed three months at the Westcliff Hydropathic Hotel in Bournemouth – a bizarre end to a career whose climax should have been his being made head boy.

Nevertheless it was a sound decision. The relief at being freed from school acted as an immediate palliative, and in Bournemouth the temptations of the underworld were conspicuous by their absence. Instead he spent much of his time playing cards and listening to the reminiscences of the elderly ladies and retired military officers who were his fellow-guests at the hotel. Yet it must be taken as a measure of the stress he had been suffering that such undemanding company should have suited him for the next three months.

Religion continued to occupy him at first; he attended the church where he had first experienced the appeal of Anglo-Catholicism, and he visited a nearby monastery with George Chambers. But the visit was not repeated, and gradually the feverish intensity of his devotions subsided. Indeed, so anodyne were his surroundings that when he fell in love with the only woman under thirty in the hotel, his thoughts turned conventionally enough to marriage despite the eight-year difference in their ages, and his gravest concern was how to explain the facts of life to her on their wedding night. The intervention of her mother, who removed her from the hotel, saved him from the embarrassment.

In June 1900 Monty's cure was judged complete and it was decided that he should spend the summer in France with his Greppo cousins – the family of Ellen Bateman, the younger of the two girl prodigies, and her husband Claude Greppo. Since the theatrical season had ended, Edward decided to take him first on a walking holiday in Switzerland which he had planned for his own health. It was not a great success. Monty once observed of his relationship with his father that their intimacy had ceased when he was three years old. 'He always regarded me as a mysterious creature and his own share of the responsibility for my existence was to him equally mysterious.'

Edward's bemusement turned to alarm when he learned that Monty had gambled away the travel money he had been given to reach France, and Virginia, equally concerned by this further sign of her son's emotional instability, suggested that he give up his ambition to go to Oxford for the calmer atmosphere of a solicitor's office. They need not have worried.

Nine months away from London and its disturbing streets allowed him to regain control of himself. By the time he reached France, the emotional crises of school and adolescence were behind him.

Ahead lay a year of coaching with the Reverend Arnold Overton in Essex, and beyond it, Oxford. The problem was not so much resolved as relocated. Never again did he give way to introspection and self-criticism. All his energies were directed outwards, towards the company in which he found himself. It was there that the conflicts took place. The criticisms he might have directed at himself were aimed at society, and the identity he might have found within himself was found in his surroundings.

In maturity he presented himself as a man of the world untroubled by doubt or inhibition, and his preferred self-description, indeed the only psychological term he would apply to himself, was 'extrovert'. Such a transformation might have been utterly convincing were it not for the continuing fear of evil which was present in him constantly as the opposite to religious faith.

Many years later he was talking to the Irish writer Terence de Vere White, and when the conversation turned to religion, Monty asked for a definition of saintliness.

'To be capable of any evil, but to choose the good,' came the reply.

'That's a very good answer, Terence,' Monty replied musingly. 'You know, I think it applies to me.'

4
The Volunteer and Oxford's aspiring dreams

In the last months of a reign which had impressed her name and outlook indelibly upon an era, Queen Victoria finally laid aside what must have been the most tedious of royal duties. Until the summer of 1900 every officer in her army from subaltern to field marshal held a commission which she had signed with her own hand. For the sons of the landed gentry that personal bond between the sovereign and her 'trusty and well-beloved servant' served as a reminder of the feudal basis of service, but for the rootless professional it was evidence that he too might consider himself a gentleman.

Nowhere was this distinction valued more highly than among the Volunteer Battalions, raised in every county to repel a rumoured invasion by the French in 1859, and maintained ever since for no more obvious purpose than to be the centre of social life in rural areas. They paraded extravagantly but drilled irregularly, and when Volunteer drafts were sent out to the Boer War they demonstrated a woeful lack of basic military skills.

On the other hand, because they represented British, and especially English, society in uniform, with local dignitaries commanding companies of their own estate servants, officered by their neighbours, the grasp of social niceties was exemplary. When young Compton Mackenzie, studying with the Reverend Arnold Overton, was invited to become a subaltern in the 1st Hertfordshire Volunteer Battalion in the autumn of 1900, his uniform included a scarlet tunic with silver lace for ceremonial occasions, a scarlet service tunic for dress occasions, a blue service tunic for undress occasions, and a mess jacket for what might be called dining occasions. It cost Edward Compton over £100, the equivalent of a clerk's annual salary, and understandably the 2nd

Battalion, officered by tradesmen from St Albans, preferred to make do with one grey uniform.

The reaction of the 1st Herts was one of tolerant condescension, as though such things were the inevitable outcome of fitting new arrivals into the old pecking order. 'Poor old 2nd Herts,' they would say as the grey uniforms stumbled by, 'of course, they haven't the officers.'

The difference between gentlemen and gentlemen was not lost on Monty. As a highly strung youth studying French and German with a rural clergyman, he must, like John Ogilvie, have 'accepted like a law of nature the proposition that the English landed classes represented the highest achievement of evolution'. Compared to the impossibly superior manner of his company commander, Henry Croft, the gentlemanly aspirations of St Paul's and West Kensington now seemed distinctly 2nd Battalion.

During his summer in France he finally discarded his ambition to be a priest. His decision not to enter the church was taken privately. It came as a blow to his Aunt Isabel, who had just taken her vows, but in the secretive manner of his schooldays, Monty affected not to care.

'When my mind was made up in youth I could not argue about it,' he recalled. 'I used to enclose myself in a kind of crystal and become oblivious of everybody. When I decided not to be a parson I could not accept such a decision as a disappointment to anybody else; it concerned only myself.'

What was left, however, was the ambition to 'make a name for myself', and in October 1900, when he applied for his commission, he also took the more serious step of beginning to compose poetry. The mood in these immature verses is a gentle, slightly vacuous melancholy, and, as in *Dreaming of Arcady*, the imagery owes something to the symbolist poetry he had read the previous year:

> For the flowers shall bury me
> And the birds shall carry me
> Over the boundless, soundless mere
> That lies between life and death.
> Four tall lilies shall carry me
> And the priest shall be a sunflower.

By chance his military duties taught him a lesson which had a bearing on his poetry. The moment of crisis in his career as an officer came with the discovery that his squad was dissolving into a shambles as he led it on a route march through a neighbouring village. Pretending an authority he did not feel, the seventeen-year-old Mackenzie ordered the group of ploughmen, gamekeepers and gardeners to march at attention, and kept them in that uncomfortable position for the next two miles. It was an important experience because, he said, 'it helped me to see myself as both actor and audience.' In other words, if he could see himself in a role, others would believe it, and the point was underlined by an incident which occurred soon afterwards.

By the time he received his commission, the old Queen had died and the document bore, not her signature, but her name stamped in purple ink and counter-signed by her successor and, on 25 January 1901, when the accession of Edward VII was proclaimed, the Hertfordshire Volunteers mounted a ceremonial guard outside the Hertford Town Hall. As the ceremony was about to begin, a police inspector attempted to move Monty's squad away from their allotted position. Resplendent in scarlet and silver lace and spiked helmet, the fledgling subaltern ordered him to desist from interfering with military dispositions and, with the backing of a senior officer, forced the inspector to withdraw.

The moral was clear: as John Ogilvie put it after his first weeks in the Volunteers, 'I am beginning to discover that form is as important in life as it is in art.' Both his poetry and his subsequent career showed that Monty took the same view.

Overton's coaching was ostensibly designed to help him pass his Oxford matriculation, a hurdle he surmounted with ease in April, but its secondary purpose was to keep him away from London and trouble. Although Monty contrived to spend occasional weekends in London in the company of Dick Hewlett and most of his Christmas holidays with Ivy Stephenson, whose sister Violet had broken his heart the previous year by preferring an actor in brown boots, there was no danger of his breakdown being repeated. His attention was increasingly fixed upon Oxford, and Ivy recognised the fact. 'You'll be forgetting us soon,' she prophesied as they walked homeward through the streets of West Kensington that winter.

His military service came to an end in August when 30,000 troops from all over Britain were assembled at Aldershot for a mock battle. It was typical of the Volunteers that the two armies managed to miss each other completely. Having encouraged his section to loose off their rifles at a party of umpires, Monty bicycled back to Beech. The laced tunic and spiked helmet had served their purpose and the role was now laid aside. His new guise was that of an Oxford undergraduate.

In the Oxford of 1901, the first motor-car had just appeared among the jingling trams and creaking coaches, but the London train was as fast as it is today. It was still possible to have one's bicycle repaired by young William Morris who would soon make cars bearing his name, and to order marmalade, quails in aspic and preserved fruit from Mr Frank Cooper himself. Undergraduates still walked arm in arm with their friends, and measured their friendships from surname to nickname to Christian name. Above all it still held the authentic glamour of influence, of being the place where the values of civilisation were formulated to be carried in person or by diktat to an Empire comprising one-third of the world's population.

The heirs to great estates went there to receive the elements of a liberal education, and the same curriculum, followed more attentively, served the would-be churchmen, lawyers and candidates for the Civil and Imperial Services. 'The Clergyman was rarely an instructed theologian,' admitted G. M. Young in *The Victorian Age*, 'but he was not a seminarist. The Scholar growing up among men destined for a public career took some tincture of public interest: the Schoolmasters, the Politicians, the Civil Servants and the gentlemen unclassified acquired the same double impress of culture and manners.'

In these surroundings, Magdalen College, although fashionable, was not untypical of the university as a whole. With no more than 160 undergraduates, of whom half were Etonians, and another quarter from Winchester, Harrow and Charterhouse, its ethos was that of the Home Counties boarding school where, unlike St Paul's, style counted for more than achievement, and an amateur interest was thought more fitting than professional knowledge. Its reputation stood high among oarsmen but not in intellectual circles. The President, Herbert Warren, a distinguished scholar and snob, made the matter plain in his welcoming address to the freshmen. 'You have come to Oxford,' he said, 'some of you to hunt foxes, some of you to wear very large and very unusual overcoats, some of you to row for your college, and a few of you to work. But all of you have come to Oxford to remain English gentlemen.'

Nevertheless it was not for its fashionable status that Monty chose Magdalen, but for its beauty. On a brief visit to Oxford when he was fifteen, he had been captivated by what is the most immediately lovely sight in the city – Magdalen Tower standing over the bridge which crosses the Cherwell, with the college gardens and buildings ranged beside it. Inside the college gates there are cloisters which are cramped and the unfinished wing of a Palladian building whose proportions are miscued, but each reveals itself through arched doorways like a stage set, and the effect of romantic improbability is only reinforced by the discovery of a miniature deer park behind the Palladian wing.

Monty's refusal to try for a scholarship left his father to pay the full cost of a Magdalen undergraduate's career and, to Edward Compton's credit, when it came to equipping his son like a gentleman, he never balked. At some unfashionable colleges it was possible to scrape by on £150 a year, but Monty's allowance was £250 in his first year and £300 thereafter, a figure comparable to all but the wealthiest of his contemporaries.

No doubt his mother was partly responsible for this generosity, but Edward was becoming rich. In the same year that Monty went up to Oxford, he sold the thin red house in Avonmore Road and spent £2000 on buying a more substantial home at 1 Nevern Square in Earl's Court. In partnership with Bode, he now owned the leases of theatres in Leicester, Huddersfield, Northampton, Crewe and Hackney, and was shortly to acquire others in Chester and Reading. They had lost money in Hackney where his performance as Davy Garrick, so warmly loved in the provinces, had flopped, but pantomimes, musical comedies and the Compton Comedy Company itself more than made up for the failure. It was a less respectable form of income than rents, but spent in the right way it became indistinguishable from the best kind of money.

Monty chose to spend the first of it on buying an engraving of Botticelli's *Primavera* and a print of the *Mona Lisa*. In later years he was inclined to congratulate himself on this selection. 'It took a strong personality in my day,' he wrote, 'to hang the walls of his room with prints of early Italian paintings.' To do so, he suggested, was to be labelled automatically an aesthete, a term 'used to cover everything from a predilection for homosexuality to admiration for Botticelli'. In Magdalen, orthodoxy was set by the hearties who hung their walls with prints of slaughtered grouse and stocked their bookshelves with Surtees. Monty, on the other hand, bought Rabelais, Verlaine and Mallarmé, entire editions at a time, and this became a passion so that at his death his library, despite repeated forced sales, numbered over 12,000 volumes. Apart from French poets, his favourite author at the time was George Meredith, of whose *Tale of Chloë* he thought 'the human pen incapable of setting down on paper a greater eloquence of passion', and although he soon transferred his affection to Thomas Hardy, the influence of Meredith's heightened emotionalism is detectable in his own early novels.

There was an incongruous air about the *Mona Lisa* propped on a mantelpiece in a sitting room furnished in subcolonial style with wicker chair, bamboo-legged table, cretonne sofa and chenille curtains, and in his first bewildered days as an undergraduate he may well have had some qualms about the choice. Coming from a day school, he felt acutely self-conscious among Etonians and Wykehamists, and no doubt fancied, like Michael Fane, that he appeared to them 'as surprising and disconcerting and vaguely improper as a ballet-girl or French count'.

Within a few weeks he had persuaded the social arbiters from boarding schools that he was 'a good egg', and soon it was apparent that 'aesthete' was too narrow a label. It was true that he wrote poetry and enjoyed arguing the merits of Hardy and Meredith with Claude Kirby, an enthusiastic follower of the arts and crafts movement; but he also played rugger with the hearties and could discuss expertly with Kenneth Fisher, a future headmaster of Oundle, the advantage of having three three-quarters in the line rather than the modern fashion for four; at the same time he was a friend of the bloods like Raymond Wavell and E. L. Coles who could always count on him to join a rag or build a bonfire in the quad from kindling, doors, chairs and lavatory seats.

Outside the college he became a member of the Strafford Club, a bastion of High Toryism, the Grid, a dining club for sociable bon viveurs, and the Oxford University Dramatic Society (the OUDS).

In each of these circles, he became the epitome of its type, and took the part with a panache that swept everything before it. Elected to the Strafford Club, he became secretary, proclaimed its adherence to Joseph Chamberlain's imperial preference policy and doubled its membership. Deciding that the ideal rag required a greased pig running amok through the college, he bought one, transported it to Magdalen and laboriously greased it, and, when it simply sat down in the quad, turned his mind to more rewarding matters. When *Isis* profiled him as its Idol, it noted that 'our Idol is self-confident, so unaffectedly self-confident that he carries conviction. Unlike many of his friends, he does things not because other people do not do them, but because he thinks they are best done in his particular way.' Another Oxford paper, the *Varsity*, suggested that 'if you wish to understand him thoroughly, study his clothing', and his clothing was flamboyant with a tendency to yellow ties worn over green shirts and white collars.

When it was rumoured that he proposed to start a new magazine called the *Oxford Point of View*, the general assumption was that it would be as shocking as the *Spirit Lamp*. 'We hope that this is not true,' commented the *Varsity*, 'we did not like the *Spirit Lamp*.' Its hopes were fully realised.

The first issue of the magazine, published in May 1902, promised to show how much 'Oxford had changed its point of view since the 1890s' and, in a phrase borrowed from Ibsen, it dubbed itself the voice of 'the younger generation knocking at the door'. At least three of the eight undergraduates who each put up five pounds towards the cost belonged to the Strafford Club, and there was more than a touch of the Young Fogey in their outlook.

'It is so easy to be abnormal and original,' Monty complained in an early editorial, 'and it is so difficult to be normal and commonplace. Here in Oxford it is more difficult than anywhere.' And then, chastising his former self, he added, 'The youthful degenerate, conscious of the suspicion of the rest of the college, and weakly trying to cultivate a liking for the poems of Verlaine or the pictures of Aubrey Beardsley, forgets that many whom he regards as Philistines have a far greater knowledge of French and a far keener appreciation of art than himself.'

The most controversial article it published – and it is a measure of the tenacity with which its editor strove for the normal and commonplace – was a plea by Robert Bridges for a reform in the pronunciation of Latin vowels. Otherwise its staple fare was the carefully responsible article in favour of imperial preference balanced by one on 'The Liberal Outlook'; it was for progress in art, but against the avant garde; and where university customs were concerned, it supported compulsory Greek, and opposed the presence of women except to decorate Eights Week. Looking back on this production of his younger self, the mature Monty rightly judged it to be 'slightly priggish, unreasonably solemn and utterly amorphous', and its lack of personality indicates the uncertainty which underlay his public performance.

Despite its shortcomings, the magazine was successful by university standards. Its first number sold 1500 copies at a shilling a copy, and although sales slowly declined, it outlasted Monty's time at university. The President of Magdalen judged it 'one of the handsomest magazines Oxford has ever produced', and writing to Edward Compton at the end of 1902 he mentioned it as 'very creditable indeed for so young a man ... if he goes on as he promises, he should come to something very worthwhile.' Warren was an entirely reliable guide to social achievement – Monty once claimed that 'only in snobbery did he achieve an authentic pre-eminence' – and so presumably this earnest espousal of orthodoxy made an impression.

So far as the President and Edward Compton were concerned, Monty's future was to be at the Bar, and the following year he began the process of eating his dinners at the Temple in order to qualify. For the next four years a vague ambition to be an ecclesiastical lawyer was periodically voiced when Edward needed reassurance.

Had the magazine fully represented his ideas, this might have been a realistic goal, but, first as a Volunteer and now as an undergraduate, he had been seduced by what Matthew Arnold called 'the life of the aristocracies with its large and free use of the world, its conversance with great affairs, its exemption from sordid cares, its liberation from the humdrum provincial round, its external splendour'. In the vacation, when the OUDS took its current production on a tour of stately homes during the summer of 1902, he stayed at Hinchingbrooke where Lord Sandwich had a Japanese garden with an erupting model of Fujiyama in the middle of it, and at Hams Hall with Lord Norton, who drank two or three bottles of port after dinner and had footmen on hand to help any guest the worse for wear up to his room. In term-time Monty gravitated naturally to the company of their heirs and relatives, the Good Eggs who were 'bonhomous, hearty, careless and rowdy'.

A Good Egg belonged to one of a few fashionable colleges – the rest being occupied by Bad Men – and if required to visit an unfashionable college like Keble he hired a coach and four to take him there in case it was somewhere miles out in the country. His high spirits were directed towards rags, whether mundanely debagging a 'quiet man' who worked too hard, or riotously celebrating the end of the Boer War.

'I see myself standing on the sloping sill of one of the bay windows of the OUDS [above a shoe-shop],' Monty wrote of the peace celebrations,

and delivering a patriotic speech to a crowd of Townees swaying backwards and forwards from the Corn Exchange to St Giles, prevented from falling headlong on top of them by the miraculous immunity which can be conferred by champagne . . . Probably piqued by failing to collect an attentive group of listeners, I decided to pique the crowd by aiming OUDS postcards at them. I was successful in cutting several townees with the sharp edges and presently a knot of them tried to break into the club . . . The next thing I remember is being knocked through the plate-glass of an ironmonger's shop. I seized the first weapon that came to hand, a frying-pan, and brought it down on the head of the nearest townee in reach . . . From the confusion of the next hours all I can recall is the magnificent blaze made by the burning cab-shelter in the Broad outside Trinity.

He did not belong to the aristocracy. He had neither the land nor the ancestry which made rioting a venial crime. On the other hand, his temperament leaned naturally towards aristocratic largeness and extravagance – it was no coincidence that he made Michael Fane the illegitimate son of an earl.

The search for a role which embodied these characteristics occupied much of his Oxford career. His abandonment of Jacobite romanticism was underlined during the Easter vacation in 1903 when he went to France in the company of Arthur Asquith and Guy Bonham-Carter. Staying at a *pension* in Compiègne, he met Osgood Mackenzie, author of *One Hundred Years in the Highlands* and creator of the gardens at Inverewe, who offered him a croft in Wester Ross where he could learn Gaelic, the language of Bonnie Prince Charlie's clansmen. Monty was grateful but let the offer lapse for want of interest. It was the concept of the English gentry which now coloured his imagination.

In his second year he began to develop the idea of Oxford itself as a natural aristocracy. Its manners – both the affectation of effortless achievement and the detestation of excessive emotion – were akin to those of the landed classes, and in age and accumulated tradition it belonged with the oldest of England's families. The undergraduate who came to this Oxford was more than himself, he was heir to a role laid upon him by the past.

'Nobody confers a privilege upon Oxford by taking up his abode here,' he wrote in the *Oxford Point of View*, 'it is Oxford who confers the honour by allowing him to do so.' The Oxford he conjured up in *Sinister Street* might be loud with the cries of bloods and hearties, but it was also an immaterial place whose immediacy dissolved in the swirling fog, where each generation of undergraduates was merely a repetition of the past, and 'the chimes in St Mary's tower struck without proclaiming any suggestion of passing time'.

The centre of that Oxford was Gunner's, or the office of Richard Gunstone, the long-serving steward of the Junior Common Room. 'Something there was in him of the old family butler, a little more of the yeoman farmer, a trace of the head-gamekeeper, a suspicion of the trainer of horses, but all these elements were blended to produce the effect of someone wise and saintly and simple.' Gunner was conservative in outlook, and an unfailing source of anecdote and tradition about Magdalen. His office, therefore, became an unofficial club for those who enjoyed such an atmosphere and valued a personality whose traits belonged to the retainer of a landed gentleman. In Monty's eyes, Gunner's was 'the innermost shrine of Oxford, the profoundest revelation of the shining truth round which the mysterious material of Oxford had grown through the Middle Ages'.

This is an extravagant compliment to pay an old college servant, but precisely because Monty's personality could take on the colours of his surroundings so easily it required a background that was unchanging. The Monty who envied the aristocrat his service to an estate and a family tradition envied Gunner for the same reason. His need for such a background was made the more pressing by the rejection of his own family's theatrical tradition.

The final break came at the end of his second year. He enjoyed acting and was clearly good at it, although the sheer number of competing interests restricted him to supporting roles in the OUDS productions. Nevertheless, his performance as Gratiano in *The Merchant of Venice* earned a remarkable tribute from Arthur Bourchier, actor-manager of the Garrick Theatre, who had come to see the production.

'Well, there's no doubt what you're going to be,' he said after the show, and immediately offered Monty a seven-year contract as the young lead at the Garrick, starting at £500 a year and rising to £2000. Over twenty years later he could still remember his astonishment when Monty turned down 'an offer I never made any young man before, and indeed I don't suppose any young man ever had such an offer'.

Enticing though it must have been, there was little likelihood that Monty would enter his father's profession. His experience of it had led him to the opinion that acting was a shallow skill and the stage itself 'a safe prosaic form of livelihood'. For someone intent on making a name for himself, it was necessary to enter a more demanding field, and it was not irrelevant that he had just read Samuel Butler's posthumous novel, *The Way of All Flesh*. The publication of the story of Ernest Pontifex's revolt against the narrow conventionality of his father was, in Monty's opinion, 'the most important literary event of my time at Oxford', and it served to crystallise his own feelings about his father and his ambitions for the future. In answer to Bourchier's shocked enquiry about the career he did intend to pursue, he replied, 'I think I'm going to write.'

What he was to write had not yet been decided. Apart from his magazine articles, he had written and discarded the opening scenes of an eighteenth-century play and a nineteenth-century melodrama, and composed several new pastoral poems. Nevertheless, when he moved out of college at the beginning of his third year, his ambitions were reflected in the surroundings which he created for himself in his rooms at 43 High Street.

The rooms were shared with his closest friend, Harry Pirie-Gordon, the only son of an Aberdeenshire laird. A tall, good-looking Harrovian,

Pirie-Gordon was Monty's opposite in that he cared nothing for the opinion of others, and he enjoyed the company of the sort of social misfits whom Monty in his orthodoxy now abhorred. One of his friends was the tiny, self-advertising Harold Davidson who, as rector of Stiffkey, was later unfrocked for importuning young women and subsequently killed by a lion at Blackpool; a few years after leaving Oxford Pirie-Gordon also took up the would-be priest Frederick Rolfe, or Baron Corvo, who viciously caricatured him as the bumbling moneybags Harry Peary-Buthlaw. Affable and unflappable, he shared with Monty a sense of the ridiculous and a taste for High Tory politics, and pursued an enthusiasm for heraldry and freemasonry which the income from estates in Wales and Scotland allowed him to do without care for the cost.

It was Monty who set the tone at their lodgings. The gas was cut off, and in its place light came from tall wax candles, brass sconces and hanging sanctuary lamps. A green tapestry embroidered with golden fleurs-de-lis and griffins' heads covered the wall. There were prints of crucifixions and madonnas by Memling and Giorgione, but the *Mona Lisa* still held its position above the fireplace. In a piece entitled 'The Undergraduate's Garden', Monty paid homage to Walter Pater's influence on his style and interior decoration. Pater had described the *Mona Lisa* as the woman 'upon whose head all the ends of the world are come . . . she is older than the rocks among which she sits; like the vampire she has been dead many times, and learned the secrets of the grave; and has been a diver in deep seas and keeps their fallen day about her.'

In the same precious manner Monty wrote of his Arundel print:

Few would wish to refuse La Gioconda the place of honour; she 'upon whose head all the ends of the world are come' may appropriately sit enthroned on the chimney shelf with her elusive smile, her arms folded so suggestively as she watches the fruitless efforts of man to see in the flame his own fiery soul. Flank her not with college shields . . . but with two austere pieces of blue or green china plates of antique shape and wrought by hand. Sometimes when you are tired of the realities of life you may light two tall wax candles, as the shadows flicker across her subtle countenance, freshen your mind with cool dreams of dead ambitions and old beliefs . . .

This was a long way from townee-bashing, and the journey owed something to the influence of a Balliol history tutor, F. F. Urquhart, known as 'Sligger', who introduced him to a more intellectually demanding circle than was to be found in Magdalen. Many of those he met in Sligger's company were to become lifelong friends, such as John

Mavrogordato, then a would-be poet, and later a professor of Greek and translator of Cavafy's poetry, and Orlo Williams, a classics scholar and later Clerk of the House of Commons.

Nevertheless, when he and Pirie-Gordon instituted a habit of giving elaborate dinners at 43 High Street, usually with roast swan, a boar's head or some other medieval dish as a centrepiece, they did not abandon their hearty friends entirely. There were large oarsmen from New College, and Kenneth 'Salt' Carlisle, captain of the university cricket XI, who gazed in perplexity at the Arundel prints and exclaimed, 'I say, Monty, you don't really *like* looking at those frightful women, do you?' And there were the jokes.

It was Harry Pirie-Gordon who successfully pulled off the famous trick of buying up the whole of the front row of stalls at the Garrick Theatre and having the tickets sent to bald men. He reported that his victims sat in a line bemused by the giggling which broke out behind them at each interval. It was Monty, however, who successfully hoaxed the *Daily Mail* with his account of how Henry Lygon was 'severely bitten in the legs, stomach and ribs by three gentlemen (sic) merely for wearing a collar with blue lines around it' – white collars being still the norm.

When a reporter was sent to investigate the story he was regaled with further details of men ragged for wearing patent leather boots or having no money, until two of Monty's friends burst into the room begging the massive Pirie-Gordon for protection against a crowd of hearties who wanted to rag them for working too hard. Before the reporter had time to digest this scene, the sound of the rowing 'push' howling for blood persuaded him to escape by climbing down a sheet from the window, and to complete Monty's triumph the *Daily Mail* gave the story a column and a half under the headline 'Ragging at Oxford – Causes of the Craze'.

The story became a favourite, both at parties and at college 'smokers' or revues, where Monty was in great demand. His power as a storyteller is almost incommunicable. It depended partly on his voice which, Terence de Vere White observed, 'had a seductive power greater than any other I have heard'. It was slightly theatrical in the clipped manner usually associated with Noel Coward, but the cadence had a springiness which invited enjoyment. His gift for mimicry created people who were utterly believable, and his eye for the absurd placed them in situations which should have been utterly implausible except that, like the *Daily Mail* story, they were all based on actual events.

By the end of 1903 his time at Oxford was running out, and even his mother had begun to wonder whether 'Monty would ever do anything but go around amusing people'. When the magazine *Isis* chose him as their 259th Idol – immediately after William Temple, the future Archbishop of Canterbury, Monty proudly noted – the writer seemed no less bemused. 'His crowded interests and occupations are almost unhealthy in their exuberance; and when he can find time to devote more than five minutes to a new occupation, the results of his industry will become palpable.' Groping for the key to his personality, *Isis* remarked:

To penetrate even deeper into the recesses of Mr Mackenzie's character, it may be said that he is at once strikingly old and startlingly young. Hardly a thought passes through his brain but comprehends some grand project . . . In debate his oratory is overwhelming, and in the bombardment of personalities his humour is most richly displayed, but when all is said and done, there remains the fact that he is very young: and when such words as 'cocksure' and 'boyish enthusiasm' are whispered, the wiseacre smiles sedately.

Whoever wrote the piece – it may well have been Pirie-Gordon, who was about to become the magazine's editor – he certainly knew his subject, for neither Monty's virtues nor his failings changed as he grew older. There were others who felt that if only he would settle down, the electrifying power of his personality would achieve remarkable things. Among them was Sligger Urquhart who, in December 1903, introduced him to Logan Pearsall Smith, the American-born critic and essayist.

A bachelor, then in his early forties, Pearsall Smith was fastidious and self-disciplined. In the austere manner appropriate to one of his Quaker background, he had set himself the goal of creating literary miniatures, beautiful in themselves and untouched by the complexities of the modern world. When they met in Sligger's rooms, Monty's future was still uncertain. He had talked of writing as a career, but he also saw himself as an ecclesiastical lawyer and, imagining that he would have a fourth year which would give him time to gain a First, as a Fellow of All Souls. Pearsall Smith was the catalyst in these amorphous dreams.

'His ability to inspire young men with the quintessential excitement of literature has never within my experience been equalled,' Monty declared, recalling the manner in which Pearsall Smith had praised the cadence of 'The Undergraduate's Garden' and delivered his verdict: 'Yes, yes, you have it in you. The authentic note of English prose sounds from time to time.'

Pearsall Smith insisted that he concentrate his energies in one area only, and in a way which captured Monty's attention, he couched his argument in religious terms. '[He] persuaded me that if I wished to be the writer of poems and plays I aspired to be,' Monty remembered, 'it was essential that I should withdraw from the world and test my vocation as sternly as if I were testing a vocation for the monastic life.' To one whose dreams of greatness sprang from a moment of revelation such an argument was irresistible.

Another undergraduate infected by Pearsall Smith's gospel of Puritan aesthetics was Christopher Stone. As a schoolboy at Eton he had published a volume of poetry called *Lusus Pueriles*, which earned Pearsall Smith's respect, and his personality, outgoing and pliable, aroused his middle-aged affection. The two of them were engaged on writing sonnets for each other's criticism when Monty appeared. Although Christopher was at Christ Church, he and Monty had met in their first term and occasionally at 'smokers', where his falsetto singing was as popular as Monty's reminiscences, but it was only now that they became friends.

In his letters home Monty started to refer casually to 'Stone the poet' or 'a literary man called Stone'. Then, in the spring of 1904, he announced that he and Christopher were to take a house in Burford, on the edge of the Cotswolds and about eighteen miles from Oxford. It was on Orlo Williams's advice that they turned aside to bicycle down the steep road into the village and over a hump-backed bridge which spanned the river Windrush. The house stood on the further bank, a small Elizabethan building lengthened by two wings with espalier pear trees and creepers framing the windows. A large garden planted with ancient apple trees separated it from the road, and the Windrush flowed through an orchard at the back. The house was named Lady Ham, and in aspect and setting it was close to perfection.

At first Christopher and Monty thought simply of living there for their fourth year, but the plan soon blossomed into making Lady Ham a monastic retreat for anyone who wanted the peace and quiet necessary to pursue the calling of literature. 'After all,' Pearsall Smith commented, 'it's in the great tradition, poverty, simplicity and the Muses.'

There was only one drawback to this plan – Monty was in love. Reflecting on this unfortunate fact some time later, his literary adviser observed austerely, 'The moral is that if one wants to start in Paradise, there must be no Eve.'

5
Romeo, Lothario and Harlequin

He was nineteen years old and still a freshman when he experienced the second of the three great momentary revelations – that of falling in love at first sight. 'I see her now as I saw her first that sunlit day in June exactly sixty-one years ago as I write these words,' he recollected.

She was wearing an organdie dress patterned with small pink flowers. Her light brown hair was drawn back over a pompadour, and when we looked at one another the roses of her face deepened to a blush . . . A year would pass before I told her of that love and heard from her that she too had loved me at first sight and that I also had blushed.

Her name was Ruth Daniel, the younger daughter of the Reverend Charles Daniel, Bursar and soon-to-be Provost of Worcester College. Apart from her sister Rachel there were no other children, and the small family was unusually close-knit. Mrs Daniel, almost twenty years younger than her husband, set a tone of bubbling humour, and Daniel himself, despite his grey beard and sixty-six years, had the breadth of interest of a man who had been William Morris's friend and still operated his own printing press.

It was an attractive household, even without the magic of undeclared love, and Monty's second year saw a growing intimacy with them. It must be admitted that his behaviour was hardly that of a young man struck by a *coup de foudre*. Neither passionate declaration nor silent ailing marred his days, and his interest, initially at least, seemed directed towards her elder sister Rachel whom he had first met in the OUDS. Yet, given his past, reticence was more convincing evidence of depth of feeling. 'I must have been afraid of destroying the magic of that moment,' he wrote, 'by letting it turn into another of those brief flirtations along the primrose path of youth's dalliance.'

It was the treacherous code of silent emotions which brought his secret love into the open. Ruth showed him a verse written by a friend:

> Happy is love expressed
> But love untold
> Is purer gold—
> Lock fast the treasure-chest

and commented on the truth of its message. Brooding over her meaning, Monty decided that she was referring not to her love but to its absence. Having reached the state of melancholy appropriate to desperate solutions, he approached Rachel and asked what he should do.

'Tell her,' said Rachel.

'But suppose she isn't in love with me?' he objected.

'The only way to find out is to ask her,' she replied. 'Somehow I don't think you will be disappointed.'

Nor was he.

'I sat down beside her on the step,' he wrote,

and told her that I loved her, and in a voice that seemed to come from out of this world I heard her say 'And I love you.' The cheek near to me burned with a minute crimson flame. I was so much overcome by the moment that I did not kiss her. I just sat in a trance. Suddenly I said, 'You must tell Rachel. You must tell your mother,' and getting up I hurried away from the house, and as it seemed to me but an instant later I was walking up George Street without touching the pavement, floating as one used to float in childish dreams.

Even in ecstasy, part of him remained audience to the actor. When he told friends about his love for Ruth many years later, he would describe it as 'one of the greatest love affairs of all time' and justify the claim by listing the three criteria which gave it such a high ranking: the lovers were young, they were both good-looking, and they fell in love at first sight.

The Daniel family welcomed him as their daughter's potential suitor, but insisted that the proprieties be observed. They were allowed to meet twice a week to take a walk together, and in a year's time, when Ruth was twenty-one, they might become engaged. Any thought of marriage must wait until Monty was able to earn enough to keep them both.

It was difficult to know when that would be. Reading history entitled him to stay up for four years, subject to the college's approval, and his plans for a career still hovered between the academic and legal professions, with writing as a sideline.

Ruth was six months younger than Monty and hardly the person to give direction to his mercurial temperament. The portrait of her in *Guy and Pauline*, which is the story of their love affair, shows her as a spiritual, sensitive girl – sensitive to the point of attempting suicide when love eventually fails – and so delicate in personality that the hero thinks of her as 'a briar rose . . . whose petals seemed to fall at the touch of definition'.

In actuality she showed herself to be rather more positive than fiction allowed. She performed in a college masque, edited a school magazine, and acted as her father's hostess welcoming the freshmen to the college. Like her fictional counterpart, however, she was deeply religious, attending church regularly and visiting the poor of the parish. Having fallen in love, her loyalties were given to her lover with the unequivocal commitment of innocence.

She wrote to him every day, and in his company gladly covered ten or twelve miles on their twice-weekly walks. On one of these excursions they visited the celebrated romantic novelist of the late Victorian era, Rhoda Broughton, whose books had once gripped Virginia Compton: 'How one longed to be in love and to be loved as her heroines were and to be equally lovely and attractive,' Virginia remembered, 'they caused a shocking discontent with oneself and one's surroundings.' But to Ruth in the perfection of her happiness, it seemed that a Broughton heroine could only have been created by someone disappointed in love.

The first shadow to that happiness came when Monty was warned by the President of Magdalen that the college history tutor, Mr Fletcher, had complained of him neglecting his work in favour of his other interests. Taking the hint, Monty withdrew from his part in the next OUDS production, but the gesture came too late to mollify Fletcher. In March 1904 Monty was informed that he would not be allowed to stay up at Oxford for a fourth year.

Attempting to soften the blow, Warren suggested to the Daniels that Monty would doubtless want to begin his career at once, but Ruth would have none of it. 'I told him,' she said to Monty, 'that your career had nothing to do with anybody except you and me.' Evidently feeling that Monty had been unjustly treated, Warren then offered to recommend him as a suitable replacement for John Buchan who was about to leave his job as editorial assistant on *The Spectator*. Monty turned down the offer with contempt, saying, 'If I did go in for journalism, it is the last paper with which I should want to be associated.'

By then Pearsall Smith had fired him with the ambition to be a poet. The deprivation of his extra year was sufficient threat to that future, but the suggestion that he should become a journalist was pouring salt in the wounds.

When he took his finals in June 1904, he had no hope of a First. Fourteen months' work had to be crammed into two, but he was determined to prove Fletcher at least morally wrong in denying him the chance of academic success. Sustained by black coffee and quails in aspic he worked till the late hours, committing to his superb memory entire pages of lecture notes. It must have aroused mixed emotions when Fletcher told him that he had not been far off a First, but he admitted to no regrets. 'It has been a lifelong habit of mine never to regret what I could not have,' he insisted, 'and to dwell instead on the disadvantage of whatever it was I had wanted if I had obtained it.' Instead of All Souls, he had Lady Ham and literature, and at the Commemoration Balls after the end of term Ruth was wearing his emerald engagement ring.

Whatever else those three crowded years at Oxford had done for him, he never denied that they had imbued him with the values of an English gentleman – the genuine, 1st Battalion variety. It was what he had wanted, but having got it he came to regard it as no less of a burden than the narrow snobbery of St Paul's. In his old age he claimed that *Sinister Street* was written in order 'to present in detail the youth of somebody handicapped by a public school and university education', and a few years after going down he tried to write a play about 'a young man with the feelings and passions of today who finds himself transported to a time when he can give vent to them, unhampered by the restraining influence of Eton and Oxford'. The truth was that, however much his manners, tastes and outlook corresponded to those of a gentleman, his passions and feelings did not.

Compared to the majority of his friends at Oxford, Monty was openly attracted to women. The difference was apparent when he and Pirie-Gordon took a holiday in Spain and North Africa during their first year. In Spain Pirie-Gordon would retire to their hotel in the evening while Monty explored the nightclubs, and when Pirie-Gordon bought a caftan as a souvenir of North Africa, Monty purchased a slave girl, and only the intervention of the British Minister eventually persuaded him to leave her behind. In London he was familiar with the Apollo, the Alhambra and theatres of their kind where the girls on stage were only separated by the pit and their amateur status from their sisters who had gone 'gay' and plied for hire on the promenade. When he went on holiday to France with some Oxford friends in his second year, it was Monty who knew which bars to visit to find prostitutes, who understood the double entendres of the cabaret girls' songs, and who acted as Pandarus when Guy Bonham-Carter decided that he must lose his virginity. Such sophistication was dangerous. Where sex was concerned the code was so hypocritical it took a real gentleman to observe it.

'Girls in your own station of life whom you hoped to marry were not seduced,' he wrote in *The East Wind of Love*.

Indeed the seduction even of girls of a lower station of life was an offence against the code of a gentleman. Sexual intercourse with girls of your own station of life who had previously been seduced by cads meant that such girls had ceased to consider the possibility of marriage with anybody. Sexual intercourse with a girl of lower station in life than your own who had previously been seduced by some cad was recognised as your prerogative, but you had to remember your gentlemanly obligation by being careful not to put her in the family way . . .

The important thing was not to be the first, or, as Henry Meats, the Mephistopheles of *Sinister Street* put it, 'Somebody else is to be the cad first, and then it's all right, eh?'

Such a code made it impossible to admit sexual feelings to romantic love, and in the great passion of his life Monty found himself trapped between the restraints imposed by his public school and university education and the impulse of natural desire. The clash came during the summer of 1904, when the happiness of his love for Ruth Daniel reached its peak.

In July he travelled down from Lady Ham to Somerset to stay with her family who had taken a house in Frome. There was a large house party whose numbers made it possible for Monty and Ruth to escape and spend the greater part of the day together. There were long drives through the lanes that threaded their way between deep hedgerows, and languorous afternoons in the garden room which overlooked the combe below the town.

One afternoon Rachel saw her sister sitting on Monty's knee in the garden room, and later scolded her furiously for behaving like a housemaid. 'From that moment,' he wrote, 'the passionate emotion of young love was tormented by a questioning self-consciousness.' The strain that Ruth was feeling showed when she reproached him a few days later for turning down Warren's offer to recommend him to *The*

Spectator, a job which might have enabled them to be married within months. It was impossible for him to contemplate marriage as more important than poetry, but that choice was obscured by the more disturbing demands of frustrated sexual desire. Ruth's innocence about her feelings had been dispelled by her sister's scolding, and thereafter she felt bound to resist his kisses. The disparity in their sexual experience exacerbated the tension, and to Monty's annoyance she began to go to church to pray to be free of impure thoughts about him. Something of the angry frustration he felt was expressed in an eloquent passage in *Guy and Pauline*:

Partly to plunge himself into a reaction and partly to avoid and even crush their spiritual divergence, Guy always made love passionately to Pauline during these days. He was aware she was terribly tried by this, but the knowledge made him more selfishly passionate. A sort of brutality had entered into their relation which Guy hated, but to which, in these circumstances that made him feverishly glad to wound her, he allowed more liberty every day. The merely physical side of the struggle between them was of course accentuated by the gag placed upon discussion. He would not give her the chance of saying why she feared his kisses, and he took an unfair advantage of the conviction that Pauline would never declare a reason until he demanded one. He was horribly conscious of abusing her love for him, and the more he was aware of that, the more brutal he showed himself until sometimes he used to wonder in dismay if at the back of his mind the impulse to destroy his love altogether had not been born.

Only marriage would cure it, but when he returned to Lady Ham Monty showed no urgency in finding a way to earn a living. He was desultory in eating the dinners at the Temple which would qualify him to be called to the Bar, and his writing turned from one project to another – dramatising a Maupassant story, versifying a French play, composing sonnets for Pearsall Smith and an epic for the Newdigate Prize. 'I must have been in a fever to accomplish something that would justify my withdrawal to Burford,' he decided. 'That I think must be the explanation of what, when I look back at it, seems an exasperating inability to make up my mind what I really did want to write, being sustained inwardly by the conviction of my own ultimate success but fretted by a continuous uncertainty about the way to achieve it.'

Ruth's awareness that writing meant more to him than marrying gave an edge of despair to their meetings in Oxford during the autumn. The pattern of recrimination and apology became ever more wearing until, in November, Mrs Daniel wrote to say that her daughter had become so overwrought that she was to be sent abroad for a change of scene.

Once he knew that she was not seriously ill, Monty's reaction was one of relief from the pressure of her expectations.

'I should like her to stay in Paris a good while,' he told his mother. 'I cannot tell you how very happy I am here . . . Really I am a very lucky person.' In the same tenor he wrote encouragingly to Ruth of his plans which included playing Phidippides, the lead role in the OUDS production of *The Clouds* by Aristophanes. The news must finally have convinced Ruth that there was no immediate prospect of his settling down. From Paris came a tiny cardboard box containing her engagement ring, and a message from her mother saying that Ruth felt she could only be a hindrance to the way he was planning his future.

In the eighteen months since they told each other of their love, she had written him over four hundred letters. On a grey January morning, he burned them all, then dropped the ring in the millpool behind Lady Ham. There were other mementoes, perhaps photographs and letters which were kept at Beech, and these were not destroyed. Throughout his life he cherished them as reminders of an ideal passion until, just three years before he died, they too were consigned to the flames.

Until Monty's marriage, Ruth continued to hope for a reconciliation, but when that hope was extinguished, she turned increasingly to religion, and eventually joined an Anglican order of nuns. Monty, on the other hand, at once accepted the rupture as final. It was the second time that he had broken the prohibition on emotional dependence, and Ruth's decision to break off the engagement was a bitter blow.

'. . . no one quite knows what I have suffered in the matter of my broken engagement,' he confided in February to a diary which he kept for the only time in his life:

. . . I have heard nothing of Ruth since. She is in Somerset, and when I think of that summer landscape bare in the pale, February sun I think of it in dismay. I have to realise somehow it was all a mistake – the wind can never wed the rain. I must make a vow not to sentimentalise the past. Outwardly I smile. Within I have that dull ache of disappointment as when one waits for a long expected, eagerly desired guest, and the bell rings bringing with it a note to apologise . . .

The bitter mood lasted through the spring – the only period in his life when he lived alone for any length of time. With only the sound of the Windrush to disturb him, he laboured at the sonnets for which so much had been sacrificed. Logan Pearsall Smith, who looked in from time to time, approved of his monastic state. Then in April, he noted that Monty was growing rather too interested in Gladys Cheatle, the daughter of a doctor who lived on the other side of the river. Despite his mentor's foreboding about the ill-effects of sex, Monty decided to invest in a canoe.

As a literary adviser Pearsall Smith was more influential. He attached particular importance to formal structure, a lesson which was learned well and is instantly detectable in Monty's novels as well as his poetry. Yet, so far as the latter was concerned, it was emotional freedom he needed rather than correctness of form.

During that spring, for example, he sent Pearsall Smith a poem entitled *Corinna* which began:

> There blooms the rathe, adventurous celandine
> In the moist February days, and lights
> The chilly landscape like small suns that shine
> In pixies' dreams asleep o' winter nights . . .

Instead of the coyness of imagery, Pearsall Smith chose to criticise the weak vowel sound at the start of a later line:

> . . . chestnuts engross
> Us with strange leaps and buoyant apples bob
> Afloat in bowls . . .

'Ugh, how *can* you begin with "Us"?' he wrote. 'Do alter the first half of the line.' Monty obliged by changing it to 'Our fancy with strange leaps and apples bob . . .' – but the quality of the poem was not materially improved.

The real flaw in the verse written at Lady Ham is the absence of authentic feeling. Despite his broken love, there is no passion and no grief. Instead there is a sense that he is watching himself being a poet, and Edmund Gosse once described them as 'Guy Hazlewood's poems, written at Plasher's Mead [the fictional name given to Lady Ham], because he was determined to write poetry'. Even a well-finished sonnet like *To the First Primrose in my Garden* is deadened by self-consciousness:

> I found thee in a sheltered garden nook
> Amid the aconites and snowdrops wan,
> The parsimonious February sun
> Must sure have lent thee that half-careworn look
> Of childish wonderment, swift overtook
> By fancied loves and fears, and life begun;
> What April-call aroused thee, quiet nun,
> That thy dark cloister is too soon forsook?

The western sky still holds a thought of rain.
The thrush is singing in the sycamore
To mellow the fast-lengthening eventide;
But fickle is the windy weather-vane,
And daffodils keep close their golden store
Which will light up the glades when thou hast died.

A quarter of a century later he dismissed such pieces as 'a versification of literary impressions', but at the time they convinced him that he had found his true vocation.

In the year since he had left Oxford, Lady Ham had been transformed. Instead of renting it as Christopher and he had intended, the death of the owner forced them to purchase it together with a nearby cottage. By a complex financial transaction they borrowed the £1400 necessary and resold the cottage – known as the Other House – for half the sum to an actor, Robert Whitworth Jones, and George Montagu, later the Earl of Sandwich. At a cost of £400, put up by Virginia Compton, the house and its surroundings were then turned into a place of walled gardens, rolling lawns, apple-green wallpaper in the dining room and tall-backed Venetian chairs in the drawing room.

With the coming of summer, visitors began to arrive. Most were old friends from Oxford and aristocratic weekenders from the Other House. Hubert Parry, who had composed the music for *The Clouds*, came to play the piano, and with a diamond pencil Roger Fry inscribed on the window which served as a visitor's book his tribute to the view of the Windrush valley, 'The fresh green lap of fair King Richard's land'. There were cricket matches at nearby mansions, picnics and parties. It might have been thought perfection, but Christopher was evidently concerned about the solitary occupant at Lady Ham. In July he wrote to his sister Faith saying that he did not think that Monty should be left alone there. The brief affair with the doctor's daughter had ended unhappily, and it may have been the state of his mind which aroused Christopher's concern.

He had begun visiting London in search of girls, and by August he was spending so much time there that he proposed to rent two rooms in 7 Grosvenor Road, a terraced house backing onto a bus depot in what was then nearly a slum. The move was made in late September, and Christopher, who had spent the summer tutoring the children of a wealthy widow named Mrs Chinnery, decided to join him.

'The astonishing thing about Monty,' he used to say, 'is the way he gets to know people. Within weeks of coming to London, he seemed to know everyone from great men to prostitutes.' They went together to the parties at which great men such as Desmond MacCarthy might be met, but Christopher used to grow weary of being woken in the early hours by the return of his friend from his nightly prowls round London's low-life.

On one of his summer visits he had picked up a commercial traveller's mistress, called Daisy. In the style of Mrs Frith and Ethel, she entranced him with stories of the underworld, and now she acted as his guide to the bars and clubs frequented by pimps and prostitutes. It was a world in which he felt free of moral restraint. His brief flings with respectable girls that summer – Gladys Cheatle and a nurse – had, as he admitted, 'made them unhappy', but in this society there was no connection between sex and marriage. He needed women and he knew he was attractive to them. The adolescent good looks had grown dramatically glamorous, and although stage-door gossip and later Capri scandal cast doubt on his sexual stamina, he had the ineffable gift of creating excitement and making life fun.

Yet there was another side to this free-wheeling exploration of the underside of society. Writing to his father on 6 December that year he referred to it with distaste, and almost as a compulsion. 'For the last year I have longed more than I can tell you to be settled,' he wrote. 'My eternal philandering since my engagement was broken off was injuring both my work and myself.' And in another letter some days later, he wrote, 'The wear and tear of a violent and oppressive imagination are such that [one] must have some soothing influence to counterbalance this. Some find it in drink, some in drugs, a few in dissipation.'

He may well have been dramatising his philandering as he did his poetry into something greater than actuality, but when Michael Fane plunges into London's low-life after leaving Oxford an explicit connection is made with his childhood fantasies:

This experience was foredoomed from very infancy. It was designate in childish dreams indelible . . . Those days of London fog when he had sat desolately in the pinched red house in Carlington Road . . . the shouting of murders by newspaper-boys on drizzled December nights; all these dreadful intimations in childhood had procured his present idea of London. With the indestructible truth of earliest impressions, they still persisted behind the outward presentation of a normal and comfortable procedure in the midst of money, friends and well-bred conventions.

A similar connection had been made between those childhood fears and his adventures in adolescence. It can hardly be coincidence that in each case the compulsive search down sinister streets was triggered by a love withdrawn – first by his mother, then by Alan Mitchell, and now by Ruth Daniel.

It was in this turbulent state that he encountered Christopher Stone's sister Faith. They had met twice before, the first time in Christopher's rooms at Christ Church, while Monty was still engaged to Ruth.

'My first impression was of a bright emerald tie and an enormous pair of eyes which seemed luminous in the darkened room,' Faith wrote in her autobiography, *As Much As I Dare*.

As he came into the light of the bay window, I saw the rose-leaf complexion, the small, pretty Cupid's bow mouth, the sloping poet's brow, and then the wan crooked smile which so surprisingly tautened the Cupid's bow of the mouth. I saw that the eyes were deep violet blue.

This then was Monty Mackenzie. I was overwhelmed by the manner in which his personality took charge of the room and everything it contained. Everything else, including myself, became insignificant. I was not at all pleased . . . I felt small and helpless, acutely conscious that no power on earth could shake the immanence of this too vivid personality. He was there, secure as a planet in our firmament. I watched him as he talked, enchanting his audience (for indeed it seemed to be instantly that).

Faith was twenty-seven, five years older than him. Tall and good-looking, with dark brows which gave her a Spanish appearance, she was then acting with Charles Hawtrey's touring company. By Compton standards, however, she was not a real actress. Her father, the Reverend Edward Stone, was a schoolmaster, as were her three elder brothers. There were also four sisters, all older than her, and Christopher, the youngest child. The pressure of bearing and bringing up so large a family had caused her mother to have a nervous breakdown, and after several painful years searching for a cure she had died while Faith was still a teenager.

Deprived of mothering herself, Faith lavished affection on her elderly father and on Christopher. As a child she was highly strung, and her nerves, which caused headaches and stomach pains throughout her life, inhibited what might have been a considerable talent as a pianist. Yet she had too much vivacity to follow the example of her sisters, who had married clergymen and teachers. 'The stage was an escape,' she said, 'not from home which I loved, but from the life which seemed inevitable.' But after five years in Hawtrey's company, she still had no more than two lines of dialogue to say, and two guineas a week to spend. She was, however, a mature woman who had had at least two affairs, and possessed sufficient wit and independence of mind to dislike being overshadowed by an undergraduate.

When they met again at a cricket match while Monty was at Lady Ham, she remained defensive, and her opinion did not change in London until, on Friday 10 November, she went round to Grosvenor Road to see Christopher, and found Monty there by himself. They had lunch together, then tea, and 'I forgot my resentment. Antagonism collapsed. I was now under the spell.' Less than three weeks later, on 30 November, they were secretly married by special licence at St Saviour's, Pimlico, with Frank Compton and a road-sweeper as witnesses.

'Handsome, charming, clever, and moreover the sister of my greatest friend,' was the description of his wife which Monty gave to Edward Compton. By themselves the first three qualities were not sufficient to make him propose so sudden a marriage, but the fourth carried more weight. He once described the little green and white room at 7 Grosvenor Road, with its view across the Thames, as being designed for love affairs. It was there on that Friday evening that he and Faith became lovers. In other circumstances she might have been one more girl whom he made 'rather unhappy', but the gentleman's code was quite clear on this point: as he told Terence de Vere White, 'it wasn't the done thing to make love to the sister of your best friend.'

The prospect of marriage threw him into a deep depression. Faith remembered that the proposal came after a late dinner in Soho; less romantically, Monty remembered his despair being suddenly lightened by seeing Alfred Lyttelton, Colonial Secretary in a crumbling Unionist government, smiling to himself as he left the House of Commons. 'If he could smile at the prospect before a Government on its last legs,' he decided, 'I too could smile at my own prospect.' With the cheerfulness of resignation, he asked Faith to marry him and was immediately accepted.

Because neither had money and their parents would impose the same delays as the Daniels had previously, the wedding had to be secret. They chose St Andrew's Day, knowing that Christopher would be at Eton for the annual Wall Game on that day. Having done the right thing, Monty hoped that they might not have to tell anyone until 'the psychological moment'. But Faith insisted that Christopher must know, and he in turn threatened to announce it publicly if Monty did not.

When he heard the news, Edward Stone replied in gentle terms: 'I can't quite approve and yet I am not furiously angry as I suppose a sensible person should be ... I can imagine the charm of a romantic marriage with no trousseau or wedding breakfast.' For Monty the crucial arbiter was his father. His mother always found extravagance in him charming, and despite her reservations she soon gave him her blessing. Edward, however, controlled his allowance, now reduced to £150 a year, and would certainly disapprove of his marrying before he could support a wife.

In his letter of 6 December Monty wrote to him with uncharacteristic frankness about his reasons

for what to you and to everybody must seem an unaccountable step. I have always had a somewhat fatal attraction to women and my love affairs have already been numerous. For the last year I have longed more passionately than I can tell you to be settled. My eternal philandering since my engagement was broken off was injuring both my work and myself. In this affair I was determined to finish for ever with half measures. You know my headstrong way, and you will understand that if I have made up my mind I will have my own way . . . If you knew how many times I have been tempted to cut myself off from society and marry some barmaid and be done with love affairs for ever, you would be glad that I have chosen so wisely.

In the same vein he had written to his mother, 'If you knew from what I have escaped for ever you would be as happy as me.'

Whatever it was he had escaped, the shadow of the sinister street or simply a tendency to chase skirts, his relief was beyond doubt. It overflowed in self-confident exuberance. His friends commented on it, and he himself could not help giving voice to his elation.

'I am happier than I have ever been or ever thought I could be,' he wrote to his mother. 'I have for the first time in my life sat down to *work* with *pleasure*. I am never idle for a moment. I shall never be idle again.' His tone was only slightly more subdued when he wrote to his father. 'Already I feel free from everything save the most earnest desire and determination to justify your confidence. If you will continue to back me up, I swear you will never regret it. If I am famous (many are convinced I shall be), you will have done a good deal more for me than fathers usually do for men of genius.'

6

The search for self-expression

'I was prepared for almost any possibility in my marriage,' Faith wrote in her autobiography, 'neglect, abandonment, even divorce.' She had some justification. When they announced the wedding with a posy of Monty's verses, letters of congratulation poured in from his many friends, and among them the phrase 'I have given up being surprised by anything you may do' recurred with alarming frequency. A Persian rug arrived from Pearsall Smith, a dinner set from George Montagu, and a brief note from a lady of the night, 'I hear you've married a straight-cut.'

The day after the wedding the drains in Grosvenor Road failed. Then Monty fell ill with jaundice. Faith judged it best to take him to her father's home in Abingdon, where Pearsall Smith found them 'very shy but looking very happy'.

In the summer they went to Lady Ham where they discovered that neither knew anything of housekeeping. Faith indeed was innocent of all domestic skills: she could not cook, hated sewing and mending, and loathed cleaning. Local women were hired to help, but she was not good with servants either, and quarrelled with a succession of cleaning-women and cooks.

None of this mattered. Instead of china or linen, Edward Stone's wedding present had been £100, and their credit was elastic. Dresses arrived from Barker's, books from Blackwell's and they lived largely on 'delicious food in jars and tins from Frank Cooper in Oxford, as expensive as could be'. Hasty though their marriage had been, they could hardly have been better matched in their taste for the best in clothes and food and the sheer pleasure they took in spending.

Monty was not the man to make good his wife's impracticality. On the morning of his wedding, he made tea and never again attempted to make anything in the kitchen. In general, Faith commented, he was 'deliberately clumsy with anything more formidable than a pen, a billiard cue, a knife and fork or a walking-stick. Sometimes he hung a picture because he was absolutely the only person who knew exactly where it should go, but it was a great business and not often repeated.'

On the other hand he did not criticise her for not being a housewife. He liked good food and comfort, but they were not of crucial importance. When Faith fell ill with colitis a few months after the wedding and was condemned to a diet of poached eggs, asparagus and biscuits, he willingly kept her company He was thoughtful in such matters, but his rarest gift was the ability to make ordinary activity significant, and to extract from the mundane business of choosing a tie or finding a cab some entertainment, some story or some theory which convincingly explained why his way was the only sensible way of choosing a tie or finding a cab. 'To have lived with him,' Faith said, 'makes ordinary life seem humdrum and ridiculous.'

The pattern of their marriage became clear during its first eighteen months. Faith provided him with the elegance and wit of an older woman. She understood his needs and adored him, and as his wife offered the sense of permanence he had lacked. In emotional terms he refused to let himself depend on her, but the helplessness in practical matters and the physical disorders which occurred in moments of stress were opportunities for her to care for him. To that kind of love he responded with charm and gaiety. 'Until the First World War Faith was more than a wife to him,' Frank Swinnerton commented. 'She mothered him, and that was what he liked.'

The role might have placed her in conflict with his real mother, for as Faith recognised, 'her devotion to her first-born son was the kind that must be lit by jealousy'. From the start, however, she acknowledged Virginia's primacy in the relationship. When Monty came down with jaundice, she sent her daily bulletins on his progress, and she constantly sought her advice on how to look after him. His care became their joint concern, and when they went abroad, Faith's letters to Virginia contained detailed reports on his physical and emotional well-being. 'I know you like to know what's going on,' she added after an unusually lengthy list of ills from Capri, 'and would feel no trust in me if you found I hadn't told you.'

In the elation of finding such a perfect wife, Monty's industry became prodigious. Within a fortnight of recovering from jaundice he had produced fifty lines of a new poem, three sonnets and a lyric. Practicality required that he mend his fences with his father, who remained alarmed by his folly in marrying without first being able to earn a living. Monty hastened to set his fears at rest, and nowhere is his ability to think himself into a role more clearly demonstrated than in this letter written on 21 December to his father:

It is inevitable that anyone who proposes to stake his fame on literature is bound to convey an impression of dawdling at first. These present years are the ones in which every great man has been criticised for what the world chooses to suppose a waste of time.

But it is significant that all the great poets were relieved from the harassing effort of earning their daily bread at this very period. A young man is laying up his experience, pruning his extravagances, moulding his ultimate idea. I should not write like this, were I not firmly convinced that one day I shall rank high among the English poets. Some intuition is given to men born poets which justifies their contempt of popular success and consoles them with the prospect of ultimate glory . . .

At Virginia's suggestion he also made a more practical appeal for his father's good opinion by rewriting a play called *Tomorrow*, on which Edward's hopes of a London success were now pinned. It was an awkward piece – half modern morality play, half eighteenth-century pastiche – but by laying aside his poetry Monty managed to have his new version ready for his father's fifty-second birthday on 14 January 1906.

Perhaps it was the youthful exuberance of his son's letter or perhaps he sensed that the play would never work, but the old trouper was in depressed spirits when he celebrated the Compton Comedy Company's silver jubilee three weeks later in Aberdeen.

'Twenty-five years' devotion to legitimate and old English comedy must be allowed to count for something,' he said wearily, 'and when I think of the plays old and new that I have rehearsed and produced during that quarter of a century I must confess that it does represent a huge amount of patience and perseverance, as well as a large amount of the inevitable worry and wear and tear and disappointment inseparable from such undertakings.' Among his audience which had gathered to present a cheque and a portrait of him in his role as Davy Garrick, there must have been some fidgeting as the hero of light-hearted romance lingered on the drab reality of long train journeys, unsuitable theatres and unresponsive audiences. 'Add to that, that we are invariably rehearsing all the time, and I at any rate have been doing all this for twenty-five years, and I think I have made out my case for work and worry and anxious times.'

It was the antithesis of the career his eldest son envisaged for himself. Indeed without Edward's example, it would be difficult to appreciate why both Monty and Frank made careless extravagance the symbol of their independence. In contrast to the academic brilliance of his elder brother, Frank had resolutely refused to work at St Paul's. Although aged only fourteen at the outbreak of the Boer War, he had seized the opportunity to run away and enlist in the Imperial Yeomanry. When he was brought back, not even the promise of a place at Sandhurst could persuade him to stay on past his sixteenth birthday. Somewhat reluctantly Edward found him work in the CCC, but Frank's temper, which later earned him the nickname 'Fiery' in the army, made it a trying arrangement. When he was eighteen he was allowed to return to a military career, and in 1906 he was commissioned into the Royal Inniskilling Fusiliers, where his demands for money to buy uniforms and polo ponies were to prove as insatiable as his elder brother's had been at Oxford.

Monty himself had gone down owing over £350 – including £102 for books and £71 for clothes – 'a very *respectable* list of debts,' he assured his mother, who paid the most pressing herself. Even with his allowance cut to £150 a year, to which Virginia added about £50 of her own, his standard of living was not appreciably diminished. His shirts still came from Edouard & Butler and, like his boots, suits, hats and the paper in his journal, they were handmade to his specification. It was as well for Edward's peace of mind that Virginia only encouraged extravagance in her sons.

Like her own mother, Virginia had a poor opinion of a girl's capacity. Since 1904 she had given Viola the leading lady's parts, such as Lydia Languish and Lady Teazle, to play opposite Edward, but this did not imply any acknowledgement of her talent; it was simply a device to prevent Edward from flirting. To inculcate the younger girls, Katie and Fay, with the proper discipline she forgave Annie Curry the gin and put her back in charge of their upbringing. Fay, however, never accepted her nanny's authority, and the old woman was finally retired for good in 1907. Virginia herself took to charity work in her retirement. Throughout her marriage she had managed both her children and herself with the same iron control, and Faith soon noted that her mother-in-law felt entirely responsible for everything to do with the family. It is clear that the stress caused by Edward's infidelity and her sons' antagonism towards him was at last wearing down her strength.

By June, Monty had enough poems to send to a publisher, Elkin Matthews. They bore the endorsements of Robert Bridges and Pearsall Smith, and in his exalted state he spoke of them as though they were already published. A month later, his friend John Mavrogordato, who was a reader with Elkin Matthews, sent him the unwelcome news that Matthews would only publish if he were guaranteed against loss.

'I have asked for them back and shall try somebody else,' he told his mother. 'If nobody will take them I shall have them printed and sell them myself at one shilling. I think I could manage to dispose of 500 all round. Rather fun too!'

Self-pity was never among his faults, and considering how much the poems stood for – the great cause in which he would astonish the world – and how certain he had been that his genius would be instantly recognised, his stoicism was admirable. Yet it did not disguise the severity of the blow. He could not bring himself to risk another publisher's rejection and the manuscript remained unseen for almost a year until he plucked up the courage to have it privately printed. He stopped writing verse until one evening in November Faith played Schumann's *Carnaval*, and the music awoke in him the idea for a poem which, he told his mother, 'is to be a sort of Wilhelm Meister, autobiographical, psychological, allegorical fantasy of some 2500 lines.' The project was never realised in poetry, which he found difficult to take up again, but in prose it can be seen as the seed of his most substantial novels.

'It was,' he recollected, 'a fussy unsatisfactory autumn.' Matthews's rebuff forced him to look seriously at other forms of writing. He had just read *Kipps* and with H. G. Wells's permission he set about dramatising it. Then an old theatrical friend of the family, Ben Greet, wrote offering him a three-year contract to join his company which performed and lectured on Shakespeare to American college audiences; by poignant coincidence his name had been suggested by Ruth's mother who, Greet said, 'spoke *very* nicely of him'. Monty discouraged him by asking for more money, and once *Kipps* was completed he began writing his first original play, *The Gentleman in Grey*.

Like Edward Compton's favourite vehicle, *Davy Garrick*, this was an eighteenth-century pastiche, set in a spa, Curtain Wells, which owed as much to Bath as the dialogue to Goldsmith and Sheridan. The story, complicated by misunderstandings and subplots, concerned the love of Charles Lovely, an upper-class highwayman, for the young Phyllida

Courteen, and it was designed deliberately to let Edward star in the sort of role he preferred.

Ever since his weary jubilee, Edward's roving eye had been kept sternly on duty by the presence of his eighteen-year-old daughter Viola as his leading lady, but now, tacitly recognising that the sacrifice of art to moral rectitude could be taken too far, Virginia had at last allowed him a new female lead, Phyllis Relph. In a sentimental manner he became infatuated with her and Monty judiciously scattered his offering with love scenes. A few days after his twenty-fourth birthday in January 1907, Monty read the play to the company. It was well received, and his father was sufficiently impressed to promise it a premiere at the Lyceum Theatre, Edinburgh, during the company's Scottish tour. 'You'll have a critical audience there,' he told his son, 'the most critical in Britain, and if Edinburgh approves you'll have nothing to worry about.'

In order to rehearse and rewrite, Monty travelled with the company to Aberdeen, the last stop before Edinburgh. After a week of full houses Edward's voice suddenly began to fade, and by the time they arrived in Edinburgh just four nights before the opening night of *The Gentleman in Grey* it was no more than a whisper. The schedule required the company to play *The School for Scandal* followed by *The Rivals* and *She Stoops to Conquer* before the new play, for all of which understudies would have to be rehearsed. Appalled by the thought of what would happen to his play if everyone were distracted by learning new parts, Monty volunteered to take his father's place. By a prodigious feat of memory, he learnt Charles Surface's part overnight and played it without a prompt, then repeated the achievement the following night for Bob Acres in *The Rivals*. They were parts he had grown up with, and like his forebears, both Bateman and Compton, he was 'a good natural study', yet it remains a remarkable feat. To top it he then learned Tony Lumpkin in *She Stoops to Conquer*, but by the time of the performance Edward's voice had returned.

The climax to a triumphant week should have come at the opening of his own play the following night. The audience was enthusiastic and the stage paper, the *Era*, gave it a friendly review, calling it

an attractive, agreeably written play, in which much skill is shown alike in dialogue and construction. Many of the lines have an epigrammatic ring and freshness, and there are dainty gems of speech which have an almost Elizabethan flavour. The comedy is full of exceptional promise ... Mr Compton made a distinct triumph and was loudly recalled at the end of each act. At the fall of the final curtain there were loud calls for the author and Mr Compton led his son onto the stage. Enthusiastic applause followed and Mr Compton said 'Was the play a success?' A unanimous shout of 'Yes' came from all parts of the house.

The most critical audience in Britain had given its verdict, yet the author himself was disappointed. 'It was not the play as I had seen it in my own mind,' he wrote. 'I began to ask myself if I was not too good an actor to be a good playwright. Was I going to write plays in the future of which the only good performance from my point of view would be when I read it to the company?'

It is not uncommon for playwrights to feel that their work has been given less than its due on stage, and the Compton Comedy Company was probably past its peak. Age and ill health must have slowed Edward down, and it was about now that he succumbed to the custom of taking on 'paying guests' – amateurs who paid for the privilege of appearing with a professional company. It is equally possible that the play may not have been as good as its author imagined – it certainly did not stay in the repertory – but whatever the cause, the timing of that disappointment was of vital importance.

He had explored the immediacy of poetry, and found it impossible to express himself. Now drama had thrown up the opposite problem and intermediaries came between himself and the audience. When he came to attempt his first novel later in the year, this question of where to place the authorial voice inevitably recurred, and the solution was to provide him with a prose style uniquely fitted to his personality and background.

A succession of illnesses followed his epic performance, and soon after he returned to the small flat at 127 Cheyne Walk which he and Faith now occupied, he came down with a severe attack of scarlet fever. As though to compensate for his imperturbability during psychological distress, he presented physical diseases in dramatic form. He rarely caught a cold but suffered 'an infernal attack of *la grippe*', diarrhoea was dysentery, and a cough bronchitis, usually accompanied by 'a touch of pleurisy'. Of the scarlet fever, he insisted that 'it had been touch and go for a time', and he did not veil the memory of the agonising pain, burning throat and delirium brought on by a temperature of 106 degrees. He was kept isolated in the Western Fever Hospital for seven weeks, and during the enforced idleness the anticlimax of his play's performance and the disappointment of his poetry evidently preyed upon his mind. On the suggestion of his old friend Claude Kirby, he decided to pay Blackwell's to publish his poems, and almost as soon as he was released from hospital at the end of May his father set him to rewriting *Tomorrow*, now called *The Eighteenth Century*, for a London production. Although he undertook the work, his thoughts were elsewhere, and when the play ended its run in September, he wrote to his mother,

I'm in rather a tangle of mind at present, and am seriously thinking of being ordained next year. But I'll give the idea time to settle firmly. That's why I want to get away to the sea and the solitary places, and be near a church that I like. The ordination idea is not a new one, but has recurred more frequently of late. I rather fought against it at first, but I think the vocation will be too strong.

The boyhood urge to be a parson had given way to the urge to write poetry, and it cannot have been chance that it should have returned once he began to doubt whether he really were touched by poetic genius. The moment of conversion had convinced him that his life had a special purpose, but the means of expression still remained hidden.

It was to the sea and the solitary places of Cornwall that he chose to go. His old friend of adolescence, Sandys Wason, had been appointed to the combined livings of Gunwalloe and Cury, and he now invited Monty and Faith to stay as paying guests at the Cury Vicarage. It was a large house, kept indifferently clean by several ladies of the congregation who competed for the favour of looking after Wason. Monty and he would play two-handed bridge in the evenings, and occasionally Wason would demonstrate his skill as a cook, but it could not be described as comfortable.

Monty's poems came out early in October, shortly after he and Faith had arrived at the vicarage, and the reviews were not slow to follow. One of the earliest appeared in the *Scotsman*: 'A volume of rich promise,' it ran. 'The author attempts many forms and succeeds in nearly all. He has great imaginative gifts, and his verse is full of delicate fancy.' Monty was encouraged but tantalised by its brevity. 'If it's worth saying so much,' he demanded in frustration, 'why isn't it worth saying more?'

Others were longer, and a few equally appreciative, praising especially the beauty of his words and phrases. The general tenor, however, was a complaint of emptiness of emotion or, as the *Daily Chronicle* brutally wrote of one sonnet, 'In a style like this it is impossible to express anything whether in fourteen or a thousand lines.' When *Country Life* declared that 'of real passion or feeling Mr Mackenzie's effusions do not give a single hint . . . his work is inspired by literature not life', Monty recognised that he did not possess the original genius which is immediately hailed by reviewers. 'It was no doubt gratifying to be told by various critics that my poems recalled Herrick or Rossetti or Keats or Spenser or William Morris,' he observed, 'but I did not want to recall any of them. I wanted to express myself; reading coldly through my poems I decided that they only expressed my cleverness. My poetry was not really inspired, it was a pastiche. It was on a par with my ability to write good Greek iambics or good Latin prose once upon a time.'

It was a double failure, as a means of self-expression and as the road to fame. The Church might repair the first, but he was running out of options if he were to make his name in literature. 'I was not prepared to be one more literary amateur,' he wrote. 'If I were to go on writing I must feel completely confident of my ability to become a recognised figure of literature.'

Before the last of the reviews was in, he took an evening walk down to the water's edge at Gunwalloe Cove. Depressed by failure and confused about the direction he should take, he was gazing out across the black waves when his eye was caught by the faint beam of a glow-worm in the grass beside him. He was in a mood for omens, and its defiance of the overwhelming night crystallised his determination to succeed. Returning to the vicarage, he waved aside Wason's offer of a game of two-handed bridge, and by the light of two tall candles sat down to write what he thought of as the ideal performance of *The Gentleman in Grey* and what turned out to be his first novel, *The Passionate Elopement*.

He wrote every evening and by the end of 1907 he had 30,000 words of what he estimated would be a total of 120,000. However, the book took another twelve months to complete, and considering that he had the outline of the plot, the main characters and substantial portions of dialogue clear in his mind, it was slow progress. Religion rather than literature was his dominating interest for much of that year.

By this time the crisis in the Church of England caused by the upsurge in Anglo-Catholicism had lost some of its urgency. There were still cases of bishops and patrons who hounded Anglo-Catholic priests from their parishes, but most tolerated ritualism sufficiently for an accommodation to be reached. And those priests for whom accommodation was intolerable had usually gone over to Rome. In Cornwall, however, the battle continued to be fought with bitterness. The county was predominantly Methodist and its influence encouraged Low Church Anglicanism. There was in consequence fierce resistance to an Anglo-Catholic priest who attempted to substitute Holy Communion for Morning Prayer or to introduce coloured vestments, incense and bells, and the celebration of saints' days. The nature of the Cornish themselves gave their fierceness a special edge.

'They are a secret people and rarely disclose their thoughts,' wrote the Reverend Bernard Walke, a leading Anglo-Catholic who held a living at Polruan and later at St Hilary. When his friend Wason came into conflict with both bishop and congregation after the war, he was alarmed on his behalf. 'Knowing the cunning and ferocity that Cornish people can show when their religious passions are aroused,' he said, 'I was daily expecting to hear of an attack.' They were not empty fears. Wason was to be physically bundled out of his vicarage by his congregation, and some years later Walke himself had his church broken into and vandalised by fundamentalist Protestants.

Walke thought of his fellow priest as a vague and unworldly White Knight, and his eccentricities as 'a manner adopted to conceal from all but his most intimate friends a nature too shy and at the same time too intolerant of the commonplace to meet with the world's approval'. In very similar terms, Monty pictured him fictionally as the Reverend Mr Dorward who was 'impelled to guard against the jeers of the unbelievers what he held to be most holy by diverting towards his own eccentricities the world's mockery'. Most of his Cury congregation had left him but, oblivious to the empty pews, he performed all the offices with the same meticulous attention to detail that once kept guests at a dinner party waiting while he created a centrepiece for the table with spring flowers placed in a top hat. Yet he was no less courageous than Walke in seeking to establish his beliefs in the hostile surroundings of Cornwall.

For a would-be priest they were stirring times and inspiring friends. On Walke's recommendation Monty decided to test his vocation first by becoming a lay-reader, and he received his licence in January 1908. 'The idea of your being a lay-reader is delightful,' his father-in-law wrote approvingly. 'What a breeze of fresh air you will bring into the business.' It was an opinion with which Monty concurred. 'I am starting a Sunday school run on my own lines,' he told his mother, 'almost as much like an ordinary Sunday school as a pig to a pea.'

His religious beliefs had lost the intensity of adolescence, with rationalism and ethics now taking the place of relics and rites. 'I don't think theology is of any use till one has an ethical standard,' he wrote to his mother, shortly after receiving his licence. '. . . Christianity should mean Humanitarianism.'

His Sunday school reflected this new outlook. Rather than teach the catechism, he took the children for walks in the course of which he would tell morality tales about the plants and birds they encountered, and he invented a game for them called Judgment Day. Each child's actions were rewarded or punished with coloured counters – white for kindness, red for cruelty, yellow for jealousy, green for thoughtfulness and so on. These were slipped unseen into money-boxes which were opened at random intervals – 'remember the Day of Judgment comes unexpectedly' – and the tallies noted down.

By Faith's account, he was a mixture of Joyce Grenfell, exclaiming during a talk on 'contentment', 'Now children, hands up anyone who's heard a primrose grumble,' and the Pied Piper, always followed by a flock of children as he led them along the cliffs or down to the beach. His class started with three children but within weeks numbered twenty-three, and the Methodists began to grumble at his success. Then Walke asked him to preach a series of sermons at the mission church in Polruan during Lent, and by Easter, Monty could write to his mother: 'I had splendid congregations – over 140 every time – not bad in a place of 1200 on a weekday.'

His subjects were not specifically religious – capital punishment, tradition, faith, hope and charity were some of the subjects – but his preaching had an electrifying quality: half a century later one member of his congregation could remember not merely his sermon on Browning's poem *The Statue and the Bust*, but also its moral, 'sin if you must, but above all do something'. In his novel *The Parson's Progress* he described a preaching technique whose stroboscopic effect must have been very similar to his own: 'He relied almost entirely upon an accumulation of emotional and eloquent flashes to produce an effect in his listeners' minds that a steady light had all the while been illuminating the subject on which he had elected to preach.'

His reputation began to spread, and invitations to preach came from vicars in parishes nearby. Unfortunately, Faith did not share his enthusiasm for spiritual matters. In consequence she found herself left out of his discussions with Wason and Walke, and lacking the advantage of teaching their children she never came to know the people of Cury well. Because Wason was a bachelor, she was expected to act as housekeeper, a task for which she had a profound aversion, and her unhappy relationship with servants resulted in her having to do the chores herself. In February she wrote to Virginia that one of Wason's female admirers was taking over and 'all the other "ladies" of Mr W's acquaintance are mad with jealousy. I get very tired of priest worship.'

She was tired too of Cornwall and its remoteness from city life, and she was bored with having nothing to do. That March, Christopher succeeded in letting Lady Ham, and Faith seized the chance to go and clear out Monty's books and furniture. She was away for over two months and so missed not only Monty's Lenten services but also his success as Antonio in a production of *The Merchant of Venice* put on in Fowey by Arthur Quiller-Couch. Despite the long absence she did not enjoy herself, and she was hurt when, instead of begging for her return, he urged her to stay longer in London if she wished. 'I wish you hadn't had such a rotten time,' he wrote soothingly when she complained. 'I only said not to come because Christopher wrote twice to me that you didn't want to come back – or at least hinted it very strongly.'

When she returned, at the end of May, it was not to Cury Vicarage but to a new house Monty had found in Gunwalloe. It was a tiny, four-roomed cottage – 'no bigger than a walnut,' he said – called Toy Cottage. Although it looked charming with its thatched roof and tiny garden, it was full of fleas, to which Faith was wretchedly susceptible and he was utterly immune.

Fortunately another house soon caught his attention, only fourteen miles from Gunwalloe, but on the north coast of Cornwall. Large and square and built in the Georgian style, it stood on a hill overlooking the Hayle estuary, surrounded by elm trees in which clouds of rooks roosted. 'A great, gloomy house,' Walke thought, and with ten bedrooms Rivière, as it was called, was far beyond the young couple's scope. However, the Compton family needed a new country house, having sold the bungalow at Beech, and with a tactful reference to the proximity of the golf-course for his father's benefit, Monty easily persuaded his parents to take it for seven years.

It was understood that he and Faith would have the top floor to share with Christopher, who would come down to keep her company, but this plan never materialised. Having returned to his post as tutor to the children of Alyce Chinnery, Christopher was falling in love with her. He only came once to Rivière, and then quarrelled with Virginia for ordering Faith about, and left immediately afterwards. When he wrote to tell Faith he was thinking of getting married, she replied with four words on a postcard, 'Not to Mrs Chinnery!', but it was so. The marriage to an Edwardian beauty twenty years older than himself was very happy, but it took from Faith her closest companion.

The spring of 1908 was Monty's first in Cornwall and the burst of wild flowers enchanted him. The towans, or sand dunes, were carpeted with cowslips, there were bluebells in the beechwoods, blue hydrangeas beneath the pine trees, and the steep banks along the lanes were starred with primroses and white-petalled flowers the Gunwalloe children called adder's eyes. In that mild climate it was not only wild flowers which flourished. His Gunwalloe neighbours grew subtropical flowers in their gardens as well as richer and earlier blossoms of daffodil, iris and lily than were found elsewhere.

The art of bulb growing provided common ground for Methodists and Anglicans, natives and incomers, and its possibilities suddenly ignited Monty's imagination. He had created a garden at Beech, and there had been some formal flower-beds among the lawns at Lady Ham, but it was only now that he saw himself as a gardener. William Search, the Lady Ham gardener, was installed in a cottage near Rivière, and for the next two years he became the instrument of Monty's dedication to growing bulbous irises and a daffodil that might one day win a First Class Certificate at the Truro Flower Show. It was a dedication which effectively displaced preaching, and the following Lent was spent in the garden rather than the pulpit. Even his Sunday School work lost its attraction and began to seem motivated as much by annoying the Methodists as by teaching Christian behaviour.

'I suppose what was happening,' he thought in retrospect, 'was that, although I would cling to Toy Cottage and those children for some months yet, my imagination was beginning to decide that one passion must gradually die and be replaced by another passion. So it has been all my life . . .'

For a time it seemed that his novel would suffer the same fate. It had been put aside first for his Lenten services, and again in the summer while Rivière was being furnished, and it was dropped once more in the autumn in favour of another play for his father. Even when he took it up again he found it difficult to concentrate while Search was mulching the iris bed, the vicar of Penzance was attempting to book him for the following Lent, and a pile of unpaid bills was growing in the drawer.

It was Faith who made it possible for him to finish the manuscript. An upright piano had been installed in a little room at the top of Rivière, which she called the 'bower', and Monty discovered that her playing was prophylactic against distracting thoughts. 'I would be half listening to the music,' he explained, 'and half considering what my characters were going to do next or how I was to describe a piece of natural scenery; the vacancy would be filled by music.'

Once he had made this discovery, he bought all Beethoven's, Schubert's, Schumann's and Chopin's piano music, and piano scores for all Beethoven's symphonies, and put her to playing. For the first time since they came to Cornwall, she had something useful to do, and the music which helped him to write also served to heal the rift which had begun to appear in their marriage.

He wrote in the evenings, beginning after dinner. Faith would play until midnight, then go to bed leaving him to write for another two or three hours. So concentrated was his attention that he failed to notice that his wife was pregnant. Faith herself kept it secret until on the eve of his twenty-sixth birthday he wrote *Explicit* at the end of the pencil-written manuscript. By then she was four months pregnant.

The novel, provisionally entitled *Curtain Wells*, was sent first to John Murray, because the head of the firm, an Oxford contemporary, had specifically asked to see anything he wrote. As with his poems, Monty allowed himself the luxury of anticipating the enthusiastic letter of acceptance. It made Murray's refusal none the easier to accept. He tried two other publishers with the same result. Then at his parents' request three authors, one of whom was Henry James, all asked their publishers to give it special attention, but it only came back faster than before. Over the next eighteen months, another six publishers were to follow their example.

The reason for their refusal is understandable. In technique it was a replica of a light eighteenth-century novel, the action robust, the tone ironical, and the style episodic, with the author commenting on the characters and events in each set-piece. It was recognised as a *tour de force*, and as such often liked by publishers' readers who nevertheless saw no good reason for publishing a book that owed nothing to the twentieth century.

This renewed failure must have been the harder to endure in the light of Christopher's success in following up his volume of schoolboy poems with the publication of a novel called *Scars* which Pearsall Smith judged to show 'real objective power'. He was certainly not made happier either by news from another aspiring young writer, Hugh Walpole, that *his* first novel, *The Wooden Horse*, had been accepted for publication. Walpole had been visiting friends in Cornwall the previous September, and having heard that Monty was a poet asked him for his opinion of this work. Monty briskly assured him that he should stick to school-mastering for he would never be a novelist. 'I found it difficult to understand how publishers could be so stupid,' he confessed. 'If Hugh Walpole could get that unpromising first novel of his accepted . . . why should my first novel be so steadily refused?'

As though these galling considerations were not enough, his father threatened to cut off his allowance unless he made an attempt to earn a living from the theatre. In May 1909 he reluctantly agreed to go to Chester to produce a theatrical pageant, but while he was there Faith suddenly went into premature labour.

'A sword ran through me,' she wrote. 'Too soon. Too soon. A month too soon. The baby clothes were swept away, the doctor called, and after an eternity of undrugged agony the son was born, dead. Never again, I swore.'

She may have known that Monty did not relish the prospect of fatherhood. She had delayed telling him of the pregnancy to begin with, and now she was anxious not to worry him with news of the stillbirth. It was Christopher who sent for him. He hurried down to her father's house in Abingdon where she had gone for the confinement, and arrived, she noted, 'looking pale and tired'. His sympathy for her grief was immediate, and she found his presence comforting, but for himself his feelings were mixed.

'In my case,' he wrote, 'the prospect of fatherhood had been clouded over by the insecurity of my financial position and the uncertainty evoked by the first refusal of my novel. I had hoped for a daughter, for whom I had chosen Corinna as a name; it was almost a relief when I was told that the stillborn child was a boy.'

From earliest childhood Monty had armoured himself against disappointment by persuading himself that he had not really wanted what was refused him. It is, for example, hardly possible to tell from his autobiography of the anguish caused by the failure of his poetry and his priestly vocation. In the loss of his child, the only sign of emotion is his insistence that he had 'never felt the faintest desire for a son', and that 'a son of mine would have been handicapped . . . by a father with what might be called an excess of personality'.

Having persuaded himself, he had little difficulty in persuading Faith that it would be a mistake to try again for a child, as her sisters were urging her to do. As her own account shows, she was anxious to be persuaded, but she was less successful than him in suppressing regrets. Twice she tried to adopt babies to fill the gap that had been left, and in the May of later years she was sometimes struck by thoughts of the boy or the tall young man who might have been her son appearing before her. They were, however, passing dreams. For the most part she accepted the argument, and eventually she understood that Monty would allow no rivals.

The tragedy altered the balance of their marriage. Without the child and with nothing to occupy her, Faith found Cornwall intolerable. When she went back to Rivière that summer, Monty had dropped the role of novelist and persuaded himself that his creative urge was best exercised in gardening. Ignorance restricted her participation to standing guard with a butterfly net to prevent a pest called the daffodil fly from landing on the bulbs. In the spring of 1909 Edward had backed a musical called *The Arcadians*, which was to run for two years and bring in enough money to calm even his doubting mind. The cellars at Rivière were stocked with champagne, the cigar boxes with Corona Coronas, the garage with a Mercedes costing £2000, and Monty with enough bulbs, plants and shrubs to assure his future as a gardener. He spent hours listening to the Reverend A. T. Boscawen talk about celmisias and to Percy Williams about hybridising daffodils. He contributed knowledge-able articles to gardening magazines, travelled to flower shows and corresponded with seedsmen in North America, New Zealand and Australia. And he lectured Search meticulously on the matter of creating raised beds for bulbous irises. There were no half measures. Having seen himself as a gardener only the ideal would satisfy him.

Faith's visits to London and to her relatives became longer. She returned at Christmas when she might have hoped to have his attention during the quietest part of the gardening year, but he was involved in the Liberal campaign in the general election held in January 1910. This was a debt of gratitude to Quiller-Couch, most fervent of Liberals. He had cast Monty as Hamlet in a production which he directed at Fowey in December, and on the basis of a growing friendship Monty had sent him a copy of his poems. To his gratification, there came back a warmly worded letter of praise, whose sincerity was confirmed in 1912 when Quiller-Couch included one of Monty's poems in the *Oxford Book of Victorian Verse*. Only once before had Monty deserted the romantic Conservatism he had espoused as secretary of the Strafford Club, and that was in the general election of 1906 when anti-Unionist fervour briefly made every young man a Radical. Then he spent a day conveying voters to the polls, but to help Quiller-Couch he spent the three weeks after Christmas speaking for the Liberals all over Cornwall.

It must have been at this time that Faith began to understand why his friends kept saying they had given up being surprised by anything he did. The gap between imagination and reality hardly seemed to exist. He wanted to be a poet – and he was writing verses; he saw himself as a priest – and he was in the pulpit; he dreamed of being a leading literary figure – and he wrote a novel; he imagined himself a famous horticulturist – and his garden was laid out with 3000 varieties of flowers and shrubs.

So far reality had not measured up to imagination, and there was a note of impatience when she wrote of his plans to her father on the last day of the year. 'The latest castle in Spain is that Monty is to play Hamlet in New York,' she wrote, then added carefully as though wishful thinking were a masculine failing, 'but it is only a vision.'

One of his dreams, however, was about to become more substantial. In the spring of 1910 Philip Sergeant, who had once tried to seduce him with decadent literature, returned from Hong Kong to join a literary agency. After yet another rejection, Monty sent him *Curtain Wells*, and returned to cultivating his garden, while Faith went back to London. She was still there in May when Monty wrote to her: 'A mysterious man called Secker came into Sergeant's office and said he heard they had a novel by me. He's going to set up as a publisher next spring and is taking the *Curtain Wells* typescript away with him. Sergeant thinks it may lead to something.'

7
Writing the perfect performance

If the mysterious man called Secker had had his way, *Curtain Wells* would already have been published. He had read the manuscript a year earlier when he was working as a junior reader for the publishers Eveleigh Nash, but his strong recommendation that they should buy it was overruled by the senior reader, Mrs Maude Craven ffoulkes. It helps to explain Secker's enjoyment of Monty's book to know that he found something quietly satisfying in fate's choice of a name like Mrs Maude Craven ffoulkes for a lady whom he described as 'statuesque and of generous proportions'.

He himself was small and neatly made, and he had the engaging habit of laughing silently at a joke until the tears ran down his cheeks. Of more immediate significance, he had also inherited £1000 and was determined to 'turn my little legacy into a golden key which would open the door into the world of publishing'.

Having served his apprenticeship with Nash, he decided to set up on his own, and early in January 1910 the ground floor and basement of 5 John Street in the Adelphi, just off the Strand, became the headquarters of the new publishing house of Martin Secker Ltd. One of his first steps had been to track down the 'eighteenth-century' novel he had so much enjoyed, and when Monty came up to London for the Temple Flower Show at the end of May, Sergeant took the opportunity to introduce him to Secker. They liked each other at once. Both delighted in absurdity, and Secker made an ideal audience for the mimicry and exaggeration which decorated Monty's conversation. From that basis grew a friendship which flourished for more than half a century.

Their trade requires publishers to be at once commercially and aesthet- ically minded, but they are rarely equally proficient in both. Secker's bias was towards the aesthetic. Typography fascinated him, and he understood that the appearance of a book contributed materially to the pleasure of reading it. He accepted without reserve Monty's wish to keep some vestiges of archaic spelling, like the ending 'ck' in 'magick' and 'musick', and features of eighteenth-century printing such as the joined 'ct', and the turnover or anticipatory word at the foot of the right-hand page. 'All these things, I think, give the book character,' he wrote agreeably, 'and help to create atmosphere.' In the choice of title he objected to *Curtain Wells*, but was admirably encouraging about both Monty's alternatives. 'I like the flavour of *The Passionate Elopement*,' he commented, 'both that and *A Tragedy in Porcelain* are good titles – and it is difficult to know which to decide upon.' Where relations were so harmonious, it hardly mattered that he could not afford to offer his first author an advance.

To the author's father it did matter. Edward had been maintaining Monty ever since university. For six years he had paid him an allowance. He provided him with a house in Cornwall and financed his enthusiasm for gardening. He had used his friendship with Henry James in an attempt to persuade an established publisher to take his novel, and now he saw him pinning his hopes to an unknown without sufficient money to pay an advance.

In June, the same month that the Secker contract was signed, he decided to pull some strings to get his son a proper job. He and Bode were backing a play called *The Bishop's Son* by the popular novelist, Hall Caine, and he put Monty forward for the supporting role of a young priest for which he would be paid ten pounds a week.

Given the underlying rivalry in his relations with his father, it was inevitable that Monty should have taken the offer to be 'something like an ultimatum'. With the utmost reluctance he went off to the Isle of Man to be vetted by Caine, but once there he could not help flattering the author outrageously – 'he can take a cargo of that,' he informed his mother – and so secured the job. As a bonus he added to his collection of stories a superb imitation of a middle-aged, maidenly author living in a red-brick villa called Greeba Castle.

Within a matter of days, Monty's fortunes seemed to turn dramatically. Encouraged by the sale of *The Passionate Elopement*, Sergeant sent the dramatisation of *Kipps* to the actor-manager James Welch, who was encouraging about the prospect of putting it on in London. Monty promptly went to see H. G. Wells and received his grudging permission for the play to be mounted should Welch decide to take it.

'Since last week,' Faith wrote to her father,

Monty has been to town, settled his novel with a new publisher, Secker – to come out in January – talked over *Kipps* with H. G. Wells – been over to the Isle of Man, seen and conquered Hall Caine – got a part in *The Bishop's Son* which comes on in September, and so settled our affairs very nicely for the year and has now returned to his beloved garden . . . I suppose the new publisher will die before January, and *The Bishop's Son* will fall through and Welch won't want *Kipps* at all, but we hope for the best.

Secker did not die. Apart from that her forebodings were well founded. *Kipps* never appeared, and *The Bishop's Son* closed after a week. What she did not foresee was more serious. Edward had backed a friend's bill for £2000, and was suddenly required to find the money. Coming on top of the failure of Caine's play it was more than he could afford, and in an effort to retrench he finally stopped Monty's allowance.

In the past Monty had always turned to Virginia at times of financial stress, but in that summer she had been sent to Sicily to recuperate from what seems to have been a nervous breakdown. A number of family tensions had boiled over in quick succession and Edward's financial worries were apparently the last straw.

The most explosive trouble came from Frank. A year earlier he had been stationed in the Mediterranean with his regiment. Their tour of duty took them from Crete to Malta, where he bought two polo ponies and then wrote home for money to pay for them. Edward paid, but with a bad grace. A few months later the regiment was ordered to the Far East. This time Frank's demand for more money to buy new equipment drew a severe letter in response. Frank had never learned his brother's self-control, especially where their father was concerned. In a fury he resigned his commission. He came home without a job, and was eventually forced to join the Compton Comedy Company at the very bottom of the ladder as junior prompter. For the next six months there was open hostility between father and son. Virginia, who had always taken the part of her sons, attempted to act as peacemaker, but Frank was incapable of moderating his anger. When he had saved up enough money, he left the company and emigrated to Canada, where he took an engagement with a touring company going to Australia.

It is conceivable that another source of tension came from her second daughter, Katie, who was in love with a member of the company called John Austen. Virginia may well have opposed the match, for the moment she left for Sicily Katie seized the chance to marry John Austen in secret.

Finally her nephew Frank Greppo, who had been found a job as stage manager for *The Bishop's Son*, suddenly vanished at the end of the play's run. Nothing was heard of him for months until a letter arrived to say that he had enlisted in the army and been sent to India. By then Virginia had broken down. 'Her nerves are all gone to pieces,' Faith observed. 'Poor little thing, she takes everyone's troubles to heart as though they were her own.'

In the expectation of a long run for *The Bishop's Son*, Monty and Faith had taken a flat for six months at 27 Church Row, Hampstead, the home of the artist Muirhead Bone. Deprived of the allowance that had sustained them for so long, they rapidly fell into debt. In September Faith wrote to her father asking for a loan of fifty pounds with the promise that 'you can be quite certain that his position is assured now and he will never look back'.

This was optimistic, but being in London restored her confidence in their future. Optimism was justified when in the same month an Irish actor called Shiel Barry, who had been in Hall Caine's play, helped him to find work with a cabaret revue called the Follies. Its formula of songs, skits, and chorus girls was not original, but in Harry Pélissier, its creator and chief comedian, it had a star of enormous appeal.

His character lay in his childlike features swollen to gross proportions by good living. He hated to be thwarted – when he saw a notice saying 'Keep Off – Wet Paint' beside the freshly painted floorcloth of one of his shows, he took a running leap into the centre of it and jumped up and down on it like a boy in a puddle. In the manner of a Hollywood mogul, he was extravagant in parties, gifts and cars, but mean in wages. However, extravagance in any form was always a recommendation to Monty, and when Barry introduced him he did not restrain his power to charm. Pélissier immediately swept him up into his entourage. Officially he was to write lyrics for the new Follies show *All Change Here*, but he was also expected to provide entertainment from dawn until late at night, and to rehearse the chorus girls. All for six pounds a week.

On Monty's twenty-eighth birthday in January 1911, *The Passionate Elopement* was published – a handsome book with wide margins, elegant type and a peacock blue cover. Although not numerous, the reviews in the first few weeks were warmly indulgent. The *English Review* was not untypical: '*The Passionate Elopement* should be read slowly from the smiles and extravagance of the opening chapters through many sounding and poetical passages to the thrilling end of the Love Chase. The quiet irony of the close leaves one smiling but with the wiser smile of Horace

Ripple who meditates on the colours of Life.' *Country Life*, which had condemned his poems, gave him particular pleasure by comparing it to *Barry Lyndon*: '. . . in the kindliness, the humour and gentleness of the treatment it comes as near to Thackeray and to Thackeray dealing with the same subject, as any man has come since Thackeray.'

Elated by these comments, Monty offered to forgo all royalties if Secker would spend his profits on advertising. It meant that he was entirely dependent on Pelissier's meagre salary, but throughout the spring the name of Compton Mackenzie repeatedly appeared on the literary pages and leaped boldly from advertisement panels in newspapers, magazines and even the underground. Almost certainly the publicity helped generate more reviews, and by April he and Secker could claim that *The Passionate Elopement* was the best reviewed first novel of the season. It was only a start, but he was beginning to make his name.

Later critics were inclined to regard this first novel as something of a freak. In *The Nineteen Hundreds* Reginald Auberon described it as 'a false start', and Leo Robertson's appraisal of Compton Mackenzie's work argued that 'it betrayed no features by which one could predict the course his subsequent writings would take'.

However, once it is recognised that he had already made two false starts in poetry and drama, it becomes apparent that *The Passionate Elopement* contains in crude form the essential features of his later fictional style. The clue comes in a significant change of emphasis from the stage version.

As in the play, the setting is fashionable Curtain Wells, ruled over by the nonpareil of high fashion, Beau Ripple, with attendant courtiers such as the Earl of Squall and Sir Jeremy Dinner, and minions like Filigree the goldsmith and Crumpett the confectioner. The plot still revolves around the competition for the love of Phyllida Courteen, although in the book she is won, not by the hero Charles Lovely, but by the villain Francis Vernon. However, soon after he began writing, Sandys Wason gave Monty an eighteenth-century commonplace book compiled by a forebear, and later Monty himself found a copy of Christopher Anstey's verse satire on spa society *New Bath Guide*, from which Smollett had borrowed ideas for *Humphrey Clinker*. The background was in consequence more detailed and convincing than on stage, but paradoxically the characters were infinitely more artificial.

From the first chapter, when Curtain Wells is described as 'a tolerably attractive stage for the marionettes who postured and declaimed upon its boards', the puppet-like nature of their lives is repeatedly underlined.

Phyllida dancing a minuet 'felt that she was a doll whose gestures served to amuse a genteel audience of monocled Gods', and watching her Charles Lovely is 'himself suspended from a longer cord and dancing for the amusement of a higher power'. The voice of the author commenting on the events emphasises the fact that he is the string-puller. Such interventions are usually at the expense of the hero: thus of Charles falling in love, he observes confidentially, 'Let me tell you that the heart of the Lovelys are all of a piece – and 'tis of cardboard', and after Lovely's fight with a bookseller, the author declares boastfully, 'I hope you will not deny this scene was in the very true vein of heroism. Aye! Aye! 'tis full of bombast as you very properly observe ma'am or sir; but that is the part of a hero. He must follow the Prince of Denmark's directions to the players.'

The action is divided into a series of set-pieces as precisely ordered as the gavottes supervised by Beau Ripple – from the measured pace of 'The Pump Room' through 'The Confidante' and with accelerating tempo to 'The Love Chase'.

The technique owed much to the eighteenth century, but it was also the solution to the problem of self-expression which had confronted him from the moment of his 'conversion'. Poetry had demanded authentic emotions which he could not express, while drama had required inter- mediaries who distorted his ideas. By adopting the style of Smollett and Fielding, he could express himself through the author's voice but without becoming involved in the action, or through his characters, who became intermediaries under his complete control.

'I remember the sense of freedom at escaping from the thrall of narrative verse into narrative prose,' he wrote of this first novel, 'and the elation of writing dialogue that no actor would have to speak and in speaking destroy that dialogue as I heard it being spoken in my head.'

In several respects the result is the best of his comedies. The style is enormously elegant, the writing has the freshness that comes with hand- ling a story for the first time, and the wit is very sharp. The emotions are small but they have the polish and pathos of the harlequinade which is performed at one of the Pump Room entertainments:

First the Columbine had pirouetted across and made a light fantastic entrance into the shadow of the house at the entrance corner. Presently came the Pierrot with a lantern swaying atop of a long pole . . . Then came Harlequin, dancing almost more beautifully than Pierrot, and a quiet murder was done in the laurel shadows around the house. Pierrot lay dead and Harlequin the slim and debonair assassin had donned his vizard. Columbine wept awhile until the lights were turned up, when everybody agreed that the whole performance was in the best of taste and vastly well executed.

The success of *The Passionate Elopement* set the course of Monty's future. He was to be a novelist, and not only that but 'a leading literary figure', which required him to find a more substantial theme for his next novel. It came from one of the duties assigned to him by Pélissier, the rehearsal of the chorus girls.

The popularity of the previous Follies had persuaded Pélissier to put on *All Change Here* at the large Alhambra Theatre, which normally housed the scantily-clad ballet. There were as a result almost a hundred girls to rehearse, and Monty's notebook was soon filled with lists of names and comments: 'Lily Clarke – attractive, sings well. Cora Trivett – massive. Gwen Sesson – contralto, ladylike. Chrissie Maude – Old Maid.'

The 'Old Maid' beside the last name referred not to her looks, which were striking – blonde hair and slanting, catlike eyes – but to her role as one of four elderly ladies transformed by the magic formula of *All Change Here* into short-skirted girls dancing ragtime. Even before the revue opened, Monty was in love with her.

Chrissie Maude was twenty-four, born and bred in Islington where she still lived with her crippled sister and widowed mother. Her career as a dancer had begun in provincial pantomime, risen briefly to Covent Garden, then sunk to the Alhambra where the ballet was, properly speaking, a legshow. Until the Ballets Russes came to London in 1911 and revolutionised ballet, the gap between it and the chorus line was not impossible to cross.

Yet it was not for her dancing or her looks alone that Monty was attracted to her, but for her storytelling. In the strange line of tale-spinning women who won his affection, from Mrs Frith onwards, Chrissie Maude was Scheherazade. She told her stories with wit and detail, and with a pungency of language which captivated him: 'She ought to have worn crêpe in her nose – her brains was dead'; 'With his temper he needed his hair nailed down'; 'Always grinning at you, like he wore his teeth outside.' In the evenings after the rehearsals were over he used to take her and sometimes Lily Clarke, her close friend, to a bar in Leicester Square called the Café de l'Europe. There they drank Guinness and gossiped of Chrissie's past, of the Alhambra, of dancers' love affairs, dressing-room vendettas and the wiles of stage-door johnnies.

In his youth he might have listened to such stories with a voyeurist's, or auralist's, fascination, but now that capacity to become the participant in another person's adventures enabled him to transform them into the raw material of fiction. The tales of the Alhambra were to appear in five novels, and from Chrissie herself he created the most enduring of his heroines.

She was ruthlessly unsentimental about men – they either wanted to spring it on a girl or were plain soppy – and she would normally cut short their advances with a brisk 'Who cares?' or 'You must be potty.' But she could never have met a man like Monty who had the seductive power of taking on the personality of his companion and returning it enhanced by his own vitality and imagination. With the Reverend A. T. Boscawen he had been the ideal bulb-grower, with Logan Pearsall Smith the dedicated sonneteer, and with Chrissie Maude he was Harlequin, the spirit of gaiety and mischief.

He used to organise elaborate trips to the zoo for her and the other dancers, just to see the expression on the giraffe's face, and visits to the skating-rink, just to annoy the instructors, and he would take her to parties travelling not in a hansom but in a salmon-coloured taxi, just for the colour of it. In the opinion of one of Faith's friends, she was the great passion of his life, although it might be truer to say that she was the perfect complement to his favourite role. He was certainly the decisive catalyst and probably the love of her life.

He had already made two unsuccessful starts on a second novel when Chrissie's stories and personality began to merge with the memory of an encounter in Cornwall with a hard-faced farmer who had just got married. His wife had been a barmaid in the Leicester Lounge, a pick-up bar in London, and he insisted that Monty come back to meet her. She was a peroxide blonde with a sad Cockney voice, and a few days later she fled back to London, but Monty remained intrigued by the circumstances which could have persuaded her to exchange a London barmaid's life for marriage to a gaunt, teetotal Methodist living in a desolate farmhouse in Cornwall. A few weeks after the publication of *The Passionate Elopement*, he was returning late to the Church Row flat when he realised that the two pictures had crystallised into one.

'I sat down at my desk on that February evening,' he recalled, 'and was granted the third of three transcendental experiences . . . the experience of conceiving the whole of a long book in a few seconds of time.'

The book was *Carnival* and in it Chrissie Maude became Jenny Pearl, born in unlovely Hagworth Street, Islington, who grows up to be a dancer. She falls in love with a young dilettante, Maurice Avery, but is deserted by him when she will not become his mistress. In despair she first allows herself to be seduced by an old lecher, then apathetically falls into marriage with Trewhella, a Cornish farmer who, twisted by jealousy, shoots her when Maurice reappears.

He intended to keep Jenny on the page from the moment she was born – a Flaubertian technique, signalling the seriousness of his approach – and the composition of a character sufficiently solid to carry such a weight demanded far more of him than the marionettes of Curtain Wells. Nevertheless, it began well. Arthur Ransome, then aged twenty-seven but already tweedy and bucolic, was in Secker's office when Monty came to read his first chapter. At the conclusion Ransome threw country restraint aside and leaped to his feet exclaiming, 'This is genius!' Thereafter the writing continued more slowly and in conditions of extraordinary stress.

All Change Here had not been a success. The idea of the Follies belonged to intimate review, and it was overwhelmed by the vastness of the Alhambra. The show came off in January, and Pélissier began work on its successor at once, but his lyricist and by now boon companion was needed more often than before to fend off the phantoms of failure. 'I guessed that the malaise which now constantly oppressed him was his premonition of adolescence,' Monty remarked none too kindly.

There were huge banquets at his home in Finchley, immense quantities of brandy and champagne throughout the day and long drives through the night in his Daimlers. Monty began to grow irritated by his childish enthusiasms and glooms, but Faith, who had only just met Pélissier, was enchanted by the excessiveness and the emotional immaturity. 'The sweetest thing in men,' she confided to her diary.

In the spring of 1911, she and Monty were forced to retire to Cornwall when the tenancy of the Hampstead flat ran out, but within a few weeks Pélissier summoned them back to share a flat with him at 45 Pall Mall. Since it was he who paid the rent, this arrangement aroused the deepest suspicions in the minds of the schoolmasterly Stones, and Edward was directed to communicate their fears.

'She seems to be immensely smitten by his social qualities,' he wrote to Monty in May, 'but I should doubt very much whether he is the sort of person you would care to be thick with . . . I am quite sure that this scheme ought to be abandoned. Please let me know that it is so without delay.'

Indignantly Faith denied the insinuation of immorality, and the quality of her love for Monty leaves little doubt that it was unfounded. On the other hand she thrived on the good times – 'fond of drinking, dancing and men, and loathe housework' was her self-description at the time – and with Monty devoting himself increasingly to Chrissie, she had no inhibitions about extracting enjoyment from Pélissier's attentions and his mogul way of life. On the whole it was a harmonious arrangement until Pélissier fell in love with Monty's sixteen-year-old sister Fay.

Like Monty, she had at first been brought up by Annie Curry, who had been forgiven her drunkenness in return for her strictness. Finishing school in Paris had given her a taste of freedom, and now she begged to be allowed to join the Follies. With Monty's help she became part of Pélissier's company in June.

It was, everyone agreed, an uncommonly hot summer. Monty ordered a white suit from his tailor's and wore it to take Chrissie and her friends to the races or the zoo. Sweating in his shirt-sleeves, Harry Pélissier watched his newest Folly, dressed like a choirboy and looking no older. 'She had a baby face,' commented Faith succinctly, 'but her violet eyes were not a baby's eyes.' There were feverish weekends at Finchley, then as the temperature climbed higher, Pélissier arranged a different trio – himself, Fay and Faith as chaperone – and the long Daimler took them away to the coolness of the seaside.

Monty apparently paid no attention. He was too preoccupied even to write *Carnival*. A chronic shortage of money had forced him to borrow £100 from Pélissier and he was obliged to finance expeditions with Chrissie from winnings on horses backed at long odds. His mornings began with the study of form in the racing papers, then having placed his bet, he strolled to the corner of Pall Mall to be shaved by Mr Edwardes, who wielded a shaving brush made from the bristles of a Siberian hog and a solid French razor rather than a cheap, hollow-ground German affair. The afternoons were spent with the girls, and the evenings at the Ballets Russes where Nijinsky was dancing or at the theatre. He had no time for other distractions. When Faith attempted to prevent Pélissier from seducing Fay on an August afternoon in Margate, she was accused of jealousy and sent back to London. She complained to Monty who told her not to be absurd.

'I have always made it a rule to avoid the emotional tangles of other people,' he said sagaciously, and immediately broke his rule when he learned that not only had Fay been seduced but that Pélissier intended to marry her.

He tried to enlist his mother's support in forbidding the marriage, but to his annoyance she found no objection. 'My mother,' he explained, 'like her own mother, thought that a girl could not be married soon enough.' Her opinion was not altered by learning that the proposed husband was twenty-two years older than her daughter, an alcoholic drinking a bottle of brandy a day, and given to various depravities that her son could only hint at but consisted in fact of a long history of bisexuality. In old age she blamed herself bitterly for her stupidity, realising too late that the marriage ruined Fay's life. In this case even she could not pretend that it had been good for the character, and she could only console herself with the thought that 'God cares for children better than parents'.

Thwarted by his mother, Monty then tackled Pélissier, but the mogul was in love and not to be dissuaded. In a fury Monty resigned from his employment, at which Pélissier bleakly reminded him of the £100 debt. It was the beginning of a winter of troubles.

He attempted to get the money by betting forty pounds on an aged gelding called Pillo. It romped in at 8 to 1, but the bookmaker welshed. He had to sell a library of books acquired since he was sixteen. Still there was not enough. He turned, as always, to his mother. Her marriage allowance had run out and she felt unable to turn to Edward, but even now she did not fail him. She borrowed £100 from a friend, Ethel Long, gave him the money and Pélissier's debt was paid.

As a result of the quarrel they had to leave the Pall Mall flat and return to Rivière, which at least had the beneficial effect of allowing him to concentrate on *Carnival* once more. Taking up the habit established by *The Passionate Elopement*, he wrote to Faith's piano music, and continued long after she had gone to bed, scribbling in an increasingly disjointed hand until the early hours of the morning. The next day Faith often found she could hardly wake him from his sleep. Money troubles weighed heavily on him. The horses were their only form of income, and he grew cautious, not betting more than a pound or two. Sometimes Faith heard him call out in his sleep and sometimes she found him lying awake rigid with worry.

'It seems wrong of me not to earn money and keep myself,' she confessed to Virginia, 'but honestly if I give up my time and life to him . . . I'm incapable of doing both. I do feel without conceit that I'm earning my keep.'

On her side the trouble was more than financial. There was the emotional strain of his affair with Chrissie Maude, and in returning to Rivière and to the habit of playing while he wrote, she was reminded of the circumstances of her pregnancy. Yet, after six years of marriage she had arrived at a clear understanding of their partnership. In her old age she wrote the outline of a short story about a married couple living in a grim Cornish house, and it could serve as a précis of her relationship with Monty at this time:

They are still devoted, but for him life has extended, while she with a dead baby remains almost static, but adoring. He has had an affair with a little actress or ballet girl, and Laura [the wife] has not only behaved well but admires the girl ... He has been gay in London and enjoyed the company of stage girls. This is his nature of which she was always aware, though with great faith in him, and reliance on her own love and good behaviour.

In that autumn of shared worry and strain, a bond was created which in some sense survived throughout their marriage. It is easy to see how much Monty owed Faith in love, loyalty and support, but less easy to appreciate that she no longer expected to be paid in the same currency. Monty's coin was the energy, the excitement, and the vulnerability of a boy, and with that she had learned to be content.

Throughout September and October he worked unceasingly to finish the novel. Just before the end he won £120 on the Cesarewitch, a sum which relieved them of financial worry, but if *Carnival* were a success, betting would become a thing of the past. Unable to pay an advance, Martin Secker had offered him a royalty of 20 per cent up to 5000 copies, and 25 per cent thereafter. In mid-November he wrote the final sentence, 'The seabirds wheeled about the mist screaming dismay,' and his dreams of wealth and literary reputation now lay with the life and death of Jenny Pearl. The book was published two months later, on 17 January 1912, his twenty-ninth birthday.

8

Carnival in London and New York

Within a month of its publication Monty and Martin Secker knew that *Carnival* had achieved the uncommon double of popular and critical success. In the February bestseller lists it ran second only to Baroness Orczy's latest adventure of the Scarlet Pimpernel. The literary journals measured it by the highest standards and the gist of their opinion was expressed by Rupert Brooke in a review for the *Westminster Gazette* which ended, 'It is not a great book – but it might have been.'

The middlebrow magazines had no reservations. 'We suppose some people will call *Carnival* an unpleasant book,' wrote the *Illustrated London News*. 'That is not the way it strikes us. It is very tender, very sympathetic to one of the most touching and pitiful things in the world – the opening heart of a woman in unworthy surroundings.' And *Punch* concluded its laudatory review with the words, 'As for the style, I will only add that it gave me the same blissful feeling of security that one has in listening to a great musician – the knowledge that every tone will be exactly right.'

By the spring *Carnival* had reached that rare level of popularity at which its language passed into the slang of the smart set. Lady Diana Manners, later Duff Cooper's wife, began the trend by making Jenny Pearl's defiant 'There's nothing wrong with this little girl' her own catch-phrase. Then, according to the *Sketch*, 'For six months everybody . . . used to talk the talk of Jenny, the heroine of *Carnival*.' Her slang became the slang of 'the set', that is both the beautifully fashionable, like the Manners girls, and the intelligently fashionable, like the Asquiths and Bonham-Carters. It was no longer Cockney but a 'Jennyism' to say 'don't be soppy' or 'any old way' or 'I must have been potty'.

Where the smart set led the rest followed, and for the next fifty years the story continued to be popular in many different forms. During that time it sold more than half a million copies, and was turned into three films, two stage plays, and two radio productions. The heart of its appeal lies in the encounter between Jenny and Maurice Avery, the most romantic and moving of ill-starred romances.

The limitations of Jenny's character are made plain in the course of her early career as a dancer. She is impatient, lacks imagination and cannot think clearly, but her tart and unsentimental comments reveal an instinctive intelligence and a clear-eyed understanding of people. When Irene Dale, a fellow dancer, attempts to deny wanting to marry her boyfriend, Arthur Danby, Jenny exclaims scornfully, 'Oh no, it's only a rumour,' and Irene's feeble assertion, 'My Danby's a gentleman,' draws the withering qualification, 'Yes, when he's asleep.'

From her first encounter with Maurice, his flaws are no less apparent, but so also is her power to transcend them. 'She liked his complexion and deep blue eyes. She liked better still his weak, girlish mouth and white teeth. She liked best of all his manner, which was not too easy although it carried some of the confidence of popularity.' Although her lack of subtlety and his quickness to take offence give rise to misunderstandings and quarrels, the reconciliations and the growing immensity of happiness do change them until they come within sight of a largeness of character in which a lasting love might be possible. There is a brooding knowledge that in the end Maurice must behave like a spoilt boy and Jenny must break rather than bend before misfortune, but until then it is possible to imagine that love will indeed conquer all, even their inadequacies.

The relationship is conveyed largely in dialogue, but the backgrounds are described with the visual intensity of an early silent film. Maurice tells her of his love for the first time as they are driving home in a cab, but it is not so much his words which suggest the mood as the moment when they arrive in Hagworth Street.

At the end of the road, under the tall plane tree where once Jenny had danced, they sat in the old hansom cab, while the steam rose in clouds from the horse and the puddles sang with rain and the driver smoked meditatively. The world was fading away in sounds of traffic very remote. The wetness of the night severed them from humanity.

Occasionally the emotion in these backgrounds lapses into lushness, but at its best it achieves an effect which is almost surreal, as in the counterpointing of the ballet girls' warm companionship with the predatory whores shadowing the Promenade.

They all appear alike. Their hats are all too large, their figures are too brutal, their cheeks too lifeless. They are automatic machines of lust waiting to be stirred into action by pennies. Under the stars they achieve a pictorial romance, but on the carpet of the Promenade they are hard and heartless and vile. Their eyes are coins and their hands are purses.

The balance to these atmospheric backgrounds comes from the sharpness of tongue of Jenny and her friends. It was his mastery of dialogue that Frank Swinnerton especially praised in *The Georgian Literary Scene*. 'The Cockney passages are among the best things in modern writing,' he commented, 'for here Mackenzie's strong humour and power of improvisation are at their freest.'

Many novelists before him, most notably Dickens, had introduced Cockney characters, but their speech had always been rendered phonetically and the proliferation of apostrophes, dropped h's and transposed v's and w's, put a visual barrier round the words. The Cockney of Jenny and her friends was suggested simply through the phrasing – a technique learned from his dramatisation of *Kipps* – and its directness could be heard uncluttered by punctuation. Generally it is used in bursts of dialogue, but an extended example comes when Jenny's friend, Maudie Chapman, describes her chance visit to the Tate Gallery:

Well, we had a good look at the pictures, *which* we didn't think much of, and I slipped on the floor and burnt my hand on a sort of grating, and then we couldn't find the way out. We *couldn't* find the way out. We got upstairs somewhere and I called out 'Management,' and a fellow with his hair nailed down and spectacles said, 'Are you looking for the Watts?' and I said 'No, we're looking for the What ho's!' and he said 'You've made a mistake, miss, they're in the National Gallery,' and Madge, you know what a shocking giggler she is, she burst out laughing and I didn't know where to look.

The weakness in *Carnival* which most critics noticed was the change in balance once Jenny marries Trewhella and moves to Cornwall. Without the sharpness of the London voices the heavy background becomes overpowering and melodramatic, a fault compounded by her murder on the last page. Despite this, it remains one of the best love stories in the canon.

The connection between the modern, vibrant story of Jenny Pearl and the polished marionette show of his first novel defeated most reviewers. Either they set the latter aside or, like Hugh Walpole taking his revenge for Monty's slight, they regretted his venture into gritty realism: 'We do not want him to be a realist,' Walpole wrote. 'He is a creator of dainty and charming fineries: he is one of our most delightful humorists. The arid area steps of Mr Arnold Bennett are not for his pen.' Monty noted the barb and did not forget.

The connection, however, lay in the author's standpoint which, despite a more immediate sympathy with the fate of his characters, still retained traces of the puppetmaster's aloofness. In one brief scene – the morning after Jenny's seduction – the sentiment, like the language, reverts precisely to that of his first novel. 'Columbine, leaden-eyed, sat up in the strange room where over an unfamiliar chair lay huddled all her clothes . . . suddenly she flung herself deep into the pillow and, buried thus, lay motionless like a marionette whose wire has snapped.' More generally, however, the author adopts the tone of a critic presenting an indictment of the social and sexual customs which brought Jenny to her death.

'When for the first time she was given the world to look at,' he comments of her education, 'her finite vision and infinite aspirations were never set in relation to each other. Her soul was a singing bird in a cage. Freedom was the only ideal. She was given a telescope and nobody had taken off the shutter. She might have been moved by Catholicism, but nobody gave it to her.'

This was the tone of the great triumvirate of H. G. Wells, Arnold Bennett and John Galsworthy who bestrode the literary scene. To reflect upon the shortcomings of society was the sign of the serious writer, and Monty followed suit, adding two particular criticisms of his own. The first was directed at the lack of spiritual teaching in popular education; the second, and by far the more controversial, was aimed at the hypocrisy of pretending that women did not feel sexual desire except in love. 'Men have built up a convention of fastidious women to flatter their own sexual rivalry,' he observes before Jenny lets herself be seduced. '. . . [The male] generally fails to perceive that when a woman cannot find a man who is able to stimulate her imagination, she often looks for another who will gratify her senses.'

In many sections of society this was perfectly well understood, in the circles formerly frequented by Edward VII, in the theatre, and among the clients of Marie Stopes who offered sexual advice as well as birth-control information to the poor, but to the middle class, which still held to the gentlemanly belief that while making love 'Ladies don't move,' it was a shocking suggestion. It caused the *Illustrated London News* to fear that *Carnival* might be thought 'an unpleasant book', *The Spectator* to damn 'its frank disregard of the conventional canons of taste', and the President of Magdalen, who had received a complimentary copy from the author, to regret that he could only look at the cover as he suspected the contents would prove 'more frankly passionate than I quite like'. But it did no harm to sales.

As the fame of *Carnival* spread in the early months of 1912, accolades came from men who had already made their name, such as J. M. Barrie welcoming 'a brother author among the tribe', and Gustav Holst bemoaning the distraction from his own *Carnival* composition caused by reading Monty's. There were first nights, parties and a huge *Carnival* ball given by him and John Mavrogordato for the ballet girls of the Alhambra.

From one of these parties came the opportunity to acquire a house in London when John Jacob Astor's secretary, Captain Gerard Tharp, told him he was giving up 6 North Street (now Lord North Street). It was built round two sides of a courtyard, and consisted principally of three Elizabethan cottages which in the eighteenth century had been converted into a love nest for Lord North's mistress.

He could move in on 1 April, but to decorate it as Monty conceived it should be required more money than Secker had been able to pay in royalties. In Cornwall, three years earlier, Faith had borrowed £500 from her future inheritance of £3000 from her father's estate in order to pay off their debts, and on the strength of Monty's prospects she now arranged to borrow the remainder, paying Edward Stone interest of 5 per cent. From Tharp they obtained orange curtains made of linen which were to follow them to their next four houses; they bought Samarkand rugs for the drawing room, black wallpaper decorated with golden willows for the study, the portrait of a grave Elizabethan to look down upon the dining-room table, a grand piano, a chandelier, and six bay trees for the courtyard. Like Lady Ham, it was perfect, almost theatrically so. For the next twenty-five years, Faith was to have a hand in decorating all Monty's houses, and few things testify so clearly to their fundamental accord than their shared preference for these settings of vivid colours and carefully contrived effects.

To go with the improvements, they acquired the services of a cook, a housemaid, and a trainee secretary called Nellie Baker. She was the adopted daughter of Mrs Stone, and having grown up a difficult and rebellious child, she had been continuously shuffled around the family until Faith and Monty gave her employment.

The rewards of success made the summer of 1912 even more glorious than its sizzling predecessor. They were invited to dinner with Arnold Bennett, to lunch with Edmund Gosse, and they entertained Norman Douglas, whose *Siren Land* had just been published, and who told them tempting stories of Capri. Their presence improved any party, for they were the ideal guests, handsome, quick-witted and charming. But once the evening was over, they went their separate ways, Faith to bed and Monty to dance with the ballet girls. Sometimes she would wake in the early hours of the morning to 'find him hanging over the bed with a paper cap on his head and a harlequin's wand in his hand'. Life, she concluded, was 'more amusing than ever'.

As a popular young writer, Monty was drawn into that intellectual ferment which later prompted Virginia Woolf to assert that 'on or about December 1910, human nature changed'. The trends in modern painting and poetry to which she referred were gathering strength and Monty explored them with some enthusiasm. He went to an avant garde meeting to hear Ezra Pound, but was unimpressed by his American accent and shouted recitation. He was invited to address a dinner to honour Marinetti, the Italian futurist, and was dismayed that his own mocking improvisation of a futurist poem on the Piccadilly underground should be taken seriously. He attended the Post-Impressionist exhibition, but found it too ridiculous not to be able to tell a dogfight from a woman swimming, and decided to keep the *Mona Lisa* in her position of honour. Criticism of the old ways attracted him, but not revolution. His own contribution to poetry that year was a collection of children's verse, scanned and rhymed, called *Kensington Rhymes*.

The literary circle in which he felt immediately and enduringly at home was the Savile Club, to which he was elected in June. Its motto, 'Sodalitas convivium', might have been his own. Conversation was prompted in the dining room by the custom of eating at two long tables, but it was not discouraged even in the card room or billiard room. To a raconteur of his compulsive and compelling nature, it needed no other recommendation, but it was also a cause for pride to belong to a club of which R. L. Stevenson and Algernon Swinburne had once been members. Like Gunner's, it enshrined a tradition which he admired, and its members constituted an aristocracy within which all were equal, not unlike the bloods of St Paul's.

In those months the dreams he had entertained since adolescence began to come true. 'The summer of 1912 blows in my memory like a flower of time that was,' he wrote, 'it is for me the last rose of a London that vanished during the First World War.'

The gauge of his success was his relationship with his father. Instead of dreams of glory he had palpable achievement, and the change this made was apparent when the management of the Haymarket Theatre in London asked him to consider writing a play for them. Knowing Edward's frustrated ambition for a London success, he grandly assured him, 'If this Haymarket commission comes off, I shall write a part for you – a comedy part – and stipulate that you play it – if you like!'

It may be doubted whether an actor-manager of thirty years' experience would have relished the thought of a role being offered to him only because his son stipulated it. However, the opportunity never arose, for in May Gerald du Maurier pressed him to dramatise *Carnival*, and once the play had been sent off, the idea for a new novel began to germinate.

The previous year he had found in Muirhead Bone's flat an engraving of a seedy row of houses, entitled 'Sinister Street'. The scene and the title had already appeared in one of the poems he wrote while at Oxford:

> And he was lost within a town,
> Empty of lamps, not populous,
> With streets that sloped for ever down
> Into dim courtyards cavernous.
> No staunch policeman wandered here
> With comfortable steps and slow.
> No friendly postman could appear
> To save him from a hiding foe,
> And so he moved with beating heart
> Along the sinister, unknown
> Deserted street . . .

It was called 'The Child's Epic of the Night', and its subject was the nightmare that haunted him in childhood. When he sat down to begin his third novel in July, the first words he wrote were the title, *Sinister Street*. No physical street of that name appears in the book; Monty himself referred to it as 'a symbolic title', but it is indisputable that it designates the street which terrified him in his dreams.

If terror of the night was the starting-point of the book, its theme, as he told his father-in-law in February, was to be religion. To this news Edward Stone replied encouragingly that 'Mrs Humphry Ward has done something in that line, although not nearly enough,' but late-Victorian moralising was not Monty's intention.

In *The Altar Steps*, part of a religious trilogy written after the war, he made explicit a theory which informs *Sinister Street*, although it is not stated. A child's nightmares, he believed, arose from 'the soul's perception of evil'. Although gradually obscured by education, culture and the use of reason, the horror and attraction of those early fears later developed into the adolescent's urge to explore the forbidden and the adult's temptation to choose evil rather than good.

The struggle between good and evil was the theme he set himself when he began to write the story of Michael Fane whose life bore such a marked resemblance to his own. It was a theme which only a great writer could achieve successfully, but that was the role he had assumed. He could no more visualise himself as an ordinary writer than he could an ordinary poet, playwright or gardener. The only flaw in the performance was his willingness to let it be interrupted by more frivolous pursuits, and like his first two novels *Sinister Street* was soon put aside.

His agent, now J. B. Pinker, informed him that an American impresario, William Brady, wanted to produce a dramatised version of *Carnival* in the United States. Gerald du Maurier had reluctantly decided that the role of Avery was too small for a male star, but Brady wanted the play for his wife, Grace George, so long as the author was prepared to make some changes. To succeed in America, his mother's country, Monty was prepared to drop everything and make any changes that were required. He made only two requests, that a part should be found for his brother Frank, who was still acting in Australia, and that Chrissie Maude and Lily Clarke should be brought over from London to help create the atmosphere of the Alhambra.

From the moment he arrived in New York in September, he was enthralled by it, and at once he saw himself as a New Yorker, living in a house on the Hudson or an apartment in the Metropolitan Tower. 'I do *love* New York,' he told Faith. 'It makes me extraordinarily fertile with ideas and fills me with renewed energy. I intend to live in America for eight months out of twelve and visit every state in turn.'

The United States responded in kind. Appletons had published *Carnival* earlier in the year, and he was deluged by interviews and invitations. Magazines like *McLure's* and *Metropolitan* commissioned stories from him, and Brady, a diamond-ringed gambler and baseball promoter, was so pleased by his speed in rewriting that he paid for both Frank and his wife Peggy to come from Australia. However Grace George forbade him to do the same for Chrissie Maude.

Warmed by so much appreciation, he found that even French Lick, Indiana, where Brady was taking the waters, had the appearance of 'a delightful American Carlsbad', and to his mother he wrote exuberantly, 'I think your country is perfectly delightful. I have received nothing but the most perfect hospitality. Miss Grace George knocks to pieces *any* English actress and I won't have anyone but her playing Jenny over in England. Brady is charming . . .'

His enthusiasm was sustained by the bright prospects of the play which was to go on tour for a few weeks in November before opening in New York. Originally there had been hopes of getting John Barrymore to play the part of Maurice Avery opposite Grace George, but when that fell through and no suitable actor could be found, Monty took the role. This was a mistake. Unable to watch the play himself, he was forced to rely on Brady's advice about the changes that were needed. He spent long nights after the performances tinkering with the script to suit Brady's latest ideas, and simultaneously attempted to complete his stories for *Mclure's*. Meanwhile the audiences' opinion of his play deteriorated in parallel with his opinion of Grace George's acting, and with Grace George's opinion of her husband. What Brady thought was not entirely clear until they reached Philadelphia, where he paid off the cast and bought a baseball team instead.

Monty hastened back to New York and just before Christmas wrote to Faith begging her to join him. 'But give up the idea that you're coming to the first night of *Carnival*. I don't see my way to altering the play to make a sentimental appeal. Frankly I'm bored with it and anxious to get on with *Sinister Street*. I get fearfully fed up with acting. Never again!'

The *cri de cœur* was what Faith had been waiting for. To fill the absence she had paired up with a wealthy, effervescent American, Tessie Brennan, with whom she attended tea parties and poetry readings, but the purpose of her life was looking after Monty, and only he could fill that gap. She scribbled in the flyleaf of a notebook a wistful verse:

> In his chair
> I could never bear
> Not to see him sitting there
> With his tumbled hair;
> Writing things I love to hear.
> I could never bear
> Not to see him sitting there.

Within days of receiving his letter she was on a liner to New York. When she arrived early in January 1913, it was Frank who met her. Monty was prostrated by sciatica.

Ever since his feat of learning his father's lines before the opening of

The Gentleman in Grey, he had been subject to attacks of what were then called neuritis, or pains in the joints of his legs. Although it was not properly speaking sciatica, that was the term he used later because it was the sciatic nerve which was attacked. The onset of pain coincided with a state of nervous exhaustion and usually depression, but these psychological factors were exacerbated by damp surroundings and draughts. Their increasing severity had forced him to buy an immense padded chair with a swivel-rest at which he could write, but nothing had prepared him for the violence of this bout which lasted almost a fortnight with spasms of pain so acute that even half a grain of morphine was insufficient to deaden them.

Faith found him pale and thin, but greatly cheered by her arrival. The knowledge that she was needed softened the blow he had to deliver: they were to leave North Street immediately. She hated the thought – 'it's like burying a beloved child,' she told Virginia, who was given the job of letting it and storing the furniture – but there was no alternative.

'It's absolutely necessary for him to go and get baked, the doctor says,' she wrote. 'He is such a precious and wonderful thing that he is worth taking care of, and I suppose he has suffered about as much pain as anyone else that's ever lived in his short life.'

They discussed plans to go to Arizona, to join some people who had bought a ranch called Hollywood in California, or to try Bermuda, one of the islands Monty had been collecting in imagination since childhood. On the wall of the hotel bedroom there hung a steel engraving of the rocky coast of Capri and with memories of Norman Douglas's stories of the island to add substance to the picture, Monty took the decision to recuperate by the Mediterranean. The nearest he ever came to open regret was over the lost opportunity to get in on the ground floor of the Californian film industry. Although he never wanted to be on the stage, he always felt that he would have enjoyed being a film star.

Shortly before they left New York, Martin Secker's partner, P. P. Howe, sent him a piece of advice that others were to echo and re-echo for most of the rest of his career to no observable effect. 'My dear old chap,' he wrote,

I think you ought to chuck all this reputation-making and go to live somewhere nice and quiet where you can write *books*. What's a success in the theatre anyway, and what's the use of getting a thousand dollars for a short story if it bores you to write a short story? Write some of the books that want to get themselves written and at the rate of one a year they'll keep you all right ...

They arrived in Naples in March 1913, and went to stay in Sorrento while Monty caught up on a backlog of stories for *Metropolitan* magazine. Every evening he and Faith sat on the cliffs dropping bits of paper over the edge while the sun set across the sea. To Faith it seemed as though simple amusements were all that he wanted, but presumably he was gradually shaking off the tumult and disappointment of the United States in preparation for a return to *Sinister Street*.

On one of these journeys to the clifftops at Punta di Campanella, he found a little terracotta head of the goddess Minerva lying among the crimson blossom of wild sweetpeas. Omens and portents always carried weight. Across the bay lay the island of Capri. They had letters of introduction from Douglas. It was clearly time to make use of them. The following day they took the ferry across to the island which would be their home for the next seven years.

9
The greatest talent
of his generation

From the Naples ferry Capri had the appearance of a dark green whale. The colour came from the olive woods which covered most of its surface. The head rising bulbous from the sea was Capri proper, and the smaller bump of the tail was Anacapri. The difference between the two ends of the island was clearly defined: the guardian of Anacapri was St Anthony of Padua, patron saint of lost causes, and its hills appeared to be a misty golden-green, while Capri venerated St Costanza, a matter-of-fact fisherman's saint, and the views were sharply contoured in silver and blue. The Anacapresi were regarded as backward and rural, and the Capresi as smart and cosmopolitan because it was at Capri that the Naples ferry arrived.

The centre of life in Capri was Morgano's Café. Its terrace, looking out over the blue sea, stood conveniently close to the top of the funicular railway, enabling residents to inspect visitors as they came up from the landing place below. The visitors themselves were hardly aware of the inspection, for the first moments as they emerged from the funicular into the piazza were overwhelming.

'Wherever we looked there seemed to be dizzy pinnacles of rock, crowned by Gothic castles,' Monty remembered.

The white columns of distant pergolas made us think of Greece. A Judas tree flamed like a great rose of solid blossom against a passionate blue sky. Round us, in a jingle of bells and laughter and cracking whips, stood so many people, natives and foreigners, who from living in Capri had achieved such a brilliance of effect as butterflies and hummingbirds achieve from competing with the light and colour of the tropics.

Thinking that they had come only for a fo[...]
the Faraglione Hotel. But they did not remain[...]
introductions from Norman Douglas gave the[...]
the émigré society of Capri, and soon they we[...]
gossip and scandal.

The Germans who arrived in the 1870s wer[...]
Capri a benign climate and a tolerance for sexual [...]
stern regime had discouraged. They were foll[...] ....lux of
British homosexuals after the Oscar Wilde case, by Russian anti-Tsarist
dissidents, aesthetic Americans, intellectual Scandinavians, by artists and
writers of every nationality, and by anyone else who had a private income
or a remittance contingent upon their staying a long way from home.
The native Capresi sold them land for villas, provided them with dom-
estics and lovers of both sexes, but made the bulk of their living from
olives, goats and fishing.

Norman Douglas had gone there first in 1888 and he looked back to
that period around the start of the century as a time of innocence. 'In
those days it still possessed some of the dreaminess and remoteness for
which it had been famed,' he wrote in *Materials for a Description of
Capri*. 'It was a restful place, full of lovable freaks of various nationalities
who lived contentedly on next to nothing, gave each other unpretentious
dinner parties and took no notice of the annual invasion of Teutonics . . .'
That society was already changing when the Mackenzies arrived, and
the straw in the wind was Count d'Adelswaerd-Fersen, known as Count
Jack.

Half French and half Swedish, but wholly a pederast, he had just
returned from a period of exile. Like his parties and his opium habit, his
interest in young boys was a little too ostentatious to be amusing. When
the *municipio* heard that he had already been imprisoned in France for
offences against minors, he had expelled Fersen for a few months in
order to protect the singularly robust morals of the Capresi.

The Mackenzies met him at the home of two elderly American ladies,
Kate and Saidee Wolcott-Perry. Many years before, when they first came
to Italy, they had hyphenated their names and lives, and now having
adopted Count Jack as their pet, they were at one in believing him the
victim of a gross miscarriage of justice. To the Mackenzies' amusement,
they found that the gentle, hospitable pair were conducting a feud against
another of the people Norman Douglas had sent them to, an ancient
American satyr, called Charles Coleman, who believed Count Jack
capable of anything except amiability. Coleman's studio was home for

on of young girls, and his hospitality was as prodigal as that
foes.

Around this central feud a cloud of minor quarrels, slanders and
innuendoes floated up in American accents which sounded to Monty's
ear like oboes, in English accents like 'gurgling clarinets', and in Italian
like a 'welter of tenor brass instruments'. Having nothing else to do, the
creation and spreading of gossip were full-time activities, so that the
elderly churchwarden who took round the collection at the English
church was said to pocket half of it, a respectable retired major was
confidently assumed to have black silk sheets on his bed the better to
show off 'the snowy amplitude of the female form' – this was Norman
Douglas's contribution – and affairs both heterosexual and homosexual
were multiplied beyond the extremes of stamina. There were two especially sure sources of gossip. The first was John Ellingham Brooks,
who shared a villa with Somerset Maugham and E. F. Benson, and for
twenty years had known or guessed everything that had happened on
the island.

Brooks became the Mackenzies' most assiduous visitor, and one never
resented but treasured for his diffidence and charm. His avowed purpose
in life, though never completed, was to translate a collection of Greek
epigrams and the sonnets of Hérédia, but he was more conscientious
about his real goal of living without work. Both Benson and Maugham
made him presents and he was a perpetual diner-out, offering in return
an appreciative audience to his hosts' stories and a selection of news and
delicate bons mots delivered with a charming hesitancy in his speech.

Their other source of information was a bosomy Edwardian beauty,
Gwen Gallacher, later immortalised by Monty in *Vestal Fire* as Mrs
Ambrogio, in whose clipped English county speech the wildest specu-
lations became not merely credible but authoritative. She adored her
fictional portrait, which was so precise that everyone referred to her as
Mrs Ambrogio, and after her death no one could quite disentangle her
real self from the double Monty had created. Both of them kept bitches
which were trussed up in chastity belts when in season. 'Everybody's
immoral in Capri,' Mrs Ambrogio, and perhaps her original, would
explain of this. 'It's the air. Dogs. People. All immoral. Can't help it,
poor dears.'

Apart from these diversions there were personalities like Dr Axel
Munthe, the great Swedish physician and fantasist who claimed to have
halted a cholera epidemic in Naples single-handed; Maxim Gorki, with
whom Monty used to go to the cinema; and the Anglo-Catholic architect,

Edwin Cerio, who designed and owned the most beautiful houses on the island.

The visit lasted two months, and by May when they returned to England, they had rented a house called La Caterola in the hills on the north side of Capri. It was still the custom for northern Europeans to flee the heat of a Mediterranean summer, but they had an additional reason for leaving.

Since the débâcle in America Monty had been idling. He had written some magazine stories and another forty pages of *Sinister Street* between parties and gossip at Morgano's, but it was not enough. Martin Secker had scheduled the novel for autumn publication, and under the threat of this deadline, he went straight to Rivière to concentrate on writing. By July it was obvious that he could not complete the 400,000 words he had in mind, and accepting the inevitable Secker agreed to publish it in two parts. Volume One, entitled *Youth's Encounter*, therefore ended with Michael Fane eighteen years old and waiting to go to Oxford. Nellie Baker, who had typed *Carnival*, came down to do the same for *Sinister Street*, and on 5 August 1913 the last chapter of the typescript was sent off to the printers.

While waiting for publication, Monty stayed with Martin Secker at Bridgefoot near Iver in Buckinghamshire. A superb Queen Anne house, it was to be a refuge at different times for both him and Faith. On this occasion, however, he was there alone. Faith had returned to Nevern Square where Harry Pélissier was dying from cirrhosis of the liver. Fay was with him, but preoccupied with their one-year-old son Antony. It was Virginia, helped by a nurse, who looked after him until Faith came to share the burden for the last six weeks of his life. Monty, who hated sick-rooms and had never forgiven Pélissier for marrying Fay, avoided the house, and shortly before Pélissier died he went to stay with Max Beerbohm in Italy, leaving Faith to follow later.

The first volume of *Sinister Street* was published on 1 September, at which date it should have been available in all the leading bookshops and circulating libraries. Of the four great circulating libraries, however – Mudies, *The Times* Book Club, Boots and W. H. Smith – the last two initially refused to order copies of *Sinister Street*, nor did Smith's order it for their 1500 bookshops. Their motives were partly a commercial dislike of two-volume novels, and partly a Puritan urge to censorship.

In the frontispiece, Monty quoted Keats's observation that 'The imagination of a boy is healthy, and the mature imagination of a man is healthy; but there is a space of life between in which the soul is in a ferment.' In his picture of public-school life the existence of homosexuality loomed large and the adolescent's fascination with the further boundaries of sexual excitement was vividly portrayed. Fortunately for Monty, his favourite paper, the *Daily Mail*, made the censorship front-page news, and the consequent publicity forced the libraries to cave in.

The heavy guns of morality continued to thunder until the end of the year, the heaviest piece being contributed by Canon Edward Lyttelton, Headmaster of Eton, who argued in a long letter to *The Times* that 'sanity and upright manliness are destroyed, not only by the reading of obscene stuff, but by a premature interest in sex matters, however excited . . .' Angrily Monty fired back with the assertion, 'If a boy exists who can possibly read it, he will find himself left at the end with a definite prejudice in favour of the Christian religion.'

Caught up in the bombardment was Edward Stone, who had accepted Monty's dedication, still thinking that *Sinister Street* belonged to the Mrs Humphry Ward school of literature. His son, Ned, was one of Lyttelton's housemasters and insisted that he withdrew his name, but when he asked Secker to do so, Faith sent him a withering letter accusing him of moral cowardice. Gallantly the old man wrote again to Secker, cancelling his earlier letter: 'I am sure I ought to stick to my colours and I am anxious not to cast any possible slur on the book, however much I may wish that certain episodes had been less highly coloured.'

As was to become the inevitable accompaniment to stress, Monty was struck down by sciatica, but from his bed he reiterated to his father-in-law that the great thing in the book's favour 'is that it pays a shining tribute to the influence of religion. I know no other writer with my influence who does that now in novels.'

In later years he was inclined to present *Sinister Street* as a criticism of society in general and public schools in particular, but at its conception and immediately after publication his comments make it plain that the religious impulse was uppermost.

In order to trace the development of the struggle against evil from its earliest manifestation in nightmare through the adolescent urge toward sexual exploration to the adult's choice between good and evil, he decided to adopt a novel technique. Not only did he keep Michael Fane on stage throughout, as he had done with Jenny Pearl, he also restricted the reader's awareness of events to Michael's experience. Thus the child's terror was recorded with a child's awareness, and the adolescent's adventures without an adult's hindsight.

'I was more successful in avoiding psychologising about his thoughts and behaviour than I had been over Jenny Pearl,' he commented, 'and also in keeping out any suggestion of comment direct or implied by myself as author. I wanted Michael Fane's attitude to life to remain what it was at the time.'

Almost of necessity, therefore, he was bound to keep the story within his own experience. So Michael's nightmares occur in a thin, red house in West Kensington, where he is bullied by a domineering nanny. His adolescent adventures take place at the nearby public school of St James which in every respect is St Paul's, and he later goes to St Mary's College, Oxford, which is a replica of Magdalen. Even differences in family background reproduce Monty's circumstances as a child. Mrs Fane is the mistress of the Earl of Saxby, and both Michael and his sister Stella are illegitimate. Thus his mother is frequently absent and he has no father on which to model himself, but only an obscure sense of being special and an outsider. Grafted onto these familiar emotions is Michael's adolescent calf-love for an aspiring actress called Lily Haden, and in the second volume it is the news that she has been seen soliciting on the Promenade that prompts him to search for her through the slums of London.

He had set himself a formidable task. To recreate times past, as Proust was also doing in *Swann's Way*, published in 1913, and Joyce was to do in *Portrait of the Artist as a Young Man* three years later, demanded stylistic innovation and a willingness to trace the roots of the present back into childhood as remorselessly as Freud and the pioneer psycho-analysts in Vienna. After the war Monty, like other writers, read Jung and Freud with interest, and later with distaste, but in these pre-war years he, Proust and Joyce seem to represent an anticipatory reflex. Of them all, it is *Sinister Street* which most clearly parallels the main body of psychoanalytical theory at the time in linking childhood trauma with adolescent sexuality and in illustrating the trauma through dreams.

To catch a sense of childhood in the first sentence, as Proust did, 'L'antan je me suis couché de bonne heure. Parfois, à peine ma bougie éteinte, mes yeux se fermaient si vite que je n'avais le temps de me dire "Je m'endors ..."', or like Mackenzie, 'From a world full of daisies as big as moons and mountainous green hillocks, Michael Fane came by some unrealised method of transport to the thin red house ...', or like Joyce, 'Once upon a time, and a very good time it was, there was a moocow coming down along the road ...', amounted to little compared to the development of the inner idea of the child in maturity.

Given its author's assertion that any boy capable of reading it should end with 'a definite prejudice in favour of Christianity', the essential yardstick of *Sinister Street* must be the realism of the choice between good and evil in the growing child. Michael himself believes that 'he could not remember any period of his life when the speculum of hidden thought had not reflected the shadow of evil which overcast the manifestation of most ordinary existence'. And if the shadow is not convincing, neither will be the rest of his life.

In purely pragmatic terms, evidence of success can be found in the consciousness of generations of schoolboys that they were reading a wicked book. The fifteen-year-old Cyril Connolly, who later turned decisively against its author, kept a copy hidden by his bed and could quote it by the page. George Orwell, who discovered it there and stole it, remembered Connolly being beaten for having it. It may well be that some of its aura of wickedness came from the opinion of schoolmasters, but without doubt for four or five decades it ranked high on the index of forbidden adolescent literature.

The nature of the wickedness is suggested rather than stated but it is immanent from the earliest haunted days when Michael 'had come to take pleasure in the grotesque and macabre'. It is conveyed by a game of alternately tormenting and cherishing a pet kitten, and by his mingled thrill and horror in a newspaper story of murder, and in bullying his sister until she cries so that 'as he hummed his way downstairs he thought sensuously of the imminent reconciliation'. School and the excitement of boyhood drive away the shadows, and the only reminder of its existence comes, as it did with Monty, in his guilty pleasure in the schoolgirl's humiliation and the cabin boy's beating.

Adolescence is when it breaks through the surface of appearance, and most especially in Michael's encounter with Brother Aloysius at an abbey where he has gone on retreat. They are picking blackberries together when the monk moves towards him and exclaims,

'Feel my hand, it's as hot as hell' . . . Michael looked at the questioner's pale face, at the uncomfortable eyes gleaming blue, at the full, stained mouth and the long feverish hands dyed with purple juice . . . 'Yes, you with your big girl's eyes, just like a girl I used to live with. Oh you needn't look so proper. I expect you've often thought about girls. I did at your age. Three months with girls, three months with priests. Girls and priests – that's my life. When I was tired of women I became religious, and when I was tired of Church, I took to women. It was a priest told me to come here to see if this would cure me, and now, damn you, you come into Chapel and stare and set me thinking of the Seven Sisters

Road on that wet night I saw her last. That's where she lives, and you look exactly like her, God! you're the image of her.'

His attempted assault on Michael comes with stunning suddenness, but also as something long anticipated, just as Michael's pleasure in the monk's degradation is an emotion which has been lurking from the beginning. It is at this point that *Sinister Street* achieves its preliminary goal of creating a realistic sense of evil, precisely because it is present not simply in the person of Brother Aloysius and his tales of the Seven Sisters Road, but in Michael himself. Nor does it arise merely from a schoolboy's guilty interest in sex. Both the writing and the psychological coherence with which it has been traced from childhood make the discovery of a sadistic streak in himself entirely convincing and chilling.

'The "motif of utter foulness" is one of the most uncanny things in the book,' the young Edmund Wilson wrote to his friend Alfred Bellinger, 'you feel that you are not walking on solid ground, that it may give way at any moment and let you into the sewer.'

The hidden presence of wickedness makes the real world a thing of appearances, and its insecurity sets the rest of Michael's youth in context. That he should be emotional, brooding, uncontrollably high-spirited and liable to despair is because he is confronted by a choice between the absolutes of good and evil while trying to live in a world of make-believe. And that, it may be said, is the adolescent condition.

The charged style of writing and the repeated reference to time which has ceased to move reinforce the unreality, yet the story is placed in the mundane actuality of West Kensington. The slang, the games, the relationships and the society are so precisely caught that to most critics it appeared that Mackenzie was telling the story not just of a youth but of that rootless salaried class which Michael and his creator despised but belonged to by education at least.

In an article for the *Outlook* late in 1913, Ford Madox Hueffer (later Ford) associated the name of Compton Mackenzie with those of D. H. Lawrence and Ezra Pound as the young hopes of literature. The first volume of *Sinister Street* contained 'the history of a whole class, a whole region, during a whole period of life,' he wrote; and he concluded that:

Possibly *Sinister Street* is a work of real genius – one of those books that really exist otherwise than as the decorations of a publishing season – exist along with *L'Education Sentimentale*, *Fathers and Children*, *Heart of Darkness* and *The Purple Land*. One is too cautious . . . to say anything like that of quite a young writer. But I shouldn't wonder.

Forty years later, in the foreword to the French translation, André Maurois picked up his words and declared, 'Ford Madox Ford ne s'était pas trompé. Le livre a duré . . .'

In March 1914, when the Mackenzies were back in Capri, Faith wrote to her mother-in-law that they had just been reading Henry James's article in the *Times Literary Supplement* called 'The Younger Generation'. 'Dear Henry James,' she commented, 'so kind if only one could understand him.' It was fair comment. In his famous survey of the literary scene, he picked out Hugh Walpole, Gilbert Cannan, Compton Mackenzie and D. H. Lawrence as the rising stars and likely successors of Conrad, Galsworthy, Wells and Bennett, but cloaked his reasons for doing so in language so opaque as to defy easy comprehension.

While Ford had been impressed by the universality of the novel, James concentrated on it purely as literature. In his article he drew a distinction between the techniques of saturation, or slice of life, and selection, or extract of life. He suspected that *Carnival* belonged to the former, and of the first volume of *Sinister Street* he wrote, 'Youth has clearly been Mr Mackenzie's saturation.' However, he suggested that the latter did show a different emphasis. He noted that it was constructed in episodic form which he compared to pearls loosely strung together, and 'in the case of each of the pearls fished up in his dive . . . his mind has had a further iridescence to confer. It is the fineness of the iridescence that on such occasion matters and this appeal to our interest is again and again on Mr Compton Mackenzie's page of the happiest and the brightest.' In particular he commended the use of language, 'positively caring for his expression as expression . . . positively loving it in the light of what it may do for him'. He could not be sure until he had read the second volume whether there actually was 'a controlling and a pointed intention' holding it all together, but he suspected that Mackenzie belonged with the practitioners of selection and thus on the side of the angels.

Such praise delighted Monty, although not quite as much as the more immediately intelligible comment which James made two months earlier to his agent, J. B. Pinker: 'He strikes me at any rate as, putting one or two aside (or rather as putting Wells only . . .) as very much the greatest talent of the new generation. And the modernity of him. It is such a happy and unexpected change to be interested!'

The second volume did not appear until November 1914, but Michael Fane's Oxford career and his subsequent search for Lily Haden in the underworld need to be considered as one with the earlier book.

Most critics recognised a change in atmosphere from the concentrated self-regard of Michael's adolescence to the widening assurance of an undergraduate. 'Quite simply,' Schofield Thayer pointed out in the American magazine *Dial*, 'as a child Michael was unique, while at Oxford and in the underworld he is one among many.' With the advantage of knowing the author's undergraduate career, it can be seen that he divided up his own experiences between Michael Fane and two friends, Maurice Avery (who had appeared in *Carnival*) and Guy Hazlewood (who was to appear in *Guy and Pauline*). Thus Maurice starts a magazine called the *Oxford Looking-Glass*, and is invested with energy, vanity, untidiness and superficial charm, while Guy who takes a house called Plasher's Mead, indistinguishable from Lady Ham, is sensitive, a poet, and unaffectedly attractive. Michael Fane is thereby reduced to the role of passive observer. In his last term at Oxford he has a room with a big bay window which 'hung over the street like the stern-cabin of a frigate, and as Michael sat there he had the impression of being cut off from communication, the sense of perpetually leaving life astern'.

It is this vantage point which gives the Oxford section its special flavour. In place of the earlier intensity, there is the golden sweetness of nostalgia. Of all his settings, this is the most famous, the Oxford of mist-wreathed streets, of bonfires in the quads, of rags, aesthetes and hearties – a standing wave of youth in the river of time.

His prose was decorated with epithets of excessive abstruseness, such as fuliginous, desquamating, feculent, tintamar, and fum, and it was growing luxuriant. In *Carnival* he had described a May morning in these terms: 'Great swan-white clouds breasted the deepening azure of May skies. The streets were dazzlingly wet with the night's rain, and every puddle was as blue as a river.' In *Sinister Street* the same scene became: 'A snowy aggregation of cumulus sustained the empyrean upon the volume of its mighty curve and swell. The road before him stretched shining in a radiant drench of azure puddles.'

In middle age Monty was inclined to disparage *Sinister Street* for its literariness, yet despite the lush elaboration, his effects were carefully arranged, and James was correct to argue that he made his expressions work for him. In his description of a November evening in Oxford, for example, the atmosphere is built up with some care through a contrast in pace between exterior and interior scenes, through the references to fog which frame each shot of the street, and through the very rhythm which juxtaposes such words as 'tea-tray gothic' and 'municipal ampelopsis':

Michael went on up the High and stood for a moment, watching the confusion caused by the fog at Carfax, listening to the fretful tinkles of the numerous bicycles and the jangling of the trams and the shouts of the paper-boys. Then he walked down Cornmarket Street past the shops splashing through the humid coils of vapour, their lights upon the townspeople, loiterers and purchasers who thronged the pavements. Undergraduates strolled along linked arm in arm and perpetually staring. How faithfully each group resembled its forerunners and successors. All had the same fresh complexions, the same ample green coats of Harris tweed, the same grey flannel trousers. Only in the casual acknowledgements of his greeting when he recognised acquaintances was there the least variation, since some would nod or toss their heads, others would shudder with their chins, and a few would raise their arms in a fan-like gesture of social benediction. Michael turned into the Broad where the fog made mysterious even the tea-tray gothic of Balliol, and Trinity with its municipal ampelopsis. A spectral cabman saluted him interrogatively from the murk. A fox-terrier went yapping down the street at the heels of a don's wife hurrying back to Banbury Road. A belated paper-boy yelled 'Varsity and Blackheath result', hurrying towards a more profitable traffic. The fog grew denser every minute, and Michael turned round into Turl Street past many-windowed Exeter and the monastic silence of Lincoln . . . Seven o'clock chimed suddenly, and Michael hurried to college, snatched a black coat and a gown out of Venner's and just avoided the sconce for being more than a quarter of an hour late for hall.

Michael was glad he had not missed hall that night . . . it would have been a pity to have missed hall when the electric light failed abruptly and when everybody had just helped themselves to baked potatoes. It would have been sad not to have seen the Scholars' table so splendidly wrecked or heard the volleys of laughter resounding through the darkness.

'By Gad,' said Lonsdale when the light was restored and the second year leaned over their table in triumphant exhaustion. 'Did you see that bad man Carben combing the potatoes out of his hair with a fork? I say, Porcher,' he said to his old scout who was waiting at the table, 'do bring us some more baked potatoes.'

'Isn't there none left?' enquired Porcher. 'Mr Lonsdale, sir, you'd better keep a bit quiet. The Sub-Warden's looking very savage – very savage indeed.'

Scenes such as this left such an indelible mark that many of its readers remember *Sinister Street* simply as a university novel. Indeed in Fane's Oxford, Monty created a myth which coloured the imagination of undergraduates there for more than half a century. 'There is no book on Oxford like it,' Max Beerbohm declared. 'It gives you the actual Oxford *experience*. What Mackenzie has miraculously done is to make you feel what each *term* was like . . .'

In itself this Oxford is a masterpiece of evocation, yet so far as the book as a whole is concerned, if Christianity were really to triumph over evil, and if as James hoped there actually was a pointed intention, the widening focus of Michael's life had to close in again on its original theme. At this crucial point, however, it is apparent that there has been a shift. Evil no longer lies within him and behind the façade of reality. Instead it lies plainly in the modern world and 'the great complication of machinery fed by gold and directed by fear' which sustained Edwardian society. 'Something akin to Don Quixote's impulsive dismay Michael experienced in his own view of the twentieth century. He felt the need of a constructive ideal of conduct to sustain him through the long pilgrimage that must ensue after these hushed Oxford dreams.'

This shift alters the balance so that Michael's picaresque journey through the sinister streets of Islington and Westminster in search of Lily has the character of social exploration rather than confrontation with a destructive power within him and all humanity. Only once is its presence suggested, in a chance encounter with a prostitute:

Michael shuddered at the monstrousness of her femininity: he seemed to have been given a glimpse of a mere mass of woman, a soft obscene primeval thing that demanded blows from a club, nothing else. He apprehended how in a moment men could become haters of femininity, could hate its animalism and wish to stamp upon it. The physical repulsion vanished when the sound of her footsteps died away.

The violence of this woman-loathing outburst is the logical outcome of Fane's upbringing. By being treated as a passing aberration rather than a crucial element of his mature self, his actions are deprived of their moral, or psychological, engine. Instead they are designed to show that the gentlemanly code which makes him offer to marry Lily is hollow and that the only sure guide is the church, but there is little conviction about it. In an epilogue to the second volume, Monty admitted that Michael Fane was growing up 'and for me his interest begins to fade'. Perhaps age is the reason for the shift of evil from the inner being to society outside, but the reader is no less aware than the author that something vital is lost in the protagonist.

'There is only one tragedy for youth,' a mysterious stranger says to Michael in the last lines of the book.

'And that is?'
'Age,' said the stranger.

'And what is the tragedy of age?'
'There is no tragedy of age,' said the stranger.

In *Sinister Street* Monty consciously set out to write a great book, and for all its flaws he succeeded. 'It is lavish, it contains rhodomontade; it is literary, sentimental and florid,' wrote Frank Swinnerton. 'But it has no timidities, it is large and confident; it is a picture of something more than a single life. It is a record of a departed generation.' It was one of the very few pre-war successes to hold its popularity through the 1920s and 1930s, thereby drawing an undue concentration of fire upon its author from critics of the next generation. And its influence was enormous, though not often beneficial.

F. Scott Fitzgerald, who announced in the preface to *The Romantic Egotist* that he intended to be 'intellectual and echo H. G. Wells and improper like Compton Mackenzie', was the best known and worst affected. 'He was drunk with Mackenzie,' Edmund Wilson observed, and *This Side of Paradise* is a deliberate attempt to translate Oxford to Princeton and Michael Fane to Amory Blaine. The enticing charm of that privileged Oxford was reflected more surely in *Brideshead Revisited*, and as John Raymond pointed out in the *New Statesman*, none of Waugh's aristocratic undergraduates bettered their original, Arthur Lonsdale:

Lonsdale really possessed the serene perfection of a great work of art. Michael thought to himself that almost he could bear to attend for ever Ardle's dusty lectures on Cicero in order that for ever he might hear Lonsdale admit with earnest politeness that he had not found time to glance at the text the day before, that he was indeed sorry to cause Mr Ardle such a mortification, but that unfortunately he had left his Plato in a saddler's shop where he had found it necessary to complain of a saddle newly made for him.

'But I am lecturing on Cicero, Mr Lonsdale. The *Pro Milone* was not delivered by Plato, Mr Lonsdale.'

'What's he talking about?' Lonsdale whispered to Michael.

'Nor was it delivered by Mr Fane,' added the Senior Tutor dryly.

Lonsdale looked at first very much alarmed by this suggestion, then, seeing by the lecturer's face that something was still wrong, he assumed a puzzled expression, and finally in an attempt to relieve the situation he laughed very heartily and said: 'Oh well, after all it's very much the same thing.' Then as everybody else laughed very loudly, Lonsdale sat down and leaned back, pulling up his trousers in gentle self-congratulation.

'Rum old buffer,' he whispered presently to Michael. 'His eye gets very glassy when he looks at me. Do you think I ought to ask him to lunch?'

Stylistically, the restriction of the narrative to Michael's consciousness influenced Dorothy Richardson, whose dozen novels entitled *Pilgrimage* took the technique one step further in pioneering the use of stream-of-consciousness narration. However, of all the novels which it influenced the only one Monty was proud to acknowledge was *Dusty Answer*, Rosamond Lehmann's story of a girl growing into adolescence.

Any consideration of *Sinister Street* must attempt to estimate how far it is autobiographical. Although he explicitly and repeatedly denied that it was autobiography disguised as fiction, the sheer accumulation of incident and circumstance borrowed from his own life makes a blanket denial impossible to believe. That the shape of Michael Fane's inner development reflected his own is confirmed first by the psychological detail of each succeeding stage of Michael's growth, and secondly by the shift from internal to external motivation at the period when the author suppressed what he felt to be the unacceptable side of his own personality. And at the age when Michael Fane becomes a passive observer, his energies divided among Guy Hazlewood and Maurice Avery, his creator likewise became protean, capable of taking on any personality but his own.

On his way back to Capri in September 1913 Monty stayed with Max Beerbohm at Rapallo, who wrote to their mutual friend Reggie Turner, 'Compton Mackenzie came and was a great success. I like him for being such an actor-r. All that part of him is delightful and quite atones for the veneer of Oxford.' On his return he gave a great dinner for thirty of Capri's fishermen and coachdrivers, and, as an actor should, caught the romance of the occasion in his dress, a broad-brimmed black hat and flowing cape pinned with a golden clasp. It was his last public appearance of the year, for the autumn of social and literary success was followed by a winter of pain. The intense and recurrent agony of his sciatica was in a sense the counterpoint to his dazzling public performance – an unmistakable private reality which could not be escaped – and it was in this light that he understood it. 'The fearful vitality . . . must be paid for,' he once wrote to his mother. 'One cannot be given so much without paying. That is why I welcome pain. It justifies my pride and my belief in myself.'

Its immediate cause in Capri was La Caterola, the house he and Faith had rented. It was damp and faced north, and for days he lay in bed either arched with pain or exhausted in the aftermath.

'This small house is a curse,' Faith wrote to Virginia. 'Sometimes I do lose courage. To see him suffering so much destroys the nerves . . . He *fears* nothing, but he wants so to be well and do all the great things that are in him.'

She decided to consult the great Dr Munthe who lived in Anacapri. Although gradually going blind, he still possessed the successful consultant's talent for telling patients what they wanted to hear, and when Faith asked for advice he assured her that the pain in Monty's legs was unlikely to lead to paralysis, and that an early death could almost certainly be avoided, but that, as she told Virginia, 'he must be spoiled and watched and coddled (unobtrusively)'. With medical confirmation that she must do what she most wanted to do, Faith's confidence returned and soon Monty too improved. 'What a darling he is,' she informed his mother. 'There never could be anything so absolutely fine and beautiful, and only you could have done it.'

In the spring Monty rented a tiny cottage in Anacapri with a sunny outlook called Il Rosaio. With the warmth his health was restored completely and, a sure sign that he was in spirits, his clothes began to blossom. 'Yesterday he put on his white suit with an orange and lemon effect of waistcoat and tie,' his wife wrote in February, 'and went to tea with the Perrys (just returned from a trip around the world) and they decorated him with wreaths of orange paper flowers from Honolulu. He looked such a lamb!'

That spring he took the path which Michael Fane was beginning to tread and made the decision to join the Roman Catholic Church. It was, he stressed, 'not to be regarded as a conversion but as a submission, a logical surrender to an inevitable recognition of the fact that Jesus Christ had founded his Church upon the rock of Peter.' He made it clear to the priest who instructed him that he could not alter his schoolboy conviction that the orders of the Anglican priesthood were genuinely Catholic and in the apostolic succession. He refused, therefore, to accept them as invalid. On 14 April 1914 he was received into the Church, but felt no great elation at the fact. As he had discovered when preaching in Cornwall, the spiritual intensity and the sense of evil which had haunted his youth were fading except on the pages of *Sinister Street*.

He had begun the second volume early in 1914, while he was still sick, but even after his recovery he remained fearful that the great work of his life would be cut short. The knowledge that the cup was at his lip drove him to write with growing urgency among the distractions of Capri society. Then, in June, an Italian fisherman showed him a report in a newspaper that the Archduke Franz Ferdinand of Austria had been assassinated at Sarajevo. At once his presentiment of impending disaster became concrete, and he declared that the murder would lead to war.

He and Faith immediately returned to England where he ensconced himself in Martin Secker's house to complete the last chapters of *Sinister Street* before the holocaust came. He wrote and revised until dawn when the finished pages would be taken away to be typed and set up at the printers. On Tuesday 3 August, he was writing at midnight when Britain's ultimatum to Germany expired, and hearing the rumble of trains in the distance he could imagine them carrying soldiers and munitions for shipment to Europe.

He was, in one sense, too late. *Sinister Street*, like *Carnival*, was addressed to the pre-war society whose standards, aspirations and failings were those of the gentleman. The apotheosis of that society came in its response to the violation of 'that scrap of paper' which guaranteed Belgian neutrality. To keep one's word no matter what the cost and to fight, not for personal gain but for justice, embodied the highest virtues of the code, and in the patriotic fervour which swamped the recruiting stations there was in truth a 'now God be thanked' vein of exhilaration as though life's inner aim had been revealed.

Monty too was caught up in the mood. Anxious to share in 'the greatest moment in the history of my time' he laid aside *Sinister Street* to try to obtain a commission in the regiment which wore the Mackenzie tartan – the Seaforth Highlanders. All his efforts were rebuffed. 'We don't want married subalterns of thirty-one,' a friend at the War Office genially replied. 'Your job is to keep us amused by writing books.'

Gradually the urgency began to leak from his drive to finish *Sinister Street*. He spent a day visiting Gilbert Cannan in Surrey, who took him to see D. H. Lawrence who was living close by at Chesham. Having read *The White Peacock* and his poetry, Monty was predisposed towards Lawrence, and he was immediately attracted by his appearance, pale-skinned and full-lipped beneath a reddish moustache, and by the neat elfish way he swept the floor and made the tea. Most of all he was delighted by Lawrence's habit of giving himself up to emotion, whether bawling up the stairs in a sudden fury, 'Frieda, Frieda, will you get off that bloody bed and come down and talk to the Cannans and Compton Mackenzie,' or overcome by Monty's suggestion that elms were melancholy trees: 'I'd never thought of it before, but those elms are dreadful. You've quite upset me, you have really. Frieda, it's those bloody elms that are driving us mad.'

The meeting of three of James's four young lions gave Monty one of his most popular Savile Club stories. Hardly any exaggeration was needed to make an absurd double act from Lawrence's high-pitched, excited Midlands voice forbidding his wife to talk about the war, 'The first time she mentions the war I'll put her out of doors,' and Frieda grinning contentedly and boasting in her thick, German accent, 'Lorenzo is so violent, so fierce.'

Monty neither admired nor liked Cannan, who had a facile style of writing and a literary gentleman's manner, but such feelings were almost always expressed obliquely. Thus Cannan's only part in his tale was to sit in portentous silence through the conversation about trees, hoping that it would be thought the silence of wisdom but really 'because he did not know one tree from another until they were made into furniture'.

His opinion of James's fourth lion was equally disparaging. Hugh Walpole's maidenly demeanour and breathless social climbing offered him ample scope to make his feelings known. 'You know what Hugh's entry in *Who's Who* should be,' he observed gently to Frank Swinnerton that year, 'eldest daughter of the bishop of Edinburgh; recreation – mountaineering.'

Although he always ascribed any ill-feeling between himself and Walpole to the latter's jealousy, insisting that for his own part he felt nothing more than amusement, his irritation at being bracketed with a writer whom he despised was clear enough. A year earlier, Walpole had poured scorn on the first volume of *Sinister Street* in an American magazine, concluding his attack with the words, 'Mackenzie, in spite of his cleverness, is no good.' Shortly afterwards, Secker, who published them both, was giving lunch to Walpole when Monty came over to their table and told Walpole that his novel, *Fortitude*, 'might have been written by a schoolgirl'. Responding to the jibe, Walpole took his next book to another publisher, letting it be known that his reputation would suffer if his name continued to appear in the same list as Compton Mackenzie. Monty, however, had the last word.

It had especially irked him that Henry James should have compared *Sinister Street* with *Fortitude* in his *TLS* article, and when he visited the Master in October 1914 he made a point of asking him his true opinion of Walpole's writing. Subsequently his impersonation of James fretfully hunting the precise epithet like a collector in pursuit of an elusive butterfly was always reckoned to have caught the man to the life. Thus, according to Monty, James's real opinion of 'our dear young friend, Hugh' was that 'so far he had written absolutely nothing at all,' and his mimicry gave the verdict a horrible ring of authenticity.

'Monty was mischievous rather than malicious,' Swinnerton commented of this duel. 'I don't think there was any malice in him. He was very sensitive to other people's faults and Hugh did leave himself open to teasing. On the other hand Monty would also laugh at himself, and with friends he could almost let himself be seen as an impostor.'

Swinnerton was another of Secker's stable, and initially at least he seemed more likely to side with Walpole. He was small and, as a young man, rather withdrawn, which led him to disapprove of Monty's exuberance. With the success of his own novels, his confidence blossomed, revealing both a genial temper and an acute ear for affectation. He particularly cherished a visit to John Galsworthy in the country when he was greeted by the great man rising from his place at the end of a long table and exclaiming gravely, 'I say, Swinnerton, this is very sporting of you, very sporting indeed.'

This sort of anecdote had an irresistible appeal for Monty, and his friendship with Swinnerton, as with Secker, was built around the exchange of such moments of absurdity. Unlike many of Monty's friends, Swinnerton retained a certain reserve in the face of the other's charm. In a revealing phrase he described Monty as possessing not so much a gift for friendship as 'the power of establishing a ruthless intimacy of understanding'. This was recognisably the same quality which Faith described as 'the gift of belonging wherever he goes. If he plays with children he plays as a child; if he talks to the Commander-in-Chief he talks as one general to another.'

It was understandable, therefore, that Henry James should have found the high opinion he had formed from Monty's books strongly reinforced by meeting him. Indeed he spoke so warmly of him to Virginia that she thought his feelings might eventually be transformed into cash.

'I hope his form of interest will develop into leaving Monty anything he has,' she wrote to Faith early in 1915. 'Poor old chap he has angina pectoris himself.'

James, however, was only concerned that Monty should be his literary, rather than his financial, heir and restricted himself to advice on style – the mistake of keeping so slight a character as Jenny Pearl at centre stage in *Carnival*, and the importance of selection over saturation. The effect was to be seen in Monty's next novel.

Disappointed by his repeated failure to get into the war, he returned to Capri in November 1914 without even waiting for the publication of the second volume of *Sinister Street*. The Channel ferry was filled with khaki, and even Italy, which had so far remained out of the war, was beginning to mobilise.

Capri, however, offered a new distraction. Thanks to Edwin Cerio, who was both its owner and architect, he and Faith had found yet another perfect home. Perched on a south-facing cliff, three hundred feet above the sea, it was called Casa Solitaria. Below the house a half-moon terrace carved out of the cliff allowed them to look straight down into the translucent green sea. The house itself was furnished with tall Venetian chairs, a gigantic baroque mirror and Maxim Gorki's table which measured seven feet across, but little else until they shipped out their own belongings from London. A studio perched on the roof which could be reached only by outside stairs provided a spectacular panorama which traversed from the Sorrento peninsula in the east across the sea and the Faraglione rocks to the hillside of Monte Solaro in the west.

Of all the spectacular places they lived in, Casa Solitaria was the pearl. Apart from its beauty, its remoteness enabled Monty to work, free from the beguiling company at Morgano's. The only flaws were an uncertain water supply and the disturbing motto picked out in tiles above the fireplace: 'Nec tecum nec sine te vivere possum' (I can live neither with you nor without you).

In Capri the war was still far off. The gossip concerned Count Jack and the Wolcott-Perrys, who had just come back from an around-the-world tour. It had been organised to demonstrate the old ladies' faith in their hero, and with their faith confirmed, they were proudly confident that he would behave as a hero should by returning to France to join his country's fight against the invader. Gossip took a more cynical view, and the excuses which Count Jack found to keep him in Capri provided Morgano's with one of its staple amusements.

As a souvenir of Thailand, he had brought back with him a Siamese cat, and when early in 1915 she had kittens, he gave two to Monty. These, the first of a succession of Siamese cats which he kept all his life, were named Guy and Pauline. Since both were female the names were not wholly appropriate, but their significance lay elsewhere. On New Year's Eve, he had begun his fourth novel, and the kittens inherited its title.

The subject of *Guy and Pauline* was the tragedy of the love he and Ruth Daniel had shared and shattered. It was written in the expectation that he might still get into the war, and that if he were to be killed this would be his swan song. The Guy of the story is Hazlewood, who had appeared in *Sinister Street* as a friend of Michael Fane at Oxford, and is now attempting to write poetry at Plasher's Mead – Lady Ham in fictional form. Across the river lives the Reverend Francis Grey and his three daughters, the youngest of whom is Pauline. Over the space of two years, they fall in love but are increasingly tormented by unsatisfied desire until Pauline has a nervous crisis and Guy leaves for London. The sentiment was not restrained, but he imposed upon it a structure of extraordinary tightness. The entire book occupies a span of two years; each chapter covers a season, divided into three sections with a month to each section. The story was told from the alternating points of view of the two lovers, the change occurring at the end of each month. There had been criticism of *Sinister Street* for its looseness of construction, and this structure was aimed at showing that 'I could tackle as difficult a piece of construction as any novelist could set himself, by composing a sort of violin and piano sonata'.

In all his more substantial novels, the passage of time played a major role; sometimes, as was to happen in *Vestal Fire*, it almost provided the plot itself, while in *The Passionate Elopement* it had been used as a frame for the action. Nowhere, however, was it so intrinsic to the shape of the story as in *Guy and Pauline*, and by forcing him to compress action within set limits it also served as a response to James's request for more selection. It is possible too that the very artificiality of the structure made it easier for Monty to write about emotions which had still not lost their sharpness.

With this book his confidence in his powers reached its height, and the proof lay in the manner in which he regarded his father, the old provincial actor-manager still hoping for his first London success. When Pinker sent him Henry James's opinion that he was 'the greatest talent of the new generation', Monty had immediately passed it on to his father as a present for his sixtieth birthday. Instead of admitting that his son had beaten him, Edward wrote back as though he were still a boy. Having congratulated him on 'the most gratifying encomium of your gratifying career', he urged him to

treasure it, preserve it and, as I am sure you will, continue to be worthy of it and to merit it . . . I commenced my birthday by studying *Richelieu* for two solid hours – 'oh good old man, how well in thee appears the merit of the antique world' (Shakespeare). 'Go and do thou likewise' (*not* Shakespeare, but nearly as good). God bless you.

Now, in the spring of 1915, Edward Compton was about to mount one more assault on the capital with *Sir Roger de Coverley*, and Monty wrote in exasperation to his mother:

You see, he doesn't realise that public taste has entirely changed. If Sir Roger were a success, *Sinister Street* would be a failure. He can't have it both ways, I'm one of the people who has helped to make a thing like Sir Roger *impossible* in London – the provinces are different . . . Why he can't retire on the laurels I bring him, I can't understand, but I suppose he wouldn't understand that.

There were other reasons for the old man's final failure. He was tired and ill, and a year later he was found to have cancer of the throat. The unconscious rivalry was coming to an end, and in one of his last letters to Edward, Monty inadvertently revealed how completely he felt he had displaced his father. 'Had you not been an actor,' he wrote, 'I am sure you would have succeeded as a novelist – heredity will out.'

This letter, with its implication that the son had become the father, was part of a pattern. It was the Mackenzie regiment – the Seaforth Highlanders – in which he had wanted to serve, and it was with the Mackenzie coat of arms and motto 'Luceo non uro' (I shine but I do not burn) that he now ornamented the clasp of his cloak and the plates of his dinner service. He had always refused to be a Compton, either professionally by working in the theatre or personally by adopting Edward's cautious ways. But now that his independence was established he was reaching back to the forebears of the Comptons and, unconsciously or not, creating a background for himself which was Highland, romantic and unmistakably Mackenzie. It must have seemed a good omen to find that Cerio had decorated Casa Solitaria with a motif of thistles.

On 4 April he received a letter from his old friend Orlo Williams, who was on the staff of General Sir Ian Hamilton, Commander of the Mediterranean Expeditionary Force. The Force was about to make a landing on the Gallipoli peninsula and, it was hoped, march on Constantinople and eliminate Turkey from the war. As Williams remarked, 'the possibilities of this show are romantic to a degree,' but for Monty the real romance lay in his other news. Seeing Hamilton with the second volume of *Sinister Street* in his hands, Williams had told him of its author's anxiety to be in the war. Hamilton replied that he would find Monty a job if he could persuade Eddie Marsh, Winston Churchill's secretary, to have him made a marine. Churchill was then at the Admiralty, and the prime begetter of the Dardanelles expedition.

Wasting no time, Monty sent him a telegram and within days Marsh had him gazetted as a lieutenant in the Royal Marines. In his nervous excitement at the news Monty came down with the severest attack of sciatica he had suffered since New York.

'I've never spent such a heartrending day,' Faith wrote to his mother.

He was half delirious all day, talking of regiments and Turks. I suppose I oughtn't to harrow you with all this, but I want you to know how hard it is being for him. The commission came so easily, it seemed as if everything had fallen into his lap; but now all this luck is counter-balanced by his tragic suffering. He *must* go. I think he will die if he doesn't, and I am dreading losing him.

Next to the need to finish *Guy and Pauline*, his gravest anxiety was, characteristically, the need to dress correctly for war. He felt as though he were again at Colet Court, dreading the possibility of being found in a jacket of Irish tweed rather than blue serge. Faith's feelings were in the same vein. 'What on earth was going to happen to him out there?' she remembered thinking. 'Who would mix his Sanatogen and see that he didn't sit about in the damp? I took the flannel sheets he slept in and joined them up to make sacks, but how could I be sure that he would use them?' An officer on sick leave sold him some basic equipment in Capri, but his anxiety about dress was not alleviated until he found himself accepted as part of the General Staff at Gallipoli.

There was still almost one-third of *Guy and Pauline* to write, but between bouts of pain he drove himself so hard that four weeks later the novel was finished. On 4 May there was a dinner party to celebrate its completion. 'I could not honestly claim that, when the guests bade me good-bye that night,' he wrote later, 'I had the least premonition they were saying good-bye to somebody whom they would never see again. Looking back at that party now, I can recognise that it marked the end of a period in my life.' The next day a telegram came with orders to report at once to the Base Commandant at Alexandria.

He scarcely had time to bid Faith farewell, and take a ferry across to Naples from where the boat to Alexandria was about to leave. It passed beneath the cliffs of Capri in the evening light, and standing on the deck Monty could see the white blur of Casa Solitaria, and fluttering above it the golden flag of Scotland with the red lion rampant. Entering the shadow of death he was flying his true colours.

From the terrace Faith watched the lights of the steamer dissolve into the night like a glow-worm. She too was nervous and dreaded the possibility that she might not see him again.

'I never did see exactly that person who had completely filled my life for ten years,' she concluded in her middle age. 'The war changed us all, and I changed no less than he.'

10

Z is for spy

When Compton Mackenzie went to war, his wife was not alone in fearing for his safety. A more sober mood had begun to succeed the fervour of the first months of war. There was a dawning awareness of the loss contained in the casualty figures from the western front. A generation of young men was being thinned out, and the first to go were those most deeply imbued with society's values. It was their sense of style and readiness for sacrifice which carried them earliest to death. With them was being killed an ethos, and society was beginning to understand its double impoverishment.

Rupert Brooke had died of sunstroke on service with the Gallipoli force, and the stature of Monty's reputation was such that his death would have been accounted an equal loss. 'There are plenty of men to serve on the Staff,' his old friend Bernard Walke had written from Cornwall, 'but there won't be another Compton Mackenzie, and the world won't thank you if you break up your health and are unable to help reconstruct things after the war.'

Walke was a friend, but the *Manchester Guardian* took a similar line in its review of *Guy and Pauline* later that year when it declared that 'The future of the English novel is to a quite considerable extent in his hands.' Henry James, the Master himself, wrote exhorting him to 'keep the Muse hovering, irresistibly fascinated about you, and yes, yes, yes, as I said before, go on making all the fine life you can against the all that's being unmade.'

In the United States his fame stretched beyond the East Coast where university students like Edmund Wilson and Scott Fitzgerald not only admired his work but could assume that friends would share their enthusiasm. Even a Midwesterner like Sinclair Lewis expected his audience to be familiar with Monty's reputation, and could indicate the level of sophistication attained by the heroine of *The Job*, simply by stating that she acquired 'a library of H. G. Wells and Compton Mackenzie and Anatole France'.

Had the fears of his wife and friends been realised, it is reasonable to suppose that his reputation today would have stood in something like the same light. There would have been the same criticism of his luxuriant style and, especially after *Guy and Pauline*, of his priggish heroes, but he would have been seen as *the* novelist of pre-war days in whose works, as Lascelles Abercrombie wrote in the *Manchester Guardian*, 'We seem to be watching the strangest of all modes of evolution, the dissolution of one century's character to make way for the character of another century.' The persistent criticism of social and sexual mores would have fallen into place between Samuel Butler and D. H. Lawrence, the steady progression of the author's voice from godlike observation to the point of displacing the character's thoughts would have put him as the source of stream-of-consciousness writing, and most of all the mixture of sensuous spirituality, of high living and the demimonde would have been taken as the exact reflection of the Edwardian era.

The mimetic quality which stands out so clearly when *Carnival*, *Sinister Street* and *Guy and Pauline* are taken together might in the end have marked him as too much a man of his period to reach that topmost rank of writers bestriding different times and societies, but no one would have questioned his consistency. His survival blurred this picture, and his protean character almost obliterated it, for as society changed so did he. In the course of time every current of twentieth-century thought left its mark upon him, and his style of writing adapted itself so well to the post-war audience that it came to bear scarcely any trace of its old lush tone.

The first and great change came with the discovery that the large arena of war provided him with a more satisfying stage than literature. As he put it, self-disparagingly, in *Gallipoli Memories*, 'My writing which I had originally regarded as a pleasant little accomplishment, was already beginning to show signs of becoming a drudgery. [After a month] the war was providing the first holiday I had enjoyed since I was up at Oxford.'

Initially, however, Monty was tortured by the shortcomings of his uniform, consisting as it did of breeches which were too large for him, a service tunic and a cap without a badge. During the journey from Capri to Alexandria to the Gallipoli beachhead and at last to Sir Ian

Hamilton's headquarters on HMS *Arcadia*, his emotions varied between those of 'a schoolboy who has gone to the wrong terminus on an August Bank Holiday' and 'a fourth-form boy in a prefect's study'. His fears were partially allayed by the warmth of his welcome on boarding *Arcadia*, and especially from Orlo Williams, who introduced him to the General Staff and then to Sir Ian himself.

Hamilton was tall and spare in build, and instead of the more usual massive cast of military features had a narrow, sensitive face. He was like Wolfe in his love of literature, and so nerveless in his courage that the distinguished war correspondent Henry Nevinson regarded him as 'an example of the rare type which not merely conceals fear with success, but does not feel it'. Yet there was also a lack of psychological ruthlessness which prevented him from imposing his will upon others, both superior in the case of Lord Kitchener and subordinate in the case of General Stopford, when doubts afflicted them. It was characteristic of him that he should be prepared to discuss the Gallipoli situation with a newly-arrived author disguised as a marine, and, when Monty asked him why Kitchener had failed to grasp the strategic importance of the Gallipoli peninsula, Hamilton answered with a fatalism which was equally characteristic. 'Lord Kitchener,' he said, 'is a great genius, and like every great genius he has blind spots.' 'At that moment,' Monty used to say, 'I divined with absolute certainty that we would never take Constantinople.'

A more immediate concern was to find a job. Eventually he was given employment as a filing clerk in counter-intelligence, compiling lists of suspected enemy agents and indexing information. It was not a demanding task, and he found more amusement in the other members of the intelligence staff.

Some colleagues, such as Eddie Keeling, an exquisite from the Foreign Office with whom Monty had acted in *The Clouds* at Oxford, he enjoyed simply as congenial spirits, but in Aubrey Herbert, an orientalist and fluent Turkish speaker, and George Lloyd, an ambitious young Conservative MP and ardent imperialist, he found two types which were to exercise a disproportionate influence on his outlook.

Both combined homosexuality with an admiration for the strongly male society of the Ottoman Empire, a coincidence which led Monty to theorise that nations had a sex – England, Germany and Spain were masculine, Scotland, Greece and France were feminine – and attracted adherents of complementary taste. It was a theory which was developed at length when he became a Scottish nationalist.

He was always mildly contemptuous of Herbert, whom he described as 'shuffling about loose-gaited, his neck out-thrust and swinging from side to side . . . holding forth passionately about the woes of the Turks and the beauty of their character, gripping my arm from time to time and exclaiming, "My dear, we *must* do this," or "My dear we *must* do that."'

On the other hand, he was fascinated by the banked-up fire of Lloyd's idealism and rigidly controlled sexuality, and evidently found there some correspondence with his own cast of mind.

'Dear, delightful George Lloyd,' he declared in *Gallipoli Memories*, 'if anyone could have converted me to imperialism it would have been you with your passionate sincerity and high purpose and infinite serious-ness. No man whose career I have been privileged to study when only half-carved has given me so much personal satisfaction in his ultimate achievement.'

By 1929 when those words were written, he had become Lord Lloyd of Dolobran and High Commissioner for Egypt and Sudan, but then his public career abruptly declined and with the thwarting of ambition his private passions gradually broke free from restraint. The intense sym-pathy with Lloyd's character and fate aroused in Monty can be gauged from the manner in which he wrote of them in *Thin Ice*, the outstanding novel of his old age.

Two weeks after Monty arrived the General Staff were transferred to tents pitched on the Kephalo promontory on Imbros, an island some dozen miles from the peninsula.

'I'm out here having the time of my life,' he wrote to his mother. 'I've been mildly under fire and nearly wrecked in a small boat, but feel frightfully fit.' And to Faith he declared, 'I've never enjoyed myself so much in my life.'

The schoolboy exuberance took longer to dissolve than the schoolboy nerves. The latter disappeared when he overheard Regular officers ex-changing bitchy gossip about General Sir William Birdwood's lust for medals, and recognised that they were 'of like jealousies to authors, actors, painters, prizefighters, ballet girls and barmaids'. His ensuing ease of mind was considerably aided by the arrival of a proper uniform. It was not until the landing at Suvla Bay on 6 August that his spirits were abruptly sobered.

Hamilton's first assault on the Gallipoli peninsula had been launched at its most southerly point, Cape Helles, with the intention of capturing the dominating heights of Achi Baba. Thirteen miles further north, Australian and New Zealand forces also landed and established what became known as the Anzac bridgehead. These attacks gradually broke down into stalemate during May and June, and Monty was in a position to see their last, ineffectual stages. At Sir Ian's request he took the place of the official war correspondent Ashmead-Bartlett, who had gone home, and although his two reports for the British press of the June battles made the most of every gain, they could hardly disguise the impregnability of Achi Baba. In his own words, he was 'a butterfly in the graveyard of Gallipoli'.

Yet in the three weeks he spent on the peninsula, he was able to register the sights and sounds of war on what Henry James described as 'the sensitive plate, your imagination, your tremendous attention'. There was the toyshop impression of Cape Helles from the sea with gunsmoke decorating it like cotton wool, and the men looking like lead soldiers. On the ground he noted the choking odour of decomposing bodies, and with a writer's passion for accuracy tried to find the precise simile for the different noises made by passing shells: some sounded like horses whinnying, others like the wind blowing in telephone wires and others still like 'the chirruping of goldfinches'. Finally there was the gratifying discovery that under fire he could summon up a fatalistic detachment by telling himself that 'if destiny intended me to be killed at Gallipoli, it would mean that I had done the work required of me in this world'.

In preparation for the Suvla Bay landing, the head of counter-intelligence, Colonel Wyndham Deedes, sent him to the island of Lesbos opposite the Turkish mainland in order to foment rumours of an intended assault there. This was more to his taste than filing and cross-indexing, and he did the job sufficiently well to sow doubts in the mind of the enemy commander, Liman von Sanders. In the course of his visit he witnessed an expert controller of spies, C. E. Heathcote-Smith, the vice-consul on Lesbos, debriefing his agents, and recognised at once that the art of reaching past the outer layers of personality, which consisted of boasting and lies, to the real information within was one that he himself possessed.

He returned to headquarters in time for the landings at Suvla Bay, some miles north of the Anzac bridgehead, which were designed to straddle the peninsula cutting off the Turkish troops in the south. Hamilton had been reinforced, but the new divisions were poorly led and their generals delayed so long after they got ashore that every element of surprise was lost. To Monty this dismal failure was more than a tactical defeat. 'An absurd phrase went singing through my head, *We have lost our amateur status tonight.*' And in *Sylvia Scarlett*, written in

1918, Guy Hazlewood expresses a similar thought: 'Gallipoli saw the death of the amateur, and a conservative like myself feels the historical tragedy of such a death . . . this waning moon was the last moon that would rise upon the old way of thinking, the rare old way of acting, the old, old merry England built in a thousand years.'

It was the watershed of Monty's life. The set of values within which his books had been placed was condemned to the past, and he could echo the words that Henry James had written to him in June: 'All that material we were taking for granted . . . now lies there behind us, like some vast damaged cargo, dumped upon a dock and unfit for human purchase or consumption.'

His despair at the tragedy on the hillsides and at the ineptitude of the generals – well named Stopford and Sitwell, he noted – quickly showed in his health. On 12 August his sickly appearance was so obvious that Hamilton immediately ordered him on leave to Athens. 'I don't want to lose another of you young writers,' he said, with Rupert Brooke's death still fresh in his mind, and the same evening Monty sailed from Gallipoli.

Despite his sickness he staggered up on deck to see the Acropolis glittering in the morning sunshine beyond the Phaleron where his ship docked, and from that moment he was caught up in the romance of discovering scenes with which his classical education had made him utterly familiar. His first exploration of Athens was cut short by a fortnight in a clinic being cured of dysentery, but convinced that the Gallipoli expedition could not quickly succeed he determined to find an excuse to stay in Greece. His speciality was intelligence and fortunately the political situation put a considerable value on his talents.

Greece was still neutral, but the logic of the Gallipoli campaign – to attack the southern flank of Germany and Austria-Hungary – was putting her under increasing pressure to declare herself on one side or the other. King Constantine, who was brother-in-law to the Kaiser, inclined towards Germany, a leaning shared by the court. On the other hand the Prime Minister, Eleutherios Venizelos, strongly favoured the Allies, and as the reformer who had brought a measure of democracy to the country he enjoyed immense popularity. In elections held in June 1915 his party was returned with a large majority. However, the issue was complicated by the gains Greece had made in the two Balkan wars in 1912 and 1913. These included much of Epiros, Macedonia and Salonica, as well as Venizelos's native island of Crete. The landward territory had been taken from Bulgaria, and both Germany and the Allies were prepared to buy Bulgarian support for their cause by forcing Greece to give back some or all of her gains. The situation was momentarily clarified when Bulgaria sided with the Central Powers, but a fortnight later, on 1 October, an Allied force under the French general, Sarrail, was summarily landed at Salonica near the Bulgarian border. Whether to protect Greek neutrality or coerce her into alliance had yet to be seen, but a patriotic Greek could find good reason for supporting or opposing either side.

While the issue still hung in the balance, the battle for public opinion in Greece was of paramount importance, and the Germans had a master propagandist in the admirably named Baron Schenk von Schweinburg who financed two Athens newspapers and was thought to exercise secret influence over many more. Initially it was proposed to put Monty up against this champion as chief of British propaganda, but his brief experience of counter-intelligence had given Monty a taste for cloak and dagger work. He was relieved therefore when the Foreign Office appointed someone else. The approach from Major Samson, known as R, and head of intelligence in Athens, was more to his liking.

Samson was all that Monty wanted a secret service agent to be. In appearance he was a quiet, courtly man who wore large hornrimmed spectacles. His cover was impeccable – the administration of a fund for refugees whose office happened to be opposite the headquarters of the Greek General Staff. But behind the mild exterior lurked a mania for secrecy. Lying in his hospital bed, Monty was deeply impressed by the stealthy way Samson entered the ward, by his surreptitious manner of speech, and by his wide staring eyes, liquid with hidden secrets, which his glasses magnified to enormous size. He wrote later:

No one is better aware now than I am how ridiculous R and I were as we talked in whispers about our mysterious work on that sunny Athenian afternoon, but on the afternoon itself I was still captivated by the infinite romance and excitement Athens promised, and if R had shown the least inclination to behave like an ordinary human being, I should have been quick to resent the implication that the secret service was not what I, as an impressionable writer of fiction, wanted it to be.

The whispers told Monty that he could have the post of head of counter-espionage, or 'B' work, in Athens, the moment R could rid himself of the present incumbent, Major Monreal, or M, who was rapidly heading for a nervous breakdown. Monty accepted the offer gratefully, and in accordance with secret service policy was required to choose a letter of the alphabet by which he would be designated for operational purposes.

'I shall call myself Z,' he told his new chief. Since A and Z are the least anonymous letters in the alphabet, Monty's choice might have given Samson a flicker of concern, but he did no more than warn him that as an additional security measure he should burn the blotting paper used to blot the sacred initial so that no one could trace it back to him. Then satisfied that the supreme importance of secrecy had been appreciated, he silently left the room.

Within twelve months, Z was the best-known pseudonym in the eastern Mediterranean. Monty had it stamped at the head of his stationery. British intelligence in Athens was designated simply as the Z Bureau. The British military attachés in Athens, Salonica and Alexandria all agreed that Z's reports were compounded of hysteria and gossip, and argued the point expensively in long cables home. At the same time the French military attachés and the Bureau des Renseignements both quoted Z's information to authenticate their own. Baron Schenk's newspapers carried regular items of shock and horror about Z's activities, and satirical reviews featured Z as a wicked bogeyman terrorising the city. The king complained to the ambassador about Z's behaviour, the ambassador cabled the permanent under-secretary about Z's duties, and the head of the secret service doubled and tripled and re-doubled the funds for Z's organisation.

The first step had been to get rid of M, who fortunately soon reached the point of behaving like his namesake in the James Bond adventures and was laying plans to assassinate enemy agents. Major Samson cabled the news to Captain Mansfield Cumming, or C, the head of the secret service, who immediately had M transferred to Malta. A brief return to Gallipoli enabled Monty to secure the approval of his nominal superior, Wyndham Deedes, for his new employment. At the first opportunity he transferred the headquarters of counter-intelligence from Major Samson's office to the British School of Archaeology, thus establishing his independence from the start. As the new head of what was still delicately called contre-espionage, Monty's prime task was to keep track of enemy agents and informers in Greece. Files and index cards were the basic tools of the trade and his own agents were required to produce a constant supply of information to confirm and update what was already recorded. The question-book contained a never-ending list of queries and commands:

1. Who is Madame P— who often visits the office of Baron Schenk?
2. Clarence to see smuggler in Piraeus, formerly employed by Russian S/service, and find out his conditions for working for us on contraband spotting.

3. For Clarence. You reported a certain N— to be a German agent. Give source of information and reasons for such a statement. *I do not expect section chiefs to bring me this kind of information. Z.*
4. Has Hoffmann who is reported to have returned lately from a second visit to Germany via Sofia come back to the Piraeus?
5. Spiro Aga reported by French as enemy agent; wants to go to Tripoli and Egypt. He must be shadowed for a week and a report sent in.

The responsibility for keeping these reports up to date fell to F. W. Hasluck, the librarian of the British School of Archaeology, and it was his superbly analytical mind which made the system effective. Monty's chief assistant was a former sanitation engineer in Constantinople, Charles Tucker, who spoke half a dozen languages but whose most important duty was the typing up of agents' reports and the coding and decoding of telegrams to and from London. In addition there were about forty agents in the field, operating chiefly in Greece and Bulgaria, but later in Turkey as well. They were mostly Maltese or Levantine, that is, the children of British and Mediterranean parents. Monty quickly learned the essential secret of intelligence – that the sort of people who provide information are by nature unreliable. To remind himself how much imagination played in the compilation of their reports, he gave them pseudonyms like Byron, Milton and Tennyson.

Their self-appointed chief was a thickset heavyweight called Cauchi, who arrived in Athens bulging with ill-concealed revolvers and violent fantasies. 'He offered me a hot, damp hand,' Monty wrote of their meeting, 'and I heard for the first time that richly larded polyglot voice, saw that immense hooked nose, that sleek bulk and luculent hair, and smelt that mixture of perspiration and musk.' He gave him the pseudonym Clarence, and for the next year was driven to extremes of irritation and ridicule by him.

Within eighteen months over 23,000 names were entered on their files, and this vast library, known as the Black List, constituted the chief resource of Monty's counter-intelligence. By itself, however, it would not have explained his vault to notoriety.

By a freak of circumstance, the eastern Mediterranean was a military wasteland commanded by three different headquarters at Alexandria, Cairo and Salonica, with the Royal Navy also attempting to impose its will from Malta. The intelligence community was no less confused. The Athens station was answerable to Mansfield Cumming, head of what was then MI1(C) and later MI6, who was in charge of all intelligence and counter-intelligence outside the empire. Colonel Vernon Kell ran

MI5, which was concerned with counter-intelligence inside the empire. Grafted onto these peacetime organisations were MI2 or military intelligence under General George Macdonogh, to whom the military attachés reported, and naval intelligence under Admiral Reginald Hall, to whom the naval attachés reported. All of them jockeyed furiously to expand their spheres of influence, and 'Blinker' Hall, in particular, was known as a merciless poacher of other people's agents.

So long as this confusion persisted, there was scope for an independent-minded adventurer to follow his own inclination, and in doing so, Monty not only secured unprecedented notoriety, he transformed the craft of intelligence. His revolutionary step concerned the Black List, and he considered it the dullest and one of the most reprehensible of his activities.

It stemmed from the fifth of the sample queries in the question book, that concerning a suspicious person wishing to travel from Athens to Egypt. Worried by the ease with which agitators and spies were passing from Greece to Egypt, the authorities in Alexandria wanted some control to be exercised over their movements. In December 1915, A. J. B. Wace, director of the British School of Archaeology, suggested that they should only be allowed to travel with a visa which Monty would approve. Building on this suggestion, Monty established a visa department at the legation to examine the applications. It was staffed with his agents who used the department as a cover and the application procedure to add names and backgrounds to the Black List from information supplied by the intending travellers themselves.

By January 1916 the set-up had been approved by the Foreign Office for use by British legations and embassies round the world, and by the end of the war it had been adopted by all Allied countries. 'So from that practical and simple suggestion of Wace's about Egyptian passports,' Monty concluded, 'sprang the control round the world which would serve as a cover for intelligence, or more crudely espionage . . .' The cover was so perfect that, according to Kim Philby, as late as the 1940s the head of the British intelligence operations in a foreign country was still usually disguised as the passport control officer, and even in the 1960s the names and fingerprints of visa applicants to the United States continued to swell the CIA's Black List. Indeed wherever visas are still required, it is in large part because they are so useful for intelligence work.

Although he appreciated the importance of the monotonous accumulation of information, Monty knew that most of it came from lies and gossip, from the disenchanted and the misinformed. He was, therefore, in immediate sympathy with a would-be informant claiming to be employed at the German embassy, who refused to communicate through any of his agents because their 'heads are full of beans', meaning wind rather than energy. The man, later nicknamed Davy Jones, proved to be the embassy's porter, and at their first meeting in December 1915 he won Monty's susceptible heart: 'from the first moment I saw the little man with his mousy hair and pale, ragged moustache, his very pale blue eyes filmed by suspicion and furtiveness almost as if by a visible cataract, I recognised in him the authentic spy, the spy by nature.'

He could describe gesture and mood as tellingly as build and feature, so that the emotions of the German military attaché, Major von Falken-hausen, were as clearly identifiable as the appearance of a new visitor at the embassy door. Understandably Monty regarded with some pride his achievement of meeting Davy Jones three times a week for over six months without arousing suspicion. The Athens of those days was a town of some 200,000 inhabitants; there were few cars, and since the horse-drawn carriages slowed to a halt going up a hill, it was easy to shadow a suspect.

These frequent interviews gave him the key to the German organisation of espionage in Greece. They confirmed his suspicion that the highly visible Baron Schenk was not the controller of the central ring of agents. He could also eliminate von Falkenhausen whose information came principally from sympathisers in the Greek army and at court. On the other hand, by the spring of 1916 the index card for Alfred Hoffmann, a commission agent at the Piraeus, was bulging.

By that date also, Monty had achieved effective control over the entire station. Although he was nominally only in charge of the 'B' work – counter-intelligence – Major Samson, the head of 'A' work, or espionage proper, had withdrawn to Alexandria, and the ambassador, Sir Francis Elliott, in cabling to London habitually referred to intelligence in Athens as the 'Z Bureau'.

Most of this was due to the sheer force of Monty's personality in a role which suited him. His friend Frank Swinnerton summed up the qualities he brought to the work: 'The quickness of his mind, the power he has of establishing what is not so much friendship as a ruthless intimacy of understanding, his sense of the picturesque, all made him enjoy his work as a boy enjoys playing at pirates.'

In professional terms, however, he was so innocent that he did not even know who his chief was, and in January 1916 a report which he drew up on espionage in Greece was sent, not to Mansfield Cumming, but to Blinker Hall and naval intelligence. This drew a furious cable from Mansfield Cumming promising to recall him if it ever happened again.

In the three books of memoirs devoted to his career as an agent, *Athenian Memories, Greek Memories* and *Aegean Memories,* Monty was not modest about his achievements, but independent confirmation came from several sources. The first and most important was the French, whose policy in Greece was assertive and expansionist. They provided two-thirds of the forces based in Salonica, and an intelligence department of commensurate size in Athens. Under Captain de Roquefeuil, who had friends in the French government, the latter was designed to be as much an instrument of policy in Greece as the CIA in a Central American republic today. The sheer size of the French operation constantly threatened to give them control of Allied activity in the area, and it was to Monty's credit that he preserved the independence of his small, under-funded station, while the military attachés did not.

He succeeded through a gesture of large and well-calculated generosity. When de Roquefeuil arrived in December 1915, Monty offered him full access to the crown jewels of espionage – his Black List – and the value of that gift was sufficient to secure a degree of cooperation between the two organisations which the disparity of their resources would otherwise have made unthinkable.

The second judgement on his performance came from one of the founders of MI5 and Kell's right hand man, Major Eric Holt-Wilson, who arrived in Athens in March 1916. One of the duties of MI5 was to vet the other intelligence operations, and Holt-Wilson's arrival was a sign of how alarmed Mansfield Cumming had been by Monty's disloyalty in sending his report to naval intelligence. He came at a critical moment for Monty, who had overspent his February allowance by no less than £600. The prospect of an examination brought on an acute attack of sciatica, but from his sick-bed he briefed Holt-Wilson, who then went through the Black List, the organisation of agents and the visa office. The result came ten days later in a cable from Mansfield Cumming. It informed him that Holt-Wilson's report had been 'highly favourable', he was promoted to the rank of captain, the £600 deficit was written off, and his income was increased from £350 a month to £1200.

The last formal verdict was delivered by Lord Denman, who came out in June 1916 as a government troubleshooter. His visit was made necessary by the attempts of the Greek royal family to persuade the

French and British governments to rein in their respective intelligence establishments. Constantine's brother, Prince Andrew, was sent to Paris and London, and succeeded in convincing George V that the Z Bureau was conspiring to overthrow his cousin, King Constantine. Under pressure from the Crown to withdraw Monty, the Foreign Office sent out Lord Denman to report on the situation. He was unequivocal in recommending that Monty be left where he was, and he later told Faith that 'the most dramatic thing in the war was the way [Monty] had created the secret service organisation in Greece.'

What made the initial 'Z' hateful to King Constantine was the public manner in which Monty hurled himself into Greek domestic politics. All the Allies and the Germans took sides in the rift which opened between Constantine and Venizelos, but they did so as foreigners serving their own purposes – Monty joined in as a supernumerary Greek.

The presence of a large number of foreign troops at Salonica – over half a million by the end of 1916 and still rising – exacerbated the division between the king and his prime minister. Venizelos had welcomed them at first as a bulwark against invasion by the Bulgarians, but in favouring the Allies he had a larger objective in view. Venizelos was a Cretan and his idea of Greece was maritime. All his diplomacy was designed to realise the dream of a Greater Greece whose territory would include the coastline of Turkey, especially around Smyrna, and which would therefore be the controlling power of the eastern Mediterranean. It was this dream which set Monty's imagination alight. To have a hand in restoring the glory of Greece whose history he had absorbed into his schoolboy bones, and whose poetry had almost reduced him to tears, that was a calling on the grand scale, and Venizelos himself, tall, blue-eyed and eloquent, commanded his utter devotion. In the absence of any clear policy from London, he had no difficulty in persuading himself that the interest of Britain coincided with those of Greater Greece: both demanded the defeat of Turkey and her German ally, and in peacetime a benevolent power in the eastern Mediterranean would guarantee the British link with India through the Suez Canal.

To the king and to conservative opinion, Venizelos's dream was sheer adventurism, and the Allied armies represented a threat to Greek independence rather than a promise of her future greatness. An echo of their distrust can be found in Dr Douglas Dakin's pithy opinion, expressed as recently as 1972 in his history, *The Unification of Greece*: 'Venizelos remained always the opportunist he had been in Crete . . . he had changed his tactics even to the extent of what appeared to be a change of principles in order to retain leadership. Of principles, however, he was totally devoid.'

In October 1915, Venizelos was forced to resign, and a royalist government under Prime Minister Gounaris attempted to buy off Bulgaria by the cession of territory. At the same time it adopted a policy of strict neutrality towards the Allies. Throughout 1916, tension grew as the French made it plain that they expected a more benevolent attitude. To achieve it they were prepared to support Venizelos if necessary, but with their own ambitions in Syria and Smyrna, they had no wish to encourage a Greater Greece. British policy, hamstrung by the growing weakness of the Asquith government, was simply to contain French expansionism.

It became the goal of the Z Bureau, therefore, not only to track down German, Turkish and Bulgarian agents, but to restore Venizelos to power. Although Britain was the junior partner, Monty was seen from the start as the instigator of the policy of destabilising the royalist government. On 17 January 1916, the government newspaper *Embros* reported that 'Some days ago an Anglo-French organisation of Secret Police was established in Athens. The different bureaux under the directorship of Mr Markentzen have been removed from the Pension Merlin, their original centre, to 3 Visarionos Street.' A few days later *Neo Hemera* referred to him as 'Professor Makenzy, director of the Anglo-French police'.

Monty was delighted by the publicity. 'The papers on the German side have been devoting much attention to me,' he wrote gleefully to Faith, 'and I am followed night and day, so far as they can. It's very entertaining.' Despite the dampness of an Athens winter his health was excellent and, a sure sign that he was on top of events, in March he wrote asking her to send out 'the two white suits (by Forster's) and white trousers, also my light-coloured ties and new white felt hat'. There probably never was a less secret secret agent, nor one who enjoyed it more.

His notoriety required him to have what even then was known as a 'minder' or bodyguard, and he chose not a thick-shouldered bruiser, but a beautiful slim-hipped Evzone clad in a white kilt. With this Adonis sitting in the front seat of his open-topped Sunbeam and Monty in his immaculately cut white suit and white felt hat in the rear, royalist reporters and spies should have had little difficulty in following him. Even if they did lose him, he would reappear sooner or later at the Panhellenion brasserie to eat half a dozen prawns and a zabaglione and to brief a pro-Venizelos journalist with some scandal about court officials dealing in contraband goods, before strolling down to police head-quarters to browbeat the sadistic Captain Chryssopathi of the Palace police into releasing a British agent who had been arrested. In the evening he could often be found in a nightclub, if possible one featuring a revue with a skit on himself. There was one he especially enjoyed. 'An absurd creature in a Cameron kilt cut like a candle-shade entered with eight secret policemen, each of them with a big drum, and sang a song about their dark and cunning deeds, the refrain of which was a sort of "Hush, hush, here comes the bogeyman!"' They all wore huge monocles painted to look like eyes, and on the word 'Hush' they banged the drums and lifted the monocles to their eyes. 'The actors always knew when I was in front,' he recalled with pleasure, 'and exerted themselves to play with added verve, and as most of the audience also knew I was present, we were all very jolly together . . .'

Hidden behind these calculatedly public appearances was the super-vision of thirty or forty agents, liaison with the French, the debriefing of Davy Jones, endless reports to other intelligence agencies and to London and, rather unexpectedly, the organisation of Serbian counter-intelligence. This last brought him into conflict with the dreaded Black Hand secret society, or Tserna Rouka, which had assassinated King Alexander and Queen Draga in 1903, and from then on controlled Serbian politics. Not the least surprising twist in Monty's extravagant career as a spy was his proposal to Mansfield Cumming in 1917 to turn the forces of the British secret service against the Black Hand, which was then operating out of Switzerland. That may have been the moment when someone in the Foreign Office wrote in his personal file, 'This officer has too much initiative, but should make an ideal Number Two.'

His disregard for royalist sensibilities was too flagrant to be tolerated. There were numerous death threats. One day the wheel came off a car in which he was travelling at high speed, and on another occasion a boulder dropped onto a road just before the Sunbeam passed by. He was, however, protected by something more than luck and his decorative minder. To injure an Allied officer would undoubtedly have been taken as a hostile, pro-German action, and whatever they may have felt, the Palace and its police were in the last resort impotent.

The diplomats in the British embassy referred to him half-admiringly as 'Pirate' or 'Jolly Roger', and asked him to let them know when Britain had declared war on Greece, but the military attachés found his conduct detestable. Brigadier 'Fairy' Fairholme nursed the conviction that the king was about to come out openly on the side of the Allies, and was only prevented by the activities of the Z Bureau which, he reported back to MI2, 'is in my opinion responsible for a good deal of the unpopularity of our cause out here'. Next to annoying the royalists, nothing pleased Monty more than annoying Fairy. He discovered by chance that Norman Douglas, well-known for his pederastic activities as well as for being the incarnation of anarchy, was Fairy's cousin, and thereafter he made the Brigadier's life a torment by threatening to have Douglas sent out as an agent.

In June the royalist government ceded Fort Roupel to Bulgaria, and in reprisal the French announced that their fleet would blockade Greece unless the Greek army was demobilised. Presented with a *fait accompli*, the other Allies – Britain, Italy and Russia – felt bound to fall in with French demands. Monty, however, saw the chance to aid Venizelos's return to power and persuaded Sir Francis Elliott to broaden the ultimatum by including a demand for new elections. To his annoyance the king bought time by accepting these terms. Although neither demobilisation nor elections took place immediately, a fuse had been lit at the end of which either the king or the French would explode.

While the touchpaper still fizzed, the Z Bureau pulled off two spectacular coups. The first was the capture of the German mail carrying secret reports from their Athens embassy to the Admiralty in Berlin. Several earlier attempts had failed, usually through bad luck, but once because Clarence forgot his pseudonym and so could not pick up his instructions from the post office where they had been sent under his false name. Low comedy continued to hang about the actual capture, for the courier wandered unscathed through a succession of carefully laid ambushes involving disguised policemen and camouflaged taxis until in desperation Clarence crudely coshed him and stole the precious envelopes. Even then Monty felt it was not quite the triumph it should have been. Not only did the information simply confirm what he already knew about the close links between von Falkenhausen and the court, but the Foreign Office refused to embarrass the king by leaking the documents to the press as Monty urged. And when a private letter from the queen to her sister in Berlin turned up amongst the other papers, the Z Bureau was reprimanded for interfering with royal correspondence. However the French, who had a weakness for dramatic action of this kind themselves, were deeply impressed by the effectiveness of his operation, and this was to pay dividends in his second great coup.

Throughout the first half of 1916 the evidence from Davy Jones and other informants had revealed with growing clarity that Baron Schenk's organisation ran few, if any, spies, and that a separate network reporting directly to Berlin was operated by Captain Alfred Hoffmann. In September, shortly after the mail was captured, Monty persuaded the French to join him in staking out all Hoffmann's known haunts. For three days he supervised a massive search in Athens and the Piraeus which ended with the chief German agent promising to surrender himself to Captain Mackenzie personally.

The 4th of September was something of a red-letter day according to *Greek Memories*. In the morning Monty interviewed Baron Schenk – 'typically Teuton, with a big nose, fleshy neck and that pork-like texture of the skin which is so frequent among Germans' – who, before being deported, expressed gratifying amazement at the successes of British intelligence, and in the evening the dumpy figure of Captain Hoffmann approached him in the street and gave himself up. 'He was as much surprised as Schenk when I told him . . . the amount of money devoted to counter-espionage by the British intelligence service.' After further courtesies Hoffmann was interned on Malta from where he wrote appreciatively of Monty's kindness.

The one flaw in this day of unbroken success came from a report of the huge search operation filed by the egregious Paxton Hibben, stringer for the Associated Press:

Unauthorised arrests, Greek as well as Austro-Germans, by Anglo-French secret police aroused deepest indignation Athens, even endangering complete accord shortly destined change entire aspect military situation Balkans. Novelist Compton Mackenzie, head British secret police, dressed like chorus man cerise silk handkerchief peeping from sleeve directs operations from security British Legation operations, some fifty automobiles filled hired gunmen armed to teeth engaged effecting arrests.

This account was part of a vendetta conducted by Hibben, the majority of whose reports ended with the information that 'the chief of the British secret police has been recalled'. His authority for this statement was Fairy Fairholme who had been strenuously recommending it to General Macdonogh, head of MI2, ever since Monty had proposed recruiting Norman Douglas for the Z Bureau.

In October 1916 it seemed as though Fairy had at last had his way, for the War Office announced that the Athens operations had become too big for a marine captain to run. Brigadier E. A. Plunkett was to take charge and Captain Mackenzie was to return to London on a month's leave. He was due for leave, but the timing was dictated by the latest turn in the Greek situation which made it vital to give a detailed briefing to his superiors in London. More territory had been ceded to Bulgaria by the royalists, provoking a surge of nationalist resentment, and Venizelos sailed to Crete where he set up a provisional government. Those of his supporters who could find transport followed him there, while Venizelists in the army went to join the Allied forces at Salonica. Nothing stirred Monty more deeply than the ardour of those soldiers who risked all for Venizelos's cause. 'The selflessness of their patriotism was complete,' he wrote, 'for at this date there was no guarantee of any future for them. They hazarded their chances of promotion. They forsook their homes, their families and their friends . . . they flung the world away for an ideal.' The completeness of their sacrifice sealed his own commitment to a Greater Greece.

On his journey home – blighted in memory by the nightmare of losing his marine cap and thus having to be incorrectly dressed – he was able to witness the monstrous offspring of the frontier controls to which his visa office in Athens had given birth. For all the hatred of officialdom and the insect state which suffused his later life, there was a period when the name of Compton Mackenzie carried as much weight in the underworld of bureaucracy as it ever did in literature.

The need to protect his literary reputation never left his mind during these hectic months. *Guy and Pauline* had been reviewed assiduously, with lavish praise or outright condemnation, but its sales came as near to a flop as he had known. Convinced it was his best work, Secker had printed 20,000 copies, but three years later, when he had still not sold out, he wrote regretfully, 'It is quite clear it did not please the public, though I think it contains some of the best things you've written.' His praise paid no bills, and shortly before he returned home, Monty told Faith to go to London to wait for him and, he added, 'I want you to keep my name before the public. This exile cannot be good.'

For his own part he had made time, despite the unceasing demands of counter-espionage, to write some short stories which Pinker had sold for him, and the greater part of a novel entitled *No Papers*. This was based upon the story of a cabaret girl called Trixie Ellwood who had been denounced to him as a German spy. He went to see her perform and immediately called off his agents. She had blonde hair and long legs – a pale imitation of the vibrant Chrissie Maude, but sharing with her the ability to recreate vividly scenes from her show business past. Most of her career had been spent in the nightclubs of southern and eastern Europe and officially she was stateless, but having acquired the image of an ideal Britain, fair-minded and free, she had become British by imagination and wanted nothing so much as a British passport. Ever responsive to a romantic dream, Monty ensured that she was given one, and when she made use of it to leave Greece, he began to make a novel from her story. It was still not complete when he returned to face his chief, whom he knew only as C.

Captain Mansfield Cumming RN remains a shadowy figure despite his claim to attention as the founder in 1912 of what was then known as the Special Intelligence Section and later became MI1 (C) and finally MI6 or the Secret Intelligence Service. However, it speaks volumes for his personality, and perhaps for his successors', that all subsequent heads of MI6 should have adopted his initial 'C', his habit of using green ink to sign his letters and, it may be confidently surmised, his invincible taste for a *Boys' Own Paper* version of reality. Those reports from agents of the period which have escaped from official censorship into public records read like pulp thrillers, and it is noticeable how Monty's own reports changed after his encounter with C from dull accounts of financial stringency and the minutiae of visa administration to highly-coloured tales of rivalry with the French and skulduggery in the streets of Athens. In this respect the advantage of being in charge of Serbian counter-intelligence enabled him to spin the villainies of the Black Hand secret society and the possibility of effecting a strike against its agents in Switzerland into a plot which Dornford Yates would have been proud to acknowledge. It was a telling coincidence (if it was coincidence at all) that the headquarters of the secret service should have been located at 2 Whitehall Court, which was also the address of the Authors' Club.

The chief of the secret service wore naval uniform and an eyeglass, and his hooked nose and chin threatened, Punch-like, to meet in front of a thin-lipped mouth. Although he had nursed a grievance against agent Z ever since he had inadvertently sent his first report to naval intelligence, C found that Monty in the flesh, spinning tales like a wizard of ambushed couriers and blown spy rings, was irresistible. 'I thought this would happen,' he confessed at the end of a two-hour report. 'I had intended to make myself extremely unpleasant, but I knew that when I saw you I should probably find you a man after my own heart and fall on your neck.'

The esteem was mutual, for Mansfield Cumming was not only a hopeless romantic, but a hero in courage. He took Monty through to his study where the portrait of a young man wearing the uniform and tartan of the Seaforth Highlanders was hanging. This was his only son, killed when the car he was driving ran off the road. C had been sitting beside him and was trapped by the leg beneath the overturned car. His son's body lay beyond his reach, and thinking the boy's life could still be saved, he had sawed away his own mangled leg with a pocket knife in order to crawl over and cover him with his overcoat. On that basis of common admiration was built a personal and professional friendship which survived until C's death in 1922. When Monty dedicated *Poor Relations* to 'the mysterious Captain C' in 1919, C thanked him warmly for the honour, and added, 'You told me once all chorus girls liked your books and I am afraid that I must plead guilty to belonging to the same category – I hope it doesn't show any particular evil tendency.'

In operational terms, therefore, the visit to London was a complete success. The lines to C were disentangled, funds were increased to over £2000 a month, and the Z Bureau was given additional staff, among them the American essayist, Edward Knoblock, and C's own protégé, a young Seaforth Highlander called Murray Molesworth. The threat of supersession by Brigadier Plunkett was lifted, and that officer left soon after Monty returned to Athens. So far as policy was concerned, he was less successful. He made an unavailing effort to behave like de Roquefeuil by leaking details of the failure of British foreign policy in Greece to Sir Edward Carson in the hope that he could use the information to force Sir Edward Grey, the Foreign Secretary, into action or resignation. Carson half-promised to bring about Grey's downfall, but before he could do so Asquith's entire government was overthrown by the machinations of Lloyd George and the Tories.

The least happy effect of the visit was upon his personal life. Apart from some leave in Capri in September and November 1915 he had not seen Faith for eighteen months, and the exchange of letters, censored and delayed, could hardly serve to bridge the disparity between their experience of war.

In Capri the mood had become sharply chauvinistic following Italy's entry into the war in September 1915, and Faith, stubbornly clinging to pre-war friendships with Germans and Austrians, was cold-shouldered by the super-patriots of Morgano's. The boycott depressed her. She returned briefly to England, but an attempt to be of use to the war by working in a canteen only convinced her of her ineffectiveness. In November 1915 she went back to Capri when political pressures forced Monty to leave Athens for two weeks, but once he had departed to the war she was alone again. From this isolation she was rescued by two friendships of enduring importance.

One was with Norman Douglas, the first in a distinguished line of homosexuals of both sexes to discover in her a strength of character and sharpness of wit which owed nothing to her husband. In the summer of 1916 she typed his novel *South Wind*, and to Douglas's later benefit recorded in her diary the frequent occasions on which they dined together. She also recorded her growing intimacy with the Anglo-Italian Caracciolo family, and especially with the two teenage girls Isabella and Bianca, and their brother Nini. Since she had begun learning to sculpt and he was a painter of promise, they shared a common interest, but Caprese gossip soon discerned something more. Perhaps J. E. Brooks gave Monty a hint of what was happening, for his letters to Faith carried increasingly urgent commands for her to go back to England, but she did not leave until she knew that he too was on his way to London.

When they met again that October, there were bridges to be built between them, but caught up in his crusade for Greece, Monty had no time to repair the damage.

On 3 November he started on the long journey back to Athens, while Faith remained behind in London. Norman Douglas had been charged with indecent behaviour with two youths he had picked up in the British Museum, and she was a key witness in his defence. To bolster their case, the police claimed that he had been seeing the boys during the summer, and in particular on 7 July. Faith could testify that so far from being in London on that day he had dined with her in Capri, and had noted the fact in her diary. In the face of her evidence, the case was thrown out, yet it must have taken some courage to let the diary be used in his defence, for the full entry read: 'Typed all day (*South Wind*) N[orman] D[ouglas] lunched. Nini to dinner ◇.' The meaning of the symbol – that they had made love – could easily have been guessed. It was marked beside most of his visits to Casa Solitaria during the summer of 1916, and when she went back to Capri in March 1917 it soon reappeared.

In Athens the long fuse lit by the French ultimatum in the summer finally exploded in December with a demand that the Greeks immediately transfer their artillery to Allied control. This time the government refused outright, and in an orgy of patriotism, the royalists took to the streets attacking both Venizelists and Allied officials. Early in December, the French navy, accompanied by a British squadron, landed soldiers to reinforce their demands and fifty *matelots* and thirty marines were killed before order was restored. Among the lesser damage was the destruction of Monty's house and with it the manuscript of *No Papers*.

He himself had been forewarned of the danger, partly through natural sources of information like his agents and the French, and partly through the supernatural in the form of the gift of two peacocks, always a bird of ill omen for him, and the appearance of the ace of spades upside down when his cook told his fortune. The cook could give only a general indication of what lay ahead, but de Roquefeuil, thanks to the trust that had been built up between them, gave his friend a clear picture of the control he and the military intended to impose upon police, trade and communications.

During the war and after it, Monty was often criticised for being too much under French influence, but at this crucial moment he immediately appreciated the vital fact that all sources of information would shortly be in French hands, and that his continuing independence required him to have his own lines of communication. He had long ago noted that the telegraph cables to Turkey, Greece and Alexandria all met at the island of Syra, and without further delay he commandeered a ship to take himself and over one hundred agents, sympathisers and retainers from the Piraeus to this new centre of operations. No single action gives him a better claim to be taken seriously as an expert in the game of secret agency than this decisive move. By contrast the professionals – Fairy Fairholme and another newly arrived military attaché, Brigadier G. F. Phillips – stayed in Athens and were forced to take shelter with the rest of the embassy in a requisitioned liner, where the French kept them isolated from affairs in Greece for the next three months.

In novels like *The Three Couriers, Extremes Meet* and *Water on the Brain*, Monty always portrayed espionage as a comical activity, appealing chiefly to the immature and inadequate. Such scanty evidence as is available in public records strongly supports such a view. Thus on Syra, Monty interviewed Armenian carpetbaggers, Venizelist sympathisers and agents from Salonica and Athens, and came to the conclusion that the Greeks were still not complying with the latest Allied demand that the army be demobilised and all weapons handed over. On 15 January 1917, Fairy cabled General Sir George Macdonogh, head of military intelligence:

In this connection, the telegrams which have been pouring in from Z at Syra . . . are quite misleading. He has been repeating all the gossip of irresponsible agents or interested partisans, to the effect that the evacuation movements are quite illusory, that the greater part of the effectiveness of units moved has remained behind, that the guns sent south are all old Turkish or Bulgarian guns . . . I can assure you that this is all rubbish.

In this he was backed up by Phillips, who confirmed that the Greeks were fulfilling Allied demands and that 'reports chiefly gained from paid agents are much exaggerated'. Macdonogh replied soothingly that 'the question of withdrawing Compton Mackenzie is under consideration and will be settled one way or the other before you receive this letter. His reports have been taken with a very large lump of salt.' There was no immediate answer, but then came a brief and embarrassed telegram from Fairy saying that the Greek government was to be asked 'to explain certain deficiencies in numbers of men going south' (for demobilisation). A fortnight later, on 26 February, Phillips had to cable the melancholy news to Colonel Buckley, Macdonogh's deputy, that fewer rifles had been handed in than first thought, and that most were old and out-of-date. 'To my mind,' he concluded in soldierly fashion, 'it's a very dirty game that is being played.' His outrage found a sympathetic ear in Buckley who cabled back, 'It seems to me that one really wants private detectives to see who *is* carrying rifles' (italics added). There was, and presumably still is, some excuse for Monty's belief that the excessive secrecy of intelligence services is a defence not against potential enemies but against public ridicule.

While the military attachés and the director of military intelligence consoled each other with thoughts of Z's imminent recall, Z himself was enjoying the most triumphant episode of his highly coloured career in espionage. Within two months of landing on Syra on 6 December, he had brought under his power the entire surrounding group of islands known as the Cyclades. Scattered between Crete and mainland Greece, from Andros in the north to Santorini in the south, these twenty or so blocks of white lava rise like quarry walls from the water of the Aegean. The majority of them measure hardly more than a dozen miles across, and in climate and setting it would be hard to imagine a more attractive kingdom to rule over.

Each island had its own demarch or mayor, appointed by the royalist government, who controlled the police and local administration, and Monty's first concern was to ensure that they switched their allegiance to Venizelos. Some were forcibly kidnapped by raiding parties and Venizelist demarchs put in their place, others willingly declared their support for the provisional government, and all accepted a system of passport control and submarine surveillance under the auspices of British military control officers.

Although some of these officers, like the eighteen-year-old Wilfred Macartney, in charge of Kythera, were scarcely old enough to shave,

Monty could fairly claim by February that the Cyclades were securely in his control. Lest the point should be missed, he changed his stationery heading from 'Z Bureau, Athens' to 'Director, Aegean Intelligence Service, Syra', and wrote to tell all his friends of these latest achievements.

The sheer romance of acquiring an archipelago of one's own tended to obscure the tactical importance of his actions in boosting the Venizelist cause when it was at a low ebb. Sympathy for Venizelos was strongest in 'New Greece' – the territory acquired in the Balkan Wars – but the Cyclades were the first part of Old Greece to desert the royalist cause and declare for him. The Greeks did not forget, and to judge by a biographer's necessarily partial experience, Compton Mackenzie's name is as readily known in Greece as a Venizelist as in Britain as a novelist.

For a few months he lived as a governor should. C had authorised him to charter a vessel to carry him around his province, and in typical style he did not commandeer a trawler or a tug but Prince George's royal yacht, the *Aulis*. Clad in the elegant white summer uniform of a marine officer, which Forster's had cut for him, and wielding the slim swordstick which C had presented to him, he steamed in palatial style from Syra to Mykonos, and later, as his influence grew, to the Dodecanese and Samos and Rhodes. Outside his headquarters in Syra there stood a new minder in place of the beautiful Evzone. This one, the young Macartney was impressed to see, was 'a huge Anatolian in baggy trousers and black waistcoat, armed to the teeth with a smart automatic rifle, two Mauser pistols and a knife stuck into a silken sash wound round his middle.'

Then he was in his glory, plotting to bribe the Vali of Smyrna into giving up the town to the British, running spy rings in Turkey and mainland Greece, and gracefully accepting the Legion of Honour from the French, and the Order of the White Eagle from the Serbs.

There were tragedies amidst the comedy. In May 1917, for example, an entire ring of agents in Turkey was uncovered and executed, and Monty raged at the incompetence of the military who ignored information bought at the risk of agents' lives. Yet even in this dire strait, he responded in a grandly romantic manner. His chief agent was still alive and in the hands of the Vali, and to secure his release Monty sailed into Smyrna with two sacks prominently displayed on the deck of the *Aulis*. He landed and went to the Vali's residence where he explained that each sack contained a rock and a close friend of Enver Pasha, leader of the Young Turks. These two hostages were survivors from a sunken Turkish destroyer and, properly speaking, were prisoners of war, but Monty courteously assured the Vali that they would be drowned at sea if his agent were executed. Although it was not strictly relevant, he also repeated his former offer of one million pounds in gold for the surrender of Smyrna. With equal courtesy the Vali refused the bribe, but promised that the agent would not be killed. With mutual expressions of goodwill, Monty returned to the *Aulis* and its two trussed hostages, and took them back to Syra with his mission accomplished.

Both friends and enemies agreed that he was theatrical, but he acted with the confidence of a professional who has worked hard for his success. Had he been simply showing off, his subordinates would certainly have hung back, but as it was they took their roles with the same panache.

Molesworth, supervising port control at Syra in his kilt, was the most conspicuous, a fact commemorated by his commanding officer in a genial sonnet which began:

> Molesworth, thy kilted form among these islands
> Has thrilled extremely the Aegean gentry,
> Who never having visualised the Highlands
> Stare mutely as a Venizelist sentry . . .

And ended:

> And still thou are the cynosure of glances
> And still the object of speculation.
> Yet Molesworth, truth compels this sad confession,
> What's underneath is Syra's main obsession.

As stylish as Molesworth's kilt were the mordant observations on all things military made by John Hope-Johnstone, who was Monty's closest friend during this time. Tall and spare in build, he would in a later age have been recognised instantly as a hippie. Wearing wire-rimmed glasses and carrying with him a flute which he never quite mastered and copies of *War and Peace* and *The Charterhouse of Parma* which he never ceased reading, he had been walking to Baghdad when war broke out. He had returned immediately to London where it was decided that his short sight and unconventional mind qualified him for nothing but intelligence work, and his arrival in Syra was another sign of C's favour. What most endeared him to Monty was his unremitting scepticism, and in the midst of a deadly attack of sciatica and dysentery, when he had convinced himself and everyone else that he was about to die, it was Hope-Johnstone who gently objected, 'You can't die yet, you haven't read *War and Peace*.'

Knoblock cultivated a similar detachment, but combined it with a gift for instant intimacy, making him the perfect emissary to the offended military attachés in Athens. It was he who passed on to Monty, who swiftly passed it on to C, Brigadier Phillips's private observation that Brigadier Fairholme 'has the brains of a linnet', and Fairholme's purely personal opinion that Phillips 'hasn't the brains of a puffball'. This was the Aegean Intelligence Service's style – an intoxicating mixture of drama and unabashed self-esteem.

Their position was too good not to arouse jealousy. Intelligence in the Dodecanese was already established under Professor J. L. Myers. As a Proctor at Oxford before the war, he had once fined Monty for dropping a shoe on a policeman's head, and when crossed was still inclined to behave like a don faced with an unruly undergraduate. However, by acquiring control of his funds, and by periodically letting him steer the *Aulis*, for which he had a passion, Monty gradually brought Myers and the Dodecanese under his sway. In Crete, the military control officer was another don, Professor J. C. Lawson, who not only refused to cooperate with his nominal superior, but let it be known that he considered the Aegean Intelligence Service to be nothing more than a theatrical touring company. This was an underhand jibe, aimed partly at the behaviour of its director, and partly at his arrival on Syra with five French cabaret girls among his camp-followers. Nevertheless he too could be tweaked into submission by the purse-strings.

The envy of subordinates was a pinprick compared to the menace of the army and the navy. During his absence from the mainland, military intelligence in Salonica laid claim to his network, and because Fairy managed to persuade the Foreign Office not to let him return to Athens, he could not defend it. At the same time Blinker Hall, director of naval intelligence, decided that Aegean intelligence must fall within his bailiwick, and insisted that its operation be placed under the control of the admiral commanding in the area. This should have ended Monty's independence, but by using the full force of his charm he won *carte blanche* from the admiral to do as he wished, and in June he wrote triumphantly to Faith, 'Have just won a terrific victory and am now supreme head of all intelligence in the eastern Mediterranean.'

Then, a few days later, the French forced King Constantine to abdicate in favour of his less Germanophile son, Alexander, and Venizelos was recalled as prime minister. For a little over a month Monty lived on the brink of realising his wildest dreams. With his hero ruling in Athens and himself in charge of the eastern Mediterranean, the French could be checked, the Italians bought off, and the British bulldozed into building a Greater Greece than even Pericles had imagined. By the autumn the dream had vanished.

C needed a network on the mainland, and appointed Colonel R. C. Temple, a Salonica intelligence officer, to run it. Because funds for the Aegean now started to come through Temple rather than Monty, Myers regained his independence, and other reluctant members of the network – military control officers, customs officers and consular officials – became less amenable to Z's direction.

At the same time he lost his firmest ally in the embassy at Athens when the ambassador, Sir Francis Elliott, demanded to be recalled in protest at the French action. While he was away the central pillar of Monty's organisation – the visa office – was taken over by the embassy. He fought bitterly to regain it, and had the junior officer who handed over control court-martialled, but it made no difference. 'I'm being treated like a naughty child for being right about Tino [King Constantine] from the beginning,' he complained angrily to Faith. Whatever their motives, political or personal, the diplomatic and military authorities whom he had treated so high-handedly in the past were determined not to give him back his power base. With the loss of the visa office he was finished. In August a telegram arrived from C, 'Regret inform you that you are recalled from your post and are to return immediately and report here.'

His departure from Syra was deeply emotional: British officers tendered their resignations, Greek agents wept, Levantine interpreters kissed him, and many did all these things regardless of nationality or trade. There was good reason for their emotion. For just over two years he had woven round them a magic in which a boy like Macartney could rule an island, a lavatory salesman like Tucker could capture German couriers, admirals could be duped and generals cheeked, kings could be deposed and history made. Every one of them became larger than life, because all their actions were invested with the intensity of his dramatic imagination.

C welcomed him back like a prodigal son, and immediately suggested giving him responsibility for setting up a new network in north Africa. When that proposal was lost in War Office politics, he suggested another: Monty should become his assistant, and once peace had returned and the depredations of Macdonogh, Hall and Kell had been seen off, he would take over as head of the secret service.

He must have been tempted. The role of spy suited him and he had enjoyed being both inside and outside the law. 'The only thing that's bothering me,' said his fictional *alter ego* John Ogilvie at the end of his career in espionage, 'is that I feel I shall never want to go back to writing, living is so much more enjoyable.'

However, he was sufficiently realistic to know that he was not cut out to be part of an organisation, and the relentless infighting and jealousy he had already encountered robbed the proposition of much of its appeal. Besides, he could not afford it. Two years had passed since the publication of *Guy and Pauline*, and in that time it had sold only 15,000 copies – a failure by his standards. The Greek government had promised compensation for the destruction of the manuscript of *No Papers*, but he could not be sure that the money would be paid. Had it not been for an unexpected £500 paid by Brady for the film rights of *Carnival*, and a £400 loan from Knoblock, the combination of his own and Faith's extravagance would already have ruined him. It was imperative, therefore, that he write a book.

He requested sick-leave and, sympathetic as always, C gave him four months. He never returned to active service, and his military career may be said to have ended when he stepped aboard the boat-train *en route* to Capri at the end of October 1917.

For his service to the Aliied cause, he had been decorated by the French and the Serbs. In the spring of 1918 the Greeks recorded their appreciation with the Order of the Redeemer. Another twelve months passed before his own government acted. In March 1919 he was awarded an OBE.

I Monty aged four, facing the imminent departure of his mother on tour

2 A family group: Monty's mother and father, Virginia and Edward Compton, with three of their children: (left to right) Frank, Viola, and Compton Mackenzie

3 His paternal grandfather, Henry Compton, at the height of his powers
4 Virginia and Isabel Bateman soon after the Henry Irving affair
5 Fay Compton about to become James Barrie's heroine
6 Frank Compton, c.1956, after 50 years on the American stage

7 The student actor, at Oxford: Monty as Phidippides in *The Clouds*
8 As Gratiano in *The Merchant of Venice*
9 The aesthete's study at Magdalen, with the Mona Lisa

10 Monty soon after his marriage

11 Faith (née Stone) his wife

12 Monty as Sunday school teacher (in breeches) at Gunwalloe, 1908

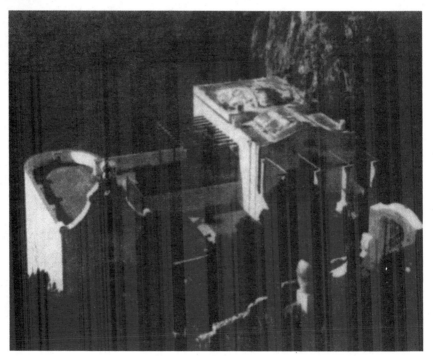

13 Uniform by Forster's, swordstick by 'C'; Monty with friends in 1917
14 'The power of establishing . . . a ruthless intimacy of understanding.'
Captain Z, 1917
15 Casa Solitaria, three hundred feet above the waves

16 Lord of the Isles: on Herm with Hamlet and James Eastwood
17 In Ireland for the Tailteann Games, 1924: (left to right) G. K. Chesterton,
James Stephens, Lennox Robinson, W. B. Yeats, Compton Mackenzie,
Augustus John, Edwin Lutyens, taken at Oliver St John Gogarty's house

18 The Lord Rector, Glasgow University, 1932, with Sir Robert Rait and Sir Iain Colquhoun
19 Nationalists and novelists: with Eric Linklater at the Fort William Mòd, 1932

20 On trial: Faith and Monty leaving for the Old Bailey, 1932

21 Virginia Compton in old age
22 At Castlebay, Barra, for the filming of *Whisky Galore*, 1952

23 His last great adventure: Monty on the Ganges
24 Friends and admirers: (left to right) John Betjeman, Martin Secker, Lord
Horder, Terence de Vere White, with a bust of Monty by Mikhail Katz. The
photograph was taken on Martin Secker's ninetieth birthday in 1972

25 '. . . one of the sights of Edinburgh': Monty outside 31 Drummond Place

26 The television personality: filming inside 31 Drummond Place, 1957

27 '. . . a barber had opened up shop in your beautiful house': publicising
'Lilian's', 1959
28 With Chrissie, soon after their marriage, and Lord Boothby, at a Foyle's
luncheon for *On Moral Courage*, 1962

29 After his marriage to Lily in 1965

30 The last photograph: Monty at eighty-nine, shortly before his death
31 The ruined church and chapel of St Barr, Eoligarry, in Barra where
Monty is buried

II

Loss of faith

The Capri to which Monty returned had changed dramatically from the island he had left in 1915. He arrived on the heels of news of the Italian defeat at Caporetto, and the chill despair of the casualty lists brought to the Capresi an experience common to all Europe. Their desolation was repeated in the empty hotels and unoccupied villas of the foreigners.

Of those who remained, every one had been touched in some degree by the great events outside, even if by no more than the interruption of their incomes and remittances. The Misses Wolcott-Perry had in addition to suffer the humiliation of witnessing the cowardice of their one-time hero, and for his part Count Jack Fersen was forced to cocoon himself in opium against their expectations of bravery. Only Maxim Gorki, who had left to take part in the Bolshevik revolution, had found better fortune in the passage of time.

The last months of waiting in these sad surroundings were the hardest for Faith. She had struck up a friendship with Axel Munthe who had moved from his clifftop house in San Michele to a Saracen tower called La Materita. Here he kept a grand piano on which Faith would play accompaniments while he sang Brahms *lieder*. Neither this, nor her longing for Monty to return, nor Capri gossip, could keep her from seeing Nini Caracciolo. She was thirty-nine years old and he, intense and passionately devoted to her, was barely twenty. He accompanied her home from parties or visited her studio, he came to dinner or sat gazing at her as she played the piano. Occasionally she tried to raise barriers against him by having people to stay, but when they left Nini would return and she would welcome him back. To her it was a conditional love affair which would end when Monty appeared, but some circumstances were outside her control.

At the end of August 1917, a fortnight before Monty was due to arrive from Athens on his way to London, she found herself pregnant. In desperation she resorted to the peasant girls' solution of violent exercise to induce a miscarriage. This succeeded in its object, but plunged her into the depths of depression. Monty only stayed for two days, and, it would seem, guessed nothing before he went on to report to C in London. He came back for good in the last week of October and made no objection when Faith introduced him to Nini in the company of his young sisters Isabella and Bianca.

At the beginning of November he settled down to work on his fifth novel, *Sylvia Scarlett*, and for the next ten days Faith continued to find opportunities of meeting Nini, at best to walk with him through the olive groves, at worst to exchange a glance across the piazza. Some of the gossip must have reached Monty's ears because on 11 November he forbade her to see the boy by herself. Accepting the decision, she told Nini and they said goodbye beneath an olive tree where they had often met. To occupy her mind, Monty gave her the manuscript of *Sylvia Scarlett* to type, but Nini had no such distraction. Night after night, regardless of the weather, he waited by the olive tree hoping she would pass. It was a cold and stormy November, and his health was frail. On the 19th J. E. Brooks, who always knew everything, came to dinner at Casa Solitaria, and mentioned that Nini was seriously ill. Faith sent an anguished message to his parents and the answer came back in a scribbled note, 'Nini sta gravissimo.' He died the same night.

Grief-stricken, Faith went to the Caracciolos' house the next day to see her lover's body: 'Lying like an angelic child among flowers,' she wrote in her diary, 'violets and cyclamen strewn on his breast. Always the sardonic corner to his mouth. The room next door was full of people and I knew some of them were watching me.'

What all Capri had known Monty now knew as well, and in the circumstances his immediate reaction was admirable. He ordered flowers, and went to the funeral with Faith so that the gossips should see them together. In the days that followed, he was very gentle with her. He wrote her a poem mourning Nini's death, and let her talk late into the night about him. When she sensed Nini's presence in the house, he said that he felt it too, and at dinner parties he was quick to change the flow of a conversation if it veered towards sensitive areas. 'M so sweet, so sweet,' she wrote. Attempting to alleviate the pain, she returned to the studio and began modelling a head. First it was a baby's head, but soon it began to resemble Nini. Even then Monty's behaviour remained kind and reassuring.

How painful the discovery of Faith's love affair really was for him can only be deduced from the knowledge of his vulnerability to those women he depended on. It had been tacitly agreed that his own infidelities did not count. On the other hand Faith, as Swinnerton had observed, was his mother as well as his wife, and however controlled he was on the surface, his inner reaction to her infidelity was the same as it had been to his real mother's betrayal in childhood – the sundering of emotional ties between them. He concealed the break as much from himself as from Faith by immersing himself in a frenzy of writing. Through November, December and the better part of January, he ground out over 3500 words a day until, five days after his thirty-fifth birthday, he cracked physically and emotionally.

A fierce spasm of pain in his leg brought the book to a halt, but instead of passing away it was followed by others in unbroken succession, and only repeated doses of morphine served to dull an agony which continued for almost two months. The attacks may have been aggravated by the stress of war. In *More Than I Should*, Faith remarked on the contrast between 'the natural ascendancy' of his character in pre-war days and 'the almost unnatural passivity' he displayed on his return from service. Yet Monty's own account points to the immediate cause being Faith's betrayal.

According to his autobiography Axel Munthe visited him in March and advised him neither to abandon his wife nor to overlook her infidelity, but to follow a third course. 'Why don't you both admit that marriage in the conventional sense is no longer possible? Why don't you give freedom to each of you to live his or her own life and yet agree to live together in friendship as man and wife?'

It is plain from Faith's diary that this scene is a dramatisation of a process of discussion and disentanglement that continued through the spring. Nevertheless it accurately described the resolution of his conflict between the wish to behave well and the need to punish her. Once this solution had been arrived at, the continuous emotional pain, registered by his sciatica, gradually became sporadic, although a year later attacks were still occurring at little more than fortnightly intervals.

For the rest of Faith's life the public appearance of their marriage was of a civilised friendship. They often shared the same house, and went to the same parties. Monty continued to trust her judgement and liked her to participate in each of his new adventures. He wrote to her regularly;

when he could he paid the enormous bills which she ran up, and he never forgot their wedding anniversary. The observance of their bargain presented little difficulty to one so accustomed to private self-discipline and public performance, but Faith was less experienced in these matters. It was also true that during their marriage she had given herself up more completely to him than he to her. There were, in consequence, flaws on her side of the bargain.

Away from him she could sustain the illusion of emotional independence and she would quote Kahlil Gibran's verse:

> Give your heart but not into each other's keeping
> And stand together, yet not too close together.

But it was an imperfect pretence. Once in his presence her spirits soared at any attention and wilted at each rebuff until, irritated by the intensity of her feelings, he contrived an excuse to send her away again. A quarter of a century was to pass before she was emotionally independent of him.

The agonising pain of his sciatica brought work on *Sylvia Scarlett* to a halt with 20,000 words left to write, and it was not until July, almost six months after his breakdown, that the book was completed. The long delay forced Secker to publish it in two parts: the first, called *The Early Adventures of Sylvia Scarlett*, came out in August 1918, and the second, *Sylvia and Michael*, was to appear the following January. To add to his domestic grief, Secker had told him with uncharacteristic bluntness that the writing was not in the same class as his earlier books, and the reviews for the first volume confirmed his warning.

At first glance the book marked a fundamental change from its predecessor. *Guy and Pauline*, written three years earlier, was manifestly a continuation of *Carnival* and *Sinister Street*, that is to say, the language was poetic, the love story pointed to the sexual hypocrisy of the gentleman's code of behaviour and Guy Hazlewood was, in the words of the *Westminster Gazette*, 'a repetition of Mr Mackenzie's young men, inert, un-moral, emotional, almost a bore'.

What gave rise to this criticism, and to an article entitled 'The Prig as Hero', was Guy's habit, shared with Maurice and Michael, of feeling intensely and taking those feelings very seriously indeed, but doing nothing to translate them into action. The emotional vacuity was also beginning to infect his style, and a passage in which Guy listens to Pauline and her two sisters playing a trio together shows how close he had come to using words for effect rather than meaning:

Monica in a white dress sat straight and still with pale gold hair that seemed the very colour of the refined, almost rarefied accompaniment upon which her fingers quivered and rippled. Something of her own coldness and remoteness and crystalline severity she brought to her instrument, as if upon a windless day a fountain played forth its pattern. Margaret's amber dress deepened from the shade of Monica's hair, and Margaret's eyes glowed deep and solemn as the solemn depths of the violoncello over which she hung with a thought of motherhood in the way she cherished it . . . Of [Pauline], as she swayed to the violin, nothing could be said but that from a rose-bloomed radiance issued a sound of music.

On the other hand, the style was admirably suited to convey the other Mackenzie ingredients of heightened sensibility, idealised setting and lurking evil. Secker treasured two criticisms in particular: S. B. Mais declared it to be 'easily Mackenzie's highwater mark. It is, I think, the most completely rounded-off piece of fiction I ever struck . . . Meredith would have been proud to have fathered *Guy and Pauline*.' Wilfred Meynell, on the other hand, insisted that '*Guy and Pauline* is the cruellest and most poisonous of Compton Mackenzie's books. Far too clever and far too dreadful to be read, or if read to be tolerated by healthy Humanity.' In 1915 it would have been easy to argue that, confronted by Henry James's alternatives of saturation or selection, Compton Mackenzie had opted for selection.

At 200,000 words *Sylvia Scarlett* was twice as long. Its heroine had already appeared in *Sinister Street*, as the spirited lesbian companion of Michael's girlfriend Lily Haden, and this vast, picaresque tale fills in the details of her life from childhood and marriage to her escape into prostitution and thence to a career as a singer and cabaret artiste. In the course of adventures in the United States, South America and eastern Europe, she takes two girls under her wing – first Lily Haden, then Queenie Walters, whose career is based upon Trixie Ellwood, the Athens cabaret singer. When the war comes they are trapped in Moscow, but Sylvia accompanies Queenie to Bulgaria and steers her through the maze of difficulties which stand between her and a British passport. Then with the help of Guy Hazlewood, who dies shortly afterwards leaving a note of farewell for Miss Pauline Grey, she rejoins Michael Fane, now with the Red Cross in Serbia, and having nursed him back to health accepts his proposal of marriage.

The differences between this book and those in which Michael and Guy first appeared are striking. While the latter are middle-class products of public school and Oxford, Sylvia is the daughter of an illegitimate

Frenchwoman and an English artisan, and her education comes largely in the nightclubs and streets of London. In literary terms the gulf between them is even wider. Compared with *Guy and Pauline*, the language is plain and abrupt – Monty blamed the speed of composition and the habits of compression picked up in wartime from writing telegrams – but more crucially the polished, episodic style of his earlier books has become a series of highly cinematic scenes and the emotion is cruder, leaning frequently towards sentimentality. Indeed Michael's proposal of marriage after rescuing Sylvia from drowning is made almost to the sound of the Wurlitzer:

Then suddenly he turned to Sylvia and took her hand. 'My dear, when I dragged you up the beach yesterday, I thought you were dead, and I cursed myself for a coward because I had let you die without telling you. Sylvia, this adventure of ours, need it ever stop?'
'Everything comes to an end,' she sighed.
'Except one thing – and that sets all the rest going again.'
'What is your magic key?'
'Sylvia, I'm afraid to ask you to marry me, but will you?'
She stared at him, then saw his eyes, and for a long while was crying in his arms with happiness.

In outlook, however, *Sinister Street* and *Sylvia Scarlett* were not far apart. Although only the reader knows it, Michael and Sylvia share the same Saxby grandfather, but they are more than cousins; they look alike and search for the same goal of an ideal to guide them through life. Both fall in love with Lily Haden, though Sylvia's lesbianism is here sanitised to celibate companionship, and discard her because of her vacuity. Even as they criticise society, each envies the security of a friend enjoying a privileged position within that society, and it simply confirms the pattern to find that both friends – Alan Merivale and Jock Airedale – are evidently based on the same person, Alan Mitchell. Indeed Sylvia so resembles Michael that one reviewer, Douglas Goldring, concluded that 'she is not really a woman but a young man'. In other words, Sylvia belongs to that group of characters who expressed the author's own opinion about society and its failings, and in common with her predecessors many of Sylvia's adventures, notably in Spain and the United States, are borrowed directly from the author's own experience.

Considering his state of mind in the immediate aftermath of the bureaucratic putsch which toppled him from power in the eastern Mediterranean, as well as during the near-dissolution of his marriage, the book is remarkable for its energy and life. Swinnerton described it as 'a harlequinade', and D. H. Lawrence found it 'witty and amusing', but even Monty, iron-willed though he was, could not entirely prevent the circumstances of its composition breaking through.

'This was the first novel affected by weariness and disgust of war,' he wrote in a foreword when it was reissued in 1950, adding in order to explain the poor reviews, 'and most of the critics at that date . . . still thought war should inspire lofty and romantic thoughts.' But it is not the fighting and slaughter which disgusts Sylvia, it is the politics and bureaucracy of war or, in her own splendid exclamation, 'It was just to redeem mankind from the sin that creates Foreign Offices and War Offices and bureaucrats and shoddy kings and lawyers and politicians that Christ died.' In short, her disgust is aimed at the very people who brought low the director of the Aegean Intelligence Service.

In her weariness with life itself, Sylvia must have been equally the vehicle for Monty's feelings. Late in the book she explains, as he often did, that her powers of assimilation are exceptionally swift, and then confesses, 'I've laboured towards religion, digested it with horrible rapidity and see nothing in it now but a half-truth. In art the same, in human associations the same, in everything the same.'

Given the emotional and physical battering he had experienced, this mood is not surprising. Whether he sensed it or not, in July 1918 his former life was coming to an end. His marriage had almost broken up and would never regain its old intimacy. A naval surgeon who came to examine him for a Medical Board witnessed one of his sciatica attacks and promptly recommended that he be invalided out; thus although he was not formally discharged until the end of the year, his brief but dazzling career in uniform was effectively over on the 30th. His father died from throat cancer on the 27th after months of agony, and despite Monty's apparent absence of emotion, it removed the stimulus of his psychological rival. Finally he concluded what may be called the last of his early books and there was to be a dramatic change of tone in his next work. Like Sylvia, the achievements of his past had lost their significance, and the comments of the critics on her early adventures merely rubbed the point home.

When the first part of *Sylvia Scarlett* appeared in August 1918, its 12,000 copies quickly sold out, but nearly all the reviews contained a note of disappointment, even puzzlement, which was struck most clearly by the *New Statesman*:

After every volume by Mr Compton Mackenzie since his first, one has looked up and asked perplexedly: what is wrong with this distinguished, graceful and entertaining writer? He has knowledge, he has charm, he knows how to write, but the reader is not quite convinced . . . And this new volume leaves one in the same perplexity asking the same question.

The fault lies primarily with his central characters who, with two exceptions, are unnaturally passive. The exceptions are Jenny Pearl and the young Michael Fane – a girl of limited ability and a boy – two people in whom a lack of psychological autonomy might be expected.

The failure to flesh out his protagonists went back to his initial problem of where to place the authorial voice. Having aligned it with the central figure's consciousness, as he did from *Sinister Street* onwards, it was inevitable that that person should be invested with many of the author's characteristics. But here Monty's personality proved a handicap. The protean nature which took on another person's character was stymied when it was turned upon its fictional counterpart, like a mirror turned to face another mirror. Unable to borrow from someone else's personality, he was also frustrated psychologically by his deliberate distaste for introspection following the crisis of his adolescence.

The emptiness of his main characters was almost overcome by his extraordinarily acute powers of observation and the vivid memory which enabled him to recall not only past incidents but past emotions. The technique was reinforced by the heightened quality of the language, and it was when this quality was removed in *Sylvia Scarlett* that the first widespread doubts were expressed. The weakness of relying on memory in this way was noted perceptively by Frank Swinnerton in *The Georgian Literary Scene*:

A novelist using, with however much skill and finesse, the skeleton of his own life and memory, tends to leave his central figure a colourless nonentity, a something to which experience occurs. For himself that central figure is filled in by substantial memory – by egotism; but for the general reader the central figure, a name only, represents a vacuum. He has traits, but no character. He may suffer, but is not objectively present.

There was, however, a compensating strength for this flaw, and it lay in the dramatic vigour of the surroundings and of the lesser characters. A more assertive Fane would have dissolved the languor of Oxford, a stronger Hazlewood would have upset the balance of love with the ethereal Pauline, and a more coherent Sylvia would not have experienced so picaresque a life.

Despite the poor reviews for the first part of *Sylvia Scarlett*, Monty had no sooner finished the last part than he began researching his next book. This was to be called *The Dark and the Fair*, and its subject was to be his experiences in Gallipoli and Greece. With an author's foresight he had carried away from Syra three crates of secret service papers, and in August and September he began to wade through them. As was his custom, he also began to look through back numbers of the *Gentleman's Magazine* for suitable names for his characters.

He and Faith were still tentatively feeling out the pact they had agreed in April. Usually each went to see friends alone, although they entertained guests like Brooks and visitors like the poet Herbert Trench together. Faith used the studio on the roof of Casa Solitaria for her sculpture, while Monty wrote below at Gorki's huge desk. A third inhabitant was Faith's adopted sister, Nellie Baker, who arrived in May to act as secretary. One of her tasks that autumn was to make a list of all the characters in his books so that he could keep track of them for the truly grand project he now had in mind. 'I myself had designed *Sinister Street* to be one of two preludes to a complete survey of contemporary society in which the personages of a large and complicated series of books were to be shown in youth,' he wrote in *Literature in My Time*. The survey was to be called *The Theatre of Youth*, and on 18 October 1918 Monty wrote to Secker that he planned to include within its scheme a separate series of six volumes about the war, to be called *The Chronicles of Argos*, later renamed *The Labyrinth*, 'and if I live long enough I shall write another magnum opus called *The Theatre of Age*, and then die in peace.'

It was his intention to make *The Dark and the Fair* the first volume in *The Labyrinth*, but after almost three months of reading and planning he was still unable to find the right way of dealing with wartime Greece and his part in it. What he had witnessed, as *Sylvia Scarlett* makes plain, was the end of the old England he knew and the beginnings of the modern or, in her word, 'Hunnish' state, in which individuality was subsumed within the laws and regulations of officialdom. To write of that on the scale of *War and Peace*, which was his inspiration, was impossible in his present exhausted state. Besides, the events were too real and too recent to be reduced to fiction; even ten years later he had to admit that 'I have never been able to find the necessary detachment.' Perhaps, too, the death of Edward Compton had removed some of the impetus to prove himself as a serious author.

On 26 October, just eight days after outlining his tremendous scheme to Martin Secker, Monty abruptly turned from it and began to write *Poor Relations*, the first of his purely comic novels. The decision gave him an enormous sense of relief, and immediately the mounting crescendo of sciatica from which he had been suffering died away. Two weeks later the war ended and Europe followed his example, giving up serious business and concentrating on having fun.

For a time it seemed that Capri would regain its pre-war gaiety, as the artists and the homosexuals began to return, among them the Russian sculptor Mikhail Katz, who took on Faith as a pupil, and Reggie Turner, as witty and beguiling as in Monty's schooldays. The first parties were given and the villas began to fill up. But the mood had changed. Before the war a certain decorum had prevailed, even at Count Jack's hallucinating parties, but the new arrivals recognised no limits. They sniffed cocaine and ether, they gave parties which scandalised the native Capresi, war profiteers from Naples ate till they vomited, drunken British officers forgot they were gentlemen and picked fights with the waiters, and the first lesbians made their appearance fishing for girls and quarrelling over their catches in Morgano's. They danced to jazz rather than ragtime, drank cocktails in place of wine, and their humour had a cruel edge – when a young Russian dancer shot himself outside the house of the American girl who had spurned him, the general reaction was summed up by Faith – 'no one knew he had any brains until he blew them out.'

A wealthy young Dutchman called van Decker gave a series of fancy dress parties at one of which it was rumoured he had danced a *pas seul* naked but for a strategic bunch of roses. Having missed the party Monty could tell the parish priest who complained of the scandal that he was sure the rumours were exaggerated; when he discovered they were not, he went to the next in the scanty tunic of a Greek boy. At another party two large Russians stripped to the waist and wrestled, but won more applause for their singing. Monty nicknamed them Bim and Boum, but their real names were Nadegin and Mariasces. They quickly attached themselves to the Casa Solitaria household – Boum indeed attached himself so closely to Nellie Baker that Monty felt bound to announce their engagement. It turned out to be a false alarm, and Boum left. His friend Bim, or Nadegin, stayed and became first Faith's lover and in course of time the most loyal of all her companions. Physically he was large and clumsy, and in appropriately Slavonic fashion he was given to glooms and passionate indignation, and more attractively to tidal surges of affection in which Faith was swept up and comforted. Monty recognised an ineffective quality in him which he thought Chekhovian, and certainly he hovered for years on the verge of success as a singer without ever quite showing the urge to achieve it. Nevertheless he was pre-eminent in kindness and in his company Faith found solace for the double loss of her lover and her husband. She played piano accompaniments to his singing, and when Nini's head was finished she began a relief of Nadegin.

Capri gossip credited Monty with several affairs but only one was of any consequence. On the evening of Armistice Day he rounded off the celebrations at Morgano's by making a bravura speech in honour of the colours of the Italian flag – its spiritual green, its immaculate white and its courageous red – and at its conclusion was submerged beneath the bearded embraces of a dozen Capri worthies, at which he fainted. Rather than walk the long road back to Casa Solitaria, he let Ann Heiskell take him home and put him to rest in her daughter's bed. That gesture of hers symbolised the nature of a relationship which began in the summer of 1918 and was to last almost four years.

His liaison with Ann Heiskell is worth noting because her portrait appeared in *The Four Winds of Love* as Athene Langridge, who marries Monty's alter ego, John Ogilvie, and is the mother of his only child. In real life, she was a tall, classically beautiful West Virginian with a calm, straightforward manner, who found it equally impossible to disguise her feelings or to impose her will upon her two children. It was her unavailing efforts to reason with her six-year-old daughter, Diana, which first attracted Monty, and her maternal role played an important part in his feelings for her. Diana became his great favourite – he dedicated his children's book *Santa Claus in Summer* to her and her younger brother Bobbie – and it would seem that Ann simply enveloped him in the same mothering love that she gave her children. Monty's need for that pristine affection was never far from the surface, and when he came to portray the relationship in *The Four Winds of Love*, it was that aspect which was most evident. Athene is loved not just as a woman, but as a mother – she too has a six-year-old child – and to underscore the relationship, she bears the same name as John Ogilvie's mother.

The Heiskells were old acquaintances. Morgan, the husband, was a talented photographer who in 1918 was away in France attached to the American army. He and Ann were childhood friends who had married young, and his wife was just beginning to understand that his mild, generous qualities were not enough to satisfy her. At the age of thirty he still lived on an allowance from his parents, and his dependent position was emphasised when they took a villa in Capri in order to be near him.

In Capri an open marriage such as the Mackenzies had arranged did not provoke condemnation, merely gossip, and far away in Casa Solitaria they could ignore what was said in Morgano's. Monty and Nadegin often played chess together, and they all met regularly as a quartet for meals and drinks at the cliff-side house. Even after Morgan Heiskell returned in time for Christmas 1918, the four of them still occasionally gathered together, and it was soon apparent that rather than create a fuss Morgan was prepared to be wilfully blind so long as Monty and Ann were discreet.

Having broken the bond of middle-class propriety at which he had been protesting ever since leaving Oxford, Monty now took another step away from his pre-war existence. In January 1919 he signed a contract with Cassell's for six books with an advance on each of £1500 for publication and an option of £1000 for serialisation in Cassell's magazine.

It was a blow to Secker, but hardly unexpected. Monty blamed the poor reviews for *Sylvia Scarlett* on Secker's decision to publish in two volumes, and he was infuriated to learn that he had only printed 12,000 copies of the first volume, which sold out within a week. Ever since *Carnival*, Monty had resisted offers from larger publishers, but in the post-war world of paper shortages and printing delays, it was clear that a tiny firm like Secker's could not take the risks to generate the income required by a big-selling author. Nor did he have a house magazine which could enable him to offer a serialisation fee. Monty arranged that he should have two further novels, but the old partnership which had made both their reputations was at an end. As it happened, the penultimate Secker novel, *Poor Relations*, which was published in October, proved to be one of their most successful collaborations, selling more than 30,000 copies in three months.

Never again was Monty to know a year like 1919. The second part of *Sylvia Scarlett* came out in January, followed in March by the reprinted first part. Together they netted him around £2000 in British sales and £2000 on his American advance. In April the Greek government unexpectedly sent him a cheque for £4103 6s 10d, as compensation for the loss in 1916 of the manuscript of *No Papers* (valued at £3500 – consisting of an expected £1500 British advance and £2000 United States advance) and the destruction of personal belongings. On its publication in October, *Poor Relations* earned him £3500 in British and American advances. With beer at one shilling a pint, a cheap meal at five shillings and a clerk's wages around £350 a year, the purchasing power of a pound was approximately fifteen times what it is today. In other words, his income was not far short of £180,000 by contemporary values.

With money allied to his dramatic imagination, there was almost nothing he could not do. When Martin Secker came out to stay with him in December, Monty took him to see a new property he had bought called Citrella, part of a valley beneath Monte Solara. Looking down into one of the steep gorges splitting the mountainside, Secker suggested that Monty keep some Barbary apes there. 'I'm sure you could get a pair from Gibraltar,' he urged.

That sort of expenditure appealed to him more strongly than the suggestion of Lloyd Osbourne, R. L. Stevenson's stepson, who advised him to buy land in the Riviera, the untouched area around Juan les Pins for choice, since it was sure to become more valuable.

'How right he was!' Monty commented in his autobiography. 'But I was never tempted by the prospect of buying anything – land or book or picture – because it would one day be worth its weight and more than its weight in gold.'

He had no need to think of investment since his imagination was an asset as nearly inexhaustible as the golden goose. During Secker's visit they had come to an agreement by which the publisher could still profit from the most successful author he had discovered. Since each of Monty's books was worth at least £3500 in British and American advances, Secker proposed to buy the copyright for that sum so that he owned it whoever the publisher was. 'The great attraction,' he wrote later, confirming the agreement, 'is that I gradually acquire a list of books which bring me in a steady income from sales.'

To Monty the advantage was having the money in hand at once, and having completed his second book of 1919, *The Vanity Girl*, in just under three months, he knew he could easily write at least two a year. Secker had also suggested that Monty should buy an interest in the firm – a suggestion they both eventually agreed to drop – but in November when the idea was first floated, Monty wrote breezily to his mother: 'I buy for £3000 a third share of his business and so, as publisher, become owner of a third of my copyright again. Rather an ingenious arrangement. I aim at £10,000 a year, then I shall be fairly content. I've got such masses of books to write that I believe I shall end like Dickens by not writing any plays at all. There is a curious similarity between my position as the son of an actor and Dickens, and neither of us writing plays.'

Despite this evidence of the direction of his literary ambitions, his imagination was turning, like Stevenson's, to the South Pacific. From childhood he had collected islands in imagination, and with the wealth he could now command there was nothing to prevent imagination becoming reality. Large orange volumes of the *Pacific Pilot* blotched the shelves of his library, and in December, having come to his agreement with Secker, he placed an advertisement in *The Times*: 'Novelist requires for long voyage expert shorthand typist, healthy, young, good sailor, not afraid of luggage or savages; small salary and all expenses paid.'

A purist might argue that if he were to write like Dickens, he needed to be settled in a society which he could know as intimately as Dickens knew London. Yet he absorbed impressions so rapidly that a sedentary life was always impossible for him. Besides, the experience of war had shown him that to create something in real life was more satisfying than creating it on the page. A third and more immediate reason for his growing wish to leave Capri was the social change since pre-war days. From about 1918 to about 1921, Capri suddenly became a fashionable watering-hole for the international sapphic set. One of the earliest to discover it was a young pianist, Renata Borgatti, whose powerful playing earned Faith's admiration: 'A young girl of the hockey type,' was her vivid description, 'with the face and figure of a woman, the eyes of a boy, the voice of a man, the strength of an orchestra and a velvet touch.' They became friends, and occasionally gave musical evenings at Casa Solitaria with Nadegin singing.

She was followed by Mimi Franchetti, the beautiful, auburn-haired daughter of Baron Franchetti, a composer of operas. In the portrait he made of her in *Extraordinary Women*, Monty suggested something of the shock which her clothes caused in 1918:

her short, accordion-pleated skirt made the long-skirted bourgeoises shudder and crick their necks to stare after her rifle-green jacket and waistcoat, her double collar and her black satin tie with coral pin, her long jade cigarette holder and slim ebony stick, and that rippling hair lustrous and hatless.

Responding as she did to a vivid personality, whatever the sex, Faith included her on the Casa Solitaria guest list, and Monty, who had been observing the lesbian jealousies with covert amusement, was suddenly precipitated into the drama. Mimi was voracious in pursuit of women and cavalier in disposing of them, with the result that she was, in Faith's words, 'usually the centre of an emotional storm at full blast'. One evening in March 1919 Monty, Faith and Nadegin returned from a party to find that Casa Solitaria had been burgled, yet apart from some jewellery the only items missing were a cheese and a bottle of absinthe presented to her by Mimi. A photograph of Faith had been taken from a drawer and placed upside down on the dressing table.

For weeks the mystery made an essential appearance in cocktail party small talk, and Monty helped to keep it there with his account of Faith's visit to Naples where she went to consult a clairvoyant about the crime. She took the ever-obliging Brooks with her for company, but the staff of the hotel where they stayed, mistaking their purpose, put them in adjoining rooms. To Brooks's alarm, there was also a connecting door. 'I'll lock it on my side,' he whispered agitatedly to Faith, 'and you lock it on yours.'

The general assumption, confirmed by the clairvoyant, was that Renata had committed the crime, imagining that Faith had some lesbian interest in Mimi, but the picking over of possible motives did not properly cease until August, when attention was diverted from the burglary at Casa Solitaria by the arrival of the magisterial Romaine Brooks. In the face of her magnetism all previous liaisons became conditional. She had visited Capri twenty years before as an impoverished art student, and Brooks had been so captivated by her boyishness that he had married her. Since then she had discovered her true nature, inherited a fortune from a Pennsylvania coalmine (from which she paid an allowance to Brooks on condition he remained in Capri), and developed an undoubted talent as a portrait painter. Faith found her 'a figure of intriguing importance, because for the first time I met a woman complete in herself, isolated mentally and psychically from the rest of her kind, independent in her judgement, accepting or rejecting as she pleased movements, ideas and people'.

Faith was one of the people she accepted, and she proved a staunch friend that autumn. In the summer Nellie Baker became pregnant, and once she had finished typing *The Vanity Girl* she left to have the baby in England. In September, some weeks after she had gone, Faith learned that the father was Vittorio Caracciolo, Nini's younger brother, and by an unfair twist the news came almost exactly two years after her own miscarriage. The fragile materials of music-making and sculpture lessons from which she had tried to build normality since Nini's death crumbled to dust. She took to her bed and lay for days in a darkened room. Monty brought her clothes from Rome where he had gone with Ann, but the blossoming of his affair only deepened her depression. 'Oh God, I'm so lonely,' she wrote in her diary as one day of misery succeeded another.

It was Romaine Brooks who took her in hand. She came to visit, bringing her a Japanese fan as a present, and having seen her state insisted that she must leave Capri at once. She arranged for Faith to stay in Paris with her friends Richard and Lilian Wallace, who were wealthy art collectors and patrons of that literary society which included Sylvia Beach and James Joyce.

With half the money from the Greek compensation, Faith departed for Paris late in October. Her spendthrift tendencies became pronounced when she was unhappy, and D. H. Lawrence, who knew her later, concluded that her extravagance was in part a weapon against her husband. In that case, her bitterness against him that autumn was intense, for she spent wildly even by her own standards while she was with the Wallaces. After two months her spirits were restored, and she moved to London and more moderate living in a house in Markham Square.

In her absence Monty did no work beyond maturing and discarding plans to explore the South Seas. Having failed to find an adventurous secretary, he tried to get a commission for an illustrated travel book with Morgan Heiskell taking the photographs, and Ann presumably also on hand. Then he decided to colonise a deserted archipelago, called the Kermadec Islands, four hundred miles north of New Zealand. All that was certain was that he wanted to move on. Although his disenchantment with post-war Capri began with the lesbians, it soon found other sources. Aldous Huxley arrived on the island with an intellectual girlfriend, and they were followed by other harbingers of new literary fashions.

'I object to living on Capri because every quill-driver in England apparently thinks that is the key to success,' he told Christopher Stone in 1921. 'I dislike the literary world, and if I want to talk about civilisation, I prefer to talk to a doctor.'

He was in part to blame for the invasion, for he could not refrain from telling people how delightful Capri was, how cheap and how warm. When Secker recommended it to one of his promising young writers, Francis Brett-Young, Monty assured him that he would shortly be able to rent the tiny cottage of Il Rosaio, which he and Faith had once taken and where the composer Respighi was now staying. A few months later, in December 1919, D. H. Lawrence wrote reminding him of a promise made in 1914 to find him a cottage on Capri, and again Monty urged him to come at once.

Francis and Jessica Brett-Young were inclined to be earnest. He had given up a medical career for writing, and could never forget what a privileged and risky calling he had adopted. For this Monty could rarely resist teasing him – 'Nobody,' he used to say, 'can discuss literature with Francis and avoid the impression of a consultation' – but the barbed quality of his Walpole jibes was missing. Brett-Young had two assets which Walpole lacked: the first was a wife, and in Jessica's case a wife who lived her life through her husband; the second was genuine modesty. He was deeply touched that someone of Monty's reputation should trouble to help him find a house, and he was almost immune to the teasing.

'No successful writer can ever have treated an unsuccessful one with greater kindness, consideration or courtesy,' he recalled many years later, adding that 'his talk was even more brilliant than his writing . . . a little cruel sometimes one must admit, but if one is as clever as Monty it is hard not to be cruel.' When Monty dedicated *Literature in My Time* to him in 1935, Francis wrote back in delight, 'How pleasant it is to think that, though we are members of one of the most spiteful and jealous professions on earth, we can still with complete honesty call each other friend.'

Lawrence could never make so solid a companion. The life expectancy of a friendship with him at this period was about eighteen months, and even at the height of intimacy a part of him observed the other person with the unforgiving gaze of a specimen-hunter. Yet he possessed an emotional enthusiasm which was as attractive as Monty's physical vitality. During the brief span of their friendship there was a certain symmetry in the way they cast their spell upon each other, maintaining all the while a novelist's detached fascination with the idiosyncrasies of the other's character. As Brett-Young noticed at the time, 'Mackenzie and Lawrence react on each other as a kind of irritating stimulus.'

Lawrence also had dreams of going to the South Pacific, and they discussed plans by the hour – picking islands from the *Pacific Pilot*, and selecting suitable vessels for sailing there from advertisements or from the sea below the terrace of Casa Solitaria. In letters to friends, Lawrence admitted, almost reluctantly, it seems, that he enjoyed Monty's company.

'Compton Mackenzie has a nice villa here and does the semi-romantic – but I like him, he's a good sort'; 'I like Compton Mackenzie as a man, but not as an influence'; and 'Compton Mackenzie is here – a man one can trust and like.' But to his closest correspondent, Catharine Carswell, he offered a glimpse through a more appraising eye:

We lunch or dine sometimes with Compton Mackenzie, and he is nice. But one feels the generations of actors behind him and can't be quite serious. What a queer thing the theatre is in its influence. He seems quite rich, and does himself well, and walks a sort of aesthetic figure . . . in a pale blue suit to match his eyes and a woman's large brown velours hat to match his hair.

When this letter was published, Monty austerely pointed out that it was a blue tweed suit and a hare's foot hat. All the same, even Brett-Young felt moved to comment on his style of dress. He too mentioned the blue suit, adding details of the ivory-coloured silk shirt, and flaming orange tie that went with it, but it was Monty's evening wear that moved him most profoundly.

'To see Mackenzie enter the Café Morgano in a black or a white sombrero and voluminous cape, lined unless I am mistaken with blue velvet, was one of the sights of Christendom. He managed it as the great Victorian actresses managed their gowns.' (Many years later Brigadier Bernard Fergusson invited Monty to dinner at Edinburgh Castle, and the soldier who drove him home in the evening was equally impressed by the cape and the black sombrero: 'Ye ken who we had in the car last night?' he was heard boasting the next day. 'It wuz Dracula!' Monty was unamused.)

His display showed that despite occasional attacks of pain Monty was in good form, and to both Lawrence and Brett-Young he proved a generous friend. He lent the latter £300 to buy his villa when its lease ran out, and early in 1920 he began pressing Martin Secker to take on Lawrence as an author.

Because *The Rainbow* had been prosecuted for obscenity during the war and withdrawn from circulation, Lawrence could neither get it republished nor find a publisher for his next novel, *Women in Love*. 'I think he will go mad if he does not have something in print soon,' Monty wrote to Secker who reluctantly agreed to take the risk of a further ban in order to do something 'to rehabilitate the author'.

'I feel instinctively that anything to do with D. H. is rather dangerous,' he told Monty in April 1920, 'but I am prepared to take the risk, fortified by what I know are your wishes that I should give him another chance.'

Friendship never prevented Monty from finding anyone ridiculous; in fact, his ruthless teasing was its inevitable accompaniment, and he enjoyed imitating Lawrence's falsetto enthusiasm. A favourite account occurred as they were discussing pre-Socratic philosophy in the crowded piazza, and Lawrence suddenly exclaimed in his high-pitched voice, 'We've got to give up thinking with our minds. What we have to learn is to think' – with a dramatic gesture towards his fly-buttons – 'here.'

Next to the South Seas, sex was the predominant topic of their conversation. Their views could almost be taken as the representation of the old and the new, the Edwardian libertine and the post-war sexual ideologue. The importance he attached to the phallus made Lawrence something of a purist about its use, and he disapproved of homosexuality, Mediterranean morals and James Joyce. 'This *Ulysses* muck is even worse than Casanova,' he exclaimed after Monty had given him copies of the *Little Review* in which Joyce's work was being serialised. By contrast Monty took the pragmatic view that sexual adventures would always be infinitely variable, often enjoyable and unfailingly absurd, and that the only rules were those of good manners. It is typical that one of the few chills in their friendship should have arisen when Lawrence felt that Monty had slighted him on New Year's Eve in Morgano's by giving all his attention to some rich Americans while 'we sip our drop of punch,' he told Catherine Carswell, 'and are the Poor Relations at the other end of the table – ignored – to our amusement.' The rich Americans were the Heiskells, and according to Monty's account of the incident he had arrived with Ann just ahead of Morgan, and with only a few minutes to arrange their next meeting had seen Lawrence and signalled to him that he needed to be left alone. 'Lawrence should really have known,' he insisted, 'that it's impossible to seduce a married woman in ten minutes if other men come up and interrupt.'

When they came to write about love, there was again a symmetry of outlook, as Lawrence noted in comparing the solutions they selected for their heroines in *The Lost Girl* and *Sylvia Scarlett*. 'How we hang on to the marriage clue! Doubt if it's really a way out. But my Alvina, in whom the questing soul is lodged, moves towards reunion with the dark half of humanity. Whither your poor Sylvia? The ideal? I loathe the ideal with an increasing volume of detestation – all ideal.'

It was a significant difference. The dark half of humanity was what Monty had turned away from, and in particular the dark half of himself. Sexual desire had proved disastrous to Jenny Pearl, Michael Fane and Guy Hazlewood, and it was noticeable that Sylvia Scarlett's adventures led her to declare, 'I represent the original conception of the Hetaera, a companion. I don't want to be made love to . . .' To judge by his relationship with Faith and with Ann Heiskell, his ideal love was all-enveloping, all-giving and maternal. By contrast, Lawrence exalted the sexual and the tempestuous exchange of instinctive passion. In his eyes the perfect union between man and woman could only be found in simultaneous orgasm. The significance lay in what each thought was the cause of the other's belief. Monty suspected that Lawrence protested too much, and when he portrayed him in *The Four Winds of Love* as Daniel Rayner he described his strident espousal of male sexuality as stemming from his 'innate homosexuality (always debarred from expressing itself by an equally strong respectability).' In his portrait of Monty in *The Man Who Loved Islands*, Lawrence depicted him as an overpowering egotist. 'He wanted an island all of his own, not to be alone on it, but to make it a world of his own,' he wrote.

These, however, were their innermost thoughts, which could only be expressed in print. In company they succumbed to each other's charm, sang duets of 'Barbara Allen' off-key while Brooks hammered out accompaniments on Faith's piano.

It became a habit for the Lawrences and the Brett-Youngs, accompanied by Gilbert Cannan's wife Mary, to meet at Casa Solitaria on Sunday afternoons, occasions which Francis Brett-Young remembered as:

the most delightful of my literary memoirs: Mackenzie, the incomparable mimic reducing us to an incapable stage of laughter by his imitations of the great and ludicrous figures of our time; Lawrence providing his version of Maud Gonne intoning Yeats' *Innisfree* to the accompaniment of an Irish harp, or singing in his oddly tuneless falsetto, French folksongs . . .

It must have been the pleasure of the memory which tempted Francis into an uncharacteristic and dangerous moment of pride. He continued:

One day Mackenzie said half-jokingly, 'Do you realise that exactly one hundred years ago Keats and Shelley and Byron were all together in Italy?' If he wished to make a comparison in kind the allotment of roles was not difficult: Mackenzie himself was more than a little Byronic, Lawrence had affinities with Shelley. As for Keats – well, as Mackenzie generously pointed out, 'You, my dear Francis, like Keats, were once a medical student.'

Such is the protection of goodness of heart that even after a lapse of twenty years, he could not feel the compliment's little sting.

The trio broke up in March when the Lawrences moved on to Sicily. Soon after they left Monty received a backward-glancing letter, signed 'DHL': 'Don't let us lose sight of one another. We are opposite in most things. But opposite poles are not inevitably mutually related. Don't let the world matter – it doesn't matter. I think we met well in Capri – I'll see you again before very long. Let us weave fate somehow together.'

For many months to come their letters continued to echo their dreams of the South Seas, until in 1922 a card arrived from Rarotonga: 'If you

are thinking of coming here don't. The people are brown and soft.
D.H.L.' It was addressed to Compton Mackenzie, Isle of Herm, Channel
Islands.

12

The man who loved islands

Any island, it seems, would have suited Monty as a retreat from the post-war world. When he came to London in June 1920 he was still set on going to the South Pacific. He tried to persuade a film company to provide him with a craft and a camera so that he could sail away and make *Mutiny on the Bounty* on location. And later that month he wrote to Lawrence that he had at last found the boat to match their dreams, an 84-foot ketch weighing 134 tons, named *Lavengro* after George Borrow's picaresque novel. Since it would cost 7500 guineas to buy her, she was, Monty commented to Brett-Young, 'well-named, because [the purchase] will be by Borrow,' but for someone of his financial well-being nothing was impossible.

Nevertheless, the moment that Secker, anxious not to see his golden goose disappear to a coral atoll, showed him *The Times* advertisement for Herm and Jethou, he leaped at the chance to acquire these more readily available islands. They were being offered on a sixty-seven-year lease from the Crown, and without bothering to inspect them, he applied for them both. On 30 August he heard that his application was successful.

Even by his standards it was a cavalier decision, and one that he soon came to regret. On the other hand, his summer in England made escape from the irritation of society appear even more attractive than in Capri.

The least tolerable aspect of that society was the attitude of the literary critics. They had given *Poor Relations* a surprisingly warm welcome. Although this story of a popular playwright called John Touchwood is not so accomplished as later comedies, its schoolboy jollity obviously caught most reviewers off guard. As the only prosperous member of his family, Touchwood is the target for a barrage of ingenious attempts to wring money from him, all of which he subverts by his own guilty generosity. For the first time since *The Passionate Elopement* there was no autobiographical background – the nearest model was Edward Compton's subsidies to his brothers and sister – and the absurd situations which lurked in the background of his other novels were here strung together to make up the story. It was the puppet-show without the puppet-master's voice.

In the *Athenaeum* Katherine Mansfield judged it 'the most excellent and amusing reading' and welcomed its author's descent 'from his cloudy, thunderous eminence into a valley where we hope he may be tempted to linger. Here to our way of thinking is his proper climate, and here he has every appearance of being most admirably at home.' In similar though more acid vein, the *New Statesman* declared, 'Mr Mackenzie started as the hope of the English novel, and he has written a first-rate book for a railway journey. Many a writer who has set out with an ambition no less exalted has come to a far worse end.'

Not everyone was pleased. Thomas Wells of Harper's, his American publisher, wrote to Monty's agent, Eric Pinker, J.B.'s son and successor, 'These chapters are no more Mackenzie than they are like any one of a number of second-grade English and American writers . . . The writing is commonplace and the reading dull . . . Mackenzie ought to be persuaded to chuck the manuscript into a drawer and forget it.' Harper's published his books for reputation rather than sales, which were consistently poor in the United States despite the critical acclaim they received. Although Monty convinced Wells that *Poor Relations* was worth publishing, it was not a success, and he was subsequently taken on by George Doran who later merged with Doubleday.

Determined to alternate the comic valley with the serious heights, he followed it up with *The Vanity Girl*, a further instalment of *The Theatre of Youth*, which also sold well. Set in Edwardian days, it is the story of the actress Dorothy Lonsdale's successful campaign to marry the Earl of Clarehaven. West Kensington and St Mary's College, Oxford, reappear, and Lily Haden and Sylvia Scarlett have walk-on parts as Dorothy's theatrical colleagues, but like scenes and characters in a serial they are little more than familiar traits – West Kensington's genteel snobbery and Lily Haden's vacuous sensuality. Bounding along in his familiar episodic style the story is not as bad as the reviews suggested, but largely because the critics, having praised him as a comic novelist, were intemperate in their hostility to his serious style. When it appeared in May 1920 Katherine Mansfield damned it as a potboiler and a betrayal of his art, and this opinion was generally shared. 'Unless he rouses himself Compton

Mackenzie's candle is burnt out,' the *Sunday Chronicle* stated bluntly, and the *Westminster Gazette* echoed the sentiment: 'As the work of a writer in regard to whom Henry James once expressed the liveliest anticipation, it does not exist at all; it represents the abandonment of serious intention altogether.'

There was one notable exception to this chorus. Rebecca West, notorious for the razor edge of her reviews, was warm in her praise. 'That book catches wonderfully – because it is not a world into which the literate can penetrate easily, and it is so absurd that almost any writer would be tempted by his regard for human dignity into setting it down as a little less absurd than it is.'

The stream of hostility wounded Monty and he was correspondingly grateful for her kindness. When they met early in July, a month after his arrival in London, he assured her that *The Judge*, the novel she was then writing, was excellent. This was not only gratifying but enabled her to discount H. G. Wells's judgement that it was an addled egg. She was then twenty-eight, already a novelist and journalist of repute, and too striking a personality to remain exclusively Wells's mistress. It was not surprising, therefore, that in the summer of 1920 she should have made, in the phrase of the time, 'a dead set' for Monty. It clearly disconcerted him. Although she was a vivid and beautiful woman, he found her complexion unattractive, not rose-leaf but hispid, or fuzzy, and he did not expect her to respond to his gallantries quite so enthusiastically. Hastily abandoning London, he shut himself up in Bridgefoot, Martin Secker's house at Iver, and tried to finish *Rich Relatives*, the successor to *Poor Relations*. Undeterred, Rebecca followed him, and according to Swinnerton was to be seen striding out to the garden in search of him while Monty, bent over to escape detection, scuttled back to the house, hidden by the garden wall.

This absurd episode had its consequences later in the year, when she and Faith went to Capri together to stay at Casa Solitaria, and it was symptomatic of the emotional tangle he was caught up in before he went to live on Herm.

In London Monty had stayed with Faith in Markham Square. There he met both her smart homosexual friends, including the young Ivor Novello and the still younger Noël Coward, and the latest Compton star, his sister Fay, who that summer was appearing in James Barrie's *Mary Rose*. Catching the expansive, spendthrift mood of the moment, he indulged in what he called 'squandermania', or spending lavishly on luxuries – a pigskin dressing-case for himself, a morocco leather case inlaid with tortoiseshell for Faith, thirty-five silk ties from Edouard & Butler, and pearl shirt studs at forty-five pounds each from Garrards. Lavish as his squandermania had been, it was soon surpassed by his mother, who was beginning to indulge an urge to extravagance held in check during thirty-five years of marriage. In 1915 she had started a small organisation to help unemployed actresses find work and to give them shelter. After Edward's death she had it formally incorporated as a charity under the name of the Theatre Girls' Club, and bought 59 Greek Street in Soho to provide cheap lodgings for the girls. In 1920 she sold her share in five theatres to Milton Bode and took on the lease of the Grand Theatre in Nottingham, for much the same reason as her mother had taken on Sadler's Wells – to provide work for her daughters, specifically, Viola and Katie.

It gives some clue to the strength of Virginia's character that she could organise her two married daughters in this manner. Viola, in particular, was at thirty-four a strong and gifted woman herself with what Faith described as 'an impassioned energy which stops at nothing, which is defeated by nothing'. Since her marriage to Henry Crocker and the birth of her son Nicholas, she had played character roles rather than leads, but she was rarely unemployed.

The middle daughter, Katie, was overshadowed by her two sisters, and for a Compton was remarkably passive. Her one act of defiance had been to marry John Austen, but thereafter she was the dutiful daughter.

Had Fay not established her reputation beyond doubt in *Mary Rose*, she too might have been brought in on the Nottingham scheme. Indeed much of her disastrous private life since Pélissier's death left her a widow at nineteen can be seen as an attempt to secure some emotional independence. She neglected her young son Antony, and to Virginia's dismay embarked on a succession of love affairs culminating in a failed second marriage. 'I deeply, deeply blame myself for so many of her failings and her sins,' her mother agonised some years later.

By a not uncommon irony, her public image which was founded on the portrayal of Barrie's sexless creations, beginning with Peter Pan in 1915, was the reverse of private reality. Although she remained incurably unfaithful to him, her third marriage to Allen Quartermaine in 1922 was to be the happiest, but it was only in middle age that she achieved a real measure of contentment.

It was a sign of the changing times that Virginia should have envisaged her daughters' future with a repertory theatre rather than a touring company. Cinemas and music halls were taking over many of the buildings the companies once visited, and their trade had not recovered from the interruption of the war, when travel had been difficult and unreliable. However, when the Nottingham theatre opened in September, it was with the Comptons' old standby, *The School for Scandal*. On 4 October it was followed by *Columbine*, Monty's dramatisation of *Carnival*. Jenny Pearl was played by his sister Katie, but a part had been found, at his request, for her original, his old flame Chrissie Maude.

She too had changed in the ten years since they sat together in the Café de l'Europe drinking Guinness after the Follies. In 1915 she had married Monty's scholarly friend John Mavrogordato, and in reaction to his family's disapproval of her Cockney accent and unzippered language she became extremely grand herself, buying clothes only in the most expensive shops and refusing ever to walk when a taxi could be found.

'It's a good thing he has money,' Secker told Monty. 'I think Chris will become a great stickler for the proprieties, and rather quick to take offence ... she is the *grande dame* and very Ikey about money, to use her own expression.' Performing was in her blood, however; after the birth of their son Nicolas she went back to the ballet in Drury Lane and when that came to an end she was delighted to have a part at Nottingham.

It must have been a strange experience seeing their love affair performed before them, and the old emotion, if it had ever entirely died, came to life again. Faith, who was helping with the wardrobe before her departure for Capri, felt a familiar despair, and when John Mavrogordato came up from London for the dress rehearsal, there were long bitter conferences between the two men. On opening night she watched as Monty stalked restlessly round the theatre, then 'sat alone in a box, pale and beautiful. I almost forgot the play looking at him'. At the party afterwards she 'felt bored and cross. I wanted to put him to bed and have him to myself for a moment'. But none of them could recreate the passions of pre-war days.

Faith was no longer the person he looked to for support, and his desire for Chrissie could not survive the opposition of his friends. When he proposed escaping with her to his retreat at Bridgefoot, Secker sent a telegram saying that he was tired of his house being used as a hotel, and Mavrogordato remained in Nottingham to haunt their movements. When the play transferred to London, Chrissie left the company and returned to her husband.

It was a gloomy time, relieved only by the news in December that Ann Heiskell had left Capri for a holiday in Paris. Monty went to see her at once, then tried to persuade her to come to Herm. However her husband, for so long complaisant, now also began to protest – jolted into action, it later transpired, by Rebecca West, who had revenged the slight on her by telling him of Monty's plans. From Capri Faith warned Monty not to let Ann join him in Guernsey, where he had gone to supervise the improvements to his island.

'It will be a *fatal* step if she is allowed to go to Guernsey. You will be most horribly compromised,' she wrote. 'M[organ] says he'll divorce her if she does. And he *may* turn nasty any time, and his story is that he hasn't condoned anything, and hasn't believed there was anything to condone. (I encouraged him in this of course.)' Monty heeded the warning, and in the face of the double threat of publicity for him and the loss of the children for Ann, the affair was broken off.

It was from troubles such as these that Herm seemed to offer escape. Although it lacked the romance of a coral atoll, it had other compensations. It was island-sized, being about five miles around and a mile and a half long. At the northern end there were superb shell beaches, overlooked by two small hills which were studded with prehistoric stones. A narrow road ran southward along the spine of the island through meadows and a farm to end in gorse and heather above a high cliff. There were clumps of Monterey pine, silver poplar and yew trees, and the banks of the steep road up from the harbour grew thick with primroses, bluebells and, later in the season, foxgloves. At the top of the harbour road stood the Manor House, a heavy, castellated structure, 'as ugly a building as may be seen in Europe' in Monty's opinion, but possessing a huge walled garden. Down by the harbour, a dozen cottages and an old inn called the White House were grouped close to the shore, and across half a mile of sea lay Jethou.

There was never any doubt that living there was going to be an expensive proposition. The island had been owned by Prince Blücher, whose German blood led to his eviction in 1914, and in the intervening years the farm had been allowed to deteriorate. The buildings were also in disrepair, and the Manor House required such extensive renovation that Monty decided to live in the White House until it was ready.

What he had not reckoned on was the curse that the Blücher family had left in response to their unjust removal, ill-wishing whoever took their place. Monty always felt that Herm had a brooding, haunted atmosphere, and his spirits, already lowered by the events of the autumn, were depressed still further when he landed on the island in December. He had made a brief visit early in September, but in winter it had a bleaker appearance. There was a community of around thirty people, including farm labourers and their families; Captain Attewell, the factor, who was loyal but stupid; Captain Mauger, the skipper of the island's boat, *Watch Me*, who was expert but rude; and Harding, the farmer, who was invaluable but elderly and often ill. Monty almost immediately added to their number by hiring two gardeners, a carpenter called George Macdonald, whose skill in building and repair became the island's greatest single asset, and a valet named Thompson who had developed during his previous employment with the Marquess of Lansdowne a Napoleonic manner and a tendency to drink too much.

'Whichever way I look I see a clouded horizon,' he wrote to Faith before he had even moved in. 'But I suppose it's all designed to help me work and give me the spur I need.'

By way of reply a letter came from Nadegin in Capri, late in December, saying that Faith was severely ill. She was suffering a prolonged and severe menstrual haemorrhage which left her anaemic. The resultant mood of deep depression verging on paranoia had been too much for Rebecca West, who left to rejoin Wells in Naples, leaving Nadegin to cope, helped occasionally by visiting friends. A succession of quarrelsome doctors exacerbated rather than cured the problem, and early in January 1921 the despairing Nadegin sent telegrams to Monty and Christopher Stone saying that her life was in danger and one of them must come at once. Knowing Nadegin's tendency to emotional excess, Monty decided that the danger was not very real. Pleading variously island business, financial problems and literary pressures – 'I cannot afford to produce anything but a solid work after *Rich Relatives* or else I shall become affiché as a light novelist' – he urged Christopher to go in his place, and to forestall any protests he took to his bed with 'an unusually fierce attack' of sciatica. Christopher was furious, but Faith, when she heard of Monty's reaction, was not surprised. 'The last person to be sent for is Monty,' she said; 'he would break down and be in agonies of pain as soon as he arrived, and what would be the use of that?' The haemorrhage, presaging the change of life, continued intermittently for the better part of two years, and only a long course of X-ray treatment eventually rid her of a frightening and painful affliction.

The 'solid work' Monty referred to was a religious trilogy comprising *The Altar Steps*, *The Parson's Progress* and *The Heavenly Ladder*, in which he proposed to describe the spiritual journey of Mark Lidderdale from a nightmare-haunted childhood by way of Anglo-Catholicism and the priesthood to conversion to the Roman Catholic Church. It was quite deliberately a withdrawal from the inconsequences of *Poor Relations* and *Rich Relatives* and a return to the pre-war style of autobiographical detail, beautiful writing and high moral tone. He began it in January 1921 and the work was to occupy him, with breaks for two light novels and a children's story, for the next three years.

During his first year on Herm there was a prolonged drought from March to October, and both crops and beasts suffered badly. Nevertheless, having reconciled himself to it, Monty took to the role of landlord with enthusiasm. He read forty-three books on farming, bought two Shire mares from his old friend George Montagu, now the Earl of Sandwich, and in a tone suggesting generations of landed gentry in his background, he wrote to Faith in the spring: 'In about three years we reckon to have this place in really good heart. I expect to have six mares, and I shall buy a two-year-old entire [stallion] this autumn.'

To supplement the *Watch Me*, whose engine was unreliable, he ordered a new motor-boat called *Aphrodite*, at a cost of £2000, and hired his former chauffeur in Athens to be her engineer. In her inaugural voyage she came second in the London to Cowes race, but Monty only had the use of her for two years before selling her at a £500 loss. Sick and far away though she was, Faith had a clearer picture of Herm's problems than he.

'You will never get any income out of Herm,' she wrote in reply to his letter, but she recognised that it had become the enthusiasm of the moment and, gratified that he should again want to discuss his schemes with her, she was ready to fall in with his mood.

'Monty was thirty-eight,' she wrote in her autobiography, 'yet he was still a child. Monty wouldn't ever grow old. He would die young, beloved of the gods, and not only of the gods – not by any means.' When he wrote to her of his agricultural improvements, of his steers, heifers, hens and pigs, she replied indulgently, 'You are so technical. Pigs farrowing! I thought it was a kind of plough.' And the same maternal note entered her correspondence to Virginia after she visited the island for the first time in June. 'It suits M so well, and he looks such a darling in his kilt. Of course he enjoys running his kingdom, and he is in his element as the benevolent despot. But it takes a lot of energy and a lot of money.'

The kilt was an augury of the future. Encouraged perhaps by Molesworth's insouciance in wearing his in the Cyclades, he had assumed the Mackenzie tartan from the start of his occupation of Herm. He also acquired an enormous Great Dane called Hamlet, and to complete the trappings of the lord of the isles, on his birthday the employees formed a band consisting of flute, mouth-organ and drum and played 'For he's a jolly good fellow', after which there were sports and the presentation to him of an inscribed silver coffee pot.

To Faith these were the appealing idiosyncrasies of her Monty, but when she confided her thoughts to D. H. Lawrence in the course of a warm and affectionate dinner in Capri in 1925, he made them the basis of *The Man Who Loved Islands*. Given Lawrence's genius and Faith's confidences, such a portrait might be expected to throw some light on the enigma of Monty's closely controlled character. Despite the malice with which he dwelt on Monty's fondness for flamboyant dress and for showing off his knowledge of farming matters, it is evident that Lawrence was genuinely fascinated by the mystery.

The islander, he suggested, was in search of a refuge from 'the terrors of infinite time'. It is for this reason that he tries to create a perfect unchanging world around him in which everyone is happy and kind and adores him. For this, sacrifices have to be made: emotions must remain superficial because 'anyone who wants the world to be perfect must be careful not to have real likes and dislikes' and he must restrict his attention to each passing moment because 'the moment is your little islet of time'. If he loses hold on this surface reality things lose their shape, and time 'begins to heave and expand in great circles, the solid earth is gone, and your naked dark soul finds herself out in the timeless world . . .'

As it happened Monty *was* subject to these sudden terrors. He had felt them in Cornwall, and was to do so again by the standing stones on Herm. Such places, he wrote in *The Parson's Progress*, had the power

to strip from man the accumulation of his experience, and to give him the mind of a child or a savage that is still susceptible to the most secret hostility of Nature. Gradually he once more succeeds in overlaying or blunting his perceptions by summoning to his aid the faculties of reason and judgement, the resources of education and the experience of civilisation until he is able to scoff at such an irrational panic; but for a little while he knows again the terrors that he thought had fled for ever when he left childhood behind him.

In childhood Monty had built elaborate barriers in his mind against the endless terrors of the night, and Lawrence was probably not far from the truth in imagining the islands to be a similar protection. Being Lawrence, he also understood that because the terrifying is fascinating as well, it may be sought in being shunned, and he imagined his islander living on ever smaller and less populated islands until on an empty rock in the Hebrides 'he derived his single satisfaction from being alone, absolutely alone with the space soaking into him'. Monty, however, always found other people an essential part of the protection. His egotism was never the sterile quality Lawrence pictured, but an urge to entertain and win affection. As Francis Brett-Young once remarked, 'The last thing you should do is to apologise for being egoistic, since egotism of your kind is one of your major charms.'

He knew that his sociable self was a performance, and his friends knew, but the shared knowledge was part of the pleasure because after all everyone's public behaviour was a pretence. Underneath, as John Ogilvie concluded, 'People were either lovable or comic or pathetic,' but beyond that their behaviour was a pose which was often absurd, sometimes disgraceful and occasionally admirable. This awareness of the divided self, and the importance he attached to the public performance, are the essential keys to his personality.

'It is his habit to dramatise everything in the world from Compton Mackenzie to the last person he met in the street,' wrote Swinnerton of him at this period. 'There is something old and yet charmingly immature in his manner; a boyishness that is quite half-composed of worldly wisdom. His demeanour, although never imperious, is lordly. His talk has none of the floridness of his longer and more studied prose passages; it is high-spirited, droll, full of a sense of audience.'

He felt most at ease with those, like Swinnerton, who understood that he was performing, and enjoyed it. It was an understanding he found more frequently in women than in men, because, he argued, being essentially passive they perceived all activity, and especially male activity, as a pose.

The private self he preferred to ignore. 'We are all as ugly as the demons of Hell if we are allowed to see ourselves as we really are,' says the Rector of Nauncepean in *The Parson's Progress*. His opinion about this inner being seems not to have altered, to judge by a comment in a book of his old age, *On Moral Courage*: 'Even when the Delphic admonition – Know Thyself – has been heeded, the knowledge may be so depressing that the trappings of the projected self are retained to hide and warm the nakedness that reality seems likely to reveal.'

The handicap to serious fiction presented by this attitude was clearer than ever in the religious trilogy. In style and outlook the trilogy should have come immediately after *Sinister Street*, for Mark Lidderdale is in the mould of Michael Fane, and the language is as poetic as that of *Guy and Pauline*. Next to these two, it is the most ambitious and exasperating of his serious work. It offers some of the best of his surreal settings, and several of his most deftly drawn minor figures, but in Mark, the preacher lurking in most of his central characters appears undisguised and in full flood. Several of the sermons which Monty himself preached at Gunwalloe are reprinted apparently verbatim, as are his Sunday school lessons. Yet its merits almost outweigh its faults.

His picture of the off-stage life of the Anglican clergy is as busy and detailed as his portrayal of ballet girls unfrocking in the dressing room. A rich frieze of mission priests, political bishops and amateur monks go trooping through slum missions, fashionable London churches and makeshift abbeys. There is a nice vignette of Sandys Wason as Father Dorward saying a Mass for Shakespeare's soul 'with a special intention for an improvement in modern poetry,' and a respectful tribute to Robert Dolling as Father Rowley.

Although it is self-evidently a novel about the search for spiritual truth, its account of religious life is as political as Trollope, with Anglo-Catholic priests manoeuvring to slip a surreptitious invocation of the saints into the service in order to soften up the congregation for a devotion for the Blessed Virgin without their first alerting the rural dean to what is going on. Of Mark Lidderdale's inner, spiritual existence, however, there is nothing. As the critic Leo Robertson remarked in a perceptive summing up:

If he had passed through that travail of the spirit in which his adversary was himself and not foul-minded parishioners and overbearing bishops; if indeed in an arena of the soul remote from controversies about forms of worship, his conflict had been with the very God he was seeking, the story of Mark Lidderdale might have made a great religious novel. Nevertheless it is a great novel about certain aspects of religion and a man dedicated to the religious life.

Yet from time to time the language does catch the chilling sense of immanent corruption which was at the heart of *Sinister Street*, especially in its underlying distrust of the feminine:

The old Spanish confessional began to get badly on Mark's nerves. It became a haunted thing, so that from the heart of every oaken rose and pomegranate, from every acanthus and vine peered the demoniac visage of a deadly sin. There were moments at dusk when the interior was hung with heavy curtains of purple velvet and when by some monstrous outrage on the imagination, it turned into an ancient four-poster bed, in the hangings of which even the ivory crucifix had at once a repulsive and a sensuous cachexy like a faded tuberose. At such moments the wood seemed to drip with hysterical tears and the air to reek with the subtly self-indulgent and lying and perfumed breath of feminality.

This is vintage Mackenzie, but it had no place in the 1920s. Post-war literature was defining itself by its difference from its predecessor, and one of the prime yardsticks was Compton Mackenzie's prose. The young Cyril Connolly put it succinctly with his dictum in *The Enemies of Promise* that 'the idiom of our time is journalistic, and the secret of journalism is to write the way people talk'. The kind of writing to be avoided was the mannered style called 'Mandarin', 'the style of all those writers whose tendency is to make their language convey more than they mean or more than they feel'. Showing exactly whom he had in mind, he quoted as an example a passage from *The Passionate Elopement*. Since this particular book is a pastiche on the period which gave birth to the Mandarin style, Monty could hardly be blamed for the excess of adjectives and unnecessary decoration of sentiment, but if the point were not already clear the equally young Raymond Mortimer made it so with a brilliant parody of the Compton Mackenzie style in the *Oxford Circus* of 1924, which began: 'Smiling gently at the amazing variegation of his metropolitan adventures, Gaveston crossed towards Vigo Street. Already a heartless shaft of madder light was sullenly annunciating the approach of yet another aenigmatick day . . .'

In such circumstances the trilogy did nothing for his reputation, and it proved disastrous to his sales. But even before the work was complete, it was apparent that quite apart from his literary troubles Monty had overstretched himself financially in taking on Herm. During the three years that it was his home the island consumed about £23,000 (£345,000 in present-day money). In that time he wrote two books a year which should have earned a minimum of £7000 annually – free of tax since Herm was outside the United Kingdom taxation area – as a result of his financial arrangement with Secker. But events soon conspired to make the original plan seem wildly ambitious. First the price of the copyrights had to be reduced by £500 when Doran became his American publisher and cut his advance by that amount, then Secker found himself overstretched and fell behind on the payments. In 1922, Eric Pinker took over the arrangement, guaranteeing him £6000 a year. In exchange he received the earnings of all Monty's writing plus a 15 per cent commission. At the end of three years he would pay Monty any surplus over that sum, or Monty would make good any deficit. The refusal of Cassell's to serialise the trilogy, and the consequent loss of the £1000 serialisation fee, meant that Monty was immediately in deficit. Thereafter he had to write fast and commercially in order to catch up. In response he gradually developed the astonishing regimen that he was to follow for the next forty years, beginning work at 3 pm and continuing until five or six o'clock the next morning. He was as ruthless in forcing his mind to produce as Miss Stanwell had been with his bowels. 'I find that the brain requires as strict a discipline as the stomach,' he revealed in a radio talk, 'and if my brain refuses to work it just has to go on trying until the hour of release arrives. I find that after being given such a lesson it always works better than ever the next day.'

It was this Stakhanovite Monty which made the sybarite possible, and it is astonishing that time and energy were still available to the latter after the former had completed his work. Yet he repeatedly found time to make the long journey to London in order to come abreast of the latest Savile Club stories.

By now he had graduated from a junior among the Savilian bloods to being a youngish blood himself, swopping reminiscences like marbles. From Sir Ray Lankester, the eminent zoologist, he heard a story which would have ranked as a giant Indian on the playground's scale of values. During his time as director of the Natural History Museum, Lankester had had to deal with a particularly difficult board of governors who wished to oversee each detail of his administration. On one occasion they discovered that he had rearranged a collection of eggshells without prior consultation, and summoned him to explain his action. Having heard their protests, he said with lordly disdain, 'You're making a great deal of fuss about what after all is only a collection of coloured farts.'

It was on one of these visits to the Savile in June 1922 that Robin Legge, the music critic of the *Daily Telegraph*, suggested that he write an article about the gramophone. Monty had acquired a machine by chance when his ambition to own an Aeolian organ – a pianola with stops – was frustrated by a lack of rolls, and having signed a hire purchase agreement was forced to accept a gramophone instead. His father had owned one in 1910, but then he could scarcely hear anything but Caruso or Harry Lauder through the buzz. To his pleasure he discovered that it was now possible to hear and enjoy most orchestral music, except for the piano, without distraction, so long as the listener imagined that it was being played in a rainstorm. The practical importance for him was that instead of relying on Faith to play the piano until late at night while he wrote, he could arrange a pile of records and leave it to his secretary or any of the servants to put them on. Following the *Daily Telegraph* article, however, there came such a flood of mail that he began to believe that there might be enough support to make a magazine devoted solely to the gramophone into a money-spinning enterprise.

Towards the end of 1922 he began to look for backers. 'Of all the charming fantasies of your brain,' Christopher Stone replied, commenting on the prospectus, 'this is the apogee. There may be pots of money in it – so there may be in the Milky Way.' Undaunted, Monty continued with what was rapidly becoming a passion like gardening. He squeezed guarantees amounting to £6000 from other friends including John Hope-Johnstone and eventually from Christopher as well; he canvassed advertisers among the record companies and gramophone manufacturers, and he wrote most of the first number. In addition he interrupted his religious trilogy and knocked off a quick novel, *The Old Men of the Sea* (published in 1924), to raise cash himself. On 20 April 1923, the first number of the *Gramophone* appeared on sale with the announcement, 'Our policy will be to encourage the recording companies to build up for generations to come a great library of good music.'

There were other record magazines, mostly for the trade, but none so unashamedly up-market as the *Gramophone*, which devoted itself to classical music and lobbying for uncut versions of symphonies and operas that did not fit comfortably on ten-inch records. For the first issue, 6000 copies were printed, of which 5000 were sold. Other than Monty's experience with the *Oxford Point of View*, none of the editorial staff – which also included Hope-Johnstone, Christopher and Faith – knew how to put a magazine together. The first issue was six weeks late and the second ten days. Frantic messages arrived from Herm demanding catalogues, vital bits of copy were lost and printing errors were rife. Of the third issue, which came out in August when people were away on holiday, only 2000 copies were sold. From that low point the circulation began to climb, although they still lost money. In the spring of 1924, Monty doubled the price, and to everyone's surprise the circulation went on growing until they could rely on a monthly sale of 8000 copies. In 1926 Cecil Pollard became business manager and under his direction the magazine's finances were gradually put on a secure basis.

It was Monty's masterful way of seeing an idea through that always caught Faith's heart. Her visit to Herm in 1921 had brought them closer together, and in the summer of 1922 he took refuge from the mounting burden of debts by revisiting her in Capri for three months.

This return to Capri brought the promise of a return to an earlier, pre-war happiness. The seven-year lease on Casa Solitaria was about to expire, but living in those familiar surroundings for the last time, he found it easy to enjoy Faith's company, and she, cured at last of her haemorrhages, was able to devote herself to his care without distraction.

Although Fersen and the elder of the Misses Wolcott-Perry had died, many old friends, such as Brooks and Mimi Ruggiero, the gardener at Citrella, were still alive and delighted to see him again.

New friends also arrived, most notably the twenty-two-year-old Bob Boothby and two Oxford friends, but they too carried with them a flavour of the past. Boothby had been at Magdalen, living indeed on the very staircase that Monty himself had adorned, and with his good looks, seductive voice and flamboyant charm, possessed many of his predecessor's qualities. When Boothby became MP for East Aberdeenshire two years later, he showed himself to be the romantic, rebellious Tory that Monty admired, and their friendship, though built on fleeting encounters, was to span half a century.

So contented was Monty during those months that for the first time he accepted the Caracciolo family as friends, and when Faith came to stay on Herm in November she brought with her Isabella Caracciolo. This was misguided because her presence simply intensified the competition among the maids, secretaries and other female guests for Monty's attention. Faith's brittle temper began to snap as the atmosphere became more strained through the winter. Privately she felt that it was bad for Monty to be surrounded by adoring women who never questioned the quality of his work, especially since it was his habit to read them excerpts from the previous day's writing to gauge its impact. Her attempts to convey this only irritated him, and the intimacy of Capri soon cooled. Early in 1923, Monty suggested that she would be better off in London finding premises for the *Gramophone*, and accepting the hint she left.

By then the catastrophic plunge in his financial fortunes had brought him close to bankruptcy, and the strain could only have contributed to his shortness of temper. His mother suggested relying on the power of prayer, but Faith had some justification for her tart reply: 'I don't feel it's just to plunge into wild, unprofitable schemes and then call upon God to extricate us!'

Her remark applied equally to Virginia who was hovering on the verge of bankruptcy. The Nottingham theatre had lost money from the moment it opened, and throughout 1922 and the first months of 1923 Monty sent what sums he could spare. When his money finally ran out in April 1923, he even offered to take on his father's mantle and go on tour with the Compton Comedy Company. Fortunately the Nottingham City Council took over the theatre before Virginia was bankrupted, and thereafter she devoted herself to the Theatre Girls' Club.

Under the pressure of mounting debt Monty was having to write as though on a treadmill. To cope with pressure of work, he had two secretaries, Nellie Baker, who had come with her baby Hilary to live on Herm, and a journalist called John Eastwood. For a time Faith hoped that she would be allowed to adopt Hilary, but Nellie married Eastwood and in 1922 they left the island. In her place came Nelly Boyte, who was to act as Monty's secretary for almost forty years. Her quiet adoration of him got on Faith's nerves, and during the fatal dinner with Lawrence she poured out the frustration she felt as she listened to Monty dictate by the hour articles, reviews, letters and other non-fiction to Nelly Boyte who, still weary from playing records while he wrote the night before, had then to type up both his dictation and his writing. These confessions became the groundwork for *The Two Bluebirds*, Lawrence's caricature of a once great writer complacently dictating fourth-rate prose to an adoring secretary while his wife watches, torn between jealousy and compassion that he is wasting his talent because no one dare tell him how much his work has deteriorated.

It needs to be emphasised, therefore, that Monty did not delude himself about the quality of his post-war work. He nursed the hope of returning to the grand theatre of youth and age that had been brought to a halt by his inability to deal with the war, but until then, he wrote in his autobiography, 'I could not help regarding the books I had been writing on Herm and Jethou during the last few years as marking time.'

In the circumstances it was perhaps as well that Faith did not confide her other stories of life on Herm, of the valet Thompson, Napoleonic in manner but increasingly drunk, of the rows caused by the housekeeper pocketing tips left for the housemaids, of the female guests quarrelling over their host's favouritism or neglect, of Hamlet, the Great Dane, being shot after snapping at a visitor, of the farm manager's vendetta with the boat engineer, of the Guernsey trippers swarming over the island in the summer, and of countless other ways in which reality undermined Monty's ideal world. To make matters worse he was being held to ransom by the sort of man who epitomised all that he most hated in the post-war world.

One evening in the summer of 1922 when he was walking by the northern end of the island where the standing stones lay on the hillside, he was struck by the sort of sudden terror he had felt in Cornwall. It had happened before when he was with Faith, and in her words, 'we rushed back to the house as though the devil were after us, and I believe he was.' On this occasion too, he ran away, but then responded in curiously pagan fashion, considering that he was engaged upon *The*

Parson's Progress, the second stage of Mark Lidderdale's pilgrimage. 'Next morning,' he wrote, 'I went back to where I had been seized by the panic and prayed to the spirits of the island. I wound up by telling them if they wanted somebody on whom they could vent their ill-will more appropriately than on me they should choose a profiteer of the war.'

He refused to believe that mere coincidence brought Sir Percival Perry to Herm that same afternoon. Sir Percival was as shameless a profiteer as could be found, with one fortune made from munitions and another from the purchase of Slough Dump, which consisted of acres of war surplus machinery. From that first afternoon he showed himself interested in buying Herm, but he tied Monty into such financial knots that it was a year before the island was sold. Although the transaction was complex, it is clear that Monty was diddled in the end, for he received just £3000 cash for a property in which he had invested seven times as much. His one consolation was that Jethou had been excluded from the deal, and it was there that he moved in July 1923.

Although only half a mile from Herm, Jethou's spirits were benign, and in the seven years that he had his home there he never felt anything akin to his earlier terror. In a fold of the hill which constitutes the island, there was a small wood of oaks, pear trees and Spanish chestnut, half surrounding a walled garden. Below this stood a ruin, another garden and then a small house which had to be enlarged to take his library of 10,000 books, 2000 records and innumerable crates of private papers. Apart from a cottage and a large hut, there were no other buildings, and other than his carpenter, George Macdonald, who built the extensions to the house, and two gardeners, his only dependents were a cook, a maid and a secretary. His furious work schedule did not slacken. In the twelve years between the completion of the religious trilogy and the beginning of his next major work of fiction, *The Four Winds of Love*, in 1935, he wrote twenty-three books, as well as numerous magazine articles, five years' worth of book reviews for the *Daily Mail* and twelve of monthly reviews and editorials for the *Gramophone*. Most of the books were potboilers which, by his own definition, 'is a piece of work produced not because one burns to write it, but because one happens to possess the necessary equipment to produce it in spite of not particularly wanting to do so'. Each of the books was 'as good as I could make it', and the results were rarely entirely disappointing, but nearly all were flawed by the single-paced rhythm of work produced at high speed.

Two which escape this fault are the pair of novels about Capri, *Vestal*

Fire and *Extraordinary Women*, published in 1927 and 1928. They are in essence a series of exact portraits of people on the island taking part in some of the colourful feuds he had witnessed, and he was unusually careful to ensure their accuracy. Faith wrote to Brooks, to whom *Vestal Fire* is dedicated, checking 'a long list of dates, epitaphs and details', and Monty went back to refresh his memory of the island in 1924 and 1925.

With regret he saw the devastation of hotels and villas put up by Neapolitan war profiteers, and he sympathised with the aims of the then idealistic young Fascists hoping to purge post-war capitalism of its grossness. On the second visit, his great admirer Scott Fitzgerald came to see him, and evidently sensed that he felt out of tune with the times. 'I found him cordial, attractive and pleasantly mundane,' Fitzgerald wrote to a friend. 'You get no sense from him that he feels his work has gone to pieces. He's not pompous about his print output. I think he's just tired. The war wrecked him as it did Wells and many of that generation.' To Fitzgerald's elegiac impression must be added Monty's memory of defending himself with the argument that humour was not a lesser form of fiction. That combination of nostalgia and comedy was precisely the mood that infused *Vestal Fire*.

The book occupies approximately fifteen years, from 1905 to 1920, the period in which the Anglo-American community are entertained and then divided by the elderly Misses Pepworth-Norton (Wolcott-Perry in real life) and their championship of Count Bob Marsac (Fersen). The book is made up of three parts, each divided into eight chapters, and from the outbreak of war at the halfway point the tone moves from the comic to the elegiac. Disillusioned by Count Bob's failure to go off to war, the old ladies see the passage of time slowly undermining their faith and shrivelling to absurdity the great matters of principle on which vendettas had been born and friendships wrecked. Their end, prefigured in the first chapter, is to be buried 'in the same sprawling rococo tomb which is almost a replica of their own villa' and the villa itself lies empty, where once they kept the parties going with the refrain, 'Oh dear, I hate to have folks go. My sakes! Why do perfectly good parties come to an end? Why can't we go on enjoying ourselves forever?' There is almost no plot other than the play of fleeting time upon them and their guests: the effusive young pansy whose 'subtle and passionate temperament was merely the result of infantile wind', his well-preserved mother with her 'gleaming pink nails that protruded like the points of daggers from the scabbards of her dry fingers', the flock of authors who never succeed in completing any of their works but congregate in Zampone's café 'where they always enquired warmly after one another's pregnancies before each began to talk exclusively of his own', the indomitable Mrs Ambrogio firing off machine gun bursts of gossip in a clipped voice, 'Always speak my mind. Always offending people. No brains. Take it or leave it, can't help it if they don't like me'; and the spirit of pagan self-indulgence, Norman Douglas, here transmogrified into Duncan Maxwell:

Laughter enveloped him in a cloud through which his small, deep-set eyes came glittering like two stars. He was of a florid complexion with a long tip-tilted, sliced-off pragmatical nose such as you might see in any number of eighteenth-century lowland lairds; but his magnificent vitality instead of exhausting itself in a struggle with agriculture and his subtle mind instead of wasting itself on the split straws and dusty chaff of Presbyterian theology had been allowed to swell and ripen in the sun.

There are similarities to Douglas's Capri novel, *South Wind*, which came out nine years earlier, particularly in the comedy of island rivalries and the atmosphere of moral inhibitions dissolving in the Mediterranean sun, but the difference is profound. *South Wind* delighted in paganism and pleasure-seeking, while *Vestal Fire* comes close to being a satire on both.

In a way that he had not attempted since *The Passionate Elopement*, he had made the perfect marionette show. The severe structure frames the action, and artifices like the Latin quotation at the head of each chapter put it at a further remove from reality. The pathos and the comedy lie not in the fate of individuals but in the futility of human passion.

So highly stylised and stylish a book was bound to fall foul of the thrust towards naturalism in literature. Thus Connolly, missing the elegiac shift in mood, summed it up as 'a witty and unpleasant chronicle of clique life', and of the distancing artifices observed only that they 'add nothing to the reader's emotion except the feeling that they are there for show'.

Extraordinary Women, the story of the lesbian intrigues of which Monty had been a spectator, received still rougher treatment from Raymond Mortimer when it came out in 1928. By chance Radclyffe Hall's pioneering lesbian novel, *The Well of Loneliness*, had just been withdrawn by Jonathan Cape after advice from the Home Office, and it was bad timing which enabled a comedy about female homosexuality to come out when a serious, if dull, book on the subject had been banned. 'Having had the enterprise to deal with a subject unexplored by English novelists,' Mortimer wrote, 'he might have produced an interesting book. But all I can see in *Extraordinary Women* is an expression of male pique and wounded vanity.'

Such criticism has persisted, largely because as a pioneering book it is expected also to be a tract on the subject. It is quite clear, however, that the author's attitude is precisely that of the one character whom he treats respectfully, Madame Sarbécoff: 'She had a sense of humour which compelled her to admit that she and all the world were equally ridiculous ... [She] had grasped another truth ... which was that love was no more and no less than a recognition of a vitality outside oneself.' Like all forms of sexual attraction, lesbianism had an absurdity which he happily accentuated, but the heterosexuals and male homosexuals in the story are not better treated.

Three of the four main characters are portraits of Faith's friends, Renata Borgatti (Cleo Gazay), Mimi Franchetti (Rosalba Donsante) and Romaine Brooks (Olimpia Leigh). The fourth, Rory Freemantle, was his own creation, and a grotesque. Her chin is prominent and hispid, she wears a bowler hat and a monocle, and before coming to Capri she has been a trainer of female boxers. It is her misfortune to fall in love with the promiscuous Rosalba who uses her sex appeal 'like a school-boy with a penknife, forever testing its sharpness'. Trumped by the famous Olimpia Leigh, of whom it is said 'to be loved by Olimpia Leigh even for five minutes gave any young woman ... a cachet not obtainable since the day when young women could boast of being loved by the mighty Sappho herself', Rosalba leaves the island, and in the end Rory finds consolation with an effeminate youth called Daffodil.

It is a harlequinade whose emotion is remote and charming. Rory, strangely enough, is cast as Columbine who wept awhile until the lights were turned up, when everyone agreed that the whole performance was in the best of taste and vastly well executed; Rosalba is Harlequin, the elegant, heartless spirit of enjoyment, who in the mere act of tipping a waiter could convince him 'that in accepting the note he and Signorina Rosalba ... were entering into a compact to get by hook or by crook the best out of life ... it conferred upon him the right to do everything he could to please her.' One suspects the author, too, of being half seduced by her charm, and his appearance commenting on the action adds to the unreality. Thus, having described the auburn-haired, dark-skinned Rosalba dancing with the blonde Zoë Mitchell, he comments:

It is even a temptation for the chronicler to lay down his pen at this point, and content with having brought two such beautiful young women together in a Sirenian dance, to let them stay here for ever, without trespassing any further upon their follies and fantastic emotions and obscure passions . . . But alas the pen of the novelist lives by follies and fantastic emotions and obscure passions.

Of all the books outside his grand scheme of life's theatre, these two elegant novels of Capri are the most substantial. Yet even these were consigned to the category of 'marking time'. They were followed by two secret service novels, *Extremes Meet* (1928) and *The Three Couriers* (1929), the first of which remains among the best in the genre, combining both the adventures of spy-chasing and the grubbiness of the Black List. A pair of comedies came next: *April Fools* (1930), a continuation of the Touchwood family saga which began in *Poor Relations*, and *Buttercups and Daisies* (1931). The latter was his experience of the Beech colony rendered into a joyful farce of two boys discovering the eccentricities of the inhabitants of Oak Town. Their chief pleasure is Mr Augustus Ryan, who first appears drunk in their father's bed and has an engaging habit of wrestling with the furniture. 'The furniture had suffered considerably, and indeed the only piece to put up anything of a show had been a large wardrobe which, exasperated by the behaviour of Mr Augustus Ryan had fallen on top of him in the middle of a bout and laid him out for nearly a week . . . "I had a bad ten minutes with the washstand when I got my head through the hole for the basin,"' Ryan gravely tells the boys, '"and the grandfather clock was pounding me in the back with its pendulum. However, I managed to fling myself free of the washstand and then I turned round and knocked out the clock with a devastating punch on the fleshy part of the hour-hand."'

The adherents of this farce were numerous and devoted. Duff Cooper used to keep it at hand during political crises, knowing that after a few pages he would laugh until the tears came, and P. G. Wodehouse wrote delightedly to Monty in 1946 after coming across a copy, 'I suppose it was about my seventh reading of the book, and I loved it just as much as ever. I always stoutly maintain that for sustained comic writing you leave the rest of us nowhere.'

Following the comedies came two exercises in affectionate nostalgia, *Our Street* (1932) and *The Darkening Green* (1934), the first being a fictional reconstruction of West Kensington at the beginning of the century, and the second of Beech at the same period. By now the heavyweight critics seemed to have given up trying to make sense of such variety and the books were almost ignored. In the case of *The Darkening*

Green, this is unfortunate, for its story of an illicit village love affair witnessed by a fourteen-year-old boy beautifully conveys the heavy mysteriousness of adult love as it appears to an adolescent.

Behind the appearance of versatility there was an unchanging method of working upon which his output and its variety depended. The entire book was mapped out in his head before he began writing. It required a prodigious effort of concentration which usually ended in acute nervous exhaustion. But even his astonishing powers would have been insufficient to hold the plot of a book in memory without an extremely clear structure to suspend it from. The most obvious example is *Vestal Fire*'s tripartite structure, each with eight chapters and a change of mood occurring exactly at the halfway point. The passage of time is the usual basis – so many years to each chapter – but in *Our Street* and *The Darkening Green*, it is place – a different house for each chapter. This mental construction was reinforced in the physical process of writing itself. The pages of the manuscript were numbered A 1–20, B 21–40, etc., missing out J, so that the alphabet gave him 500 pages, at which he began again AA 501–20. 'Through long familiarity,' he explained in a radio talk,

the letters of the alphabet have acquired a kind of monitory significance so that whether I be telling a story of fancy or fact I know whereabouts I ought to be when I come to any letter, and I am able without the aid of more than half a sheet of notepaper to construct a book of 300,000 words without being more than 5000 words out either way when it has been written.

The drawback to the method was that the progress through the alphabet, implying as it did a movement through time or space, tended to take the place of motivation. As a result, dramas occurred and passions developed less out of characterisation or plotting than at the dictates of geography or the calendar. It could also be argued that the segmented structure exaggerated his habit of thinking theatrically and relying on the reader to infer emotions and character from dialogue and setting. It was a habit he freely admitted, saying, 'I fancy that only readers with a dramatic sense enjoy my novels; they must be able as it were to play all the parts themselves, and grasp their life. I am not interested in creating characters of such psychological complicacy that pages of patient analysis of human motive are required to present them on the printed page.'

Pushed to the limit, the method allowed him to have *Figure of Eight*, a novel of 100,000 words, ready for the printers one month after he wrote the first sentence. But he found no satisfaction in it beyond that of doing a job. Commenting on the banality of Fay's autobiography

Rosemary, published in 1926, he wrote in the foreword, 'I doubt if she gets any more pleasure out of acting than I get out of filling a sheet of paper with words.' The only book he ever enjoyed writing, he used to say, was *Santa Claus in Summer*, his children's book. In it he wove together the off-duty lives of several dozen fairy-tale characters to make a story much loved by little girls, but considered slightly damp by little boys.

The book he wanted to write was about his war experiences, but that remained blocked, and until it came free in 1933 he was condemned to mark time and boil pots. He derived much more satisfaction from the growing popularity of the *Gramophone* and the platform it gave him to talk about music.

The *Gramophone* had in fact caught a rising tide of interest in recorded music, and through such devices as its National Gramophone Society, which acted like a book club, it undoubtedly galvanised the record companies into serving the market for complete recordings of classical music. 'The example of the National Gramophone Society has been very possibly the greatest single force in compelling the commercial manufacturers to take their courage in both hands and go forward along artistic lines,' an American journalist wrote in 1928.

Nevertheless the magazine was regarded with a certain condescension by the more serious music critics. Monty's habit of reviewing records which he listened to while writing novels was not approved of, nor was his tendency to write of a flute 'whistling like an errand boy', or a piano 'rocking gently like a boat on a sea of strings'. He was roundly condemned for attempting to give nicknames, akin to the 'Unfinished Symphony' or the 'Moonlight Sonata' to pieces which he liked, and for referring to Stravinsky as 'a tragic buffoon', an opinion he later revised. He rarely went to concerts, and in his preference for recorded music over live, there was a curious similarity to his taste for prints rather than original paintings.

In 1926 Ernest Newman attempted to cut him down to size with an attack in the *Sunday Times* upon 'the pontifical assurance with which our men of letters, and especially the minor novelists, deliver their opinion upon music'. Music criticism, he asserted ponderously, was far too complex for anyone but a specialist, and the interlopers would be better off 'keeping to the writing of novels or some other equally easy form of manual labour'. This was too heavy-handed to escape without riposte. Noting how the conflict with one novelist had been broadened to sound as though Newman were confronted by an army of writers,

Monty compared him to Falstaff: '"If I fought not with fifty of them, call me a radish; if there were not two or three and fifty, then am I no two-legged creature." No, it won't do, Mr Newman, and without a moment's hesitation I *do* call you a radish.'

He used to assert that if he had listened to experts he would never have started the *Gramophone* at all, and he continued to pontificate entertainingly, confident that he shared the tastes of his readers. 'Fortunately I have been granted exceptional rapidity of assimilation,' he declared, '. . . I have also been granted normality of experience. It may be that in a certain number of months I shall accomplish in the adventures of taste what the average man accomplishes in the same number of years, but he and I are going to reach the same goal ultimately and the only difference is that I get there first.'

Initially Monty had hoped to edit the magazine from Herm where he had accumulated both records and the latest machines with huge horns, but it was soon clear that the offices had to be in London, and Faith found suitable premises at 25 Newman Street. In the organisation which grew up she became assistant to Christopher, who was London editor, but answerable to the stream of instructions flowing from Herm and later Jethou. It was a good arrangement in that it made the best use of everyone's talents.

Like his grandfather Hezekiah Bateman, Monty had an innate understanding of publicity, and it was he who came up with the gimmicks for boosting sales – the readers' competitions, the plugs on the newly emergent BBC (by insisting that Christopher always be introduced as 'the London editor of the *Gramophone* magazine'), the Famous Names' Favourite Tunes, and the Great Gramophone Challenge which filled the Steinway Hall with Deccas, Edisons, Autophones, Cliftophones and Orchestraphones, to discover which was best. Distance allowed him an overview, and as in his gardening he preferred to deal with the strategy rather than daily routine. This was left to Christopher, to whom it came as a godsend.

In many ways Christopher had flowered too early. After the publication of his poems and novels he had rather too gratefully allowed himself to be supported by Alyce, his wealthy wife, and, in Faith's opinion, be bullied by her. Christopher himself, pliant and good-natured, seemed not to mind. The war had shown him to be conspicuously gallant, disdaining staff work for service in the trenches on the western front where he had won the DSO and the MC. In its aftermath, however, he had again been reduced to little more than companion to Alyce in her enthusiasm for dog shows and race-meetings – 'all his fine brain and cultivation wasted,' Faith lamented. By pushing the *Gramophone* job at him, Monty not only restored his self-respect, but launched him on a career which was to make him, as a record presenter, one of the most popular voices on the BBC in the 1930s. It would not be unfair to say that hierarchy suited him and that orders, whether from his wife, his colonel or Monty, relieved him of a responsibility he had no wish to shoulder.

For Faith also the *Gramophone* provided a focus. She contributed articles under the pseudonym F Sharp, which was her own comment on the caustic tone her temper was beginning to acquire. Although it came hard to her – 'I wish writing did not consume my heart's blood,' she complained – she learned to have confidence in her work. Like Christopher, she found it paved the way to other things, and four years later she began her first book, a biography of Queen Christina of Sweden. Of more immediate significance, there was a flat above the Newman Street offices where she could live and entertain a smart circle of friends which included Beatrice Lillie, Syrie Maugham and Violet Hunt.

Until then she had shuttled rootlessly between Capri, which she loved but for the absence of Monty, and Herm, which she disliked but for his electrifying presence. Elegant and forthright in public, whatever her inner uncertainties, she was the sort of person who thrived in the city, and the *Gramophone* gave her a purpose and a base there. Capri always retained her affection, but in 1924 the lease on Casa Solitaria ran out, and lack of money forced her to move into ever smaller lodgings until the two rooms she had made her home were pulled down in 1927. Thereafter she transferred her loyalties to Jethou and its garden.

Had an island been sufficient in itself to satisfy his needs, Monty would have been content with Jethou. The garden began to flourish, and the house with its extensions was made as comfortable as any he had lived in. On the eastern side of the island there was a small wood of stunted trees carpeted with bluebells and primroses where, sheltered from the wind, he could look out across the sea to Sark. It was restful, beautiful and isolated and almost at once he began to look for somewhere else to live. His first choice was Ireland.

In August 1924 the Irish government celebrated its hard-won independence by reviving the Tailteann Games at which athletic and artistic competitions were held, and Monty was asked to be a judge of the literary section. The agglomeration of sporting and artistic stars gave him more good stories than even he had hoped for. His favourite concerned Augustus John, who appeared at the welcoming dinner in tailcoat, white tie and brown tweed trousers, having forgotten to pack his black trousers. To Monty's delight, Oliver St John Gogarty, one of the organisers of the Games, confided, 'I've got a great joke on over Augustus. I've told Augustus that Dunsany [his host in Ireland] is a fierce teetotaller and for god's sake not to ask him for a drink and I've told Dunsany /that Augustus is a fierce teetotaller and for god's sake not to offer him one.' Making up for the long drought, John drank himself insensible at the welcoming dinner and did not recover until near the end when he awoke by chance as the electricity failed during a speech from the commander-in-chief of the Free State army.

'What's going on?' he mumbled.

'It's a Free State General making a speech in Gaelic,' Monty whispered.

'Thank God, I'm only drunk,' John replied. 'I thought I'd gone mad.'

To his pleasure Monty was quartered with the Governor-General, Tim Healy, at Viceregal Lodge, and he treasured Gogarty's photograph of himself with other luminaries such as W. B. Yeats, G. K. Chesterton and Edwin Lutyens. During his week in Dublin he made friends with the tenor John McCormack, and later went to stay with the publisher William Nolan and his wife Hilda in Shankill. Hilda was American and about fifteen years younger than her husband, and within days of meeting Monty she became his mistress. Together they explored much of the south and west of Ireland by car, and on one expedition to county Kerry, he found a house for sale which stood beside a tumbling river with thirty acres of beeches, Scots pines and rowans, rising up to moorland behind. It was called Lickeen. A general in India had the first refusal, but Monty was so determined to have it that he rented a house nearby called Ripley Lodge in order to be on the spot if it became available. But when the general refused to give up his option Monty abruptly lost interest.

He never explained why he should have wanted to desert Jethou for county Kerry, but twelve months later in October 1925 when another property presented itself, it aroused similar enthusiasm. He was in Glasgow to give a talk to the Gramophone Society when he heard that Lord Leverhulme's estate in the Western Isles was to be auctioned off. On the list of properties were the Shiant Islands, three superb tables of basaltic rock in the Minch among whose cliffs are squared columns like those of Fingal's Cave rising sheer for five hundred feet from sea to turf. Having just received £1000 for a serial, *Fairy Gold*, which ironically was the fictional account of his dealings with Sir Percival Perry, he decided to set aside £500 to bid at the auction.

If Sir Percival did him out of Herm at an unfair price, it would seem that Monty inadvertently did another financial magnate, the 2nd Lord Leverhulme, out of the Shiants. The auctioneers had been instructed to reserve them for Leverhulme, the original owner's son, but mistook Monty's representative at the auction for Leverhulme's. It was generally agreed that the proper price was nearer £750, and there were still bidders in the ring, but at precisely £500 the islands were knocked down to Monty's man. That stroke of extraordinary fortune decisively changed the latter half of his life.

From the beginning his feelings went much deeper than the pleasure of owning another island. 'I can scarcely remember the time when I was not a perfervid Gael,' he wrote in an article, 'Looking Northward', a few months later,

but I have never attempted to express the passion of race in words. The consciousness of being landless in Alba, coupled with ignorance of the language, forbade me out of pride to assume what I should have felt would appear no more than the trappings of a mock romanticism. So this is actually the first time I have ventured to speak of something that has long lain nearer my heart than rank or fortune or reputation.

He traced the passion back to the dreams of childhood – the insistence on being called Mackenzie and not Compton, the pride and sadness aroused by *Tales of a Grandfather*, even the membership of Jacobite societies – in fact all the dreams of the secret Monty who was opposed to Nanny, West Kensington and St Paul's. 'I count myself a fool now in middle-age,' he confessed, 'because I understand at last that what seemed the shadow was the substance, but that what offered itself as the substance was no more than a mean shadow.'

On Capri he had been the cosmopolitan expatriate, and on Herm the landed gentleman. They were not identities assumed so much as entered into, the protean temperament taking on the quality of its surroundings. But in Scotland there was something which he sensed to be already present in himself. It had led him to go to war beneath the flag of the Lion Rampant and to wear the kilt in Herm. When at last he assumed the identity of a Scot, it was with the excitement of discovering what he felt to be his true self.

13
The Jacobite becomes a Lord Rector

In June 1926 he visited his land in Alba for the first time, travelling by train to Inverness and then driving through Glenmoriston and Glenshiel to Kyle of Lochalsh. If ever he had any doubts about the hold of his childhood dreams, that drive dispelled them. It took him past scenes which had the power of talismans – Glenmoriston, home of the seven companions of Bonnie Prince Charlie after Culloden, Glenshiel, scene of the skirmish in 1719 when French troops landed to support the Old Pretender, and the castle of Eilean Donan, ruined by the bombardment of English frigates.

A ferry took him from Kyle to Tarbert in Harris at the southern end of the island of Lewis, and there he met Malcolm MacSween who rented the grazing on the Shiants. To his pleasure, and perhaps also to his relief since he was always inwardly nervous before meetings of such importance, MacSween proved to be a vital, outgoing man, as Mediterranean in temperament as he was in appearance. His wife, Barabel, was ill in bed, but waiting at the house was their eight-year-old daughter Lily. He remembered her as small and shy, glancing up from beneath dark brows, and she never forgot her first glimpse of him, smiling and strikingly handsome in blue bonnet and stockings, oatmeal tweed jacket and kilt.

The scenes on the road to Kyle must have captured the imagination, but the MacSween family, quick, warm and good-looking, were to take his heart. And then, on a still, glassy day, he saw for the first time the Shiants, outreaching every expectation of beauty as they rose green upon green, 'the bottle-green water at the base of this cliff, the greenish-black glaze of these columns, that lustrous green of the braes and summits . . . a scene of classic grandeur unsurpassed by any of the famed islands of the Aegean.' It was fit that the Gaelic word *seunta* from which Shiant was derived should mean 'enchanted'.

The emotion this Scotland aroused in him ran as deep as any he had felt since his adolescent conversion. In the mouth of John Ogilvie in *The North Wind of Love* he described it as being as fundamental as that crucial experience. 'I love Scotland,' says Ogilvie, 'and whenever and wherever I feel that glow, it sets my heart beating as women in their day have set it beating. But long before a woman set it beating, I had been stirred so profoundly by the abrupt revelation of life itself that the love I have for Scotland seems to me now the finest and perfect expression of my own vitality within the bounds of mortal flesh.'

In the years ahead the charge of being a synthetic Scot was levelled at him often enough, but the extravagant toss-all-to-the-winds note in that passage has the ring of the real Mackay. It was more than a passion like gardening or gramophones – it was the great cause, like religion or Greater Greece, affording him a context and an identity. Although it was true that his idea of Scotland was culled from books and plays, it could well be argued that as a nation Scotland scarcely existed outside the imagination in 1926.

To the great majority of Scots, the British Empire, with the emphasis on British, offered an umbrella nationality which they were happy to adopt as their own. The corollary was that Scotland could not be more than a region of the Home Country, a deduction expressly recognised in 1928 by the most influential of North Britons, John Reith, when he established the BBC in his native land under the title of the Scottish Regional Service.

A large majority, especially in the industrial southwest, gave their first loyalty not to Scotland but to international socialism: as one trade union delegate argued at the 1928 Scottish Trades Union Congress, 'The national geographic area was not to be the area for the future. To support home rule would be to support the narrow spirit of nationalism, when we were all out for a broad internationalism.' A small minority, in the Highlands and Islands for the most part, did envisage an independent Scotland within the empire, and expressed the aspiration by voting for the Liberal Party which had made home rule for Scotland its policy before the war; but a country which depended upon the fortunes of a politically moribund party might be thought to belong pre-eminently to the imagination. There was a history, but neither a language nor a literature. There were ministers and lawyers who discerned national identity in the Kirk or the legal system, and teachers who found it in the excellence of the schools, and romantics who saw it in tartan or heard it in pipe music. They all felt themselves to be Scots, but as a nation Scotland was a series of personal experiences whose only common thread was the certainty that Scotland was not England. This negative definition might have continued to suffice had the Irish Free State not broken away from the Union and fought its way to independence.

In the aftermath of the war, the Scottish Home Rule Association which had flourished twenty years earlier with Robert Cunninghame Graham and Keir Hardie at its head, was revived by Roland Muirhead, who was by trade a tanner and by nature a powerful propagandist. The journalist Lewis Spence, whose writing helped to restore an interest in the Braid Scots of William Dunbar and Robert Henryson, founded the Scottish National Movement in 1926 to promote a specifically Scots culture. And in 1921 the stormy petrel of nationalist politics, Ruaraidh Erskine of Marr, formed the Scots National League, whose aims reflected his own blend of enthusiasms for a Gaelic revival, the confiscation of estates from absentee landlords and the overthrow of the English ascendancy in all its guises. It was for Erskine's magazine, the *Pictish Review*, that Monty wrote his earliest articles on the importance of Scotland to him, and the development of his own views of Scotland owed much to Erskine's.

The articles were commissioned by the magazine's editor, Christopher Grieve, who under the name of Hugh MacDiarmid became the fountain-head of the Scottish renaissance when he synthesised a new language from etymology and border dialect to make the great epic poem, *A Drunk Man Looks at a Thistle*. Its publication in 1926 made public the inner doubts and diversities of the nature of Scotland, and in so doing acted as the catalyst to resolve them:

> Whatever Scotland is to me,
> Be it aye pairt o' a' men see
> O' Earth and o' Eternity . . .
>
> He canna Scotland see wha yet
> Canna see the Infinite
> And Scotland in true scale to it.

MacDiarmid was more than a pen name, it was Grieve's other personality, pugnacious and overwhelming in its Promethean creativity. MacDiarmid would have made a new Scotland in his sprawling, contradictory image, but Grieve, though he admired and wrote an approving review of MacDiarmid's poetry, was more cautious, fearing that the emerging nationalist movement could too easily become parochial. He welcomed men of like mind, whether an exiled Scot like Cunninghame Graham – 'We will never see his like again,' he wrote, 'the human equivalent of that pure white stag with great branching horns the appearance of which tradition says will betoken great good fortune for Scotland at last' – or a Scot discovering himself like Compton Mackenzie.

'A great deal will depend in the immediate future on the evidence of return to Scotland of men of your prestige,' he wrote to Monty on 14 May 1928. 'If the old tendency of holding south is reversed, if people see that distinguished Scots are impressed by, and in sympathy with, the New Nationalism and returning to take a personal share in the work – it will be half the battle.' This letter was sent just four days after they had met for the first time. MacDiarmid was not alone in seeing the political value of Monty's name. The Labour Party in Scotland was ready to find a constituency where he could run as a Labour and home rule candidate. It was, therefore, not just as a contributor to the *Pictish Review* but as a potential home rule candidate that he was invited to Glasgow on 10 May when the leaders of a dozen different nationalist societies and associations met to discuss the formation of a National Party of Scotland.

The meeting was organised by a young Glasgow student, John Mac-Cormick, whose administrative and political talents were to earn him the nickname of 'the king-maker' and give him an influence in the National Party beyond his years. He had founded the university's Scottish Nationalist Association with the intention of putting forward Robert Cunninghame Graham as its candidate in the forthcoming election for rector. Thus the focus of that heterogeneous meeting was the elderly Don Roberto, a claimant to the Earldom of Monteith, who had once been a Radical MP and later a landowner in Argentina, though always a writer of clean and subtle prose.

'Of what we discussed that afternoon,' said Monty's mouthpiece John Ogilvie, 'I retain not a word. I was merely aware that about a dozen ordinary people were filled with creative life and that I was sharing in that manifestation ... it gave me an assurance that the dreams and fantasies of youth could be transmuted into the projects, the rational, deliberate projects of age and experience.'

It is the addictive charm of the beginnings of any radical movement that the only people who want to belong are those giving greater weight to the possible than to the actual. Eventually their dreams are bound to be crushed by the obduracy of their opponents or the realism of their successors, but for a brief moment the romantics, outsiders, dreamers and actors so encourage one another that like the founders of the National Party of Scotland their visions take on substance and something is created which never existed before.

Monty was elected to the Council of the new party, and accepted John MacCormick's request to announce Cunninghame Graham's candidature for the rectorship – a largely honorary post representing the students in the university court. It was a brave decision. The speech had to be made the following day, but in an attempt to cure his sciatica which it was thought might be caused by pyorrhoea of the gums, all his teeth had been pulled out a few weeks before and his false teeth had only just been fitted. Until he went on to the platform he did not know whether they would stay in place or how his voice would be affected. Even Cunninghame Graham, who in the past had addressed mobs in Trafalgar Square, observed, 'I would not face those "Ephesians" for anything, not that I mind a rough meeting or opposition, but Glasgow students go to make a row, quite apart from what they may think.'

There was a clamorous uproar when Monty began, but within a few minutes he had their attention and held them to the end. The students were only the first of a succession of unpromising audiences whom he captivated with his Nationalist fervour. After one meeting at which he congratulated a meeting of Free Presbyterians for being motivated by principle like himself, one listener remarked, 'It's the first time I've heard a Roman Catholic tell the people of Gairloch they were on a level with the Papists and get applauded for telling them so.' His oratory owed something to his preaching style, being fed by the impressionist garnering of facts and ideas which arranged themselves according to the emotion of the moment. He spoke rapidly and without notes – reporters estimated his delivery at about three hundred words a minute – and the cadence conveyed as much as the words. A relation who had heard Henry Compton noticed that he had the same trick as his grandfather of conveying emotion by changing key from major to minor within a sentence.

The Nationalist case was presented on a broad scale and in decisive terms. He argued that it was the saviour of an individuality which would otherwise be crushed by capitalist bankers or communist bureaucrats, and he was emphatic that Scotland must settle for nothing less than complete independence. Neither home rule, nor Dominion status, nor 'the glorified County Council' of Stormont was the solution. 'To my mind it would be better to wait thirty years and die at the end of it with every dream unfulfilled,' he declared passionately, 'than to accept such a parody of a nation's life.'

It was not only Cunninghame Graham's candidature that he launched that May evening but Scottish Nationalism as a political movement. With it the focus of his life was to shift decisively away from Jethou. Until then Scotland was the place he visited when the relentless pace of his work permitted – first to see the Shiants, and again in 1927 to discuss the issue of Gaelic records with the Gaelic scholar, Father John Macmillan, then at Ballachulish but soon to return to his native Barra.

Both *Vestal Fire* and *Extraordinary Women* had required an exceptional degree of concentration – the latter he termed 'the most exhausting book I ever wrote' – and at the beginning of 1928 there had been a race to get *Extremes Meet* finished in time to stave off a financial crisis. Since 1927 he also had contracts to provide a monthly article for *Vanity Fair*, and a weekly record review column for the *Sunday Pictorial*. Although each journey required him to stockpile articles and reviews beforehand, the amount of time he spent in Scotland steadily increased after the Glasgow meeting until it was Jethou that was the place he visited.

'I find the poet Grieve very remarkable,' Monty wrote to Faith after the National Party's inauguration, 'a little like D. H. Lawrence, but with a harder intellect and, I think, a richer genius. I hope that between us we shall be able to steer the movement out of any kind of parochialism.'

MacDiarmid responded to his good opinion by inviting him to Montrose at the end of May where he was editing the local paper. There he stood godfather with Neil Gunn at the christening of MacDiarmid's son.

Their efforts to broaden the movement's horizon bred a mutual admiration despite the complete divergence of their thoughts. MacDiarmid had once argued the need for a Scottish Fascism, and in Capri Monty had also thought that its creed offered the only hope of regenerating Europe. From that common starting point their politics had developed in different directions.

Monty argued that the English mentality was stolid, male and Saxon, and his worst fear was that the materialist genius of the Scots which had produced Adam Smith, James Watt and William Paterson would always try to find in that mentality a kindly soil for its growth. Instead he wanted intuitive, female Scotland to find her identity with her sisters, Ireland, Wales and Brittany and to form with them a federation of Celtic states. This theme, to which he constantly returned, arose from the importance he attached to 'the Scottish idea' which would embody the character of the nation. Not surprisingly it bore the lineaments of his own past rather than the reality of the present.

'For many years a sentimental Jacobitism is the emotion that has kept alive the idea of Scotland as a nation,' he wrote later that year in the *Pictish Review*,

and it is now the duty of the nationalist leaders to see that such fervour is given an opportunity for practical expression . . . every intelligent Scot must devote himself practically to the desire for political independence. All the dreams that haunt us – the salvation of Gaelic, the revival of Braid Scots, a Gaelic University in Inverness, the repopulation of the glens, a Celtic federation, and a hundred other things, will only embody themselves when we have a Scottish Free State under the Crown.

His Scottish idea was always more Jacobite than Presbyterian, and more romantic than practical. It was once genially apostrophised by Lewis Grassic Gibbon as 'a Scots Catholic kingdom, with Mr Compton Mackenzie Prime Minister to some disinterred Jacobite royalty, and all the Scots intellectuals settled out on the land on thirty-acre crofts or sent out to re-colonise St Kilda for the good of their souls and the nation.'

Despite its royalist and religious leanings, the strongest supporter of Monty's idea was MacDiarmid, whose own Scottish idea was a compound of anarchist sympathies, tempered by communism and informed by Major C. H. Douglas's economic theory of social credit. Prepared though he was to excoriate moderate Home Rulers like Sir Alexander MacEwen who were ready to settle for Dominion status, he lauded Compton Mackenzie for hitting 'upon the real ground for hope – the unimpaired, undeceivable intuition of the Commons of Scotland'. Monty for his part lavished praise on MacDiarmid's Marxist populism, declaring in the *Pictish Review* that 'his Scottish idea is precisely that for which Culloden was fought'.

Any misapprehension was a matter of detail. When MacCormick and Spence were already talking of by-elections and attracting the Tory vote, it was not the exact blueprint of utopia which counted but the passion which made one dream of such things. In the words of MacDiarmid's great poem:

> I'll hae nae hauf-way hoose, but aye be whaur
> Extremes meet – it's the only way I ken
> To dodge the curst conceit o' bein' richt
> That damns the vast majority o' men.

From Montrose Monty travelled to Inveraray Castle, to stay with the Duke of Argyll and his sister Lady Elspeth Campbell. Monty felt himself at home there, discussing religion with the duke, who was a fervent Anglo-Catholic and one-time friend of Sandys Wason, laying plans for the revival of Gaelic with Lady Elspeth, who was enthusiastically Presbyterian, and appraising the rhododendrons with both. Yet it is noticeable that while he found nothing absurd in MacDiarmid, the castle and its inhabitants were the focal points for a string of stories. In literary terms Inveraray and in particular the Great Hall, hung with claymores, stags' heads and ancestral portraits, became the Great Hall at Glenbogle Castle in *The Monarch of the Glen*. He also entertained the Savile Club with his account of the mild but pertinacious duke struggling to pin down the exact hue of the chasuble worn at St Michael's, Shoreditch, in the 1890s while the Great Hall rang with a visiting soprano's rendering of a Uist waulking song which his forceful sister had commanded from the other end of the table. When he went to the annual Mod, or festival of Gaelic music, in Inverness later that year, he enjoyed the encounter between Lady Elspeth and Lord Ashbourne who professed a passion for Irish Gaelic. 'He addressed her in Irish Gaelic; she replied in Scots Gaelic,' he noted. 'To the obvious surprise of the onlookers each apparently understood what the other was saying; nobody conversant with Irish or Scots Gaelic had ever immediately understood what either Lord Ashbourne or Lady Elspeth was saying.'

Towards the end of that summer his dream of Scotland reached a more romantic height than a sceptic would have deemed probable. Travelling on to the Shiants, he again called on the MacSweens and this time met their elder daughter. 'As we came in,' he remembered, 'I saw in the doorway of the kitchen a girl in a blue frock with a red belt. Her dark hair was parted in the middle and coiled over her ears in the fashion known at that date in the Highlands as "earphones". Her eyes were so dark as to seem black above her red rose cheeks. In that moment of meeting I knew that girl must become a part of my life.'

Christina MacSween, known as Chrissie, was twenty-two and newly appointed as teacher of the school on the nearby island of Scarp. Apart from her training in Edinburgh, her life had been spent in the Western Isles, and her soft voice had the inflections of the Gaelic she had spoken since childhood. It is easy to see why Monty was attracted to her, apart from her dark eyes. She was her father's daughter, warm-hearted and impulsive, and although she possessed a shrewd judgement of people it was continually at risk from an optimism which seemed determined to believe that everyone was essentially good and everything must eventually turn out for the best.

The flowering of this double love for a country and a girl had its effect upon his work. He was asked to give a talk on the Shiants for the BBC in August 1928, and in his exalted mood the image of the islands acquired a magic which was sensed immediately by his audience. The enthusiastic response alerted the BBC to his talent, and thereafter he became one of their surefire successes, being booked repeatedly for talks and debates despite a constant battle over fees. His style was a natural extension of the reminiscent story-telling with which he beguiled dinner parties and Savile Club gatherings, and the subjects – Siamese cats, gardens, Gallipoli, music-hall and twenty others – were almost as diverse. The mischief was removed but the evocative detail and the warm theatrical voice had the same compelling effect. The BBC once conducted a test with schoolchildren listening to the unidentified voices of a selection of broadcasters and found that Monty's was selected as 'the nicest' by twice as many votes as his nearest rival. To the more sophisticated ear of Terence de Vere White, it had 'the most seductive power of any voice I've ever heard. It made everything he said seem to be of enormous importance'.

This new career in broadcasting brought him a huge increase in fan mail, and a normal week's total of perhaps fifty or seventy letters to answer would be doubled after a broadcast. He was shrewd enough to realise that the publicity helped to sell books, and the flood of mail justified his claim to need another secretary.

When he went back to Harris in the autumn he suggested to the MacSweens that Chrissie might take on this job. She and her father were delighted by the suggestion, but it was Mrs MacSween whose opinion counted. Reserved in manner and a devout member of the Free Presbyterian kirk, she was on the face of it unlikely to approve of her daughter giving up her job as a teacher to work for a forty-six-year-old man living apart from his wife. But Monty was irresistible. Behind her reserved exterior he discovered a delight in absurdity, and needing no other encouragement he would spin out his stories of ridiculousness until she wept with laughter. 'He and my mother established a complete communion,' Chrissie's sister Lily recalled. 'He knocked any stuffiness out of her, and from the word go they understood each other perfectly.' With her consent it was arranged that Chrissie would give up her teaching and join him in Jethou shortly before Christmas 1928.

It was more than coincidence that at the same time he should have made the first break in the barrier which prevented him from writing about the war. So complete was this block that he could not even fulfil a promise made to G. K. Chesterton in 1925 to contribute an article on the war to his magazine. Nevertheless he did not abandon the ambitious scheme outlined to Martin Secker in 1918 for a series of novels on the theme of war to be entitled *The Labyrinth*. In April 1926 he told the *Daily Mail* of a book he planned to write called *Our Seven Selves*. It was to consist of seven volumes and one million words, and all save one of the titles were the same as those of *The Labyrinth*. Its scope had widened but not its inspiration.

'The theme of the book,' he said,

is the self-determination of man in relation to (1) His art, craft or profession, (2) Women, (3) Family, (4) Class, (5) Country, (6) Humanity, (7) God. The book will begin in the year 1897 and finish in the 1920s. The length of the book is due to the large stage which extends from Ireland in the West to Greece in the East, to the length of time covered by the narrative, and to the number of personages and groups involved . . . You ask what was the inspiration of it, and I can only say 'my experiences during the war'.

He had been thinking of it for eight years, he told the newspaper, and intended to begin it in 1927.

Our Seven Selves was never written. Its plan, however, is sufficiently close to *The Four Winds of Love* to establish it as the connecting link between the work he first conceived in 1918 and the great work of his middle age, begun in 1935, but the number of intervening steps explains why the barrier between conception and realisation proved so formidable.

In his spy novel *Extremes Meet*, which he began in January 1928, Monty made use of some of his experiences in Athens, and when he finished it late in February he was also able to complete the article promised so long ago to Chesterton. By the end of that remarkable year he had also finished *The Three Couriers*, another secret service book based on his own activities. To his annoyance reviews of the first one suggested that the people and events in it were largely fictional.

'So when *Extremes Meet* was published and I found that I was being patted on the back for having written a successful thriller, I felt that the only way to use my war experiences was by putting them down on paper as a true story,' he wrote. 'Perhaps I felt I owed it to myself to make it clear that my experience was the result of my own creative passion . . . I did not want it to be regarded as mere material for fiction.'

In January 1929 he began the first of his war memoirs, *Gallipoli*

Memories, whose prevailing emotion is one of valediction to the pre-war world. The backward glance was always affectionate – not for him the anti-war mood of *All Quiet on the Western Front*, or *Her Privates We*, or *Goodbye to All That*, all of which appeared in the late 1920s. In his article for Chesterton he signalled the tone he would adopt by praising Rupert Brooke and the romance of war. It was not just the passage of time which allowed him to strike such a note. The war was the last chapter of the old England he had been brought up in, and it was not until he had found a new country that he could regard its death indulgently.

Once he began work it was like the bursting of a dam. 'His whole heart and soul are in it,' Faith told his mother, 'and I've never seen him so passionately engrossed since *Sinister Street*.' The first volume carried him from May 1915 to August when he was sent to Athens on sick leave. He planned another two volumes to cover his experiences in Athens, a fourth for Syra and a fifth for the Aegean. Subsequently it was decided to compress his Athenian experiences into one volume; nevertheless it was a leisurely pace, allowing time for individual portraits, a wide political survey and the intricacies of departmental infighting.

In *Gallipoli Memories* General Sir Ian Hamilton was the hero, lean, imaginative and beset by indolent divisional commanders and obstructive politicians. There is, however, a contrary current. Writing of the Suvla Bay landings, for example, the emotion which in *Sylvia Scarlett* had been pure regret for the loss of the old Merrie England was here shot through with condemnation for its failings: 'I felt as if I had watched a system smash to pieces before my eyes,' he wrote, 'as if I had stood at the death of the old order . . . An absurd phrase went singing through my head, *We have lost our amateur status tonight*. It was foolish of me who had been old enough to appreciate the muddle of the South African War to go on believing in the practical value of the public school system.'

That dissentient note struck many readers as implying a criticism of the unprofessional romantics like Churchill and Hamilton who had imagined that the Gallipoli operation would shorten the war. It was sufficiently widespread to give rise to an absurd encounter on a remote atoll on the Great Barrier Reef. Clementine Churchill, Winston's wife, landed there on a holiday in 1939, and while she was exploring its apparently deserted beach an ancient bearded beachcomber in tattered shorts suddenly appeared and said, 'Mrs Churchill, eh? I've just been reading a book called *Gallipoli Memories* and from what I can make out your husband made a bit of a *faux pas* over Gallipoli.' Although it made a good enough tale to enter his repertory, he was indignant that his thesis should have been so misunderstood. The independent-thinking romantics were right in his opinion; it was the plodder imprinted with public school conventions who bore the responsibility for failure.

First Athenian Memories (the *First* was dropped from later editions) covered the last six months of 1915 when he was settling into his intelligence work. Like its predecessor, it was written largely from memory. The tone remained mellow, and the narrative is both amusing and studded with deft character sketches. Captain Samson appears, furtive and prone to panic, Clarence as the archetypal heavy, and Davy Jones, pale-eyed and watchful. As in his novels, they were drawn almost entirely through dialogue, one of the neatest being a vignette of his chauffeur:

Markham could not bear to disappoint anybody. On one occasion when the Sunbeam was occupied I sent down word that the Overland was to come round for me at once. Presently Markham arrived:

'You wanted the Overland at once, sir?'

'Yes, have you brought it round?'

'Yes, sir, at least no sir, not quite round.'

'It's all right isn't it?'

'Oh yes, sir. Oh yes, sir, yes, it's quite all *right*.'

'The new tyres are all right?'

'Oh yes, sir, the tyres are all right. The left front tyre is a bit wonkified. You know, sir, the outer cover's a bit ripped up. And the right front tyre, well the inner-tube I'm a bit afraid of. In fact it isn't really there at all in a way of speaking. It seemed to burst itself all up. But both back tyres are all right, except that the right hand one is perished a bit. But the car's quite all *right*.'

'You think you can drive me down to Phaleron in it?'

'To Phaleron, sir? Well perhaps not quite as far as that. In fact I think till the new tyres come the car had really better remain in the garage.'

'Then the new tyres aren't on?'

'No sir; well they haven't come yet.'

'In other words I can't have the Overland this afternoon.'

'No sir, that's right sir. Looking at it that way you really can't have it. Well sir, even with the new tyres she'll want a thorough good overhauling before she can go out again.'

Instantly recognisable and skilfully delineated, characters such as Markham could have come from his novels, and when he covered the same period in *The South Wind of Love* some of them did reappear. The dividing line between fact and fiction, rarely very wide in his serious writing, here dissolves to nothing. But without the memoirs it is difficult to imagine him grappling with *The Four Winds of Love*. The theme of the former is pre-war – the death of the old world – and with their writing he bade farewell to the dilemma faced by Michael, Guy, Sylvia, Mark and Maurice, of living morally in a hypocritical society. That society, for good or ill, was destroyed, and once he had described its death he could turn to the dilemma of dealing with the forces of mass control – bureaucracy, fascism and communism – that had arisen in its place.

The solution was one he had sensed in Greece, but found in Scotland. 'One of the aspirations of the individual human being is a background against which he will not be lost,' he wrote in *Athenian Memories*, and the perfect background, he suggested, was a small country. 'When a Briton, whatever his social status or personal ability, finds himself in a small country, he expands. His ability to grasp the whole of his environment enriches him as love enriches a man because in the act of becoming aware of his own importance to the loved object that loved object becomes infinitely more precious.'

It was of course a description of his own frame of mind. By the time he wrote it, Scotland had become the secure background he needed, and the knowledge that he was appreciated there had made his love for it greater still.

His first success had come with the result of the rectorial campaign for Cunninghame Graham in October 1928. He had spoken again on the eve of the poll and in such compelling mood that many students who had come to jeer at a kilted Englishman were caught despite themselves. Nevertheless it was confidently assumed that Stanley Baldwin, the Conservative candidate, would win convincingly with the Liberal, Lord Samuel, second, and the real race would be to get ahead of the Labour candidate, Rosslyn Mitchell. When Monty went to join Cunninghame Graham in the gloomy lounge of the Caledonian Hotel in Edinburgh, the best news he could bring was his conviction that they would beat Mitchell. The result when it came in a telegram sent his blue bonnet sailing through the air, narrowly missing an old lady's tea when it landed. Baldwin had indeed been elected with 1014 votes, but Cunninghame Graham was a mere sixty-six votes behind, and far ahead of both Liberal and Labour combined. Never before had nationalist sympathy been tested, but here, at the first opportunity, their candidate had come close to toppling the Conservative leader. Suddenly it seemed as though nationalism must exist, like a huge artesian well beneath the crust of existing politics, waiting to be tapped. Together with MacCormick,

MacDiarmid and the other Nationalist leaders, Monty and Cunninghame Graham addressed a succession of packed meetings in the week following the Glasgow rectorship at which the pressure of expectation appeared powerful enough to move political mountains. In an atmosphere of euphoria the party decided that it would contest parliamentary by-elections at every opportunity.

Although Monty himself had argued that the political campaign must take precedence over all else, he soon began to suspect that they had overestimated the strength of feeling in the country. He turned down invitations to stand as Nationalist candidate for several constituencies, and having seen the first flush of enthusiasm dissipated by Lewis Spence's ill-organised campaign in the North Midlothian by-election early in 1929, he drew away from the parliamentary ambitions of the party. By a familiar pattern of reasoning, the would-be candidates were beginning to argue for a moderation of demands for complete independence in order to widen the party's appeal. He himself wanted to maintain the union of the Crown, but rejected anything less than an independent parliament with tax-raising powers. But it was the idea, not the politics of independence which most concerned him, and in the summer of 1929 he and Christopher Grieve, together with Ruaraidh Erskine, began to explore a more perilous course, with the formation of a secret organisation called Clann Albain, or Scotland's children.

The aim of Clann Albain was to raise the consciousness of the Scots voters by undertaking politically sensitive and illegal acts. The choice of target and the method of recruiting members exercised a good deal of discussion, and long before they had decided on either, the constitutionalists got wind of what was happening. With Lewis Spence and John MacCormick on one side and Grieve on the other, the quarrel soon spilled into the press. There were rumours that the Clann proposed to seize the island of Rum or occupy Edinburgh Castle or, most strongly of all, seize the Stone of Destiny from Westminster Abbey. And there was fevered speculation about the identity of its organisers. Grieve fanned the mystery by telling the *Daily Record* that 'one of the most distinguished of living Scotsmen is the chief of Clann Albain'. By that time – the summer of 1930 – the Special Branch was interested, and Monty was interviewed by a senior police officer. His denial of any conspiracy was accepted, and indeed the Clann never had got beyond the stage of discussion. However, his name remained on the files.

The disputes did not slow the party's growth. By 1931 it had 8000 paid-up members, and after a string of failures it at last managed to save its deposit at a by-election. So great were the demands for Monty's services as a speaker that it became impossible for him to remain living in Jethou.

Ever since the nationalist conference, he had been looking for a house in Scotland, and characteristically had set his heart on buying Flodigarry on Skye, the home of Flora Macdonald. Unfortunately he was asked an impossible price, but in April 1930 his disappointment was softened by the offer of an even more romantic home.

At the Station Hotel, Inverness, which is to the Highlands what the Café de la Paix is to Paris, he encountered Lady Lovat and her children, Magdalen, Hugh and Veronica Fraser. Monty had been at Oxford with her brother, and since the Lovats were one of the great Catholic families of Scotland they had mutual friends in Ronald Knox and Maurice Baring. He went to stay with the Lovats at Beaufort Castle, close to Inverness, and his friendship with Laura Lovat was made firmer by a shared preference for the past, for Medici prints and Morris wallpaper, for gardens and reminiscence. In a way which he never remembered without affection, he was drawn into the family and an extensive network of Fraser and Constable-Maxwell relations. With the ten-year-old Veronica in particular he struck up an immediate intimacy which he treasured for the rest of his life.

The Lovats had a house called Eilean Aigas, built on an island in the river Beauly. Its first inhabitants had been the Sobieski Stuarts, two Polish brothers who convinced themselves and half Scotland that they were Prince Charles Edward Stuart's grandsons. As an alternative to Flora Macdonald they were just adequate, but Eilean Aigas's setting had a beauty which far outdid Flodigarry.

From a narrow white bridge which spanned the tumbling rapids of the river, a drive curved upwards to a bulky mid-Victorian house. It had ten bedrooms and some hideous furniture made by the Sobieskis themselves, and other than the drawing room, which Laura Lovat had decorated, it was not handsome. But Monty had chosen the island rather than the building.

'The island was incredibly, wildly romantic,' Faith recalled in *More Than I Should*:

On the north side rugged purple and grey cliffs flanked the narrow, turbulent river, small pine trees hung at all angles over the water from rock crevices. Walking against the stream up on the grassy path of the cliff, you suddenly went downhill and came upon the same river tranquil as a pool, on fine days reflecting the trees above it as though in a looking-glass. Now you were on a level with it, and a broad track shaded by oaks and larches went parallel with the tranquil stream until the round of the island had been completed; the river went mad again and rushed under the white bridge, and you would return through dense rhododendron walks up to the house.

Eilean Aigas was not available until December 1930, and Faith, driving up with Chrissie, was the first to arrive. For the time being at least, she too was going to leave Jethou in order to live at Eilean Aigas. Then came Nelly Boyte, the gardener and carpenter, and finally Monty. He felt a deserter to be abandoning Jethou and its garden – the best he had created since Cornwall – but in truth his imagination had never come to rest there.

The romance of his new home exacted a stiff price. It was far more expensive than Jethou to run. The rent was £450 a year, and for seven months out of twelve fires and boilers had to be kept burning constantly to heat the enormous rooms to a temperature which would not induce rheumatic pains in his legs. The list of servants was lengthened again by the addition of a chauffeur and two maids, and a stream of nationalist politicians, competitors at the Mod and passing friends arrived for meals and entertainment. 'The kitchen boiler burst,' Faith wrote in her diary of a not wholly untypical day, 'and the Provost of Inverness, wife and daughter came to lunch. Nerve-racking combination for everyone. M in bed with pains.'

His income was now a shadow of Herm days. His guarantee of £6000 a year from Pinker had had to be cut in half in 1926, so sharply had his sales fallen, and the move to Scotland which rendered him liable to income tax reduced it effectively by another 20 per cent. He was still earning an advance of £1500 for each novel from Cassell's, but they would only pay £500 for each of his memoirs and there were no American sales. In addition he had lost money with the failure of a new magazine, called *Vox*, which had been launched in November 1929, with Mac-Diarmid as its editor, to do for the wireless what the *Gramophone* was doing for records. However, in the aftermath of the stock market crash the wireless manufacturers refused to advertise and the magazine folded after three months. By the end of 1930 his overdraft stood at £8000 (about £90,000 in present-day terms), and he was forced to promise that it would be reduced by £1000 a year. The need for money made the literary treadmill spin faster. In addition to one volume of memoirs, he was also trying to write two novels a year, his column for the *Sunday Pictorial* (until it ended in March 1932), and his editorials for the *Gramophone*. In August 1931 he also wrote a play for the BBC called

The Lost Cause, about Prince Charles Edward Stuart, and a month later accepted an invitation to become book critic for the *Daily Mail* at £1500 a year. Like the Red Queen he was running faster and faster to stay in the same spot, but unlike her his best pace could not prevent him from slipping slowly backwards. That summer he seemed to gain a breathing-space when a would-be purchaser offered £3000 for the Jethou lease, and paid 10 per cent as a deposit, but after four months' delay the Treasury decided he was an unsuitable tenant, leaving Monty worse off than ever, since by then he had spent the deposit. The *Daily Mail* contract necessitated reading a book a day and writing a weekly column, which was more than he could properly cope with, and a crescendo of illness and pain forced him to defer his third volume of memoirs, *Greek Memories*, until the spring of 1932. By the time he began it his overdraft had reached £9000.

Next to prolonged illness nothing is more likely to sap the spirit than chronic financial worries, and there was something truly heroic in Monty's response to both. When his record reviewing for the *Sunday Pictorial* came to an end he bought himself a billiard table. He celebrated the Jethou disappointment by buying Faith a car. With less time than ever he still made forays all over Scotland to speak for the Nationalists, and when John MacCormick asked him to stand as candidate for the rectorship of Glasgow University in 1931 he agreed with scarcely a hesitation. At the Lovats' parties he entertained the adults with stories which always worked and the children with conjuring tricks which never did. Ronald Knox, who saw much of him that year at Beaufort Castle, wrote of him in a testimonial for the rectorial contest that 'he remains so young, the sort of man professors shake their heads over. In point of years he is, I am glad to say, my senior, but what a difference in essential youthfulness. I have found myself before now almost patting him on the head.' It was an apt comment, for only essential youthfulness could have persuaded a man in such straits to let his name go forward for the rectorship, and to promise that unlike his predecessors he would be a working rector attending the monthly sittings of the university to represent the students' interests.

Since candidates did not speak on their own behalf, it was John MacCormick who put his case and organised his campaign. There was an obvious risk in trying to match Cunninghame Graham's feat three years earlier, and he faced strong competition for the non-Tory vote from Gilbert Murray for the Liberals, Tom Johnston for Labour and Sir Oswald Mosley for the New Party. The contest aroused unusually widespread interest, and most newspapers took the opportunity to offer their own advice to the students, usually suggesting circumspectly what the *Inverness Courier* put stridently:

Who are Mr MacCormick and Mr Compton Mackenzie or any leading light in their trumpery party that Scotland should trust them and place her destiny blindly in their hands? The first-named, a callow inexperienced youth of twenty-odd years with only 'a gift of the gab' to recommend him, the second, a writer of English novels of a not particularly elevating kind who, after a lifetime spent in England has taken it upon himself to shed the light of his presence upon Scotland, and instruct us poor ignorant Scots what we ought to do and how we ought to do it . . . They have vapoured and pranced and postured, but have they done anything of the slightest practical value for the country or the people whom they aspire to instruct?

The answer came on 24 October, when it was revealed that Mr Compton Mackenzie had been elected Lord Rector of Glasgow University with 849 votes, eighty-seven votes ahead of the Conservative Sir Robert Horne, with the Liberal, Labour and New Party candidates trailing well behind. It was a heady triumph for the Nationalists, their first electoral victory of any consequence, and in an emotional scene Monty's arrival in Glasgow was greeted by a throng of supporters singing 'Scots Wha Hae'. It was also a moment of personal glory for Monty.

'I am the first Catholic Rector to be elected since the Reformation,' he proudly told his mother, 'and the first literary man since Macaulay, but he was a politician as well. Even Sir Walter Scott was defeated twice.' His predecessors included Baldwin, Poincaré, Asquith, Balfour, Disraeli, Gladstone and Edmund Burke – 'a long line to live up to'.

Telegrams and letters of congratulation showered upon him, and two from his English past especially pleased him. Hugh Walpole wrote warmly expressing his delight in the success of 'the Old Firm. For we are the Old Firm, you know, bound together by nearly mutual scorn and hatred.' And twenty years after Sir Herbert Warren had expressed his wounding indifference to *Carnival*, his successor as President of Magdalen wrote, 'A College as such has no literary taste, and no organ for expressing it. It is therefore possible (I don't know), that previous triumphs of yours outside the academic world have drawn no voice from Magdalen. But we all understand being elected Lord Rector.'

It was a famous victory, and in *The Orators*, written that year, W. H. Auden included a couplet which reflected the sense of excitement it aroused:

The people are stirring; in Scotland they say
That Compton Mackenzie will be king one day . . .

Monty promised the Vice-Chancellor that he would give his rectorial address on 29 January 1932, the centenary of Goethe's death. A week beforehand he was struck down by severe influenza, but dosed with pills of all kinds, including strychnine, he took his place on the platform. His sister Fay, who was appearing in pantomime in Glasgow, watched from the gallery and described the scene for her mother.

A lot of ceremonies took place – none of which I heard at all as the students were all shouting, talking, singing, whistling and cat-calling through it all . . . The next ceremony was changing Monty's scarlet robe to the black and gold robe of the Lord Rector. Bless his heart, he was dead white and obviously very nervous, which had the effect of making him look about twenty-five, and when he gave us his charming smile he looked about nineteen . . . It is a most remarkable tribute to him that during the long reading of his address, the students were practically silent – there were just a few harmless interruptions . . . There was such cheering and enthusiasm at the end of the address, and I felt tremendously proud and again very close to tears.

His speech was the distillation of everything he held most important, and he had agonised over its construction as though it were a novel. Nowhere else did he ever make so clear the roots and personal significance of his nationalist beliefs. In particular terms he demonstrated that Scottish nationalism was the natural outcome of a war which had been fought for the rights of small nations, and of the empire's declining power which, by stripping away the glamour of world dominion, showed that 'The empire might be British, but it was clear that Britain was England.'

However, nationalism as a philosophy was set in a wider context, and the centenary of Goethe's death – 'the last human being great enough to live with the world for his background' – gave him his theme. In those hundred years, material and scientific progress had widened the world immeasurably. It had flattened the boundaries of geography through travel and communication, diminished social barriers through popular education and entertainment, and extended the limits of life itself through medical and nutritional improvement. These were material gains, but they left the individual standing solitary in a vast, standardised landscape. 'Nationalism in its political aspect is essentially a reactionary theory of government,' he argued. 'It is the admission by the part of an inability to adjust itself to the whole . . . Nationalism is a demand by the soul of man to afford him leisure for the contemplation of his own destiny, to restore to him a richer personal life, and by narrowing his background to enable him to recover a measure of trust of his own significance in time and space.'

Against this lucid account of the alienation produced by technological advance, he set his own odyssey from a West Kensington childhood to the Lord Rectorship of Glasgow University. At the age of seven he had been given Scott's *Tales of a Grandfather* and found in it his own natural background:

Thence onwards I lived secretly in the past of my country: but because through the closing years of the nineteenth century and through the opening years of the twentieth, the future of which I was dreaming seemed as improbable as a Jacobite hope, I did what so many sons of Scotland were doing and abandoned myself to the pursuit of material success in that larger world which seemed to be submerging all the smaller nations.

He had nursed the dream privately, he said, until the day came when he found a sufficient number of Scots of like mind 'to give me the assurance that I was not an isolated eccentric. The vision of Scotland which as a boy I had beheld in *Tales of a Grandfather* was no longer a dream that faded when the book was closed: it was ever-present in the daily round of life.'

It is given to few adults to make real, however briefly, the ambitions of childhood dreaming. Monty may have romanticised the trail that brought him from the past to the present, but there is no doubt that his Scotland was first visualised in the inner world he created as a defence against the surrounding menace of Avonmore Road. More than any other, therefore, that hour in St Andrew's Hall, Glasgow, justified his adoption late in life of the epitaph 'Homo Felix'.

14

From dock to cockle beach

For weeks after his rectorial address Monty lay ill in bed. In chilly Eilean Aigas his influenza turned to bronchitis, which gave way to prolonged bouts of sciatic pain. The pain was accompanied by a loss of vitality, and the onset of depression. To add to his worry, his bank threatened to foreclose on his overdraft, and the Inland Revenue began an audit of his tax returns. Unable to cope, he agreed to let his financial affairs be managed by his new agent, Ralph Pinker, successor to his brother, Eric, but it did his morale no good to be told that spending £81 on shirts at Edouard & Butler was an extravagance he could no longer afford. It was in a low state of mind that he began work on *Greek Memories* in February 1932, wading through the three crates of documents he had shipped from Syra to Capri, and dictating to Chrissie.

His were not the only books to be written about the secret service in Greece. The first off the mark had been J. C. Lawson, the recalcitrant don in charge of intelligence on Crete, whose *Tales of Aegean Intelligence* was published in 1920. His reference to the arrival of the Z Bureau in Syra 'looking like a jaded theatrical company' and his suggestion that identifying armbands were routinely issued to its secret agents in Athens thus coloured subsequent accounts. His opinions were quoted by G. F. Abbott in *Greece and the Allies 1914–1922* in support of the argument that the Allied secret services were out of control and irresponsible, and by Prince Nicholas of Greece in *Political Memoirs 1914–17*, who added gratuitously, 'I have personally heard many Englishmen in Greece give a very sad narrative of the doings of the British Section of the Secret Police.' In Beverley Nichols's brash autobiography *25*, Greek royalists were quoted as saying that 'Compton Mackenzie was the evil genius of Greece during the war,' and the same sources claimed that he had twice tried to assassinate King Constantine, once by putting arsenic in his medicine and again by starting a heath-fire round his country residence. Finally in 1931 Sir Basil Thomson, self-styled Director of Intelligence (approximately head of the Special Branch at Scotland Yard) from 1919 to 1921, produced a book called *The Allied Secret Service in Greece*. From its virulently anti-Venizelist line, Monty correctly surmised that it was financed by the Greek royal family. Here too there were references to 'the vaudeville antics of the British secret service' but they were subsidiary to the central thesis that King Constantine was an immensely popular monarch brought down by the machinations of Venizelos and the French.

To Monty's fury, Thomson's book was frequently compared with *Athenian Memories*, and one reviewer concluded, 'Again and again these two authors are thus ranged against one another, and it must be said for Sir Basil that his facts are documented and not mere expressions of opinion.' Nothing could have been better calculated to encourage the use of Monty's secret service papers, and the course of Greek politics since the war gave a defence of Venizelos added urgency.

In 1920 the Venizelist dream of a Greater Greece had led to a disastrous occupation of Smyrna on the Turkish mainland. Two years later the Turks drove out both the invaders and about a million Greeks who had been domiciled in Asia Minor for generations, and the resultant turmoil continued to disrupt the country's fragile democracy up to the time that he was writing. The one factor that might have given him pause for thought was a letter he received in 1931 from Eric Holt-Wilson of MI5, who had checked out the Z Bureau during the war.

'Dear Mackenzie,' he wrote, 'I have just read with great interest your *Athenian Memories* and much enjoyed your vivid picture of those days.' Having reminded Monty of his services in the past, he continued, 'If you are writing up any further Athenian Memories and would care for any facts and dates to be checked on matters outside Greece, I have old records here and should be only too glad to read any of your MSS for you.' Discreetly camouflaged though it was, the letter was evidently fishing for information, and had Monty's intelligence instincts been at wartime sharpness he might have taken heed. As it was, he thanked Holt-Wilson for his offer of help, but said that he had all the documents he required.

In order to demonstrate the effectiveness of the Z Bureau and the soundness of Venizelos's cause, he was prepared to sacrifice the easy-mannered style of the first two memoirs. There was at least one page of documentation for five of memory; he named agents, quoted memoranda and described administrative structures. 'It is a genuinely important historical contribution,' he told Newman Flower, his editor at Cassell's, 'and three-quarters of the book is taken up with facts which have never been published.'

In its original form *Greek Memories* does in fact offer a better insight into the mechanics of running an intelligence station than any other published source until the spate of books in the 1970s about the CIA's operations. Much of it is concerned with the wearisome business of filing information, decoding telegrams and fighting rival departments such as MI2. But there are also fascinating insights into the use of misinformation, the maintenance of a Black List and, in the appendix, on the use of visa applications to gain information on suspects.

There was nothing subversive in revealing this. Experts such as Admiral Hall had already declared that the secrets of the 1914–18 war would have lost all value after twenty years, and Monty himself had expressed in *Extremes Meet* his own opinion that 'Nowadays, with wireless and aeroplanes, this kind of espionage was superfluous.' The substitution of electronic surveillance and spy satellites only underlines the continuing good sense of that opinion.

As the evidence of his wartime achievements mounted, his spirits also began to rise, and soon he was boasting of having dictated 5000 words a day. There was another surprising result. The block that had descended on his grand design for depicting the theatre of youth and age gradually disappeared. The first sign came in a letter to Christopher Stone in April, when he suddenly declared, 'I am filled with ideas for books, I never felt so full of creative desire.' Then a month later he had the name of the book he was thinking of, *The Four Winds of Love*. On 3 July he wrote to tell Newman Flower that *Greek Memories* was finished and that *The Four Winds of Love* would be about 200,000 words long, 'and will consist of four love stories, and four philosophies of life, and four decades of a man's life'. The number was different, but the writing was to show that it was substantially the same as *Our Seven Selves* which in turn was recognisably *The Labyrinth*.

Despite the return of creativity and with it his optimism about the future, Eilean Aigas was losing its appeal. To the problems of draughts and expense was added the collapse of the bedroom ceiling on top of him while he lay asleep, but more serious than the physical shortcomings were the emotional tensions within the house. It had been a strange ménage from the start with Monty surrounded by three women all dependent on him in different ways.

When they first arrived Faith had just completed her biography of Queen Christina of Sweden, called *The Sibyl of the North*, and was awaiting publication of her short stories, *Mandolinata*. Both were well received, but she found it impossible to turn her mind to a new subject, a failing which Monty found impossible to comprehend. She played the piano with Laura Lovat, and drove for miles to explore the Highlands, but never shared Monty's romantic attachment to them. In company she remained forceful and witty, and Colin Summerford, her editor at Cope and Fenwick, publishers of *Mandolinata*, and her close friend for much of the rest of her life, sometimes suspected Monty of being jealous of her social success. At Eilean Aigas, however, the mixture of tweedy landowners and Nationalist politicians bored her to distraction. 'Merciful heavens, what a deliverance!' she exclaimed after missing an influx of Inverness-shire gentry.

The strength of her continuing attachment to Monty was painfully apparent. Moving to the Highlands had meant abandoning the garden at Jethou for which she had developed a passion. When she returned to it in 1933 after three years of neglect, she was almost overcome by what had happened in her absence.

'Here was beauty gone mad most gloriously,' she wrote in *More Than I Should*:

Free for nearly three years from all restraint, climbing roses had scaled the heights, clinging to windscreens and each other, a mass of crimson, white and gold. Clematis of all kinds swept up in a tangle . . . The ground was a carpet of tulips: *iris Germanica* in every possible variety of heavenly shape and colour. The acacias in the sunk garden, now big trees, filled the air with the scent of their yellow bobbles . . . all, all in full bloom. Dear God! This was a garden in a dream.

She had given up the *Gramophone* as she had given up the garden, and although she was beginning to work on another biography, this time of Marie Mancini, published as *The Cardinal's Niece*, her single point of interest was in effect her husband. From him she was once more increasingly excluded.

He and Chrissie had become lovers in 1929, and soon she was his companion, his housekeeper and his wife in all but name. His more sophisticated friends were surprised that he should be content with someone who had so direct and simple a nature, but in Chrissie's youth and devotion he found everything he wanted. 'The older I get,' remarked John Ogilvie, having fallen in love with a girl half his age, 'the more convinced I am that men with brains are happier with wives who express for them essential womanhood.' It was to her that he talked of his worries, and from her that he received the maternal care he was accustomed to.

It was not an easy position for Chrissie. Faith had a snobbish streak and never disguised her feelings of social superiority. She was equally sensitive to slights upon her status as wife. In her presence the fiction had to be maintained that Chrissie was an employee; her employer was always referred to as 'Mr Mackenzie', and Faith was assumed to run the household.

Chrissie's arrival upset the faithful Nelly Boyte who on Herm and Jethou had had Monty to herself as secretary. Now she was relegated from taking dictation to typing, and Faith, formerly so irritated by her silent adoration, had to act as her comforter. The role added to her own tension. At times the steady drone of his voice dictating letters, book reviews and war memoirs was more than she could stand. She had screaming fits, stomach pains and attacks of giddiness. A doctor diagnosed an enlarged liver, but perhaps it was also loneliness.

'I find that whenever she stays any length of time with me, especially when I am working under pressure, she does become melancholic,' Monty wrote to Christopher in April. 'Of course were she able to run a house or even be interested in the running of a house she would be occupied, but she knows she cannot do this.' The solution, he suggested, was to involve her again in the running of the *Gramophone*. 'Everything depends on you,' he insisted. 'If you can persuade her that she is very useful, it will be a tremendous thing for her.' Christopher agreed reluctantly. Her inability to meet deadlines for copy and her quickness to quarrel with other members of the staff made her a difficult colleague, however much he loved her as a sister.

A flat was found for her in London, and since Christopher was increasingly occupied with broadcasting she was able to take over some of his work as London editor, but it was an uneasy arrangement.

Monty's financial troubles made it essential to let Eilean Aigas for the summer, and he took the opportunity to go with Chrissie to Barra. He arranged to rent a bungalow from Ruaraidh MacNeil, known as the Crookle, and promised Pinker that he could live there for no more than thirty shillings a week. It was not the sort of promise he could keep, but for a time he was free from the burden of Eilean Aigas. The surrender of two insurance policies brought his overdraft down to acceptable limits, and with destitution temporarily staved off he could afford to enjoy Barra.

While he was there he completed a short biography, *Bonnie Prince Charlie*, which was remarkable for the intemperance of his language attacking the Duke of Cumberland and any Highland chief who did not come out for the prince. However, the visit's chief significance was the contrast it offered to the mansion of the Sobieski Stuarts.

He had been there before, in the summer of 1929, when he made a pilgrimage to Eriskay, the tiny island between Barra and South Uist where Prince Charles Edward Stuart first set foot in Scotland in 1745. Even then he had conferred his stamp of approval by acquiring a dwelling – a one-roomed coastguard's hut which he bought for £60. He returned the next summer with Faith and later went on to see St Kilda shortly before its evacuation. Both these had been fleeting visits, although he had as his guide Father John Macmillan, the vast, untidy priest whose Gaelic scholarship and rumbustious character made him known far beyond his parish of Northbay. Through him, Monty met the leading personalities of Northbay, and especially John Macpherson, known as the Coddie, the schoolmaster Neil Sinclair, called the Sgoileir Ruadh – the Red Scholar – for the colour of his hair, and Ruairidh MacNeil, known as the Crookle in whose house he now stayed.

Barra was unlike the rest of the Highlands – in the phrase that Father John Macmillan liked to use, 'A ring of gold has been set round Barra.' The most southerly of the Outer Hebrides, it was both Catholic and classless: the Reformation which had swept down through Lewis and into North Uist had gradually petered out in South Uist, and left Barra untouched; and its hereditary owners, the MacNeils of Barra, had long since gone. Although only about nine miles long and four across, it supported a thriving community of some 2250 people, of whom about 400 were schoolchildren, and so, unlike most of the Highlands which were made old as well as empty by emigration, it retained the Gaelic culture intact. It lacked the grandeur of Eilean Aigas, but it contained the essence of that Jacobite Scotland which he hoped independence might create.

'Barra is a great success,' he wrote to his mother that August. 'Everybody thinks I look a different person since I arrived here.' His delight in the island was summed up by the week in which the three Lovat children, including his beloved Veronica, came to stay. All of them were packed into the cottage, and the chaos and laughter was still fresh in his mind thirty-five years later. 'It was only a week, but in memory that week seems like a month of delight.' By the time he left at the end of August, his imagination had found its new background, and it was only a matter of time before he went to live there.

Both before and after this visit he threw himself again into the National-ist campaign. At Aberdeen he spoke for an hour and a quarter, and at the annual commemoration of the Battle of Bannockburn in June he joined Cunninghame Graham on the platform and made a speech of such inspiring intensity that a party of young Nationalists led by Wendy Wood invaded Stirling Castle and having pushed the sentries aside hauled down the Union Jack. His staunch approval of her action set him further apart from the constitutionalists in the party, and later that year he ranged himself equally firmly against the growing pressure to call merely for a measure of devolution rather than outright independence.

His position as rector and the power of his oratory made him the party's most influential figure, particularly among its activists. Yet it was a narrow base. John MacCormick was manoeuvring the National Party towards a moderate stance which would appeal to the newly-formed Scottish Party composed primarily of former Conservatives looking for a form of Dominion status. In July 1933 there was a purge of those calling for full independence and Monty was powerless to prevent it. He had neither the time nor the temperament for committees and the formulation of policy, and his tortured explanation of Douglas's social credit scheme did not sound convincing even to Faith. 'But darling,' she protested at length, 'you don't understand it yourself.'

There was another limitation, which was less easily defined, but was widely shared. According to Robin MacEwen, son of Sir Alexander, a leader of the Scottish Party, 'Many people had reservations about him personally. Considering that he hadn't lived up here his breadth of knowledge about the Highlands was amazing, but there were always doubts about the extent to which he really had put down roots here.'

Any incomer would have aroused such doubts, but in Monty's case it was noticeable how frequently he referred, as in the rectorial address, to Scotland as his 'natural background' rather than the more permanent-sounding 'home'. Nevertheless, while Nationalism remained predominantly a movement rather than a political party, ideas were more important than politics, and the large meetings he addressed cheered him to the echo.

Individuals were less responsive. Lady Londonderry, then at the height of her influence as a political hostess, arranged a meeting with Ramsay MacDonald in October. At the Spean Bridge Hotel in Inverness-shire, Monty spent twenty minutes trying to breathe life into the prime minister's former commitment to home rule, but at the end MacDonald was concerned more with the opinion of Lady Londonderry – 'Tell her we've had this talk,' he said in parting, 'and I shall get a good mark.' A few days later the Duke and Duchess of York, soon to be George VI and Queen Elizabeth, came to receive honorary degrees at Glasgow University, and Monty took the opportunity of passing on another of his ideas to the Duchess: 'It would be wonderful, ma'am,' he suggested, 'if Princess Margaret Rose could be educated in Scotland, learn Gaelic and become one day Princess of Scotland, with Holyrood House brought to life again.' 'Very interesting,' said the Duchess unenthusiastically. He had no better luck with Eamon de Valera when he went to Ireland early in November. Monty tried to interest him in an economic union between Ireland and an independent Scotland. In his coldest schoolmasterly manner, de Valera discounted the possibility that Scotland could ever be independent, or that any exchange between the two countries could possibly be to Ireland's benefit. 'What about an exchange of Scots settlers in Ulster for Irish immigrants in Glasgow?' Monty countered angrily and took his leave.

The trip to Dublin was intended to be only one stop in a long itinerary, which had begun in July with the visit to Barra. There had been a summer of Nationalist campaigning, and then in September he joined two friends from the BBC – Moray McLaren, a producer, and David Cleghorn Thompson, Director of Broadcasting in Scotland – on a cultural visit to Poland. Since he and McLaren shared the belief that an early night was a night wasted, the ostensible purpose of their journey was sometimes blurred, but from Cracow he carried away one memory of supreme importance. From the tower of St Mary's Church, the hours were sounded by a clock trumpeter, the last note of whose call ended waveringly. It commemorated the thirteenth-century watchman who had blown a warning of the approach of the Tartars, but was killed by an arrow in the throat as he sounded the alarm. The repetition of that defiant, dying call through the centuries caught his imagination so forcibly that in *The Four Winds of Love* it came to symbolise the attempt of John Ogilvie to raise the alarm against the forces of barbarism in the modern world. It was that large-scale work which he intended to begin after he returned to Eilean Aigas from Dublin.

On 27 October 1933 *Greek Memories* was published and received mixed reviews, dullness being the principal complaint. The first warning that more serious exception might be taken was given by the ominous sight of a stuffed peacock at the Students' International Club in Glasgow where Monty was addressing a meeting. That same evening word came from London that Cassell's had withdrawn the book on advice from the authorities, and finally on 4 November it was announced that he would be prosecuted under Part Two of the Official Secrets Act, which covers the unauthorised communication of secret information.

By that time he was in Dublin, officially to address the Historical Society of Trinity College, whose secretary was the precocious Terence de Vere White, unofficially to enjoy himself in congenial company. He was staying, as usual, with the publisher William Nolan and resumed with pleasure his affair, begun eight years earlier, with Hilda Nolan.

'I didn't know that you smoked cigarettes,' de Vere White remarked, seeing Monty slide a silver cigarette case into the pocket of his grey velvet suit just before Mrs Nolan arrived to fetch him in the car.

'I don't,' Monty replied, 'but Hilda gave it to me, and you know women, Terence, they like to see that you remember.' The news from London put an end to dalliance. The charge itself was sufficient to catch the interest of the newspapers, but Monty's fame as a writer, newspaper columnist, broadcaster and nationalist leader made it a front-page sensation. The Nolans' home was bombarded with telephone calls from journalists demanding information and from Irish deputies offering asylum. At first the drama of his situation rather appealed to him. 'The authorities will probably try to make mine a leading case,' he assured anxious friends. 'I shouldn't be surprised if I get fifteen or twenty years.' In the same mood he told Pinker that he intended to arrive in London on the appropriate date of Guy Fawkes' Day.

Even during the committal proceedings at the Guildhall later in the month he found it difficult to adopt the proper attitude. He was delighted that one of the hearings should be in the court which Dickens used in *The Pickwick Papers* as the setting for Bardell versus Pickwick, and when he was sent for trial at the Old Bailey to be prosecuted by the Attorney-General, Sir Thomas Inskip, in person, he confessed to feeling 'rather tickled by the prospect'. At the request of his solicitor he tried to take a more sober view, and in a defence document set down the weaknesses of the government's case.

There were three specific charges against him: communicating Mansfield Cumming's name and the military initials, MI1 (C), (after the case they were changed to MI6, and for consistency these are used hereafter); giving the names of sixteen agents still employed or likely to be employed by MI6; and, finally, revealing that passport control was used as a cover for espionage. To the first of these he pointed out that Cumming's name and initials had already been published in the *War List*, an official publication, and in the memoirs of a French admiral. Of the allegedly compromised agents, he showed that most had left the service at least ten years before, including his old friend Pirie-Gordon, and that some of their names had already appeared in previous volumes of his memoirs. Of the remainder, Wace of the British School of Archaeology had never been an agent, Clarence's employment as an agent was an open joke in Athens, and Arthur Whittal, who actually was still a spy, 'will testify that his job as Passport Control Officer in Constantinople has not been hampered'. To the third charge of having revealed the use of passport offices as covers for spying, he argued that if this were really important there would have been ample opportunity for the authorities to intervene before publication since the contents of the book had been widely advertised and review copies were readily available; their failure to act, he suggested, 'argues either culpable negligence or a deliberate sacrifice of the secret service for the sake of personal vendetta'.

The significance of a vendetta lay in the relationship between MI5, who had prepared the case against him, and his former employers. Because MI5's responsibilities included policing all the intelligence agencies at home – they sometimes called themselves the constabulary of the War Department – to ensure their security was not compromised by foreign agents, there was ample scope for friction with MI6, and their differing fortunes since the war had multiplied friction to intolerable levels.

Thanks to Mansfield Cumming, MI6 had flourished. By an astute stroke of inter-departmental politics, he accepted an admiral as his successor, and in exchange gobbled up Blinker Hall's Department of Naval Intelligence. At the same time Bolshevik propaganda, which made a habit of holding the British secret service responsible for all Russia's problems, had boosted their reputation abroad to bogeyman proportions.

The fortunes of MI5 on the other hand were on the decline. Vernon Kell, by now a major-general, was still in charge. He had founded it in 1909 and, rather as J. Edgar Hoover was to do with the FBI, had in the course of time succumbed to the delusion that he was the organisation. Subordinates were hampered by over-regulation and by Kell's obsessive concern for secrecy, which was approaching paranoid dimensions. The only colleague he trusted fully was Eric Holt-Wilson, his right-hand man for almost twenty years.

The ineptitude with which MI5 presented the case at the committal proceedings, when the judge nearly declined to send him for trial at all, persuaded Monty that he could win at the Old Bailey by showing that no harm had been done to the security of the nation, and that the charge was actuated by malice. Yet this too was not the right attitude. As his counsel, Sir Henry Curtis-Bennett, explained, victory was not possible. 'The judge will tell the jury that it is not their business to say whether any harm was done by your book, but merely to say whether or not you had used information in it which you could only have obtained in the position you occupied officially.' It would be impossible to make any public protest about the unfairness of the charge because the trial would be held in camera. Besides, Sir Henry added, he had already fixed it with the Attorney-General that he would plead guilty, in return for which the Attorney-General had fixed it with the judge that he would only be fined £500 with £500 costs.

In those days Official Secrets cases were still sufficiently rare for Monty to be genuinely shocked by the revelation of collusion between the judiciary and the executive. It was this more than anything else which persuaded him that he had no chance of winning the case. As the reality sank in he wrote to Chrissie, who had remained in Eilean Aigas, 'Dearest Child, Just a line to say a bargain has practically been made and that if we don't fight, the government will not press the case, which means a fine of about £1000 but not prison.'

From her he now heard how the Coddie had written saying that 'early this morning I was in church kneeling before twelve lit candles, praying hard that God would keep him against his enemies who are very numerous', and that the Crookle had also assured her that 'there has been plenty of praying which I am sure, and I also hope in God, that he will come off top.' In those days between the committal proceedings and the trial, Barra bound itself to him more tightly than ever.

Down in London he stayed with Faith at her flat in Drymen Chambers, presenting a picture of marital orthodoxy, and it was with her at his side that he went to the Old Bailey on 12 December 1933.

'My first emotion was one of surprise at the size of the dock,' he wrote in his autobiography:

I had always fancied the dock as a cramped enclosure with just enough room to hold the accused and a couple of warders; the dock at the Old Bailey was large enough for a dozen couples to dance in it without too much of a squash ... I am not self-conscious or I might have been embarrassed by the eyes all over the Court that stared at me. Yet self-conscious or not, it undoubtedly is a bit of an ordeal five days away from one's fiftieth birthday to stand in the dock of the Old Bailey.

As Curtis-Bennett had arranged, Monty pleaded guilty to the charge. Although the result of the trial had been fixed, Inskip then proceeded to make the prosecution case, and in doing so provided the prisoner with one of his most satisfying stories. As the Attorney-General was attempting to show the danger of revealing Mansfield Cumming's name, the judge interrupted to ask how long it was since Cumming had died. Inskip was floored. The judge asked the barristers, but none of them knew. He then asked Major-General Kell who was sitting in the gallery with Holt-Wilson and other MI5 chiefs, all of them, Monty noticed, wearing long black coats. To be addressed by name, even while the court was in camera, made the security-conscious Kell squirm, but he too was at a loss. It was left to Monty to provide the information from the dock:

'My lord, with great respect, the officer in question died in June or July 1922.'

'Thank you.' And then with what Cockneys call a perishing look, the Judge eyed the rooks in the gallery. 'I *accept* that.'

I had an impression from the Judge's tone of voice that at this moment he was feeling that he and the accused were the only sane people in Court.

Monty called two character witnesses, Admiral Bill Sells, formerly the Naval Attaché in Athens, and Sir Ian Hamilton who, by an agreeable chance, had just been elected rector of Edinburgh University. To his bewilderment, each was asked whether he thought Monty was loyal to King George V. At the end of it all he was fined only £100 with £100 costs, a reduction, he thought, due rather to Inskip's prosecution than to Curtis-Bennett's defence.

The attitude of the press was sympathetic, most believing with *The Times* that his case 'is a warning to those with more important secrets', meaning Winston Churchill and Lloyd George, who were thought to be planning memoirs with the help of Cabinet papers. This may well have been a factor, and Churchill later told Monty he had indeed destroyed many papers at the time of the trial, but the real motive for his prosecution was more startling.

Faced with legal costs of over £1100, and the requirement to reimburse Cassell's for his £500 advance and £900 of publishing costs, Monty tried first to discover whether the book could be issued with cuts. MI5 replied that the existence of uncut copies would make it obvious to a foreign power which parts were sensitive, and in consequence the book would never be allowed to be published. Still thinking he must be simply the victim of a vendetta, he turned to those immediately affected by the revelations of the book, MI6 and their paymaster, the Foreign Office. On his behalf Lord Lovat approached Sir Robert Vansittart, Permanent Under-Secretary at the Foreign Office, and Sir Stewart Menzies, who had taken over from Admiral Sir Hugh Sinclair, Cumming's successor, as head of MI6. His conversations suggested that the prosecution originated not with MI5 but with a relatively junior figure in one of those organisations. Writing to Monty, Laura Lovat reported that 'Both [Vansittart] and [Menzies] agree that you have been made the scapegoat of their Depts. and are sympathetic but late.' Menzies, she added, 'seemed genuinely shocked at such "dirty work",' while Vansittart, rather more helpfully, promised to try to track down the person responsible.

When it seemed that some minor functionary was the instigator, there were moves to ask questions in Parliament, but the solution to the mystery stopped everyone in his tracks. The trail uncovered by Vansittart's enquiries led from the Foreign Office down the Mall to Buckingham Palace. Precisely what Vansittart was able to tell Lovat is unknown. All that Monty revealed was that 'Those who moved in the matter of *Greek Memories* had secured the approval of King George [V] before they took action.'

The King's interest in the matter dated back to the visit by Prince Andrew of Greece in 1916 to complain of Monty's anti-royalist activities. *Greek Memories* covered that very period, and it seems probable that either the Greek royal family or one of the pro-Constantine diplomats offended by Monty informed the King of its contents. If he did approve their suggestion that it be suppressed, it meant that the motive for prosecution came, not from any threat it posed to the security of the nation, but from the aspersions it cast upon the pro-German King Constantine. It was, as Menzies, Lovat, and almost everyone else admitted sooner or later, 'a very dirty business'.

The matter must have been conducted at a relatively junior level between the Royal Household and the Foreign Office and MI6 functionaries to whom it was first entrusted. Had there been any real threat to security, Menzies certainly, and Vansittart possibly, would have been informed. Only when it reached MI5 were senior officials involved, and had they not seen it as an opportunity to pay off old scores the case would have halted there. 'The Secret People [MI5] behaved disgustingly,' T. E. Lawrence wrote to Monty later that year. 'Two or three of us met the MI[6] chiefs and spoke our minds – and found that they resented the proceedings as much as anybody. To be "secret" for any sum of time ruins the nerves: Holt-Wilson deplores his own shadow now.'

To find oneself the victim of a frame-up involving the sovereign, the government, the security services and the judiciary would have taxed most people's sanity, but Monty had pictured the modern state as the enemy of the individual too often to be entirely unprepared. His response was to write a farce about the secret service, called *Water on the Brain* which, he declared in the preface, 'represents my own amusement at the end of it all. It is the friendliest archery: not a shaft has been barbed with malice or poisoned by vexation of spirit.'

At the heart of a tale which is as complex as an opera plot is the confusion caused by three different intelligence branches – roughly MI6, MI5, and the Special Branch – all sending agents for various reasons to the same hotel in the Highlands. Departmental rivalries and obsessive secrecy prevent them communicating with one another, and since each of their agents suspects the others of being either subversive nationalists or foreign spies, panic ensues. The comedy is rollicking rather than subtle, and it might be thought no truer to life than farce normally is. However the intelligence community found it a useful handbook. Kim Philby admitted that during the Second World War, while planning to use newspaper publicity against a network of German agents in Spain, 'My thoughts turned to General Westmacott, Director of Extraordinary Intelligence in Compton Mackenzie's *Water on the Brain*, and his dictum, "After all the whole point of the Secret Service is that it should be secret."' Apparently the dictum held good, for the German network was shamed into ineffectuality by stories which Philby fed the Spanish newspapers about its activities. In 1942 the Office of Strategic Studies, chrysalis of the CIA, made a hundred photocopies of the book which new recruits were required to read 'in the hope,' an OSS agent explained, 'that appropriate lessons would be learned by those who were smart enough to learn.' Even Monty, whom no folly of intelligence could surprise, confessed to disbelief at this story until another OSS operative confirmed it.

Even if it had been in his temperament to harbour a grievance, the threat of bankruptcy left him no time. Before the trial he had managed to reduce his overdraft to less than £3000 by realising two insurance policies. Now it had almost doubled to £5600, and he no longer had an insurance policy to act as collateral. At Pinker's insistence, and Monty never forgave him for it, he sold some of his most precious books and manuscripts – including the first volume of *Sinister Street* which Hugh Walpole bought and presented to King's School, Canterbury – and raised £370. He had to borrow £200 from the *Gramophone*, and the young novelist Eric Linklater, whom he had met the year before, lent him another £200. These sums were only enough to provide a breathing space, and from the moment the trial ended he was forced to return to the literary grind, abandoning his hopes of beginning *The Four Winds of Love*. Over the next eighteen months he wrote five books: *Water on* the Brain, Literature in My Time, The Darkening Green, Marathon and Salamis and Prince Charlie and his Ladies. In addition, he found time for his weekly Daily Mail articles, quarterly Gramophone editorials, occasional BBC talks, a two-month lecture tour in South America, and a weekly postbag of over fifty letters. He was punctilious about this last duty and could never understand authors who disregarded fan letters.

'My correspondence is a sign of my popularity,' he told his mother when she protested at the time spent answering it. 'No letters would mean people were not thinking of me.'

Such a furious pace would not have been possible without Barra. He moved there in May 1933, breaking unilaterally the lease on Eilean Aigas. Although Lord Lovat had agreed to let him withdraw from it, he had died in February before the agreement could be signed, and for two years – until another tenant was found – embarrassing letters arrived from the Lovat Estate demanding rent he could not afford to pay. From the Crookle he rented the cottage called 5 Ardveenish at Northbay for £3 a week, and his return was celebrated by what he called 'one of the supreme days of my life'.

On a sunny day in June six of them – Monty, the Coddie, the Crookle and the teachers from the three schools in the north of the island – sailed in the Coddie's boat to visit the uninhabited islands of Sandray, Mingulay, Pabbay and Berneray that necklace Barra. It was not only the beauty of the scene that caught him, but the talk that went with it. In his stories the Coddie displayed an uncanny gift for immediacy which made it seem that he had personally witnessed the events in his tale, whether they happened in myth or a century before. Thus, describing a good-looking forebear who had fought under Wellington, he remarked with assurance, 'I should say that he was the second most handsome man at the battle of Waterloo.' And John Johnston, or Sgoileir Ban, the fair-haired teacher from Greian, could summon up a picture of the sluagh, or fairy horde, who hauled him to safety when he slipped on the cliffs of Pabbay. It was he who took a pair of English ladies for a sail in his boat and, when asked how much the trip had cost, replied with a flourish, 'It will cost you nothing, ladies. I am an aristocrat of the democracy.'

In his autobiography Monty commented, 'And indeed that was one of the secrets of the joy life was to me on Barra, they were all aristocrats of the democracy.'

Within weeks of arriving there, the physical strain of his trial was beginning to fade. He was suntanned, relaxed and could write to his mother, 'No news here except of work and financial embarrassment, softened by being in a place that I love very much.'

His mother's replies, sent from the Theatre Girls' Club in Greek Street, were written in a hand which had become as spidery and nearly illegible as his own. The news they brought of the rest of her family was depressing: in the United States, his brother Frank's first marriage had broken up and he had no money to support his wife, but Monty's response was brusque: 'Peggy has ruined Frank's life and that's all there is to be said.' Viola had opened a theatre school, and Katie was touring with the Old Vic, but Fay was 'still not weaned from her love affairs' and painfully ignored her son Antony Pélissier. 'I don't think Antony has anyone to love him except me,' Virginia wrote. 'Fay has never loved him. My Mother never loved me (very likely mostly my own fault) and that fact gives me a deep, deep sympathy with any unloved child.'

The most harrowing news concerned Monty's favourite aunt, Isabel, who after being Mother Superior of the Wantage community of nuns for eleven years had suffered a nervous breakdown in 1931. Her condition had now developed into something like schizophrenia, and she was confined to a nursing home.

Ever since the Henry Irving episode, the two sisters had given each other unquestioning affection, but in her madness Isabel became hostile and suspicious even of Virginia. Then, at the time of Monty's prosecution, Virginia herself fell ill with pneumonia and almost died. She was now eighty and her recovery was slow. For much of 1933 she was confined to a wheelchair, but with her vitality and capacity for suffering on her sister's behalf undiminished. Isabel eventually died in June 1934, and at her death both stage and church paid tribute to the steadfastness of her character.

Virginia herself entered into an Indian summer in the last six years of her life, praying constantly for humility and a better temper, but remaining incorrigibly extravagant and pugnacious. She had many friends, but among her family it was Faith who loved her most deeply, since she alone could appreciate her fierce affection without being daunted by her dangerously uncertain temper. At Nottingham she heard Virginia say to an actress who was dancing around in delight at the dress she had been allocated for the play, 'That costume doesn't suit you at all, Mrs Kettle, your legs are much too fat.' When Faith suggested that this was a little cruel, Virginia replied, 'I was only trying to prepare her gently for her dismissal.'

After twelve years of poverty following the Nottingham disaster, she became in 1934 a trustee of a £10,000 trust fund raised for the Club, and without hesitation persuaded her fellow trustees, Lilian Baylis, Sybil Thorndike and Monty, that £1000 should be spent on forming a repertory company in Cheltenham to give the Theatre Girls employment.

'Repertory is the thing in the country now,' she announced. 'There are no tours, no companies that go about any more . . . I just want to say that I feel that [the money] is perfectly safe.' Then she added warningly, 'Of course I am a very bad businesswoman.' And indeed she was, because nine months later the company went bankrupt. 'Unfortunately you won't be able to get rid of me,' she told the Club's supporters, 'because I am here for life.' But nobody did want to get rid of her. More money could be raised, but she, indomitable in spirit and as sharp in sympathy as in tongue, was irreplaceable. 'Darling Mrs Compton,' wrote Lilian Baylis, 'Yours is a bit of work to thank God for, and having the right woman to carry on as you have to do is such a Blessing.'

As a mother, however, she remained equally difficult, overpowering in her affection and freezing in her disappointment. When she believed she was dying, in October 1932, she wrote to Monty tenderly:

I think you know you have been everything to me, ever since you came a tiny, little, shivering baby – so beautifully small. Well you have been a remarkable man and I ought to be (and I am) immensely proud of you, but I think my love for you is so great that there is no pride in it – if we are very very good, we are very very great and I don't think it matters about the other kind of greatness at all.

Nevertheless Monty was rarely at ease with her. His intended visits to her were often aborted by attacks of sciatica, and his weekly letters were stilted in tone, rarely straying from the subjects of work, illness and religious affairs such as the celebration of saints' days on Barra. In her company he remained a child equally defenceless against her expectation of perfection and her disappointment. In the spring of 1935, she suggested that he have the nineteen-year-old Antony Pélissier, Fay's son, to stay with him in Barra – 'You can help him greatly, he needs a wise, kind friend, a man who understands and sympathises' – and he agreed immediately, seeing himself in the role although he was still living in a small bungalow rented from the Crookle, and in the stress of working could only tolerate the most undemanding company.

The visit was a disaster. After a childhood marred by his mother's complete neglect, Antony wanted to talk about himself, rather than listen to Monty's reminiscences of his own golden youth. Their ten days together produced irritation, sermons and storms at the end of which his host sent him back south. Rather than accept realistically that Monty's temperament had never taken easily to competition, and was still less likely to do so under stress, Virginia piled on the agony. 'He was so delighted that you wanted him to come,' she wrote, 'and I was so happy with your first letter – it certainly has been a bitter disappointment. "Put not your trust in princes" etc. I was putting my trust in "Monty" – he would develop all the good, he would recognise and encourage all the good.'

All the Batemans, and Monty too, had a cold, stony look which entered their blue eyes when they felt let down, and it could be sensed in Virginia's letter to Monty.

To her dying day her judgemental temper made him nervous, but by a happy inspiration he managed at about this time to direct it to less vulnerable targets. He sent her Joseph Cowell's autobiography, and encouraged her to write down her memories of the Cowells, Batemans and Greppos. It is hard to believe that dissipation, disease and immorality were quite as rife among the Batemans and Cowells as she made out, for almost all of them seemed to succumb to drink, venereal disease or adultery. Even the innocuous Greppos did not escape unscathed: her sister Ellen, she observed, 'would have been so much happier if she were not so proud', and her niece Claudia 'would have been pretty but a difficult nose spoilt her', and her nephew Theodore 'never developed into anything more than a New York stockbroker'. But they at least were not likely to be hurt by her condemnation.

In the circumstances, the quality of Monty's writing is extraordinary, showing few signs of the pressures to which he was subject. He found a quiet reflective mood for *The Darkening Green*, written in the autumn of 1933, and a happy tone for an article in the *Daily Mail* choosing his ten most beautiful words – peril, azure, carnation, silence, heart, shadow, moon, April, apricot and forlorn. His reviews for the paper were always dictated at great speed, and the expression of his feelings was often threadbare, but he did read the books and his judgements were remarkably acute. Thus of D. H. Lawrence he wrote, 'No contemporary of my own has been able to take the English language as Lawrence has done and make of it not merely such a perfectly beautiful but a perfectly serviceable vessel to contain his own ideas.' And of George Orwell's first three novels: 'I have no hesitation in asserting that no realistic writer during the last five years has produced three volumes which can compare in directness, vigour, courage and vitality with these volumes from the pen of Mr Orwell'; and of C. P. Snow's *Death Under Sail*: 'a good specimen of the chess-problem thriller, and incidentally a suggestive peep into the schoolgirl naivety of the scientific mind on holiday.'

At Pinker's suggestion he wove out of memory a volume called *Literature in My Time*. It was written on Barra without reference books to hand. The result depressed him, and he was only just dissuaded from putting in a disclaimer that it had no real value. It was, however, widely praised for, as always, when forced to rely entirely on memory, his writing was vivid and anecdotal, and his judgement of writers against a longer perspective remains persuasive. Arnold Bennett's novels, for example, he judged to have 'succeeded in what they set out to do, but looking back at them they appear to have set out to do very little', and he selected James Joyce's *Ulysses* as 'the major piece of literature this time has witnessed . . . To my mind *Ulysses* is the second part of *Faust* written at last, and the most convincing proof ever penned of the possibility of human damnation, the profoundest revelation of evil ever set down on paper.'

The tone was in part a Catholic convert's reaction to the confessions of a Catholic apostate, but it was also a symptom of his general unease about post-war society. He theorised about it constantly and not all the theories fitted with one another, but they all sprang from his conviction that the world 'was standing at a point of evolution where the individual must surrender to the group mind. If Communism can only be fought by the inverted form of it called Fascism there is no hope for the individual.'

This pessimistic note became especially noticeable after his Official Secrets trial, and although he never admitted it, the shock of being attacked in that fashion left effects which could be detected in his writing for a decade to come. The most immediate pressures, however, began to lift in May 1934, when the lease of Jethou was at last sold, much to Faith's distress. As consolation he took her, along with Chrissie, on a lecture tour of South America organised in August by Philip Guedalla. He gave five lectures in Argentina, but as a severe attack of sciatica in Rio de Janeiro indicated, he did not greatly enjoy Brazil, nor the Brazilian papers, which announced that he was suffering from paralysis. On his return to Barra in October, he began to plan the building of his own house on the island.

The two focal points of the island were the harbour of Castlebay in the south where the Macbrayne's ferry from Oban called, and at the other end the square mile of cockle beach at Northbay where the Glasgow plane landed. It was at Northbay that Monty chose to live, first in the Crookle's cottage and then in the sprawling bungalow he built for himself.

With the Coddie's help he selected a site where the land narrows to a neck close to the most northerly point of Eoligarry. Thus the house would stand less than four hundred yards from the Atlantic beach on the west side, but overlooking the great cockle beach, Traigh Mhor, in the east. That at least was the original plan. In the event only the windows of the passage and the billiard room overlooked the Traigh Mhor.

Barra gossip alleged that the house had been built back to front, but Eric Linklater more charitably assumed that

like all good houses it had found organic life and grown beyond recognition from its original design. A mere cottage to begin with – I had seen him drawing the plan of it, and half a sheet of notepaper held it all – but then came the need to find room for gramophone records, some ten thousand or so, and a chamber was built for them, while bookshelves led a wide corridor far beyond the prime intention till it turned a corner and, for the entertainment of island friends, the crofters and their priests, opened into a billiard room that was walled with books, books uncountable, the diversity of the world in battered calf and many-coloured buckram, their close array pierced only by small round windows that looked upon the sea. A charming house with a troop of Siamese cats in the kitchen.

Suidheachan (pronounced Soo-yech-an) – the sitting-down place – was the name of the house, for it was built where one of the MacNeils of Barra who once owned the island used to take his rest while shooting. Every Sunday evening it became the sitting-down place for a group of friends including the island priests, Fathers John Macmillan of Northbay, Dominic MacKellaig, and John MacQueen of Castlebay; the Coddie and the Crookle; the Northbay teachers, Neil Sinclair and Annie Johnstone, and the young Gaelic scholar, John Lorne Campbell, and later his wife, Margaret Fay Shaw.

His working schedule, which now continued until six or seven in the morning, followed by sleep until mid-afternoon, did not allow him to enter into the daily life of Barra. A great occasion like an island wedding or the annual Corpus Christi procession, when he helped carry one of the canopies, would draw him out, and in the summer he would take a boat to explore the deserted islands round Barra. With John Lorne Campbell, he set up the Sea League, based on Michael Davitt's Land League, to fight for the inshore fishermen's rights which were being destroyed by the larger boats from England and the east coast of Scotland,

and the campaign brought him into occasional contact with the Western Isles fishermen. But it was through his Suidheachan friends that he really came to know the people of Barra.

The most striking of the group who collected at Suidheachan was the Coddie, with his crafty eyes, beguiling tongue and unrivalled store of folklore and gossip. But as Monty admitted, 'everyone in Barra was an outstanding personality'. The Crookle had been a merchant seaman, and his tales of internment by the Turks made an impression on him which was later expressed in *The Four Winds of Love*. From the priests he heard the gossip of family feuds, and from the teachers the talk of the playground. It was Annie Johnstone who gave him the story of the only boy in the school who wore a kilt and was thus nicknamed 'Compton'. Nicknames were endemic, and Monty's namesake once joined a friend with lank black hair to beat up another child who ran to the teacher crying, 'Please Miss, Compton and Hitler's after hitting me.'

The one flaw in this company was Dr Bartlett, an ebullient Liverpudlian who had fallen in love with Barra and retired there. He wore the kilt, learned a few words of Gaelic, but remained irredeemably, impossibly English. In his hearty, good-natured way, he behaved as though the islanders were a charming, feckless and rather backward people, and was unaware of the sharp wit that played about him.

In any small community, the lack of anonymity and the fact of mutual dependence breeds a certain degree of reserve and sensitivity, which the doctor evidently lacked, but having had their laugh at him most people forgave him his failings for his cheerfulness. Monty did not. To him the presence of Dr Bartlett with his Royal Stewart kilt and his clumsy behaviour was a constant source of irritation. While everyone else called him 'Compton' or 'Mr Mackenzie', the doctor alone used the English form 'Mackenzie'; he alone would try to cap Monty's stories and, in the games of knock-out pool which they played on Sunday evenings, he alone failed to observe the unwritten rule that Monty's ball was not to be knocked out. A moment of revenge came at a fireworks party when a rocket which the doctor was attempting to light suddenly went off and fizzed up his kilt, but revenge became immortal in *Whisky Galore* where Dr Bartlett was transmogrified into fussy, thick-skinned Captain Waggett.

A constant flow of visitors also appeared at Suidheachan. Many belonged to a generation younger than himself, but he bewitched them as he had his own contemporaries. At twenty-two, Terence de Vere White was already a fully-fledged solicitor and the author of his first novel, but in Monty he found someone with a necromancer's capacity to make a moment significant or a thought profound.

'With his good looks, actor's voice, easy omniscience, his sense of fun and warmth of manner, Compton Mackenzie came into my life like an avatar,' he wrote in *The Fretful Midge*:

Everything he said seemed to have extraordinary importance. It was like meeting Gogarty's fabulous ship that,

> ... from Valparaiso came,
> And in the bay her sails were furled,
> She brought the wonder of her name
> And tidings of a sunnier world.

Eric Linklater, then aged thirty-four, and at the height of his fame following the publication of *Juan in America*, was another touched by the magic which Monty created. He came to Barra for his honeymoon in June 1933, and returned to stay at Suidheachan on several occasions. Like de Vere White, he found that Monty could make the romantic real. Having observed that authors rarely have time to escape the burden of composition, he noted in *The Man on My Back* that there were exceptions: 'Byron the most redoubtable, Blunt in his Arab saddle, d'Annunzio well-known, Graham the hidalgo, and like a plume in Scotland's dusty bonnet, Compton Mackenzie.'

The power of Monty's enchantment was to let each be the person he wanted to be: to the young de Vere White, a quarter of a century his junior, he talked of books to come, of the ways of women and the lessons of fame, as though to an equal, or rather to a younger Monty who was heir to all this and could appreciate its value. Emphasising the relationship, he told the young man that he was particularly significant because he was the same age that his own son would have been.

Eric Linklater had already made his name and found his own way into the National Party for whom he fought a by-election in 1932 in East Fife with Monty's help – indeed, having been hopelessly defeated there, he had already found his own way out of the party – but he was probably the more susceptible to Monty's power. In Monty's company he found relief from the anxiety of writing – 'a persistent autogamy' he called it, 'the imagery of the male meeting twice nightly female organisation in the one system: the begetting, the load of pregnancy, the father's anxious fear, and parturition all burdened on a brain conceiving still while still in labour' – and received confirmation of his own undoubted gifts. On the occasion that he loaned Monty £200, he had gone to Eilean Aigas specifically to ask whether he would be justified in resting a future, and a married one at that, on his ability as a novelist. 'I told him,' Monty remembered, 'that I recognised in him genuine creativeness and had no doubt whatever that he was justified in backing his future as a writer.' But there was a more subtle reassurance to be found in the very confidence of Monty's demeanour, in the largeness of his own plans and the quickness of his wit, qualities displayed in a manner which implied that they were shared in equal measure by his friend.

In that friendship, the younger man can be seen repeatedly testing the older's ability and gratefully recognising its genuineness as though it confirmed his own. When Monty remarked that he enjoyed watching clouds, Linklater asked challengingly, 'Do you mean you're a nephologist?' To his delight, Monty replied without a moment's hesitation, 'No. I'm really a nephelologist, it's only the little clouds I like.' And in his dedication of *Ripeness is All* to him in 1935, Linklater wrote:

It is a large and delighted friendship; but if I do not protest it now in public, it may go unspoken for long enough. For as soon as we meet again, there will be talk on noisier subjects, more inflammatory subjects, on a multitude of very arguable subjects, and a host of inordinately comical subjects; we shall certainly not bother about a topic as quiet as friendship.

In lending confidence, however, Monty also offered a more dangerous encouragement. It was, after all, his protean gift to take on another's personality and return it, as it were, in dramatised form. In consequence his influence on Linklater's style was to reinforce a tendency to wordiness, which *Ripeness is All* showed all too clearly.

To Veronica Fraser, growing up self-assured and rebellious, he was something like the ideal elder brother – knowledgeable about books, unconventional about society and sympathetic to her changing moods. 'I am so glad you are awed by my immense age,' she wrote to him in December 1935, soon after her fifteenth birthday. 'I do hope I look it, but I'm afraid I shall always seem hopelessly young till my hair is permanently up . . . I think it is mostly through your influence that I love music and poetry and books so much – and I shall never stop being grateful to you for awakening it in me . . .'

To his former subordinate, the young Wilfred Macartney, he appeared in yet another form. Macartney had become a communist after the war, and in 1927 was convicted of spying after passing a catalogue of aircraft spare parts to a Russian agent. After eight years in Dartmoor, two with hard labour, he emerged in 1935, almost broken by the experience and conspiratorial in outlook. With genuine generosity, especially marked because Macartney's other friends shunned him as a traitor, Monty immediately invited him up to Barra to recuperate. Visitors to Suidhea-chan began to notice that the word 'bourgeois' entered Monty's talk, and his grander friends were referred to as 'the Junkers', a term he occasionally applied to himself as well. Instead of equating communism with fascism as he had done in *Literature in My Time*, he sometimes argued that it was historically inevitable, although still clinging to his Catholicism he would picture it as a purgatory mankind had to endure in order to be cleansed. And in his foreword to Macartney's book, *Walls Have Mouths*, he no longer portrayed the secret service as absurd but as a political weapon: 'It is the fear of revolution that sustains it.'

No one had more cause to be grateful for Monty's gift than Macartney. He arrived as the move into Suidheachan was about to take place in the autumn of 1935, but Monty found room for him and helped him through the readjustment to society.

'You can have no idea how much good that two months in Barra did me,' Macartney wrote, addressing Monty by his old intelligence initial, ' . . . and Zed I do appreciate your really uncommon goodness to me, the inspiration that you have been, and to put up with me in the midst of moving was too kind, especially as I get a bit heavy at times – that is the jail hang-over.' Monty did more than provide hospitality. Recognising Macartney's need to tell about his experiences, he provided him with a place to write, edited the work, and contributed a foreword and comments. Despite the excision of the rawest details, the book remained so shocking that only Monty's vigorous salesmanship finally found it a publisher in Gollancz. The result, *Walls Have Mouths*, remains one of the outstanding documents of prison life.

To be touched by Monty's magic it was necessary to admire his performance. One who failed to be touched was Louis MacNeice, who appeared in 1936 while picking up colour for his sophisticate-slumming-with-the-crofters book called *I Crossed the Minch*. He found Monty affected, and commented with dislike upon his ginger-coloured suede shoes, the Fair Isle pullover which matched the green check suit, and the posed stance on a white rug in front of the fire, 'looking like Lionel Barrymore turning into a bird, weighing himself on his feet, and poising remarks as he poised the pipe in his hand'.

Linklater also noted the theatricality, but enjoyed it in all its variety and in so doing was moved to draw an eloquent and affectionate portrait which deserves to be quoted at some length:

To see him weary is to see a lean and anguished priest; to see him well and in unfriendly company is to see him harsh and arrogant; and to see him as a host, when entertainment is his aim, is to see a varying mask of all the emotions he may elect to show, the many characters he may choose to mime. To all who admit his virtue and his charm, he is the very top and flourish of good company.

His habit, however, is disconcertingly nocturnal. He sleeps by day because to be awake in sunlight would be, for him, an irresistible temptation to botanise, zoologise, nephelologise, and do no work. When I arrived in Barra he woke before his usual time – indeed quite early in the afternoon – and I saw him first in a lounging-suit, old rose in colour with lapels of a darker hue, of a thickened silk material. But this was not dandyism, for beneath it were pyjamas and a Fair Isle tunic most violently moresque; he was two days unshaven, and his hair hung like a mother raven shot upon the nest. His clothes resemble the adjectives in a poem by Gerard Manley Hopkins: chosen for their texture and colour, and often most arbitrarily joined.

He works with the persistence of a fanatic in circumstances of considerable luxury. In a high-backed padded chair in the corner of a room, a mere closet of a room but papered with gold, he will sit through the night under a funnelled lamp, the rest of the closet an aureate dusk, a hundred or so books of reference within easy reach; while in the adjacent room, the connecting door wide open, one of his secretaries – Chrissie with her soft voice and lovely eyes, Nelly with her London kindness – will feed a pair of enormous gramophones with continuous records, progressing in a single night, as may happen, from a symphony by Brahms, through a little Cesar Franck and a few Beethoven quartets, to a Mozart concerto, and before the dawn an hour or so of Sibelius.

This arduous but mollified routine he will maintain, if he is alone, for weeks on end; but company is a temptation to which he yields. His conversation, like the delta of the Brahmaputra, flows from enormous reservoirs and will cover unpredictably far tracts of country. He was writing, while I was storm-stayed on Barra, a life of Pericles, and often he would come out from the golden closet with some fragment of Athenian gossip too good to keep; and the Ten Years' War led easily to Gallipoli, Theban treachery to German spies on Mytilene. Mackenzie, in the last war, was in charge of counter-espionage in the Aegean, and, retaining individual ideas about the Allied aims, succeeded in harassing both sides. – On both sides, he explains, there were so many bureaucrats. – Then from Lesbos to Capri was but a stride between sentences, and D. H. Lawrence the stepping-stone to an archbishop or two and London in the eighteenth century. One night he fetched from the billiard room an armful of Admiralty pilot books, and by felicitous example demonstrated the excellent prose in which they are written. And from the atolled sea between the Nicobards and Norfolk Island he found a canal to water-gardens, Covent Garden, the Edwardian theatre, and English accents.

'Cockney,' he said, 'is a dead speech. Dead as Etruscan. It rose in a world and got genteel, and died of debility like everything else that goes away from its own soil. I listened the other night to a young man in the BBC trying to impersonate Sam Weller. He was no more like Sam Weller than a marmoset's like a two-toed sloth. You remember the trial, Bardell versus Pickwick? Well, this is how it ought to be done.'

He got up, and after a false start recited with astonishing virtuosity the exchanges between Mr Justice Stareleigh and Sam Weller, the anonymous interruption, the questions of Mr Buzfuz, and Sam's response. He made Sam speak in a husky constricted voice that was like a London fog.

'But it's meant to be a fog!' he exclaimed. 'Not the shallow fog of today, but a regular pea-soup London particular. Fog in the throat. That's how Dickens used to read the trial scene.'

'How do you know that?'

'Because my father heard him, and imitated him, and I learned from my father. My father was a first-class mimic, and I'm a good one. So what you've just heard was practically the voice of Charles Dickens himself. As well as a piece of authentic Cockney.'

It was a performance appreciated equally by those on Barra. 'He was a kind man, I think all his friends knew that,' commented Ruiraidh Mackay, who often visited Suidheachan. 'Of course he liked to hold the floor and he would want to take over the talk, but he took trouble with people, and he was prepared to listen to folk like the Coddie.'

On the day that the ground of Suidheachan was pegged out in April 1935, Monty at last set himself to planning *The East Wind of Love*, the first volume of his long-deferred great work. In the same year the two leaders of the Scottish renaissance, Hugh MacDiarmid and Lewis Grassic Gibbon, combined in writing *Scottish Scene*, a gallimaufry of opinion and argument, in which the former cited Compton Mackenzie as a Nationalist who understood the essence of Scotland, and the latter cited him as a writer who could not be considered Scots. There was good reason for both arguments. His Nationalism had occupied the better part of his energy for seven years, but so far the only influence of Scotland on his writing which was apparent was a slight biography of Bonnie Prince Charlie.

Paradoxically a commission from Grassic Gibbon to write a book called *Catholicism in Scotland* diverted him for a few more months from his task. With a violence that recalled his attacks on the Kensitites of his youth, he laid into John Knox – 'that concupiscent Hun' – the founding fathers of the Presbyterian Kirk – 'the sinister collection of drunkards, debauchees and religious maniacs' – and the coming of the Reformation – 'the treachery and bloody deeds by which a collection of the blackest villains that ever defiled the pages of history drove the Queen of Scots from her throne to find captivity and death at the hands of a queen who lacked at once the essential bodily and mental characteristics of womanhood.'

His researches for this polemic made one important contribution to *The Four Winds of Love*. Among the victims of Knox's reformers was a Jesuit priest who was hanged in 1614. His name, John Ogilvie, was now to be used for the trumpeter of the twentieth century.

15

The winds of love

Like Suidheachan, *The Four Winds of Love* not only expanded from its original modest plan, but shifted in alignment so that the intended outlook was obscured. When he told Eric Linklater of his conception of it in 1932, the structure was well-defined. The action of the *East Wind* was to take place mostly in spring, and the crucial scenes were to be set in Poland; the *South Wind*'s season was summer, and Italy and France its locale; autumn was the key season for the *West Wind* and the setting America, Ireland and Cornwall, and the *North Wind* would blow from Scotland with winter as its season.

This pattern was imposed upon a passage of time beginning in the late 1890s and continuing to the 1930s. Having covered the history of western civilisation in the twentieth century, the story would reach its climax in the discovery of Scottish Nationalism and the small community as the only hope of a disturbed age.

For three years he had described this structure to each of his friends, and all had besought him to start work on it as soon as possible. Nevertheless he showed himself oddly reluctant to begin. He could fairly claim that the Official Secrets trial had delayed him, but its costs could have been met more quickly, as Ralph Pinker constantly urged, by cutting back on expenditure rather than writing potboilers. He refused to sell the Shiants or a hillside in Capri which he still owned in order to raise the money, and in June 1935 he proposed to defer the great enterprise again so that he could write a quick biography of Pericles. At this Pinker wrote in exasperation that both he and Newman Flower 'are absolutely intent on your writing The Four Winds . . . it would be a very great mistake to dive off into any other extraneous work such as biography or articles of reminiscence.'

Pericles was temporarily laid aside, but even after he had actually begun writing he was again distracted. In November the *Daily Mail* decided it could no longer afford a book reviewer, and the annual £1500 which had kept him afloat for five years was withdrawn. In desperation he laid aside *The East Wind of Love* and rattled off *Figure of Eight* in a month. This tale of eight ballet girls who had known Jenny Pearl at the Orient Palace of Varieties may be regarded as the last addition to *The Theatre of Youth*, but the plot was so slight that neither Pinker nor Flower was convinced it amounted to a novel. Angrily he replied to their criticism, 'this reception of *Figure of Eight* suggests you are both looking for an excuse to force a rupture.' But the problem concerned more than a single novel. Over the fifteen years that he had been with Cassell's his books had barely covered their costs, and adding the publisher's over-heads notionally allocated to each book produced a net loss. *Figure of Eight* was the last straw.

It was at this point that Monty revealed the true scope of *The Four Winds of Love* and the money he needed to carry it through. When he began writing in June 1935 it was to be a two-volume work amounting to 500,000 words, for which he was to be paid £3000. In March 1936 he broke the news that it was to run to four volumes and a total of 700,000 words. 'I admit that my first conception of *The Four Winds of Love* was less ambitious than it is now,' he told Newman Flower disarmingly, 'but that only means the book is a bigger and better work than I thought it was going to be.' He proposed, therefore, that Cassell's pay him £1500 for each of the four volumes.

Had the flak not still been flying round *Figure of Eight*, Flower might have found the money. He liked Monty personally and admired him as a writer – 'You are the star in Cassell's firmament,' he declared in 1933 – and he had persuaded Cassell's to guarantee first his towering overdraft, and later the insurance for Suidheachan. In these circumstances, however, he felt bound to insist on the original contract being met.

This refusal to advance any more money precipitated the most acute of Monty's many financial crises, and it is to his credit that through it all he still found time to nurse Macartney's book to publication. In March he had to borrow £200 from the Coddie and £100 from the *Gramophone* to stave off the bank, and he had just sent £600 of post-dated cheques to the Inland Revenue when he heard of Cassell's decision. 'Had I known a year ahead this was going to happen, I could have planned my books better,' he wrote in despair to Pinker. 'If I am sued by the Inland Revenue it can only mean bankruptcy, and [Flower]

must realise what it will mean if I can't meet those post-dated cheques
. . . The strain of writing this immense work is bad enough, but with all
this money-juggling it's just not bearable. My mind is working all the
time to square the circle.'

To keep afloat he was forced to sell his talisman of Scotland, the
Shiants, but there seemed no chance of avoiding bankruptcy unless new
publishers could be found. Rescue came on 4 May in a telegram from
Pinker saying that the newly formed firm of Rich & Cowan were
prepared to publish all four volumes at £1500 each, and at this news
Flower generously agreed to release him from his contract with Cassell's.
'Never did I run myself so close before,' Monty wrote in relief. 'However
all's well that ends well . . .'

The East Wind of Love was eventually delivered in August, and the
agreeable Lieutenant-Commander Rich-wrote to tell him that his literary
advisers 'are of the unanimous opinion that it is magnificent'. It was
published in January 1937 to the sort of acclaim which is reserved for
the prodigal's return. Douglas West in the *Daily Mail* explicitly measured
it against the great work of his youth, saying, 'He has given us no
comparable work of imagination since *Sinister Street*, and in scope and
insight, as well as in the quality of the experience communicated, it
surpasses that young man's masterpiece.' Looking ahead to the three
succeeding volumes, the *Evening Standard* prophesied that 'when the
race is over Mr Mackenzie will have achieved his masterpiece'. Both
papers, together with the Book Society and the Book Circle, selected it
as their book of the month.

In his dedication to Eric Linklater, 'a friend to whose friendship I owe
more than can be paid with words', he referred to the scale of the work:

I am hopeful that when the four volumes are published it will be clear that the
size of the work was demanded by the design, but whether such a design which
involves such an accumulation of incident, such an amount of discussion, such
a variety of scene, and such a crowd of characters will be approved is another
matter, and I confess that I await the final verdict in some anxiety.

This design followed from his aim of capturing the atmosphere of each
of the first four decades of the twentieth century. It was not surprising
therefore that he frequently complained of the shadow of *Sinister Street*
hanging over *The East Wind of Love*. It opens in the last years of the
nineteenth century in the public school of St James's; Michael Fane
makes an appearance, and the buildings of West Kensington continue to
haunt the adolescent mind as 'those nightmare houses which unfettered

sleep builds fast as thought'. The direction, however, is entirely different. Instead of Michael Fane trying to determine himself within society, the three central characters are all outsiders – Edward Fitzgerald, who first appears supporting home rule for Ireland in a school debate; the Jew Emil Stern, who opposes him, arguing that independence of mind is more valuable than independence of country; and John Ogilvie, who decides that 'in theory he was a revolutionary, but he had such an amount of amiable tolerance ... that even if he should have the chance of revolutionary activity he should always find it most difficult to put a number of negatively harmless people even to inconvenience.'

The outlook of the main characters remains consistent throughout the quartet of *Winds*. Fitzgerald takes part in the Easter Rising, joins the IRA and is shot by Irish Free State troops. Emil Stern becomes a communist, pacifist and rationalist, while Ogilvie searches for an ideal which will draw him from dreams into action.

The love of the *East Wind* is maternal – not from Ogilvie's own mother who has died when he was seven, ten years before the book opens, but from Miriam Stern, whose 'slim ivory beauty at thirty-seven recalled the very appearance in his mind of his own mother who would have been just her age today'. There are other passions – for a boy at school, an actress, and a Guy-and-Pauline love affair for a landowner's daughter, Rose Medlicott, which founders on the rock of sexual desire – but throughout it is Miriam who guides, supports and adores both as a mother and a woman. It is to her that the author gives the most overtly erotic feelings as she sits dreaming of the seventeen-year-old John Ogilvie:

She moved restlessly on the chair as if her body sought his body. Her lips were slightly parted as if the warm air of this starlit laden night were the breath of his kiss. She thrust her hand down to her left breast, calling it in fancy his hand and trying to imagine whether he would shrink from the softness of a breast that had sacrificed contour and resilience to maternity.

The love is consummated one night when the Stern family take him with them on a journey to Poland, but thereafter they agree to return to a friendship 'exquisitely enriched by the passionate emotion which has been added to it'. Despite the many loves which follow, Miriam Stern's is the consistent and dominating passion of John Ogilvie's life.

A second theme which is signalled in *The East Wind of Love* is his feeling for Scotland. Ogilvie's father, a son of the manse, has left his country to become a successful London barrister. He is the embodiment of reason and good sense, save for his jealousy of his good-looking son, 'that jealousy from which few men whose worldly success is founded upon the exploitation of personality remain free'. His dead mother, Athene Pendarves, however, was Cornish, and her Celtic emotion is inherited by John. When an old Highlander, Torquil MacLeod of Ardvore, invites him to stay in Sutherland, he responds immediately to

the first sight of Suilven, standing up in the west like a huge grape-dark hand, miles away above the desolate moorland. What were the mountains of Switzerland compared with that shape of stone solitary as a mammoth upon the edge of the landscape? Huddled parvenus. His first sight of the Laird of Ardvore, standing by the inn door when the coach pulled up, was not less memorable. That beaky-nosed bearded old man in faded kilt was autochthonous like Ben More Assynt itself.

The first volume ends with his intention on hearing Sibelius's symphonic poem *The Swan of Tuonela*: 'You shall go back ultimately. There lies the fulfilment of your weird.' But he also carries with him Emil Stern's prophecy that he will be a superficial drifter, 'and gradually you will sentimentalise your sentimentality, and humbug yourself with the notion that fate denied you the chance to express yourself as you wished. It will always be fate of course . . . not your own choice of the easier course.'

The second storey of this broad edifice was completed in July 1937, and was published two months later with a warm dedication to Newman Flower, acknowledging his generosity over the Cassell's contract. He added a warning that 'this volume must not be read as even veiled autobiography . . . it will be a waste of time for people to try to identify characters or search for facts in what is a work of fiction'. His insistence was understandable since the period of the book, from 1912 to 1918, carried John Ogilvie from a career as a successful playwright into secret service work during the war, first on mainland Greece (based in Salonica rather than Athens) and later in the Cyclades. Thus in addition to libel there was the risk of another Official Secrets prosecution. In fact the portraits are readily identifiable. Ogilvie's encounters with the novelist Daniel Rayner, for example, are usually word-for-word reconstructions of Monty's meetings with D. H. Lawrence, and of the character of Athene Langridge Faith remarked, 'I hope Ann [Heiskell] will enjoy the book . . . it's a most alluring portrait.'

The *South Wind*'s love is sexual, and the break-up of Ogilvie's pre-war affair with the French actress Gabrielle Desrozier illustrates the difference between the desires of men and women. The truth, as Ogilvie sees it, is contained in the aphorisms found in every language which emphasised the unimportance to a man of the sexual act compared to its importance to a woman; but humanity continued blithely to ignore such aphorisms as soon as its desire was aroused. Men still swore undying devotion, women smothered their realistic incredulity and humbugged themselves into believing those vows, still measured men's spiritual fidelity by their eagerness to get into bed with them.

Hotly pursued by Gabrielle, Ogilvie gives vent to exasperated comments such as, 'Oh dear, the readiness with which women accepted the tribute of physical interest as a sign of enduring affection' or 'Why couldn't women be content with as much of a man as they were capable of digesting? Why must they emulate the Praying Mantis and try to devour their lovers whole?' Having eluded her through the intervention of the war, he returns with relief to the undemanding love of Miriam Stern, who assures him that sexual satisfaction is not the only desire a woman values. Moved that he should have remembered their night together in Poland, she says, 'You are curiously feminine in some ways. I suppose that is part of your charm for women. We are strange creatures, extolling and indeed desiring uncompromising masculinity, and all the time wishing in our hearts that men were not quite so excessively and peculiarly men.'

The war leaves John Ogilvie drained and without a sense of direction, and his purposelessness is given contrast by Fitzgerald's commitment to Irish independence and Emil Stern's discovery of communism. A third figure, Julius Stern, Emil's younger brother and a virtuoso violinist, becomes his closest friend. When he too finds a goal in marriage and in a new career as a composer, John returns to the Mediterranean town of Citrano where he had been living before the war. *The South Wind of Love* ends with his meeting the American, Athene Langridge – his future wife.

Although *The West Wind of Love* begins in the moments following that meeting, two years elapsed between writing the last words of the previous volume and the first of this. In his dedicatory letter to Rosamund Lehmann he explained that the gap was 'due to my having been compelled by anger to write *The Windsor Tapestry* . . . On top of that I was able to secure the release of the ban on *Greek Memories* and decided to finish off that broken series by writing *Aegean Memories*.' His anger had been aroused by the circumstances of the Abdication, and *The Windsor Tapestry*, although in large part an assault on the Hanoverian dynasty, was ostensibly a defence of the duke's right to a morganatic marriage. However understandable, the break caused a loss of momentum for readers and author alike, and when he returned to writing *The West Wind of Love* in September 1939 the scheme had slipped irrevocably.

Married love, which should have been the theme of this volume, is overshadowed by Fitzgerald's participation in the Irish struggle for independence, and Ogilvie's continuing inability to find either a faith or a cause he can believe in. 'You hadn't the luck to be born an Irishman,' Fitzgerald tells him. 'If you had been, you'd have seen your road clear before you, and whatever personally had happened to you on that road you'd have taken it and stuck to it. A small country and a worldwide religion. That's the happy combination.' Athene Langridge is already married and the mother of a six-year-old son, but her husband dies, enabling Ogilvie to marry her and become the father of a daughter, Corinna. Nevertheless his attention is more taken up with the attempt to find sense in the post-war turmoil of spreading communism and the rise of fascism in Italy, in Greece's attempt to annexe the Turkish coastline and Fitzgerald's murder in 1922 by Free State soldiers. This last, foreseen by Fitzgerald at school, persuades Ogilvie to become Catholic, and it then only remains to him to find the small country. Because this volume ran to 290,000 words, it had to be split in two, the second volume being called *West to North*.

Another four years were to elapse before *The North Wind of Love* was finished in March 1944, and by then the deviation from his original intention had changed the balance of the work. The plan had been to cover the years 1926 to 1934 in this volume, when Ogilvie would have followed the prophecy of the Swan of Tuonela and returned north, ending as a Nationalist and finding the second half of Fitzgerald's 'happy combination'. Instead the span is from 1931 to 1937, and although Scottish Nationalism occupies the greater part of the book, before the end Ogilvie, like the author, has become disillusioned by the cliques within the Nationalist movement and the failure of a plan to retrieve the Stone of Destiny from Westminster Abbey. The North Wind's love is filial and, Athene having died, he is intermittently occupied with educating Corinna according to his theories. She falls in love with Sebastian, the son of Julius Stern, and Ogilvie, returning to the Greek islands, decides to marry Euphrosyne Ladas whom he had known during the war. In classical mythology Euphrosyne is the goddess of mirth, and *The Four Winds of Love* ends with the announcement of Corinna and Sebastian's engagement, just thirty-seven years after the story began. Despite the gathering clouds of war, optimism is the final note.

Of the more than one hundred books he eventually wrote, Monty ranked *The Four Winds of Love* at the top. 'It was the book that he put most of himself into,' said Norah Smallwood, his editor at Chatto & Windus, who published the last two volumes. 'He used to say it contained all his deepest beliefs, and he always considered it his best.' Certainly in scope and size it dwarfs all but his autobiography, and *The East Wind of Love* by itself stands comparison with *Sinister Street*. It lacks its predecessor's adolescent intensity, but possesses a wider range of aspiration. Nevertheless the total work fits into no conventional category of novel.

The plot is the twentieth century. It is the current of public affairs that carries the story forward, and the central characters reveal themselves through their discussions upon these events. At Gallipoli, Ogilvie comments, 'All the while that I was in the Peninsula, I was conscious of being at one with the valorous and humble . . . A portion of me, and I think the best of me, had become history.' That thought might be taken as the key to his existence. At every moment he acts as though he must be conscious of what is happening in an ever more confused world in order to belong to it. The alternative is to become a victim – the fate of a party of British stokers interned by the Turks simply because their ships happened to be in Turkish ports when war is declared: 'each, now that he was up against a world at war, more conscious of his individuality than ever, and each less and less capable of expressing that individuality.' And so Ogilvie, the Sterns and Fitzgerald talk, discuss, and hold forth about the times which are carrying them relentlessly forward.

Leo Robertson, who judged it to be the greatest of Compton Mackenzie's books, decided that it must belong to a new genre which he labelled the 'Intellective Novel'. 'It is a novel of ideas, and the light that plays about it is that of the intellect,' he argued. 'There are many works of fiction in which ideas predominate over action or emotion . . . but in *The Four Winds of Love* what we have through the central figure, John Ogilvie, and the intelligent set revolving round him is a commentary on the whole life of their time . . .'

The construction was not without its drawbacks. The frequency and length of the disquisitions hold up the flow of the narrative – Ogilvie's monologue on Scottish Nationalism in *The North Wind of Love* runs for fifty pages – and their ideas often have the threadbare quality of the pub bore. 'Music itself is in a queer state,' Julius Stern observes in 1920. 'I think we're all of us wondering where we are. All this Relativity business seems to have shaken people. Einstein had a triumph over that eclipse last year.' Finally the preponderance of comment and analysis robs everyone's emotions, with the shining exception of Miriam Stern, of their force. Although frequently spoken of, they have little effect upon actions, and they provide no depth to the characterisation. As Francis Russell Hart commented of John Ogilvie in *The Scottish Novel*, 'The result is a character who in his inner life is almost entirely sentimental or instinctive, and in his public role is tirelessly dialectical; the fusion is slight.'

However, to adapt Dr Johnson's observation, to read *The Four Winds of Love* for the characterisation is to fret one's impatience. It is the successor to *The Theatre of Youth* – monumental in span and encyclopaedic in its exploration of the influences that shaped Michael Fane's generation. *The Labyrinth* was the original and apt title when he first planned it twenty years earlier, for it reveals itself to be a search through blind alleys and passages without exits. Among the shifting crowds of background characters, and the kaleidoscope of scenes, there is a consistent thread which is only partly concerned with love, whether of people or countries. By the time his great work reaches its conclusion, it has traced to the eve of another war the history of the values of the late Victorian age, and the blankness of Ogilvie's character is the screen onto which their story is projected.

Educated to be a gentleman – that is, to use privilege justly – he is inevitably appalled by the selfishness and materialism of the Victorian and Edwardian eras. 'When war came I was exultant,' Ogilvie recalls, '. . . every black memory vanished when we entered a war from motives as near to generosity as could be imagined.' But to win the war gentlemanly values have to be jettisoned, and after it he finds the materialists occupying the position of privilege. He flirts with fascism, and declares in 1922:

As I see the world today, it is suffering from an excess of material advancement which the mind of man has not yet had time to digest. What I perceive in *Fascismo* is an effort to restore discipline and to regulate the mind of man to esteem and make full use of the wealth at his disposal. That must involve a certain amount of interference with the freedom of the individual.

He rejects fascism when it becomes a mass movement. He is romantically attracted by communism as 'a revolt against the form of present-day capitalism', but turns away because it is bureaucratic. Too fastidious to join popular movements, he is also too inhibited to explore the personal freedom of post-war morality. 'John's life lay in the gap between two periods,' the author observes. 'He was able to criticise the Victorian discipline of respectability, but not to break completely free from it. The ability to face hard physical facts which was to distinguish the youth of the next generation was beyond his imagination.' To Scotland he has been drawn since his youth and at last he finds in nationalism the background he needs in the vastness of the modern state. But the utopia he envisages for his rediscovered country is once more a closed society, as authoritarian as the *Republic* of Plato on which he cut his schoolboy teeth. It is to be governed first by an autocrat, then by Parliament elected only by trades and professions. All land, banks and heavy industry are to be nationalised, work made compulsory, films censored, professional sports banned and all schools to be located in the country. With no faith in popular opinion he is willing to encourage illegal actions to achieve his ends. The impossibility of exercising the values of his youth means that he can never again belong to society or become part of history. Trapped by the machine age he can only proclaim a warning against material progress and pin his uncertain faith in God, taking as his motif the Cracow trumpeter's dying alarms whose 'strength was in the feeble wavering note at the end. Its triumph was its failure'.

There is so much of the author in John Ogilvie that it is tempting simply to take him as a fictional representation. The differences are, however, instructive. The charm and vitality of the performer are missing (as they were for Michael, Guy and Mark); they are given to Fitzgerald. The creativity belongs to Julius Stern – Ogilvie's plays are mentioned but never described and are always disparaged – and the disciplined Miss Stanwell side of his character is taken on by Emil Stern. It is he who acts as conscience to Ogilvie, and the thrust of his accusations provides an interesting sidelight on the sort of dissatisfactions that Monty entertained of himself. They were aimed primarily at the pliancy of his character, the waste of his talent and the immaturity of his aims.

'Your mind sprawls,' Emil exclaims.

You feel, you don't think. You aspire, you cannot plan. You're living in a lumber-room. I become impatient with you now that you're closing in on forty. When you were seventeen you could carry off your romantic individualism . . . At that age your Jacobitism and Chopinism and Byronism added to your charm, but now at thirty-nine you're going to a fancy-dress ball in an unsuitable costume.

It is Miriam who provides the excuses. 'He would plunge from youth into eld, but he would never know middle age,' she thinks, and to Emil's charge that he is a butterfly, she replies, 'He may be. But even butterflies have their uses. They fertilise many flowers during their beautiful existence.'

Faith made exactly these excuses for Monty, and there is undoubtedly something of her in the piano-playing, ever-understanding Miriam, just as her family, the artistic Stones, resembled the musical Sterns in more than name. But the identification of Miriam with Ogilvie's real mother is part of a pattern of incest. It recurs in his marriage to Athene – whom he loves for her mothering qualities and who bears his mother's name – and again in the marriage of his daughter to his mother-substitute's grandson.

Implicit in the idea of incest is the urge to beget oneself, and only when this theme is set against the massive reconstructions of his life and times first in *The Theatre of Youth*, then in *The Four Winds of Love*, and finally in his autobiography, does their full significance emerge. It is in fact the logical outcome of that division of his self into actor and audience, for the self that is created on the page has the permanence which his performance in real life necessarily lacked. In a way that has rarely, if ever, been attempted, he made himself. It was the realisation of the thought implied in his last letter to Edward Compton, that he himself was his own father.

The long period over which *The Four Winds of Love* appeared made it difficult to judge the work as a whole. When it was issued as a single work after the Second World War, its purpose was no longer apparent to the critics. 'The one-time admirer of Mackenzie's early books, in attempting to tackle, in whole or in separate units, *The Four Winds of Love* is subjected to an experience of almost aesthetic despair,' declared the literary critic of *Commonweal*, who went on to condemn its length, style and characterisation, winding up with the accusation, 'Mr Mackenzie has never guarded his prose because he has always completely lacked self-discipline, and has made up in a kind of exuberance for what he lacks in definite quality.'

Those who did not know Monty, and thus had never felt his charm, were always harsher on the work than those who had listened to him talk about it. Yet even his friends had their doubts. De Vere White regretted that he had strayed so far from his original idea, while Linklater, who always insisted on its virtues, admitted that probably only three or four people other than himself had actually read all of it. 'Perhaps if I had never offered my pen to the Duke of Windsor,' Monty wrote, 'it would have made it easier for critics to judge the complete novel.'

In retrospect there may have been a hint of regret that he had compromised the chances of his masterpiece, but at the time, in 1937, there was no thought of holding back.

For Monty, as for many of his generation, the Prince of Wales had always been 'one of our kind', the dashing individualist who would break the drab, dutiful mould of King George V's monarchy. While at Eilean Aigas he had in fact met the prince when he flew in to Beaufort Castle, and was immensely gratified when Edward admired his laced Highland brogues. The Abdication he saw as a conspiracy by the establishment, and in the *Gramophone* he wrote angrily of 'a black rage which had come over me at hearing immediately after news of the Abdication the prices of the Stock Exchange read by the six o'clock announcer out of their usual order. Was that the true anodyne of a nation's sorrow, a rise in the shares of some wretched motor car company?'

Throughout the first months of 1937 he seethed impotently at the gossip which wafted up to Barra as he laboured to complete *The South Wind of Love*. The duke's marriage to Mrs Simpson in June gave him a chance to express his feelings. He sent them a telegram of congratulations, ending with the words, 'Floreat Magdalena', the motto of the college which he and the duke had both attended. To his surprise, the duke replied thanking him, and Macartney, who was staying at Suidheachan again, urged him to write a book presenting the duke's case. Macartney's involvement was unfortunate in that he later fanned Monty's suspicions of a conspiracy against him, but his initial idea bore fruit. The duke accepted Monty's offer to put his case and made an appointment to discuss the synopsis with him in the autumn. With a certain naivety Monty told his agent, his publishers and the *Sunday Pictorial*, which offered £5000 for the serial rights of the book. At the newspaper's suggestion he widened the scope from the Abdication itself to a biography of the former king, in which there would be a justification of his right to a morganatic marriage.

He employed a young history graduate from Oxford, Joyce Weiner, as a researcher, and his instructions to her showed the exactness of his memory: 'He always knew where I should go for information and what I would find there,' she remembered. 'He once said to me that the editor of the *Hungarian Quarterly* was the person to go to for confirmation of the possibility that Queen Mary was the grand-daughter of a morganatic marriage – and he was right.'

In the synopsis which he sent to the duke in September, his criticism of the prime minister, Stanley Baldwin, and the Archbishop of Canterbury, Cosmo Lang, contained a combative note which apparently alarmed the duke's advisers. At their insistence he withdrew first from the interview, and later refused to give the book his approval, although he did not condemn it. Before the research was complete, enough of the secret had leaked out for a *Daily Express* reporter to be flown up to Barra to question him, and for MI5 to begin opening his mail. Adding to the strain, Macartney suggested from London that his agent or his publisher were secretly negotiating with the government to let them vet the manuscript before publication.

'If you think this book is going through with the approval of the authorities,' he wrote fiercely to Pinker, 'you were never more deceived in your life.' At the first opportunity following publication he fired Pinker and put his financial affairs in the hands of an accountant, J. B. Watson.

In November he came to London to assure himself through Walter Monckton, the duke's solicitor, that the duke would not forbid him to write, but he was back in Barra at the end of the month when the *Sunday Dispatch* broke the story with a front page headline: THE TRUTH ABOUT THE DUKE OF WINDSOR BOOK. Once again he was in the centre of the stage. 'The whole of London is plastered with you tonight,' Faith wrote to him in Barra. 'Not only News Reviews in rows everywhere, but posters – DUKE'S BIOGRAPHY SENSATION – DUKE AND AUTHOR – all over the place.'

He began work on 10 December and by mid-February had completed 75,000 words. 'I never wrote in such a fever,' he told Faith, 'but I can't write more than 1500 words a day.' The force of his emotion concealed the fact that he was making impossible demands on his physical strength. His frame was still wiry and his hair grew thick and black, but he was fifty-five, and his way of life had never been healthy. He had passed more nights in writing than sleeping, and since the age of twenty-six he estimated that 'I have spent a sixth of the time in pain and at least a tenth of the time in torture.' Ignoring physical symptoms had become a habit, and so there was no warning when, on 18 April, he suddenly collapsed.

'His face was the colour of grey clay and he was rigid,' Joyce Weiner told Faith. 'He did not yield to Chrissie's attempts to restore him, and she was absolutely distraught . . .' For five hours he lay insensible, and he seemed so obviously in danger of dying that Faith was sent for. Yet with astonishing resilience he recovered, and within days he was writing again.

The manuscript was sent off in mid-May, but he was still frail and in pain when the *Sunday Pictorial* publicly denounced him. Instead of advertising the book's forthcoming serialisation, its issue of 22 May came out with a banner headline: THE DUKE, and underneath: APPALLING BOOK.

Without his knowledge, the benign editor who had employed him as a record reviewer had been replaced by the twenty-five-year-old Hugh Cudlipp. With a fine concern for his readers' sensibilities, Cudlipp explained that although his paper had paid £5000 for the serialisation rights, it regarded Monty's criticism of the Hanoverians too extreme to be published. Presumably Cudlipp must have calculated that there was more to be gained from a manufactured row than from printing extracts of a book which had neither the duke's authorisation nor any new details about the Abdication. If so he was wrong. When its sister publication the *Sunday Dispatch* began to serialise *The Windsor Tapestry* its readership grew by over 100,000.

'I put all I knew into the writing of it,' Monty declared, and the passion was evident in his vituperative attack on Edward VIII's enemies. Baldwin and every other politician, except Churchill, together with the entire bench of bishops without exception, where shown to be servile and treacherous and – in most cases – to have avoided military service in the war; the Labour Party was 'no more than great wobbly blancmange streaked here and there with cochineal', and the BBC's coverage of the Abdication was dubbed 'Rat Week'. In her distinguished biography, *Edward VIII*, Frances Donaldson described it as being 'full of indignation and sarcasm and illogical scores against those he took to be the king's enemies, and is almost unreadable'.

The violence of his language, not unlike that directed at Knox and Cumberland, is explained by the depth of his sympathy, to the point of identification, with the duke. Edward, he declared, had 'the genius of royalty beyond any except a dozen princes in history', and George V, who lacked it entirely, was correspondingly jealous: 'Fathers, royal and commoner, will always distrust the resounding success of a son, particularly an eldest son . . . it must be regarded as universal.' The duke's enemies were his enemies, as bleak and life-destroying as nannies.

Despite this failing, the book has a superb central section justifying the duke's right to a morganatic marriage. Its purpose is to show that such marriages took place *de facto* repeatedly under the first five Hanoverians. Unable to resist a good story, even at the risk of putting Mrs Simpson in some distinctly unsavoury company, he assembled a marvellous collection of tales of royal mistresses and lovers whose rumpled robes, coroneted elopements, legitimised bastards and bigamous marriage vows are all detailed with the gusto of a Boccaccio. This section apart, the chief value of *The Windsor Tapestry* is as evidence of the passions which the Abdication aroused.

Although he had to split the *Sunday Pictorial*'s £5000 with his publisher and agent, the book made him enough money to pay off the worst of his tax bills and to buy a house in London. Woodbine Cottage was situated in the Vale of Health, Hampstead, and minute though it was, it ranks among the perfect houses he acquired. Leigh Hunt, who once owned it, described it as a 'packing-case' for size, and Keats and Shelley both stayed there and cherished the memory of it. Whitestone Pond stood nearby and Hampstead Heath surrounded it on all sides.

The purchase of Woodbine Cottage was a sure sign of the direction in which his imagination was straying, just as the purchase of the Shiants and the coast-guard's hut on Barra had been. He had lost interest in the Nationalist Party. The politicians had pushed aside the dreamers. MacCormick's hope of merging with the respectable Scottish Party was achieved in 1934, and in the same year Christopher Grieve was expelled for membership of the Communist Party. The clash of utopian aspiration was silenced, and for a generation Monty watched the party he had helped to found become a platform for the ideas of small-town politicians. Henceforth he would restrict himself to Barra affairs. He pestered the Department of Agriculture which owned part of the land in the north of the island to plant grass to prevent sand erosion. With John Lorne Campbell he badgered the Forestry Commission not to plaster solid squares of conifer over the hillsides, and with the other motorists on the island he resorted to civil disobedience – the withholding of road tax – in a successful campaign to persuade the local authority to repair the roads. But Barra by itself was to prove too small a stage.

Having come south in May for the publication of *The Windsor Tapestry*, Monty stayed through the summer. His customary sociability reasserted itself in a round of parties and dinners. Rich & Cowan were about to go out of business, and at one party he met Ian Parsons of Chatto & Windus, with whom he signed a contract for a novel and one other book a year. Cassell's, generous to the last, let him have back for a nominal sum the titles he had sold them. Thus the two decades between the wars which had been so fraught in financial and literary terms took on the look of relative solidity at the end.

Quite uncharacteristically he made a brief visit to Oxford that summer. It was his rule never to go back to scenes of happiness, and the only previous infraction, for a college gaudy (or reunion) in 1920, had been a melancholy event. Driven by Neil MacKellaig, with his brother Dominic in the back beside Chrissie and Nelly Boyte, he now visited first a Magdalen haunted by the ghosts of his dead friends – he reckoned that about two hundred of his Oxford acquaintances had been killed in the war – and then went on to Lady Ham where he had once dreamed of becoming a great poet.

The window on which Roger Fry had written 'The fresh green lap of fair King Richard's land' was broken, but he had no difficulty in returning to the past:

I saw again in that bedroom the room as it once was. My books were again on either side of the fireplace. Twinkle, the Manx cat, was in the grandfather-chair. I was wrestling with a sonnet by the light of a reading candle. I was suddenly glad that window had been broken. On it on a June day in 1904 the Provost of Worcester had written *hoc erat in votis*, and it would be six months later in a letter from Mrs Daniel opened and read in this room that I should hear of the breaking off of my engagement to Ruth Daniel.

They drove on to Somerset, and would have gone on to Cornwall if there had been enough time. It had become 'a pilgrimage to youth', and with only one day remaining he decided to spend it at Beech, visiting again the bungalow his father had called 'Holiday Haunt' to his own and Frank's acute embarrassment.

As I looked at the wide path of the old right of way past Wyard's Farm I saw with my mind's eye that narrow winding right of way through a hop-garden. I saw my young brother and myself resentfully trudging a quarter of a mile with pails to fetch water from the brick-kiln when our own well ran dry in the baking summer of the Diamond Jubilee.

From there they went to Wield, in whose Norman church he had once served as an altar boy, and then at last returned to 1938 and the portents of another war. He never explained what gave rise to this surprising urge to return to the original scenes of his memory-sets, but it may have been the threat of destruction implied by the digging of trenches and the issue of gas masks that summer.

Neither he nor Faith believed in the efficacy of the gas masks or the trenches. Taught by the bitter experience of the previous conflict, they were convinced that only unimaginable folly could set in motion another war, and that a government capable of such folly could not be trusted in anything, not even the issue of proper gas masks.

'I know perfectly well the whole business is to keep us quiet and that masks are useless after a few hours,' Faith wrote bitterly, to which Monty replied that in Gallipoli the troops had used them for tobacco pouches. 'I hope the latest gas masks are even as useful as that.'

The pilgrimage to youth had taken him through Somerset, where he found a cottage for sale with a view across the Vale of Avalon to Glastonbury Tor. The price was only £800 and, knowing that Faith wanted a home in the country where she could exercise the passion for gardening she had learned in Jethou, he bought it.

'Faith ... always began by feeling ill at ease with a place,' Monty commented, 'and then gradually fell in love with it and went on clinging to it when she had to leave it. Thus it had been with Capri, and with Jethou most of all.' The Somerset cottage was an exception to the first part of this rule. She fell in love with it at once, and helped by Colin Summerford and Nicholas Nadegin she was installed by the end of 1938. With a touching optimism she named it Peace Close.

For Faith too the turbulence of the inter-war years appeared to be resolving itself into tranquillity. At the beginning of 1938 the first volume of her autobiography, *As Much As I Dare*, had been published amid general recognition that her writing deserved, as Max Beerbohm put it, 'that overworked, but in this case necessary adjective – distinguished'. Thus encouraged, she was writing a sequel, *More Than I Should*. Her old friend Nadegin had returned to keep her company after his wife had run off with Kerensky, the last prime minister of pre-Bolshevik Russia, and his presence gave a security she otherwise lacked. 'He's so kind and mothering,' she wrote gratefully in her diary.

In the last months of peace, Monty was caught up in another of those unlikely episodes which make it easier to understand why he treated life as a drama. Among the readers who appreciated his passionate defence of Edward VIII was the ex-Kaiser of Germany, then living at Doorn in Holland. Through an intermediary, Professor Haäs-Heye, he let Monty know that he would like to discuss the possibility of his own biography being written. Unable to resist the lure, Monty travelled to Doorn in May 1939 with Haäs-Heye, who had brought with him a pile of gardening catalogues. They met the ex-Kaiser out walking, an old man dressed in a grey Harris tweed suit, and Monty was struck by his bright blue eyes and diminutive size, not more than five feet six inches. They discussed gardening and the existence of the Loch Ness Monster, while the equerry kept dropping the slippery catalogues from the bundle he had been handed. Then Monty was taken on to the house to meet his daughter, the Princess, who sat in a boudoir crowded with pictures including a portrait of the Kaiser in white uniform, breastplate and winged helmet.

'After tea,' he wrote in his autobiography,

when we were smoking those royal cigarettes – all cardboard holder they seemed – there was a rumble from what I had thought was a cupboard. The Princess flung away her cigarette as she jumped up.

'It is the Emperor,' she exclaimed. 'He has come up by the lift.'

As she spoke the cupboard door opened, and there, framed in the entrance, stood that eighty-year-old bearded shrivelled Emperor, almost, it seemed, standing at attention beneath the picture of himself in all his glory with the famous moustaches and winged helmet of once upon a time.

At any period such a scene would be fantastic, but with events rolling inexorably towards a new conflict, it stands beyond comedy or tragedy. When Monty came back in August for a second visit, there were dark-suited Nazis in attendance and white peacocks screaming in the garden. With such ominous portents, there was no need of clairvoyance to know that war was at hand once more.

16

The blast of war

Three weeks after the outbreak of hostilities, he began writing *The West Wind of Love* in Suidheachan. With what must have been an almost overpowering melancholy, he took up the story in late 1917 just after Athene Langridge had asked John Ogilvie what he had hated most in the war. 'Stupidity,' he had answered. 'And the power for harm given to the second- and third-rate mind, and the end it becomes in itself.'

In common with the great majority of people who had fought in the First World War, he was obsessed by the folly which had permitted another war to begin. He was not deluded by Hitler. As early as 1933 he had given up a magazine column rather than undertake not to be rude about him, and from the summer of 1938 he had spoken at meetings on behalf of German Jews. Nevertheless he longed for almost any solution other than war – because almost nothing could be more stupid than that solution.

At Woodbine Cottage, a few weeks before he came north to Barra, he and Christopher Stone had given dinner to General Sir Edmund Ironside, who was about to become Chief of the Imperial General Staff, and was generally accounted one of the cleverest men in the army. To Monty's dismay he turned out to be a British Israelite – an infallible sign of barminess in his opinion – and more seriously to despise Hore-Belisha, the Secretary of State for War and promoter of Captain Liddell Hart's ideas on mobile warfare, because he wore zip-fastened boots. Outwardly Monty merely found him absurd and the encounter became one of his stock stories, in the course of which Ironside's absurdities were no doubt exaggerated, but inwardly he discerned in his attitude a contempt for innovation which was typical of those in charge of the country. They were the same people who had turned against Edward VIII, who kept

Churchill out of office, and who had allowed the war to happen. The full force of his despair was expressed in a letter to his mother – almost the last he ever sent her – written in the spring of 1940:

I cannot see this war as anything except a crime against man and a sin against God. The ultimate responsibility rests on this country, the immediate responsibility on Germany. I consider ours the greater guilt ... We should have had no war if we had not got rid of our ex-king. Indeed, it was the money power which was most instrumental in getting him out. Well, people will have to learn their lesson, and it is going to be a very hard lesson, and a very unpleasant lesson. Fortunately for my own peace of mind I have a very clear idea of what to aim at, and therefore I contemplate the inevitable catastrophe calmly. So much will be swept away that ought to be swept away.

This letter brought only a short reply from his mother: 'I have been thinking so much lately about what an extraordinarily good little boy you were, how anxious to be good.' A fortnight later, on 4 May, she died at the age of eighty-seven. A telegram summoning him to her bedside was delayed and he arrived too late to see her, but Faith who was with her almost to the end heard her asking for Monty. She more than anyone had made him what he was through the impact of her powerful but divided nature.

Affectionate and judgemental, witty and pious, she coloured his earliest years with extremes of mood which fostered both charm and anxiety, responsiveness and superficiality. At the funeral service his thoughts turned to their days together – making the garden at Beech, the holiday at Cromer, her pleasure in his ambition to be a parson – but he felt no grief.

He stayed on in London after her death, hoping for a job in the Ministry of Information which never came. For the moment he was free of literary pressure. He had completed *The West Wind of Love*, which had to be split in two because of paper rationing, and *Aegean Memories*, the last of his First World War memoirs, a revised version of *Greek Memories* having been issued in July 1939. With time on his hands he took part in a BBC broadcast about Poland and gave vent to his despair in an unscripted exclamation that he hoped a nation of shopkeepers was not about to become a nation of undertakers. The remark caused him to be banned from broadcasting on current affairs for two years, but it expressed his mood. Unable to find any wartime employment, he took up a project first offered to him in the spring, to write a commentary for a series of war pictures by a Hungarian artist, Imre Hofbauer, on behalf of the War Orphans Fund. The volume was called *Calvary,* and in it the apocalyptic note sounded in his last letter to his mother found full expression. Although it was written before the end of *The Four Winds of Love,* it may properly be taken as its epilogue. In the days when Dunkirk was about to take place, invasion seemed probable and his writing became the authentic call of the Cracow trumpeter before oblivion fell.

Hitler was not a freak personality, he argued, but the genius of 'the little man'. The war, therefore, was not just a twentieth-century conflict but

a stage in an evolutionary struggle to determine the direction to which humanity shall move for a couple of centuries . . . I believe that we may soon be witnessing the death agony of that habit of thought and system of economy too loosely called capitalism . . . I regard our period as the beginning of the reaction against the trend that was given to Western development by the Renaissance and the Reformation and the discovery of America which led to an exaggerated conception of the rights of the individual and an insufficient appreciation of his duties. The process has been accelerated by the abuse of mechanical progress from printing to flying, by the corruption of the ideal of popular education, by the institution of [humanist] theory for religious practice, by the continually growing power of money, and by the encouragement of an illusory freedom of thought at the cost of real freedom of action. The result has been that never before in recorded history was the ordinary man so completely at the mercy of his environment as he is today. The liberty that seemed within his grasp at the beginning of the fifteenth century is now further away than ever, and it is likely to recede still further as long as man elects to be the slave of self rather than the servant of God . . .

Although it was his depression about the war which brought the expression of this credo, it had been prefigured in the thought which led him to nationalism in the 1920s, and he quoted it again at length in his autobiography 'because it expresses so much of what I am feeling in 1967'. It was therefore the consistent belief of the latter half of his life. The other side of this dignified statement of reaction was a violent hatred of 'the little man' – not just Hitler, but the Babbitts, Kippses, clerks and bureaucrats of the modern world. In a furious outburst provoked by H. G. Wells's jibe that Lord Gort was 'a praying general' he declared that Mr Lewisham, Kipps and Mr Polly merged into one would become Hitler, and that had Cromwell not cured the English of dictatorship, 'H. G. Wells himself might have become an English Hitler and laid out a cloud cuckooland paradise for mankind with dive-bombers'.

Like a Savonarola he then turned on the sort of people who enjoyed gangster films and books and accused them of 'administering to themselves thrills and kicks more pernicious to moral stamina than any hashish or cocaine could supply'. It was their escapism which left Britain undefended in 1938, he implied. In similar vein he condemned newspaper readers for their 'sadistic pruriency' in responding to stories of people beaten up with rubber truncheons while ignoring stories of official stupidity 'hardly less horrible than a rubber truncheon'.

This was the dark side of his character – harsh, illogical and vituperative. Yet it was while he was in this grim mood that he visited Rosamund Lehmann and her daughter Sally, and her letter shows the other side of him. 'Oh it was a treat your visit,' she wrote. 'You don't know what pleasure it gave us both. You make me remember the kind of life that surrounded me when I was young, and fill me with nostalgia and happy melancholy. The fact is, you make me feel like myself and sometimes one forgets what this is like.'

To adapt to his friends and give back to them the best of themselves was his inimitable quality, but a protean character takes on all characteristics, and it was partly self-protection that made him hate 'the little man' so violently. In the last part of Calvary he described the despair induced by the sight of crowds of Dutch cyclists riding by as he sat in a café waiting for his appointment with the ex-Kaiser. 'If I had been told then that thousands of these people would be blown to fragments by dive-bombers in the following May, I believe that while the fleeting despair held I should have felt as little emotion as to be told of thousands of midges being devoured by dragon-flies.'

When he returned to Barra in July he found a letter from Donald Cameron of Lochiel asking him to take over the Local Defence Volunteers, soon to be redesignated the Home Guard, in Barra. Nothing could have been better designed to turn his mind from the gloomy grandeur of these thoughts. To stave off Armageddon with a platoon of elderly islanders amid a blizzard of top secret and most confidential instructions from military authorities could lead only to despair or comedy. The tone of fatuity was set by his one-time brother officer in the Hertfordshire Volunteers, Henry Croft, who, as Parliamentary Under-Secretary for War, suggested that Home Guards without rifles should use pikes against the invaders' machine guns.

When an extra consignment of rifles and Lewis guns arrived for the Barra Company of the 2nd Inverness-shire Battalion, they were followed by peremptory orders to send them back at once. Monty complied, but they reappeared a week later followed by still brusquer orders to return them forthwith and explain how he had obtained these extra weapons. 'I decided to stick to them,' he recollected, 'and surprise the enemy.'

He had a longer battle to prevent the call-up of Kenny MacCormick, his chauffeur and handyman, whom he designated as essential to the war effort on Barra, because he was the only trained mechanic on the island. For two years he fended off orders for him to report to the Ministry of Labour, to Scottish Command and to the RAF. At length the RAF threatened to send the military police to take him away. Monty countered with a warning that he would use the Home Guard and the coastguard, of which he had been appointed supervisor, to arrest the police as soon as they landed. In the end he was forced to admit defeat, but it took the full force of military and civilian bureaucracy to achieve it.

Living on an island sixty miles from the mainland made defiance easier, but it also exaggerated the absurdities of the Home Guard. Messages from headquarters in Inverness 150 miles away took up to ten days to arrive, for the telegrams were censored and the telephone was unreliable. Thus when the code word 'Cromwell', signifying that an invasion had actually taken place, was mistakenly flashed up and down the country in September 1940 the Inverness censors decided that it was too suspicious a message to pass on.

'Up in Harris the gallant [Local Defence Volunteers] under Colonel Walker . . . stood by with their thirty American rifles,' he recalled:

In North Uist MacDonald of Balranald was resolved to do or die with thirty rifles. In South Uist Finlay Mackenzie, the owner of the famous Lochboisdale Hotel, led his warriors to the beaches prepared with thirty rifles to fling the enemy back into the sea. Only the LDV of Barra did not move to take their thirty rifles from the rack and slept tranquilly all through that anxious weekend.

The island was further isolated when the War Office designated the Western Isles a Protected Area, meaning that a military permit was required to enter it. Six months later, Whitehall split the area into two so that Barra was divided from South Uist and a separate permit was needed to travel between the two. Into the midst of the confusion came an announcement from MacNeil of Barra, an American businessman rather unconvincingly deemed to be chief of the clan, that he was raising money in the United States to send five hundred Glasgow children to Barra. To this, as to all other fatuities, Monty responded with a long letter written with indignation and courtesy struggling for supremacy.

The constant stress produced a skin disease which tormented him for much of the war, and yet he could not prevent his imagination from being seduced by the romance of defending the island.

It appealed to his 'creative urge', he said, and he quickly persuaded himself that Barra was the logical place for enemy submarines to use as a base and that the show depended on him. 'I doubt if I can manage to get down to Manchester,' he told the BBC in February 1941, 'as I am OC Home Guard here and also Supervisor of the Coast Guard, and I think things may be a little lively here presently.'

Once he had imagined the role he performed it admirably, earning the congratulations of the Inspector-General of Home Guard Forces, and a compliment from one of his men. 'You enjoyed yourself with Compton,' the latter said. 'Mind you, he liked to hear his own voice, but he wasn't for ever on about drill, just the shooting and the Germans.'

His moment of triumph came in June 1941 when the South Uist Home Guard invaded across the five mile stretch of the Sound of Barra and the Protected Area's invisible boundary. They had several veterans of the First World War in their ranks and were reinforced by a platoon of Royal Engineers, but under the eyes of the GSO1 Scottish Command Monty won a famous victory.

'I trapped them at Eoligarry,' he told Christopher Stone, 'and we bagged about a dozen REs close to Suidheachan. They tried a surprise landing at Bruernish with another boat, but I had anticipated that move and we wiped out the whole lot with a Lewis gun. Simultaneously they attacked Castleby, and we again obliterated them.'

He was delighted by his success, and Faith, who was staying at Suidheachan, exclaimed, 'It's Syra all over again.' It bred a crop of stories because almost everyone had been involved – Roderick MacLeod, the Castlebay bank manager, Mr Mackenzie, the Church of Scotland minister who was one of his subalterns, and most of the able-bodied crofters and shopkeepers. Soon everyone knew that the sergeant commanding the Royal Engineers had let himself be captured because he was in love with the maid at Suidheachan, and that Dr Bartlett, who was an umpire, had attempted to tell Sguiridh that he was dead but was frustrated by Sguiridh affecting to believe that the doctor was a German spy disguised as an umpire.

At the end of the letter he said, 'One day I shall write a grand comedy called *Keep the Home Guard Turning*.' He did so two years later when it became the third novel to feature the eagle-nosed Hector Macdonald of Ben Nevis – not to mention of Glenbogle, Glenbristle, Strathdiddle,

Strathdun, Loch Hoch and Loch Hoo – Mac 'ic Eachainn to those who had the Gaelic, and the distillation of a dozen different Highland grandees known to the author. It also marked the debut of the islands of Great and Little Todday, and their denizens of MacRuries and Macroons who would achieve their greatest fame in *Whisky Galore*.

The story is built around Ben Nevis's invasion of the Toddays, ostensibly as a Home Guard exercise but in reality to recapture a left boot from the Todday company which properly belongs to his own, and the events of 29 June 1941 appear in almost every detail down to the love-sick sergeant – Fred Odd – allowing himself to be captured in order to woo Peigi Macroon.

Ben Nevis had appeared first in 1940 as a minor character in a comedy of bureaucratic confusion called *The Red Tapeworm* which Monty had written in order to salve his irritation at the flowering of wartime controls. In that volume Ben Nevis's role was merely to bemuse Sir Claud Huntbath, Permanent Secretary to the Minister of Waste, by his insistence on being addressed as Britain's highest mountain, and to intimidate him with the amaranthine hue that mantled his eagle-nose in a rage. He achieved his first independent airing in *The Monarch of the Glen*, to which Monty turned in the winter of 1940 when pain and despondency made it impossible to continue with *The North Wind of Love*. There is a certain pathos in the abandonment of John Ogilvie's heartfelt advocacy of Scottish Nationalism for Ben Nevis's trite argument against it that 'if every Scot stayed at home to run Scotland the Empire would have to be run by the English and the whole caboodle would collapse in a few years.' Nevertheless, in the series of Highland comedies heralded by *The Monarch of the Glen*, he struck a vein of humour that deservedly brought him a wider readership than he had known since the early 1920s.

Although the original of Ben Nevis was confidently recognised in many of the Highlands' more prominent landowners – Cameron of Lochiel being the most popular choice, though Lochiel himself picked MacDonald of Glengarry – it would be truer to say that he represented a type whose traits are unusually well marked. Educated at an English public school and supported by a rich English wife, Ben Nevis is genially ignorant of his surroundings and his history. He retains some words of Gaelic from childhood – 'always wish I'd kept it up' – and a few legends of the MacDonald past, but his chief expertise lies in determining the order of precedence at the Glenbristle Highland Gathering, the likelihood of county council grants being available for the repair of his roads, and the prospects for grouse-shooting and stalking. His two daughters and three sons are all as massive and unthinking as himself, and exposure to wind and rain has veined their complexions like chaffinch eggs.

In the course of the comedies Ben Nevis plays host – willingly to Chester Royde, the American millionaire who wishes to acquire a flame-coloured kilt; unwillingly to the Hikers' Union who try to invade Glenbogle Castle after he shoots a trespassing hiker's wireless; confidently to his droopy-moustached neighbour Hugh Cameron of Kilwhillie, who is burdened by bashfulness and an impoverished deer forest (these and other characteristics, such as his habit of burying a new kilt in a bog for a year before wearing it, were borrowed, like many other of his characteristics, from Angus Campbell of Dunstaffnage); and apprehensively to Mrs Florence Urquhart-Unwin who wants to hunt fairies. Although he also travels to India and invades the Toddays, he is pre-eminently a man of his place – to the Highlands what Lord Emsworth is to Shropshire.

There are no villains in the Highland comedies, and the sharpest humour is a gentle teasing. This usually took the form of an inner joke, such as the choice of Inveraray, stronghold of the Campbells, as the model for Glenbogle, home of their hereditary foes, the MacDonalds. It is not necessary to have seen the once truly desperate zeal of Highland landowners to sell their estates to appreciate Hugh Cameron of Kilwhillie's reaction to the presence of a rich American:

Kilwhillie's faded eyes were lighted up with that strange light which never was on sea or land, but is only to be seen in the eyes of a landed proprietor in the Highlands who hopes he has found a buyer for an overtaxed forest of twelve heads and a shooting lodge that looks like a bunch of tarnished pepper-pots.

However, such descriptions are always exact. When Monty demanded of his readers 'a dramatic sense', he wished them to see the scene he had before his own eyes, which was the accentuation of a meticulously observed original.

On the whole his targets enjoyed the gentle scratching – 'most humorous irony,' Lochiel commented – but on one occasion it backfired badly. In the first four comedies there is a running joke about the infinitely misty descriptions of the Highlands and Islands attributed to Hector Hamish Mackay, 'the well-known topographer and author of *Happy Days among the Heather* and *Faerie Lands Forlorn*'. The style reads like parody – 'Is that St Brendan's floating isle we see upon the western horizon? Forsooth on such a night it were easy to conjure up that elusive morsel of geography' – but is an almost exact rendering of the hugely popular Hebridean guidebooks of Alasdair Alpin MacGregor. In *The Book of Barra*, a joint compilation with John Lorne Campbell of island facts and history, Monty had issued a general criticism of guidebook writers who made 'the Islands and the Islanders conform to a sentimental preconception', but the figure of Hector Hamish Mackay made plain the particular target he had in mind.

The joke reached its climax in *Hunting the Fairies*, published in 1945, where Hector Hamish Mackay actually makes an appearance, small and kilted, 'with slightly shrivelled but well-weathered knees', and receives a moving accolade from Florence Urquhart-Unwin, gushing President of the Ossianic Society of Boston, Mass.: 'Hector Hamish Mackay's books have given me more happy hours than almost any books – except of course Ossian and Shakespeare and Longfellow and the great poets. And another British author to admire greatly is Beverley Nichols. He's so close to Nature.'

His touch in this feline mood was very sure, but MacGregor had already had enough. In his next guidebook, *The Western Isles of Scotland*, he admitted that he had in the past looked through 'coloured spectacles', but that now he proposed to tell the truth. As a guidebook to the Hebrides the result is somewhat unexpected, for it accuses the inhabitants of being lazy, dirty, irresponsible, apathetic, obsequious, drunken, obtuse, unmusical, avaricious, immoral, incestuous, and of going to bed late at night. 'I hope no one will be so foolhardy as to contradict me on all this,' MacGregor concluded from an address in Chelsea, 'for I write with some inside knowledge of what goes on, having been associated with Highland and Island affairs since infancy.'

The only two portraits to which Monty did admit were a sketch of the legendary skipper of the Macbrayne's ferries, Captain 'Squeaky' Robertson, who appears as Captain McKechnie, and a warm picture of Father John Macmillan, who became Father John Macalister, the priest of Little Todday, vast, generous-hearted and ready to solve all difficulties with his motto, 'We'll roll right over them.' Nevertheless, teasing caricatures are scattered all over the series, and this is not surprising given Monty's technique of taking the original from memory and imagining himself into the role. He had one near escape when he portrayed a Miss Donaldson who had also written a guidebook about the Highlands as Miss Lamont, an eccentric rival to Hector Hamish Mackay with distinctly lesbian tendencies. Just as the book, *Hunting the Fairies*, was going to press, he discovered that Miss Donaldson was still alive and very prone to litigation, and he had to spend an anxious day with the proofs changing her into the effeminate Aeneas Lamont.

Where the inhabitants of the Toddays are concerned, there are several likenesses to individuals on Barra and South Uist, but the most notable is the bumptious Paul Waggett. No one knowing of Monty's feelings about Dr Bartlett doubted that he was the original of the figure who stands for authority and convention in the Toddays. His grey eyes bulge with self-satisfaction and the cocksure certainty that he knows the best way of doing everything. 'Och he doesn't really mean any harm,' says Duncan Ban Macroon. 'Somebody must have told him once he was a clever boy and he's grown up on the strength of it.'

His first appearance was as the commander of the Home Guard who had inadvertently aroused Ben Nevis's wrath by keeping his boot. The combination of Ben Nevis thundering in Glenbogle Castle, of Waggett attempting to make soldiers from crofters despite their wives' habit of using the helmets as basins for the henfeed, and of Father James rolling over the difficulties that stand in the way of Sergeant Odd's engagement to Peigi Macroon, makes *Keep the Home Guard Turning* the most attractive of the comedies. Waggett's most famous role, however, came as the last outpost of law-abiding sobriety in *Whisky Galore*: 'Here we are fighting a war for our very existence as a nation, and the one idea of the people here is to get hold of whisky which doesn't belong to them.'

The raw facts of the story occurred on 3 February 1941 while Monty was lost in the maze of pain and skin irritation which had forced him to abandon *The North Wind of Love* for *The Monarch of the Glen*. The s.s. *Politician*, loaded with 200,000 cases of premium whisky for the American market in the Number 5 hold, as well as a cargo of cotton and bicycles, was steaming north from Liverpool to join a convoy across the Atlantic when bad weather blew her off course. Just before dawn she grounded on a rock off Eriskay, between Barra and South Uist, and could not be moved. The crew was taken off by the Castlebay lifeboat and given shelter by Barra families until they could be taken back to the mainland. A salvage firm began unloading the cotton and bicycles, but Number 5 hold was full of oily water making it impossible to retrieve the whisky. A customs seal was placed on the hatch and the police were warned.

Meanwhile, relaxing in the warmth of peat fires, the crew had talked of its contents, and the word was spreading. After a month the salvors announced that they had recovered as much as they could, and the wreck was abandoned. By that stage of the war, conditions in the Western Isles had almost reached the emergency levels of Great Todday, where the oldest inhabitant, Hector MacRurie, 'has made up his mind that he will shortly have to face his Maker without a dram inside him to sustain him through the ordeal'. On the night after the salvors left, a fleet of small boats was drawn to the wreck like moths to a golden light. The men improvised gaffs to hook the cases of whisky, and Tilley lamps were brought to help them see. The cases were lowered to the waiting boats on lengths of cotton stripped from discarded bales. For weeks to come the same fantastic scenes were repeated nightly in the dancing glow of the lamps, as men dressed in their oldest clothes and sometimes their wives' discarded dresses slithered around the oily decks clutching bottles of whisky. Sometimes a customs launch would appear and the boats would scatter, and occasionally the police were waiting on shore. The problem of hiding so much whisky was the biggest problem. Monty simply arranged his bottles all along the top of his bookshelves, and visiting dignitaries were careful not to enquire into their origin. Those with smaller houses had to conceal them in sheds, fields or along the shore. There were rumours that some of the old women looking for cockles were gathering bottles as well, and not every man went to his own cache for supplies. But it hardly mattered: whisky was available everywhere; the hospitality was generous, the *ceilidhs* stupendous, and the prices, for those who wanted to buy, ludicrous. 'I often think of the 30 cases for £20,' the Coddie wrote to Monty three years later. 'I shall be weeping over that bargain for ever. Every time I think of it, I have a grudge against myself. What did happen to my courage?'

There was a less pleasant side. Drunkenness became an epidemic, and in the summer an increase in police activity which led to several arrests gave rise to ugly suspicions of informers. But it was a small price to pay for a season of bounty. Bottles from the 'Polly' continued to turn up, and with them the spirit of a carnival which had attracted boats from up and down the long island and would be remembered for years until memory merged with the events of *Whisky Galore*.

The book was not written until 1946, by which time Monty was living in England, but his command of Gaelic cadences remained as secure as his rendering of Cockney speech. The plot was ready-made, and woven into it were the long-delayed marriage of Sergeant Odd, the rivalry of the two Toddays, and Paul Waggett's irrepressible lust for convention. He promoted the *Politician* to the *Cabinet Minister* and just as surely raised the events of the spring of 1941 to the level of legend. The word 'galore', from the Gaelic *gu leoir* for plenty, was made popular, and when the book was translated into French that title also became famous as the name of a thousand nightclubs: *Whisky à Go-Go*. 'A genial farce' was the most he would claim for it, but in the post-war world it arrived as the incarnation of the spirit of plenty.

The security cordon around the Western Isles made it difficult for Monty's friends to visit him. Faith came up to stay for an extended period after Peace Close was sold in 1940 to pay her spiralling debts, but she lost much of her enthusiasm for Barra after a gale knocked down the garden fence, allowing horses to browse in the flower-beds. When it became possible to rent a bungalow in the grounds next to her former home at Peace Close, she returned south to garden in a more benign climate.

Bob Boothby, then under a political cloud and about to enter the RAF, came to be restored in the company of a girl called Araminta. In the telegram announcing their arrival, her name was transposed to 'armaments', and Monty paraded his Home Guard and a couple of carts to receive what he hoped would be a substantial supply of munitions. Although disappointed as a commander he was delighted as a host, for visitors were rarer than rifles, and far too few to provide the social distraction and audience he had been accustomed to before the war. As the immediate risk of invasion receded towards the end of 1941 he began to make the complicated journey southward more frequently, and an increasing proportion of his time was spent in Glasgow and London, broadcasting frequently and picking up commissions for books.

Two were potboiling biographies – *Mr Roosevelt* and *Dr Beneš*. 'Critics always suggest that potboiling affects a writer's creative work adversely,' he said, defending himself. 'This is nonsense ... The effort to make a potboiler produce good soup helps the cooking of a creative joint.' In this case, however, he was using the potboilers as an excuse for postponing the completion of his magnum opus. Having lost sympathy with nationalism, he had also lost the conclusion to which the quartet had been leading, and as things stood in 1941, *The North Wind of Love* could only have culminated in a pit of apocalyptic gloom. By 1942 his hopes were beginning to rise, but without a cause to serve they had no focus, and the book of his life could have no proper ending.

The cause and conclusion were provided in February 1942 by a request from the Greek government in exile to write the official history of their war. The approach led to the revival of his old love affair with Greece, and John Ogilvie's return to the Greek islands to marry Euphrosyne

Ladas at the end of *The North Wind of Love* may be taken as the fictional representation of his own emotions.

The Greek invasion of Turkey in 1922 had been the outcome of the Venizelist policies he had supported so vigorously during the First World War, and with its failure his philhellenism dwindled. Scotland became his cause and in 1936 Greece slipped further from his affection when it fell under the power of the dictator Joannes Metaxas, who had once been King Constantine's firm supporter against Venizelos. That indifference vanished on 28 October 1940 when Metaxas delivered a resounding '*Oxi*' – 'No' – to an Italian ultimatum demanding virtual surrender. In the *Sunday Graphic*, which had recently given him a fortnightly column, Monty declared, 'If a single bomb falls on Athens, Rome should be destroyed.' Over the next eighteen months he took what opportunities he could to plead for more attention to be given to Greece. Few as they were, his efforts caught the notice of the exiled Greek government, and it was at the personal insistence of King George of the Hellenes that he was asked to write the history which was eventually published under the title *The Wind of Freedom*.

As he wrote he became more Greek, until he reached a point where he told Faith, 'I think I shall abandon British nationality after the war and take out Greek papers.' Despite his passion, he steered a sensitive course between the fierce rivalries of royalists and republicans, which Metaxas's regime had stirred up. He endeared himself to Greek hearts by calling for the union of Cyprus with Greece, and made no secret of his commitment to the enlargement of her frontiers when war ended. Yet it was not mere propaganda. Lawrence Durrell, an exacting critic, wrote at once to say that '. . . it is to date the one really properly documented account of this confused, marvellous and miraculous business. I am sure the Greeks will feel themselves to be in your debt for the magnificent way you have handled the anomalies of the Metaxas regime . . . you are the first writer to have put them in their true perspective for us.'

After it was published, Monty began to write regularly for the emigré paper *Hellas* and in 1944 became chairman of the League for Democracy in Greece. Time for these activities among the rush of other business was only made possible by cutting his links with Scotland.

Faith was the first to hear of his intention to move south when he wrote in April 1943 asking her to look over a house in Suffolk. For the first time in her life, Faith demurred at being plucked away from her surroundings. She felt at home in Somerset, and had built up a circle of friends who provided her with the support she needed at sixty-five. Despite completing the third volume of her autobiography, *Always Afternoon*, and occasional journalism, she was desperately poor, subsisting on dividends from the *Gramophone* and periodic cheques from Monty. The sight of her left eye was gradually deteriorating and she was prone to fits of despair about herself and the country. In her defeatist moods her condemnation of the government's handling of the war became so extreme that Nadegin would rush from the room shouting 'Traitor!' Nevertheless in more confident mood she could overlook her disabilities, and declare, 'I'm a very lucky old female. Life blossoms instead of withering.' Although delighted that Monty was coming south, she had no intention of uprooting herself to live in East Anglia. 'I don't think you seriously want a Suffolk house,' she told him firmly.

He was, however, intent on moving. At the end of November 1943 he purchased a short lease on Sudbrooke Lodge, a large and handsome house in Richmond, which had once been the home of Nell Gwyn and later Judge Jeffreys. The purchase was made possible by the sort of stroke of fortune which ought to give extravagance a good name. Early in 1943 the new publishing house of Macdonald's offered £10,000 for the copyrights of his first twenty novels. Ever since 1918 he had made a practice of selling his copyrights rather than taking royalties, but they had all reverted to him either through being allowed to go out of print or through Cassell's generosity. As a result he was now able to sell them a second time – a fact the Inland Revenue were to make much of. The sale enabled him to pay Faith's debts as well as his own, two of which had been on his conscience. Christina Roebuck, an Edinburgh hostess in the 1930s, had lent him £800 in his crisis year of 1936, and in 1942, Bryher, daughter of the millionaire Sir John Ellerman and companion of the Imagist poet H. D. (Hilda Doolittle), had made him a loan of £750. Bryher's generosity did not stop there: she sent Faith regular cheques and to the end of her life paid the cost of her journeys abroad. As Monty said, 'I cannot find any other word than goodness for Bryher's heart.'

He remained in Barra until April 1944, which was long enough to finish *The North Wind of Love* in March and to disband the Barra Home Guard so that they could plant potatoes and dig peats. There was nothing now to hold his imagination on the island. In the event he had scarcely settled in Sudbrooke before the arrival of V1 rockets in June sent him back to Barra until the end of August, but the move south was irreversible.

Once he had arrived in London he succumbed to all the pleasures which it had to offer – dinner parties with Lady Cunard, speeches to

Cambridge undergraduates, lunch with Rosamond Lehmann, negotiations with film producers, discussions with Robert Donat for a play
about Byron, BBC talks with Moray McLaren.

With Hilaire Belloc mentally ill, Monty was the senior Catholic writer,
and as such was asked to propose the toast to Cardinal Griffin, Archbishop of Westminster, at a dinner of Catholic writers. He did this
sort of thing well, although he rarely went to church – 'Father John
understands about my sciatica,' he used to say on Barra – and when he
did attend, as often as not would read a book through the service.

'Compton Mackenzie made an emotional speech,' Evelyn Waugh
noted dryly in his diary. '"Here we all are together, all different,
all divided on every issue except one – our love and homage to His
Grace. I humbly beg His Grace to give us a lead in our work." His
Grace had clearly never read anything except a text-book in his life, but was
not nonplussed.

In the wake of his magnum opus, Monty was restricting himself to
writing potboilers, such as the biography of Beneš which occupied the
last months of 1944. 'I am more free from financial worries than I have
been for years,' he told Faith early in 1945. A buyer was found for
Woodbine Cottage. In December *The North Wind of Love* had sold out
on its first printing of 15,000 copies, and invitations to parties poured
in. 'The rush of my life seems to increase all the time,' he wrote to
Chrissie who had stayed in Barra to sell Suidheachan. 'Tonight I'm
dining with Lady Juliet Duff, which means an enchanting evening back
in a civilised world.'

This was the Monty which most people remembered – sociable, vivid
and endlessly entertaining, as though untouched by the weariness of war.
'Why do people complain about having to go to parties?' he demanded
of Terence de Vere White. 'When I go to a party, I go because I like
them and I know that I am an asset.' And he was. Where other guests
might need prodding, Monty would scintillate from the start. The stories
were always about himself, and studded with allusions which showed him
at his best – 'As Venizelos used to say, "Of course Captain Mackenzie, no
one understands our country as you do"' or, "Ironside turned to me and
said, "Now Monty you would know better than anyone else."'

Few people minded. The tales were told superbly, and he took such
obvious pleasure in them that the mood was contagious. 'I met him in
London ... at a rather dreary literary gathering,' Edmund Wilson
remembered from an occasion in 1945, 'and, unexpectedly, enjoyed him
more than anybody else that evening. I was astonished, among all the

limp and the dim, to find him so cheerful and brisk, small and wiry, and full of energy and delighted with himself.'

He found his best form at the Savile Club, where his arrival began to have something of the effect of a rerun of *Casablanca* for film fans. Stories known line for line would be begged from him, and without the presence of ladies these included the more risqué ones, such as the selection of a prostitute for Guy Bonham-Carter in pre-First World War Paris, the cabaret girl urinating on a gardener from a castle wall, and the vast sexual lore of the Empire, the Apollo and Alhambra theatres.

'He was the uncrowned king of the Savile,' remembered Tom Howarth, High Master of St Paul's, who met him there after the war. 'When people knew he was coming, there tended to be a large turnout for the occasion. He conveyed a sense of exceptional vitality, and long after the rest of us were dropping he would still be talking, his pipe in his hand and whisky appearing in Homeric quantities.'

Among the club's newest members was the young novelist John Moore, then serving with the Fleet Air Arm, whose high spirits and kindness of heart made him a much-loved figure at the Savile. After the war he presided over the Cheltenham Literary Festival, and his lovingly observed novels of the English countryside brought him a small but influential following. In him Monty found a deeply congenial spirit. Their friendship was typical of the links he forged with younger novelists, none of whom were in sympathy with the critical outlook typified by Cyril Connolly and Raymond Mortimer. Among others who joined Moore in Monty's inner circle at the Savile were Richard Church, C. P. Snow, Eric Linklater and Humphrey Hare.

'I don't think there's much doubt that he felt most at home in the club,' remarked Howarth. 'I should say that he preferred chaps' company to girls'.' But it was part of his charm to suggest that each audience was his favourite. And one of his female friends remarked, with equal conviction, 'I am pretty certain that he never felt at ease with men in the way he did with women.'

With both sexes there was a conspiracy about his showing off. Norah Smallwood expressed the general view of his women friends: 'I liked to see him showing off. I think any woman does like to see a man she admires putting himself in the best light.' To his male friends it was the weakness which lightened the multitude of his virtues. 'He was of course a vain man,' Eric Linklater wrote in an obituary, 'but his vanity was curiously innocent and certainly never offensive.' The example he offered was of Monty searching for some emotion he had never experienced and finding only one. '"I've never known what it is to feel jealous. But then of course" – a brief pause to question memory – "oh no, I've never had any occasion for jealousy."'

As a Home Guard commander he had grown a military moustache, and he now added to it a small, pointed beard whose snow-whiteness was the only sign of the pain and stress of the war years. He continued to find the adoration of women irresistible. 'Ah, my dear,' he would say with a wistful smile, 'if only we had met twenty years earlier, what an affair we should have had.' At least one of the young women he said it to was prepared to roll back the years, but there was more than time involved. When a handsome, middle-aged womaniser used that phrase in *Figure of Eight*, the girl to whom it was addressed saw the excuse through the compliment. 'You were afraid of a rebuff,' she replied, 'and a man of your experience knows his vanity would not survive a rebuff. It would have crumpled you up. You would have aged rapidly.' Monty did not age rapidly. He liked to have girls and young women about him, but as one astringently observed, 'He wanted us to adore him at his feet, but not to reach any higher.' Despite these limitations, most women continued to find him utterly beguiling – as he well knew. Appearing on the panel show *Any Questions*, he was once asked, 'Which would you prefer to do: to wash up or to dry?' The rest of the panel contrived various excuses for choosing one or the other, but Monty merely smiled and murmured in that mellow, slightly clipped voice, 'When I can't find a woman to do both for me, I'll know I've had it.'

As the war approached its end he became convinced that his future lay with the film industry. He accepted an invitation to join the Scenario Institute which was intended to give direction to the British cinema, and unfolded to J. Arthur Rank an ambitious plan to make films of 'the *Iliad*, the *Odyssey*, the *Aeneid*, Dante's *Inferno*, *Don Quixote* to be made in Spain, all Shakespeare's plays to be made not only in England, but in Greece, Italy and wherever else the scene is set . . . And why do we not go ultimately to Mexico and Peru to make films of the Conquistadores? Let us go all out with half the surface of the globe at our disposal to put British films upon the map.' The response was deafening in its silence.

However he did not lose hope. *Carnival* was being filmed by the Two Cities company and he readily agreed to the suggestion of its managing director, Filippo del Giudice, that he should write a script of *Bonnie Prince Charlie* for Laurence Olivier. Neither this nor a plan to make a film of the famous murderess Madeleine Smith came to anything. Undaunted, he later teamed up with the actor James Robertson Justice to form Albyn Films with the purpose of establishing a Scottish film industry, but that project also foundered.

In December 1944 Faith was rushed into a hospital in Bristol for an emergency gall-bladder operation. He was too busy to see her until February, and after his visit it was she, not quite unexpectedly, who wrote to commiserate with him. 'I am distressed to hear of that blasted skin trouble as well as bronchitis and sciatica. You are thoroughly tired out. I beg you to spare yourself and not give in to the constant demands for your presence which will only increase with your appearance.'

The flurry of his affairs made it impossible to follow such advice. Film work and good company were not the only demands upon his time. The civil war in Greece which began in December 1944 drew a series of passionate articles from him in favour of the communist-led ELAS forces, and forced him as chairman of the League for Democracy to spend long hours attempting to reconcile irreconcilable factions within the League. In addition he had accepted commissions for three quick books – on the steel firm Brockhouse, the about-to-be-nationalised gas industry, and the building firm McAlpine's – and was in a rush to complete them. In April 1945 he moved from Sudbrooke Lodge to the fine medieval and Tudor house of Denchworth Manor near Wantage which, with customary enthusiasm, he informed Faith was 'the Perfect House'. Its large garden encouraged him to order bulbs from newly liberated Holland in quantities which recalled his neophyte days in Cornwall, but the main attraction was a large tithe barn where he could store the vast library of 12,000 books still at Suidheachan. There was even space for Christopher Stone's sizeable collection of books, and Christopher himself, who had been at a loose end since the death of his wife Alyce some months earlier, reserved for himself a bedroom at the Manor.

With the purchase of Denchworth, Suidheachan was put on the market, but Monty allowed himself no regrets. 'Barra had been as important to my life as Burford, Cornwall, Capri, Greece and the Channel Islands had been,' he asserted in his autobiography. 'Yet when the irrevocable moment has come to quit a beloved place I have no sentimental regrets. That place passes into the background of my memory from which I can summon it to be as vivid to me as if I were really living in that place once more.'

Barra, however, was not quite like the others. They had been found by chance, but Barra was the nearest embodiment of his Jacobite dreams that there was, and the place ultimately where he wished to be buried.

In leaving it he was abandoning the inner world he had nurtured in childhood.

In October 1945 a buyer was found for Suidheachan, and with the exception of a brief visit to the island in 1948 to act the *Cabinet Minister's* captain in the film of *Whisky Galore*, he was finished not only with Barra but with thirty-two years of island living.

In the same month he received an enquiry about writing a book whose scope would have daunted anyone less accustomed to the composition of epic novels. The government of India wished him to write the history of the Indian Army in the Second World War in fictional form, and was prepared to fly him to India to do the necessary research. He was about to go into hospital for the skin disease which had troubled him since the early days of the war, and was now diagnosed as ringworm. This ailment, combined with sciatica and the pace of his life, had left him so run-down that even he, who had never resisted any temptation, attempted to decline this one.

He reckoned without his old commanding officer, Sir Ian Hamilton, then aged ninety-six, who stumped up three flights of stairs to his hospital room and insisted that he accept. 'It will be,' he said, 'the perfect way to round off your experience of life.'

After that it was simply a matter of deciding when he could leave. He was committed to finishing *The Vital Flame*, his book on the gas industry, and to writing *Whisky Galore* which he did mostly in bed while trying to ignore stabbing pains in his leg. There were official duties stemming from his position on the selection board of the Book Society and his chairmanship of the League for Democracy in Greece, and he was distracted by a looming conflict with the Inland Revenue concerning the sale of his copyrights to Macdonald's.

Not until 1 October 1946 did he and Chrissie sail for Bombay. Ahead of them lay an odyssey which took some ten months and covered over 50,000 miles by road, rail and air through Burmese jungle and Himalayan mountains. It was the great achievement of his old age.

17

His last bow

He had never been entirely respectable. The actor's son became the novelist whose reputation was made by novels widely regarded as improper. He was the spy found guilty of betraying secrets, and the nationalist who whipped up militancy, the vituperative defender of an exiled king, and the radical who loathed an empire 'inspired solely by the spirit of greed, gain and competition'. Yet he had never been wholly an outsider. Half of him remained with the gentry while he haunted the demi-monde; half of him hoped to see independent Scotland as a model for the empire, and Edward VIII as an exemplar for the establishment. It was that half of him which was set ablaze by the Indian epic.

His itinerary had been composed with an eye to history rather than geography. He and Chrissie travelled first to India to catch an idea of the country which gave birth to the army. Then they flew to North Africa, Syria and Keren in Ethiopia to see the battlefields of 1940. From there they returned to India and followed the 1943–5 campaign in which the Japanese advance was halted in Assam before being rolled back through Burma to Rangoon. Singapore and Hong Kong were visited, and then the Northwest Frontier, followed by an arduous journey by train, lorry and *dandhi* – a Nepalese sedan chair – to Kathmandu.

From the moment that he witnessed the beating of the retreat by the Fifth Mahratta Light Infantry when he first landed, Monty was gripped by the romance which made the Indian Army a home for British exiles and an ideal for Indian soldiers. In its pageantry it retained the weighty grandeur of Edwardian society, but wherever he went brigadiers and generals talked to him not of hierarchy but of traditions, affections and emotions. 'Where the idea originated that Indian Army officers are particularly prone to blimpery I do not know,' he wrote in his diary, 'but it's bad biology.'

He met the commander-in-chief, Field Marshal Sir Claude Auchinleck, and the viceroy, Viscount Wavell, whom he had known as a major in the Black Watch in 1916. He dined with Nehru, and stayed with the Maharajah of Mysore, who was a subscriber to the *Gramophone*. He was crammed into jeeps and military lorries, bumped along jungle trails and over Bailey bridges, and was toured extensively around war memorials and battle sites. Trimly dressed in white cap and blazer, he seemed immune to discomfort or fatigue, and despite the physical pounding and the extremes of climate, he did not suffer a twinge of sciatica. For hour after hour he listened with intense concentration to descriptions of skirmishes, battles and campaigns, and after each new encounter he asked his informant to sign his birthday book. By the end of his tour it contained twelve hundred new names.

Not for a moment did his attention lapse. In a mess room he noted the progression of whiskers in photographs of former officers from the 'Dundrearies' of the 1850s through beards, mutton-chops and soup-strainers to the toothbrushes of the 1940s. Beside a pile of spent shells, he spotted a primula, 'the colour of *P. denticulata*, but it grew with a looser head and was perhaps a shade rosier'. And among the worshippers in a Buddhist temple in Nepal, he saw that 'babies had their eyes darkened with mascara, and even the cheeks of little boys were rouged'.

When he and Chrissie returned to Delhi in May 1947, the timetable for India's independence had been brought forward to August, and with it the nature of the book changed. It was to become larger in scope, a memorial to the old Indian Army before it was split up into the armies of India and Pakistan. In order to have a book on sale before the end of the year, he decided to publish the diary he had kept with Chrissie's help, under the title of *All Over the Place*.

The journey was, therefore, extended. They flew back to England for a few days, then returned to tour the battlefields of North Africa and the Italian campaign, and arrived back in India in time for Independence Day on 15 August. Monty had already met Wavell's successor as viceroy, Lord Mountbatten, who now became governor-general, and during the months of bloodshed that followed independence, he conceived an intense admiration both for him and his wife Edwina. He treasured a letter from Lady Mountbatten in which she had written, 'May I say it is a breath of fresh air knowing someone in a high position such as you hold has so clearly and fairly understood the real Indian picture.'

Although obviously intended to be flattering, it was not greatly exaggerated. To have assisted at the extraordinary events surrounding the end of British rule in India, and to have heard such tales of heroism, fired his imagination more deeply than any experience since the First World War, and his miraculous capacity for absorbing information was stimulated as it never had been since those days.

On his journey home he visited the Seychelles, and wrote *Hunting the Fairies* there in two months. He found it difficult to recover his concentration after this foray to Glenbogle, and the last stage of the odyssey which took him to Kenya made him impatient to be home. He met more generals, and dined with the governor, Sir Philip Mitchell, brother of his beloved Alan who had died at Lahore in 1941. Then, rather than wait for a ship, he and Chrissie flew home, and on 18 May 1948 they arrived back at Denchworth.

It had been not only a great adventure, but a patriotic service compensating for the failure of the government to employ him during the war. He was determined to do the Indian Army justice in the book, which was to be called *Eastern Epic*. Both Auchinleck and Mountbatten expressed their confidence in his ability to present a true picture of the army's achievements, especially in 1944 and 1945 when victory had been overshadowed by the war in Europe and the Pacific. It was no less important to avoid giving offence to the newly independent nations of India and Pakistan. The pressures were considerable, and long after Monty returned home he continued to interview senior officers and wade through piles of blurred carbon copies of dispatches and orders. Even after he began writing, his meticulous concern for accuracy involved a constant correspondence to check facts with military records in India. 'I am staggering along with the book,' he told Faith in October 1949, 'but it's becoming clear that I shall need two volumes. I'm rather tired, in fact very tired.'

Nevertheless John Connell was nearly justified that year in suggesting that 'he has passed through that period of disparagement and neglect which seems inevitable for any serious, creative artist in this country'. The film of *Whisky Galore*, for which he had written the script, achieved an enormous popular success, and by the end of the year the book had sold over 30,000 copies, and *Hunting the Fairies* 20,000 copies. A new edition of *Sinister Street* was brought out by Macdonald's, an eight-volume set of *The Four Winds of Love* was published by Chatto & Windus, and *Carnival* was broadcast on the radio. Among the critics the scourges of the inter-war years, Cyril Connolly and Raymond Mortimer, had turned into mature arbiters of taste, and although they attempted no new assessment, their earlier savagery was not repeated. And at least one influential critic had begun to feel that it was time to reconsider the reputation of Compton Mackenzie.

From a transatlantic perspective, Edmund Wilson came to the conclusion that the continued failure of British critics to give Monty his due was evidence of 'London provincialism'.

'Mackenzie is a very odd literary case,' he wrote to a friend in the summer of 1949:

He gets less attention now than he deserves. He has been – except perhaps in *Carnival* and *Guy and Pauline* – completely lacking in intensity and completely extroverted. I have a theory – his mother I believe was an American woman from the South, and his father a Scottish actor – that he represents a particular breed – romantic but extroverted, intelligent but superficial, quixotic but rather mild – that is due to this mingling of strains and that doesn't find any appropriate role in the English public school system in which he was brought up ... His career has been disappointing, but I would rather read him than Somerset Maugham, for he seems to me a real and rather remarkably gifted writer.

The critical appreciation of Monty's work which he had in mind was never carried out. From his comparison with Somerset Maugham, however, it is apparent that he would have pointed to the ambitiousness of Monty's canvas and his moral scope, compared with Maugham's contained and knowing stories. Presumably, too, he would have picked out the acuteness of observation which served both serious and comic novels so well, and the theatrical effects of the language of the early books.

The absence of serious attention was partly Monty's own fault. He frequently referred to himself as 'an entertainer', and the qualities on which he prided himself were those of his father. He was a professional, alert to the public taste and, declaring what he always used to deny, 'the theatre is in my blood'. Perhaps, having realised in Barra the Jacobite dreams of childhood, he could afford to let West Kensington come in, but it did not encourage any weighty reappraisal. The critical attitude was best expressed in a long article which John Raymond wrote for the *New Statesman* in 1954:

Sir Compton is a natural, unabashed Platonist. For him everything in life must conform to its quintessential Idea. If you describe a tart, let her be a tart. Let her be decrepit, let her be miserable, let us see the gin and mascara running down her old, tear-stained cheeks. Conversely a *jeune fille* should be as much *en fleur* as her creator can make her. Such a temperament finds its natural outlet in the noble art of the twopence-coloured and the writing of romances ... It has been both Sir Compton's privilege and his fate as an artist to remain a young man all his life. But in art, as in life, everything has to be paid for. The youthfulness, the gaiety, the fun, the tearing high spirits in Sir Compton's writing has been paid for at the price of artistic maturity.

The early books were largely discounted and the real Mackenzie was taken to be the writer of comic novels. 'He has a superb sense of comedy,' Raymond wrote, 'and what so seldom goes with it, a wonderful flow of invention.'

There was yet another influence which made it difficult for literary opinion in Britain to take him as seriously as he deserved. Television, which was beginning to establish itself as a medium, discovered in him a natural performer. For all his diatribes against modern technology, he was far ahead of any other writer in understanding its potential. As early as 1929 he had prophesied in his magazine *Vox* that 'Radio (to which undoubtedly will be added Television) is going to revolutionise human thought and human action as completely as did the invention of printing.' He had made his first appearance on it in 1936 when there were only about two hundred sets in the country, and by the time of its dramatic surge in popularity with the coronation of Queen Elizabeth in 1953, he was a regular, introducing concerts, reminiscing about the past and appearing on panel shows like *Any Questions*. It was not simply London provincialism he was up against but that aesthetic, as well as social, snobbery which refused to have 'the box' in the house and felt that watching it was a form of cultural slumming.

Whatever the literary world might think, the Indian Army took Monty as their champion. 'There is no doubt that it is a great book,' Auchinleck wrote to him of the first volume of *Eastern Epic*, 'one that will live ... none could have done more than you to repay our debt to the Sepoy Army.' Present at the Foyle's luncheon in November 1951 to launch the book was a full parade of generals, the commanders-in-chief of the armies of India and Pakistan, the high commissioners of both countries, and Lord Mountbatten, former Supreme Commander of the Armed Forces of India and Pakistan, who paid tribute to the eloquence with which Monty had presented the old army's achievements.

In their eyes at least he was a paladin among authors, and if he was inclined to blame any lapses of their army on the civil servants in Whitehall, it was a fault in the right direction. 'There will be mugawumps and headshakers of course,' said Auchinleck, 'but it speaks the truth, and the truth is what most people want – unless it is about themselves?!!'

The first volume carried the history up to 1942 and the first battle of El Alamein, and a few days after its launch he began work on the second volume. One morning after he had been working late, Chrissie noticed that his eye was red around the rim. 'I asked for my looking-glass,' he recalled. 'I shut my right eye to look more closely and my face vanished from the mirror.' Thus baldly did he describe the process of going blind in one eye. A retinal haemorrhage had destroyed the sight in his left eye – the stronger of the two – and from now on he had to rely on the uncertain vision of the other, which itself was slowly being obscured by a cataract.

Of his minor afflictions he made much, but in this he was stoical. 'I can think of no one else who having so lately lost the sight of an eye, could pass a longish day (and part of the night) without alluding to his loss without some trace of self-pity,' wrote Eric Linklater after staying with him at Denchworth. 'I still marvel at your self-control, and even more than that I'm delighted to recall the completely undaunted way in which you were planning this, that and the other for years to come.'

With only one eye it was impossible to complete the detailed reading and research needed for the second volume of *Eastern Epic*, a failure that haunted him. Yet with the self-control Linklater had noticed, he refused to let himself grow despondent, and instead deliberately chose to dwell on his blessings. 'I remember going to see him after visiting John Betjeman who lived nearby,' de Vere White said, 'and I was amazed by the contrast between Betjeman's deep pessimism at the age of forty and Monty's cheerful outlook at seventy. "Another very good morning, Terence," he said, "do you know I woke with the plots of six more novels in my head. That's pretty remarkable don't you think?" And he said it with a child's delight in himself.'

It was with similar delight that he received a letter in May 1952 from the prime minister, Winston Churchill, offering him a knighthood. He was to be among the first knights that the young Queen dubbed, and as he told Faith, 'I think it's a bit of a triumph to be granted a commission by Queen Victoria and be knighted by her great-great-granddaughter.'

His old friend Bob Boothby had suggested the honour two years earlier, after Churchill told him of his admiration for *Gallipoli Memories*. Time had obviously diluted the taint of the Official Secrets case and *The Windsor Tapestry*, but the timing of the offer just six months after the publication of *Eastern Epic* was also significant. It could be said that he had made amends. From Majorca, where she had taken a small cottage,

Faith wrote back with congratulations and enquired whether he intended to be Sir Edward, Sir Montague or Sir Compton Mackenzie. On 8 July he arrived at Buckingham Palace at 10.15 am, as instructed, circled the great hall with the other knights-to-be, knelt a sciatic knee before the young Queen, and emerged Sir Compton Mackenzie.

There was little chance that he would become entirely respectable. Six days later he was in the Court of Appeal arguing that the sale of copyright should not be taxed as income. It was a case he was bound to lose as the law then stood, and the Inland Revenue made much of the fact that he had sold the copyrights once before. In support of their case, they quoted the precedent of a rubber plantation where the sale of trees had been disallowed as a capital transaction, and it was in the quixotic belief that authors' earnings should not be regarded as analogous to those of a rubber plantation that Monty had appealed the case from the commissioners to the courts to the Justices of Appeal.

'Surely the author is being treated as if he was a kind of crop,' he argued in the Court of Appeal. 'The analogy is imperfect. You may reasonably expect, unless winter or summer drought comes, to go on producing crops, but you have no reasonable expectation as an author of what you will produce next year.'

Although the case was lost, it proved to be the winning of a larger war for a reform in the taxation of authors and artists in general. Because he was so well-known, the publicity generated wide interest and a crisis in the writers' trade union, the Society of Authors, which had done nothing to help during the proceedings. On one side, A. A. Milne claimed that an author who had sold twenty copyrights for £10,000 had nothing to worry about, and on the other A. P. Herbert threatened to form a breakaway union which would actually work for its members. To prevent the Society from fragmenting, John Moore, who had become Monty's cherished friend, persuaded Herbert to join a committee under Monty's chairmanship whose purpose would be to propose changes in the taxation of authors' incomes.

The reforms which they presented first to the Chancellor of the Exchequer, R. A. Butler, and then to the Inland Revenue, established the principle of spreading tax relief on authors' earnings over a number of years. It was a step for which every writer today has good cause to be grateful to Monty's quixotry.

In *The Four Winds of Love*, he had put into Miriam Stern's mouth the butterfly's defence of its wayward decorative flitting, that it had the utilitarian effect of fertilising flowers. In these later years the justice of the argument was borne out. While staying with the Maharajah of Mysore in 1946, he had talked enthusiastically not merely of listening to music but of making it, and when Walter Legge was seeking funds to found the Philharmonia Concert Society from which sprang the Orchestra and Chorus, it was the maharajah who funded its first season in 1949, and insisted that Monty become a trustee. The following year Dr Tom Walsh asked him to speak to a circle of opera enthusiasts in Wexford. He talked to them of Balfe, who had spent his early years in Wexford, and suggested that instead of listening to opera on record they should bring it back to life. It was an idea Tom Walsh cherished himself, and Monty's ability to waft a thought into other people's imaginations helped to make the realisation of his idea possible. Twelve months later Walsh put on Balfe's *The Rose of Castile*, thus inaugurating the Wexford Festival, and the part that Monty played was commemorated in his election as president of this, the most intimate and enchanting of festivals.

Even Scottish nationalism, the flower round which he had once fluttered with such devotion, seemed to blossom again with the election of John MacCormick as rector of Glasgow University in the autumn of 1950. That winter some young nationalists removed the Stone of Destiny from Westminster Abbey, just as John Ogilvie had planned in *The North Wind of Love*. He took it as an omen, and in an article for the *Sunday Dispatch* he made no secret of his sympathy for those who had retrieved the Stone.

When the Special Branch began to question his Denchworth neighbours about his movements at the time of the Stone's disappearance, it confirmed the northward turn his thoughts were taking. He was too old to live in the country, he decided, and so he and Chrissie began to explore Edinburgh for a suitable home.

The standards set by Lady Ham and its successors were high, and it was not until the spring of 1953 that Chrissie found a house that matched them. Built in 1815, Drummond Place was one of the earlier additions to Edinburgh's New Town, and number 31, standing on the shoulder of a small rise, looked over its own gardens towards the Firth of Forth on one side and on the other across the cobbled crescent to the trees and shrubs of the public gardens. There was just sufficient space on its four floors to house the great library and all Monty's personal papers. Almost ten years after leaving Scotland he returned, and this time it was for good.

The ten years' absence had seen a change. His return was no longer a search for a background, or the addition of a missing detail to make himself complete. In a curious way he was now complete in himself. Perhaps it was advancing age, but the great adventure of India and his commemoration of the mightiest force that the empire had produced had also had its effect. As John Connell noted on Monty's return from his epic journey, 'he's bustling with activity, yet he's very gentle, very urbane, very mellow'. He regarded it himself as the high water mark of his post-war years, and in a way he had not known since Gallipoli it had brought him back into step with history.

In 1954 a column in *The Spectator*, called 'Sidelight', gave him a platform for his views, and he used it to advocate the union of Cyprus with Greece. Over the next two years, as the demands for *enosis* grew stronger and boiled into the emergency of 1956, he persistently argued for the grand gesture which would bind a Greek, and still more a Cypriot, heart. From his own experience he understood the power of what Lawrence Durrell termed 'that extraordinary flower of chance, the quixotic, irrational love of England which no other nation seems to have and [which] in a fantastic way flowered in blissful co-operation with the haunting dream of Union.'

His advocacy elicited an outpouring of affection for him in Greece, which even now has not entirely faded from memory. Apart from the individuals who wrote to him, the Athenian press which had pictured him in the past as a bogeyman now applied to him the epithet 'the just', once given to Aristides, and in the years to come a street in the Cypriot capital of Nicosia was named after him. In 1958 he persuaded the BBC to make a series of films called *The Glory that was Greece*, and the producer, Stephen Hearst, wrote from Athens: 'The magic of your philhellenism has created a climate of opinion so favourable that all the planning and preparation in the world would avail nothing without it.'

Archbishop Makarios, Ethnarch of Cyprus, was among those who wrote to express their thanks for Monty's stand, and a photograph of the two of them together triggered a spasm of press rage which momentarily threatened the transmission of the series. When it was broadcast, however, it not only commanded astonishingly large audiences for what was essentially a history of classical Greece, but it became a landmark in television for its technical innovation and location shooting. Sixty years earlier the High Master of St Paul's had upbraided him for throwing away the chance of becoming a classical scholar to match Jebb and Porson, but Monty might have claimed that as a showman he had brought the subject to the attention of more people than any nineteenth-century pedagogue ever dreamed possible.

The most telling symptom of the mood in which he returned to Scotland was to be found in a single novel. Most of his books in the early 1950s were what he called 'enjoyable potboilers' – short histories of Buckingham Palace, the Chartered Bank, the tobacco industry, the china industry, and the National Trust – commissioned works that paid up to £3000 and involved a month of familiarisation and two months' writing. Although the writing is often flat, *Sublime Tobacco*, for example, is a wonderfully seductive celebration of the weed of which he had consumed by his reckoning half a ton; it was not smoking which was dangerous to the health but inhaling, he argued.

At the age of seventy-two, however, he began a far more ambitious work, *Thin Ice*, which, as he later confessed, took 'as much out of me as any novel I have ever written'. The story told by the kind and slightly stuffy George Gaymer concerns the career of his Oxford friend, Henry Fortescue, who fights to suppress his homosexuality for the sake of his political career. 'It is the perpetual thwarting of curiosity which is so hard to withstand,' Fortescue admits. 'The mere fact of divining that somebody on the other side of a crowded room was like myself has often been enough temptation for me to make sure.'

Despite early promise, Fortescue's career begins to decline after the First World War. Frustrated in his political ambition, he abandons all self-control and starts cruising in pubs and lavatories. At the outbreak of the Second World War his former expertise in the Middle East leads to recruitment into the security service but, unable to suppress his real nature, he becomes the victim of blackmail and assault.

The outline of the story was taken partly from Harold Nicolson's career, but mostly from the life of his one-time colleague in intelligence at Gallipoli, George Lloyd, later Lord Lloyd of Dolobran, who became Governor of Bombay and then High Commissioner for Egypt and Sudan in the 1920s, and whose fortunes then faded except for a brief resurgence in 1940 when he was appointed Secretary of State for the Colonies. He also used Tom Driberg's wartime experience of being arrested after a policeman found him with a Norwegian seaman in Princes Street Gardens in Edinburgh. Like Driberg, Henry Fortescue escapes being charged by convincing the policeman that the Germans would use it as propaganda if he were convicted.

Thin Ice is unique among Monty's serious novels in using the first person as narrator. As a result, the omniscience of the author's voice is replaced by the compassionate view of an old friend. The technique suited his style so neatly that it is surprising he did not attempt it earlier.

The episodic rhythm which he still held to becomes the natural effect of the two friends' sporadic meetings, and by separating the observer, Gaymer, from the main character, Fortescue, he achieved a parallax view of events which offers a depth of perspective that the single vision of Michael Fane or John Ogilvie necessarily lacked.

Its genesis lay in a remark by a barrister, which Monty overheard, that three-quarters of all suicides were blackmailed homosexuals, and like his earliest novels it contained a moral – which he had also argued in a 'Sidelight' column – that no civilised society should regard homosexuality as a more serious crime than blackmail. Yet there is also a powerful counter-rhythm to this implicitly liberal message. Henry Fortescue is the heir to one of England's great landed families, and the failure of himself and his brother, an alcoholic, to exercise control over themselves leads to the extinction of a long and honourable family line. Thus Evelyn Waugh, in an admiring review, could aptly commend the author for illustrating 'that every moral and immoral act is an act of will', while with no less justification, John Davenport in the *Observer* could judge it to be 'a powerful indictment of the present idiotic state of the English law on this subject'.

It is pre-eminently a book of age. People grow old, characters improve or warp through the passage of time, and death comes, sometimes slowly, sometimes unexpectedly as it does to Henry Fortescue in the blitz before his secret is exposed. There is an acceptance of passing time, and instead of Fane railing against the tragedy of lost youth or Ogilvie losing himself in the comfort of endless tradition, the book ends with Gaymer listening to Big Ben chiming 'as it has chimed a million and a half times since I came to live here', and across the lapse of time still gently mourning the death of his old friend.

It was no coincidence. Monty was beginning to succumb to age himself. The blurring of his vision seemed to impair his superb memory, and repeatedly he complained of the confusing bustle of people and events. 'Life after sixty is like a railway station,' he observed, and as he grew older the departures became more frequent – Norman Douglas and Ian Hamilton among his elders, Calum MacSween, John Moore and his brother Frank among his juniors, and the Coddie and Father John Macmillan on Barra. Then, in 1960, Faith died at the age of eighty-two.

There is no relationship in Monty's life more difficult to account for than this marriage. To the end of Faith's life they remained friends. He trusted her judgement, and wrote to her almost weekly about what he was doing. He marked their wedding day with a telegram, and placed announcements in *The Times* to celebrate their ruby and golden weddings.

Had this seemly behaviour been echoed on Faith's side all would have been well, but Faith was never so well-controlled. She was both exasperatingly difficult – abrasive in temper, snobbish, moody and wilfully extravagant – and at the same time quite unreasonably steadfast and affectionate, as both Norman Douglas and Virginia Compton knew. She accepted the bargain made in Capri because it was the most he would allow, but even after Chrissie's arrival had persuaded her that their former intimacy would never be recreated, she continued to want more emotionally from Monty than he could or would give. That imbalance irritated him and pained her until about ten years before her death.

From 1950 her financial hardships gradually disappeared when it was agreed that the shares in the *Gramophone* held by her, Christopher and Monty should be commuted to annuities, with the magazine eventually passing to Cecil Pollard's son Anthony. Its rising circulation, from 36,000 in 1952 to 70,000 by 1970, provided for all three of them an old age free from financial anxieties.

The death of Norman Douglas in 1952 grieved her deeply – on the night he died she felt his ghost sitting ice-cold on her bed and was terrified – and although she wanted to return to the Mediterranean the thought of Capri without him was unbearable. An attempt to find a substitute in Majorca was a failure, and in 1953 she returned to live in Campden Hill Square in London, where she wrote the last of her biographies, a life of her great-uncle, William Cory, the author of the 'Eton Boating Song'.

When Monty appeared on *This is Your Life* in 1956, Faith again gave the official picture of their marriage. She quoted Gibran's lines about a couple needing 'to stand together but not too close together', and summed it up in four words, 'Love and let live.' It was a touching performance and many viewers wrote to thank her for her words. But it was Nadegin who now kept her going. Although he never touched her imagination as Monty did, his large, kindly, clumsy presence eventually came to mean more. When she reviewed the circumstances of her life at seventy-six, it was with gratitude to him above all that she came to the conclusion that 'Life is still interesting.'

Two years later she fell heavily, and although she recovered the shock aged her rapidly. The lease on the Campden Hill Square flat ran out in 1958 and she came to live at 31 Drummond Place, but her hold on reality was fading. When Nadegin died in 1959, living itself became a torment. She entered a nursing home, and twelve months later, on 9 July 1960, she died.

There were many letters of condolence, but it was difficult to strike the right note, and only John Mavrogordato succeeded in saying what many felt. 'Many of Faith's friends and admirers regarded her for years with something between affection and fear. As she was lately, not one of them could have wanted her to go on living. But now she is gone, we know there is nobody to take her place and very sincerely we can send you our deepest sympathy.'

Monty's vitality remained astonishing. For many years he had been in the habit of staying in bed until midday, and what had begun as the consequence of writing till dawn was now the means of husbanding his strength. Yet he still averaged a book a year, and despite their diversity of subject, they were grouped around a single theme.

In *Rockets Galore* (1957), the nearest any of his comedies came to showing a hard edge, the Toddays are in danger of being overwhelmed by a Whitehall which is intent on installing a rocket range – as had just happened on South Uist – but save themselves by the discovery of a new species of seagull, created by the schoolmaster painting the originals red. It is part of the satire that the preservation of a habitat for birds counts for more than that of a habitat for people, an absurdity rendered no less telling by the repeated evidence since then that the only acceptable argument against official landgrabbing is that of ecology.

The Lunatic Republic (1959), a whimsy of moon-based bureaucrats, is a slighter book, and *Mezzotint* (1961), though a more serious novel about institutionalised racialism in the West Indies, is sounder as a plea for tolerance than as literature. In between came *Greece in my Life*, heavily padded with paragraphs from his memoirs, and *Cat's Company*, a brief autobiography centred on his love of Siamese and lesser breeds, both published in 1960.

Hatred of regimentation, whether by bureaucrats, colonialists or animal owners, was the idea that most occupied him in these last years. He disliked almost equally the town planners ('they've done more damage to London than Hitler ever did'), cars ('the infernal combustion engine') and popular culture ('the insensate vulgarisation of the sexy sixties'), but these were the twinges of old age which he would shoot down in others with the enquiry, 'What's the use of resenting change?'

The bedrock from which he did not budge was the need to resist the pressure of convention, and the last of his preaching books, *On Moral Courage*, takes nearly all its examples from this category. If *Thin Ice* is one of the triumphs of his old age, *On Moral Courage* must be accounted its disappointment, for the title is ambitious and the theme could have stretched him. But starting from an impossibly diffuse definition of the term offered by a judge – 'a readiness to expose oneself to suffering or inconvenience which does not affect the body' – he soon lost sight of his argument in reminiscences of controversies which people had once thought shocking. Yet he could state with great simplicity a moral dilemma and the courage needed to overcome it, as in his response to the threat of nuclear war:

So long as only the United States and the USSR possessed the H-Bomb, it was possible to feel that war could come only by accident. Then Britannia decided that her dignity must be preserved by making the bomb herself, with the natural result of suggesting to France that her dignity required an H-Bomb too. We may expect in due course any nation large or small will need its H-Bomb. Should they be allowed to multiply, a third war is inevitable. Should such a war come it will assuredly mean the end of civilisation. At this moment in the destiny of mankind, a tremendous gesture of moral courage by a great nation might save the world, and perhaps only Britain is capable of making such a gesture.

Such a conclusion – to use power justly rather than selfishly – may be seen as the logical outcome of the gentlemanly tenets with which he had been imbued. He joined the Campaign for Nuclear Disarmament, and became a founder-member of the Committee of 100. The lifelong conflict between the rebel he wanted to be and the gentleman he was bred to be was at last being resolved. But even before *On Moral Courage* was published he had begun to trace the steps which led to such a resolution.

On 16 October 1961, at four o'clock in the afternoon, he wrote the first words of his autobiography, *My Life and Times*. Its plan had been conceived in 1943, when he proposed to divide his life into periods of eight years, or octaves, devoting a volume to each octave, and a chapter to each year. The entire work was to be called *The Keyboard*. A different title and the addition of two more octaves were the only changes, but in giving himself ten volumes for his autobiography some critics felt that he had gone too far. 'Even Sir Osbert Sitwell needed little more than four,' wrote Nigel Dennis in the *Sunday Telegraph*. 'As for Rousseau, Gibbon, St Augustine . . .'

As though deliberately challenging fate, he proposed that the first volume should be published on his eightieth birthday, and the others at yearly intervals. 'If by God's grace I should succeed in keeping what many will think is a presumptuous time-table,' he wrote, 'I shall be eighty-nine when the tenth octave is published in January 1972.'

Such an undertaking amounted to more than an autobiography. As with his serious novels, the structure is episodic and the story driven forward by time rather than by emotion or ambition. Events and people and descriptive passages which appeared in *Sinister Street, Guy and Pauline, Sylvia Scarlett* and *The Four Winds of Love* reappear little changed and sometimes verbatim in *My Life and Times*. And the sheer scale lifts it from the understood purpose of autobiography, which is to present either an apology for or a celebration of the life of the author, to the almost fictional level of recreating that life. Instead of autobiography, it should properly be seen as the third and last piece of the mighty edifice outlined to Martin Secker in 1918, which began with *The Theatre of Youth*, continued with *The Labyrinth* and ended with *The Theatre of Age*.

Here the search for 'an ideal conduct of life to guide him through the long pilgrimage of the twentieth century' reaches its conclusion. The adolescent agonising is pushed aside, the middle-aged depression forgotten, and as though the last words of *Sinister Street* were its motto – 'There is no tragedy of age' – the tone is consistently good-humoured and well-mannered. And as John Ogilvie is recognisably the middle-aged Michael Fane, so Compton Mackenzie is no less obviously the octogenarian Ogilvie. At the end of his gigantic theatre one is left, as any great actor would want his audience to be left, with the sensation – at once uncomfortable and exhilarating – that illusion and reality are both acts of imagination.

The swell of affection which had been rising since his seventies broke with the publication of Octave One on his eightieth birthday. Congratulations on his age were mingled with compliments on the book, and several reviewers took the opportunity, like Angus Wilson, to express regret for past hostility. 'Let us hope that on his eightieth birthday,' said *The Times Literary Supplement*, 'he will at last be recognised for what he is: one of the most naturally gifted and versatile writers of the century.'

The first volume carried him to the front door of Colet Court, and both it and the second, which ended with him on the train to the Bournemouth Hydro, were received warmly for their memories of Victorian London. 'For calling up or recalling the flavour of English society at the turn of the century,' declared Marghanita Laski, 'this is the book.'

To start with the writing was easy, justifying his claim that 'the inspiration of the ambitious task I have set myself is self-indulgence'. It was familiar territory. Apart from fictional presentations, he had covered the ground at least half a dozen times before in books as various as *My Record of Music, Sublime Tobacco*, and *The Windsor Tapestry*. Nevertheless, to complete Octave Three's 110,000 words in seven weeks at the age of eighty-one was a remarkable feat.

He was by now the grand old man of letters, and the sun king of Edinburgh society, holding court during the morning in a small four-poster bed where he received close friends and journalists. Later in the day, dressed characteristically in a light Donegal tweed jacket with green corduroy trousers and bow-tie, he entertained other visitors who, especially during the three weeks of the festival, would appear in hordes.

'With the Castle, the Royal Mile, Holyrood, Rosslyn Chapel and the Forth Bridge, he is one of the sights of Edinburgh,' declared Robert Bruce Lockhart, famous for his activities as a secret service agent during the Russian revolution, and one of those who came to know Monty after his move north. 'Because of his neuritis he rarely goes to a theatre or a concert. But after their performance, the actors and the musicians come to Monty.'

Bruce Lockhart regretted the effect company had on him. 'If you are alone with him, he is very gentle, very courteous and most endearing. When his courtiers arrive to drink his whisky and to hear him talk, Monty puts on what I call his act. It is what his hearers expect of him.' More accurately, it might be said that he gave each hearer, Bruce Lockhart as much as the courtiers, the Monty he expected. 'How I give myself,' he would exclaim in exhaustion and pride when the last guest had left.

It was Chrissie who made it all possible. She had grown motherly in shape and demeanour, but with her slimness had gone her shyness. She protected him from the more demanding visitors and from his wilder assertions. 'Oh Monty,' she would exclaim, 'you're embroidering again.' The organisation of his life, like the deciphering of the scrawled manu-script of his autobiography, depended on her.

On 23 January 1962, eighteen months after Faith's death, he and Chrissie were married. The step surprised none of his friends. They had been together for almost thirty-five years, and the warmth of her personality had made each of their homes since Barra a place which visitors remembered with affection. Indeed the crush of visitors at 31 Drummond Place grew so great that it seriously interrupted his work. He needed 'a place of the hermitage style' to concentrate on the auto-biography, and in the autumn of 1961 Chrissie found a small French farmhouse called Pradelles in the department of Lot which became his summer retreat.

In 1959 Lily MacSween, Chrissie's younger sister, gave up her teaching career, and at Monty's suggestion opened a hairdressing salon at 31 Drummond Place. 'Someone told me a barber had opened up shop in your beautiful house,' Evelyn Waugh wrote in concern, 'Surely not?' Nevertheless 'Lilian's' flourished, and Lily was already helping her elder sister look after Monty when, about eighteen months after the wedding, Chrissie was diagnosed as having cancer. In October 1963, she died aged fifty-four.

Monty's grief was violent but short-lived. Eric Linklater called to express his sympathy and found him in tears. To console him he said, 'There is one thing you can do for her, Monty. You can preserve her memory in your autobiography.' Monty cheered up immediately. 'That's right,' he exclaimed, 'I shall make her immortal.'

There is unfortunately no portrait of her in *My Life and Times*. It was not a deliberate omission. He rarely succeeded in portraying people he knew in the latter half of his life, and he recognised the lack himself: 'One of my continuous regrets while I am writing this record of my experience is what I feel is my inability to bring real people to life,' he confessed. 'When I start to paint a friend as he is or was, I become as self-conscious as a schoolboy over his first essay.' Though she lacked a memorial in print, it was no coincidence that Monty's long period of marking time in the 1920s and 1930s ended soon after she came to live with him. She fired his imagination then, and later in life her care enabled him to endure the demanding journey through India and the Far East, and the still more exacting onset of blindness.

These duties now fell to Lily. Dark-haired and dark-eyed like her sister, she was more assertive in temperament, both fiercer in protecting him from unwanted visitors and livelier in her enjoyment of welcome company. There had been a bond between them ever since the moment Monty first saw her as an eight-year-old girl in Tarbert, a moment which both remembered with perfect clarity. The difference of thirty-five years in their ages was of little importance compared to the length of time that picture had been cherished. It was easy for Lily to take on her sister's role of reading Monty's near-illegible handwriting and caring for his needs, and her decisive character suited his increasing dependence. On 4 March 1965 she became his third wife.

Over the first five octaves the speed of writing enabled him to gain a year on his timetable despite the increasing difficulty in focusing what remained of his sight in his right eye. Thereafter he found details more difficult to keep in the right sequence. Yet for some critics the seventh and eighth octaves, dealing with the 1930s and the Second World War, were the best in the sequence. 'Octave Eight captures to perfection the peculiar flavour – a blend of dedication and dottiness – that characterised Britain during the last war,' wrote Charles Curran. 'It will last as long as anybody is interested in that period.'

A paradox was emerging from the reviews, which was also the paradox of his life. After more than three-quarters of a million words about himself, he was being praised for his evocation of period, but criticised for his failure to reveal anything of himself. Such criticism was misconceived. Whatever he had been in the past, he had now become his public self and to look beneath the text for the authentic Monty was absurd.

He deplored the present, but gently, he mourned the death of friends like John Moore, bitterly but briefly, and he was stoical about his own ailments. He was kindly in judgement, genial in mood, and optimistic in outlook.

A farce called *The Stolen Soprano* (1965) was interposed between Octaves Four and Five. The later volumes were a battle against growing blindness, but he still found it possible to interpose between Octaves Seven and Eight a brief biography of R. L. Stevenson and a children's story, *The Strongest Man on Earth*. He was, furthermore, always available to journalists for quotes on anything from rates to nuclear disarmament. And he could be relied upon to reminisce about the past in front of the television cameras with unfailing wit and grace.

Eight years and eight months after he began, he reached the end of his autobiography. 'My emotion as I write these last words of a year-by-year record of a long life is one of gratitude. I have been happy and fortunate, *Homo Felix*, and I am still very happy and fortunate. As I lay down my pen on this June 13th, 1970, the feast-day of my favourite St Anthony of Padua, let the two last words be DEO GRATIAS.'

Of all the acts of will by which he formed his life, this final marathon against failing sight and old age is the most remarkable. Artistically, it is essential that the double image of himself as actor and audience should be continued until the last moment, and daunting though the challenge was it seemed to many of his friends that it kept him alive. Once the autobiography was complete, his strength began to dwindle. He planned another farce, to be called *The Devil's Diary*, in which the Devil would admit that his proudest achievement was to give humanity the motor-car, but it was never written. He was indeed too blind even to make the journey to Pradelles, yet he did not let melancholy intrude.

'You and I are indeed lucky,' he wrote to Rupert Hart-Davis early in 1972, 'and blindness is little enough to pay for my happiness. I doubt if

I shall ever write another novel because trying to dictate a novel makes me as self-conscious as I was in my 'teens.' Through the summer he did some work on a collection of articles which were to be called *Pages in Waiting*. He told friends that he would dictate a coda to his autobiography to be published when he was ninety-one, but his vitality was beginning to ebb more quickly.

Cancer of the prostate had been diagnosed, and he was frequently in pain, although his public performances remained graceful. On 29 November 1972 he gave a television interview in 31 Drummond Place which taxed his strength to the limit, and it was agreed to continue filming the next day. After the crew left he collapsed from weariness, and Lily put him to bed. In the evening Margaret Fay Campbell, John Lorne's wife, came in and all three had supper in his bedroom.

'He recovered himself very quickly,' Lily remembered, 'and he was in very good form considering the day he'd had. After supper he smoked an enormous cigar, and then lay down listening to the radio.' Later that night he called out in some discomfort, and Lily telephoned the doctor who came and gave him some medicine. It had no effect, and after a time she insisted he come again. On this occasion he told her there was nothing to be done – Monty was dying. Death came in the early hours of 30 November, seven weeks short of his ninetieth birthday.

The affection felt for him could be measured in the messages of sympathy sent to his widow. The prime minister, Edward Heath, wrote personally to express his sorrow. 'He made a major contribution to Britain's literature over his long and productive life, and he will be long remembered as an author, as a broadcaster, and for his work in connection with the *Gramophone*.' The dustmen who emptied the bins at Drummond Place paid tribute, as did Cardinal Gray of St Andrew's, the Society of Authors, the ambassadors of Greece and Pakistan, the Royal Stuart Society, the Siamese Cat Club, and some five hundred other individuals and societies. The heavyweight weeklies and the popular dailies devoted equal space, the former to his novels, the latter to his lifestyle. 'He made life smile for him,' wrote Peter Lewis in the *Daily Mail*, accurately catching Monty's popular appeal. 'It did you good to see him get away with it.'

What his close friends valued was the magic that involved them in the drama of living as an ideal of themselves. That magic did not altogether end with his death.

When the plane carrying his body to Barra for burial landed on the cockle beach of Traigh Mhor, eighty-two-year-old Calum Johnston, a friend from before the war, was waiting to pipe the body home to its resting place. Undeterred by the cold rain driving in on a southwest wind, he played a lament as the coffin was carried from the plane. Accompanied by a large crowd of mourners he followed it up the steep green slope to the cemetery at Eoligarry and stood to attention while Father Aeneas MacQueen of Castlebay conducted the brief burial service. As the rites were ending, the piper began to sway, then suddenly collapsed and died on the wet turf.

There was a dramatic quality in that graveside death which those familiar with Monty's life immediately recognised. It belonged to a more romantic age when a knight might share his sovereign's fate or a harper fall by his chieftain's side. In dying thus poignantly, Calum Johnston made heroic both his own end and the burial of the man he admired.

'Monty laid up his treasure in the hearts of his friends,' wrote Bob Boothby in an obituary, and in the years since his death the warmth of their affection has evidently not dimmed. For them his power to charm the passing moment into intense experience gives him a pre-eminence that cannot be challenged.

His reputation as a novelist is less securely based. In the books written before the First World War he created an adolescent mood which will never be forgotten, and the comedies of Capri and the Western Isles contain parodies which will always seem more convincing than their originals. It is fruitless to wish that he had devoted himself to these strengths and been less prone to distraction and extravagance. He had almost every gift that a great writer requires except the belief that writing is of supreme importance.

His books enabled him to be the sort of public figure he wished to be. They brought him fame and financed, although only just, a dramatic and romantic way of living. Through them he could express his outrage and amusement at the outside world, and repeatedly, in reminiscence both fictive and factual, he used them to render his past permanent. But writing was never an end in itself. Like those other great causes, Catholicism and Scottish Nationalism, it became part of the background, a setting for his life as a whole.

In the end it is clear that his true genius was theatrical, but that instead of confining his talents to the stage he created around him a stage on which he could represent himself. However wrong it may be to compare a man's life to a work of art, the comparison is difficult to avoid in the case of Compton Mackenzie. In the quixotic, extravagant performance of his own life he achieved his real masterpiece.

Notes and sources

It would be superfluous to cite *My Life and Times* on each occasion it has been used as the source of information, but I have noted specific quotations in the text. I list below additional sources of information, and give publication details for those books which do not appear in the bibliography.

FOREWORD

xiv 'Such critics forgot': *My Life and Times*, Octave One, pp. 14–15.

1 THE FIRST STAGE

Other than the published autobiographical writings listed in the bibliography, the prime sources for the history of the Compton family are: *A Memoir of Henry Compton* compiled by Charles and Edward Compton (London: Tinsley Bros, 1879), *The Mackenzies Called Compton* by Lou Warwick (Northampton: privately published, 1977), together with information supplied by the family of Frank Compton. Theatrical background comes from Mackenzie's *Carnival, The Seven Ages of Woman* and *Rogues and Vagabonds; Ellen Terry and Bernard Shaw: a correspondence* edited by Christopher St John (London: Constable, 1931); *Henry Irving and the Victorian Theatre* by Madeleine Bingham (London: Allen & Unwin, 1978); *Theatre in the Age of Irving* by George Rowell (Oxford: Basil Blackwell, 1981); and 'Adam Smith, Beerbohm Tree and the Wages of Actors' by Michael Sanderson in *Business History* of July 1985. Mackenzie's recollections of his childhood, contained in the first two volumes of his autobiography and the reminiscences listed above, are supplemented by *Sinister Street*.

2 reviews: quoted in *A Memoir of Henry Compton*.
8 Sydney Paxton: quoted in *The Mackenzies Called Compton*.
10 'I can echo': *My Life and Times*, Octave One, p. 254.
16 'I can still hear': *My Life and Times*, Octave One, p. 149.

2 SUFFERING IS GOOD FOR THE SOUL

In addition to the family and theatrical sources listed above, the Bateman family history is extensively based upon the unpublished memoirs of her family, childhood and upbringing which Virginia Compton wrote in her seventies. Faith Compton Mackenzie, who also attended the Misses Allen's kindergarten, described it in *As Much As I Dare*. Henry James's flirtation with the theatre is described in his letters to Edward Compton and in Leon Edel's *The Life of Henry James* (Harmondsworth: Penguin, 1977). The streets of west London at the end of the nineteenth century provided Mackenzie with his most vivid memories; in addition to overt recollection they appear menacingly in *Sinister Street* and *The Parson's Progress* and affectionately in *Kensington Rhymes* and *Our Street*. The first volume of Leonard Woolf's autobiography, *Sowing* (London: Hogarth Press, 1960), and *G. K. Chesterton* by Margaret Canovan (New York: Harcourt Brace Jovanovich, 1977) are also useful for place and period.

23 'I can see': *My Life and Times*, Octave One, p. 150.
24 'I recall the gathering dread': *My Life and Times*, Octave One, pp. 164–75.
25 'I have written': *My Life and Times*, Octave One, p. 165.
26 'I can recall': *My Life and Times*, Octave One, p. 192.
26 'I can assert': *My Life and Times*, Octave One, pp. 193–4.

3 THE SINISTER STREETS OF ADOLESCENCE

The sources for the nineteenth-century public school are *A French Eton* by Matthew Arnold (London: Macmillan, 1864); *Victorian England: Portrait of an Age* by G. M. Young (London: OUP, 1936); and *Athleticism in the Victorian and Edwardian Public School* by J. A. Mangan (Cambridge: CUP, 1981). St Paul's at the end of the nineteenth century is derived from *Sowing* and *G. K. Chesterton* as well as *Sinister Street* and *The East Wind of Love*. Mackenzie's school reports come from the St Paul's School archives. A few family papers survive from this period, notably a letter on Mackenzie's tenth birthday to his father, a letter from his Aunt Isabel about his religious practices, a school notebook dating from *c.* 1896 and the MS of *Hectoma*. Anglo-Catholicism and the personality of Sandys Wason are taken from *The Parson's Progress*, *Palafox* by Sandys Wason (London: Cope & Fenwick, 1927) and *Twenty Years at St Hilary* by Bernard Walke (London: Methuen, 1935). *Fin de siècle* London and literature are derived from *Oscar Wilde* by Richard Ellmann (Berkeley: University of California Press, 1977); and *Bosie* (London: New English Library, 1965) and *Feasting with Panthers* (London: W. H. Allen, 1967), both by Rupert Croft Cooke.

32 'I was conscious': *My Life and Times*, Octave Two, p. 28.
36 Norman Bentwich: in *My 77 Years*, London: Routledge & Kegan Paul, 1962.
38 'It was my delight': 'How I Learned Not to Hate the Jews', unpublished article.
38 'Believe it or not': *My Life and Times*, Octave Two, p. 120.
39 'He was a source': *My Life and Times*, Octave Two, p. 242.
41 'I was here': *My Life and Times*, Octave Two, p. 170.
41 'In bed that night': *My Life and Times*, Octave Two, p. 115.
47 'You have been': quoted in *My Life and Times*, Octave Two, p. 242.
47 'I remember listening': *My Life and Times*, Octave Two, p. 242.
48 'Although I was not': *My Life and Times*, Octave Two, p. 255.
49 'This annoyed me': *My Life and Times*, Octave Two, p. 252.
49 'I am grateful': *My Life and Times*, Octave Two, pp. 256–7.

4 THE VOLUNTEER AND OXFORD'S ASPIRING DREAMS

Family letters which are sparse up to this date begin to increase in number. In addition to correspondence with his parents, Mackenzie's notebooks from 1900 onwards contain poems, partially worked out ideas for plays and subjects for university essays. *The East Wind of Love* covers this period in Mackenzie's life, and the history of the Volunteers is contained in Sir John Fortescue's *A History of the British Army* (London: Macmillan, 1899–1930). Published sources for Mackenzie's Oxford are the first six numbers of the *Oxford Point of View*, *Isis* and the *Varsity*. *The Windsor Tapestry* has a long description of Magdalen College at the end of the century, but *Sinister Street* is inimitable for the summoning up of atmosphere. These are supplemented by James Morris's *Oxford* (London: Faber & Faber, 1965) and *The Oxford Book of Oxford* edited by Jan Morris (Oxford: OUP, 1978). A. J. Symons's *The Quest for Corvo* sheds some light on Harry Pirie-Gordon (Harmondsworth: Penguin, 1966). The triangular friendship between Christopher Stone, Logan Pearsall Smith and Mackenzie is drawn from the unpublished correspondence of all three and *A Portrait of Logan Pearsall Smith* edited by John Russell (London: Dropmore Press, 1950).

56 'the English landed classes': *The East Wind of Love*.
56 'When my mind': *My Life and Times*, Octave Three, p. 29.
57 'I am beginning': *The East Wind of Love*.
59 'It took a strong personality': *Literature in My Time*.
63 'Something there was': *Sinister Street*, quoted in *My Life and Times*, Octave Three, p. 108.
67 'His ability to inspire': *My Life and Times*, Octave Three, p. 164.

5 ROMEO, LOTHARIO AND HARLEQUIN

Guy and Pauline is the fictional account of Mackenzie's love affair with Ruth Daniel. The unpublished sources are Mackenzie's diary, his notebooks and some letters to his mother; letters from Pearsall Smith to Christopher Stone; and the author's conversation with Terence de Vere White. Lady Ham or, in its fictional form, Plasher's Mead, still stands in Burford beside the Windrush and in the pages of *Guy and Pauline*. The turbulent months in London in the latter half of 1905, and Mackenzie's friendship and marriage, come from *Carnival* and *Sinister Street*, and from Faith Compton Mackenzie's *As Much As I Dare*. Unpublished sources are a copious correspondence between Faith and her father Edward Stone, and between Mackenzie and both his parents. The author's conversations with de Vere White shed light on Mackenzie's feelings for Ruth Daniel and his motives for marrying Faith Stone.

69 'I see her now': *My Life and Times*, Octave Three, p. 103.
70 'I sat down': *My Life and Times*, Octave Three, pp. 147–8.
73 'From that moment': *My Life and Times*, Octave Three, pp. 198–9.

76 'Guy Hazlewood's poems': letter to Compton Mackenzie quoted in *My Life and Times*, Octave Four, p. 236.

79 'My first impression': Faith Compton Mackenzie, *As Much As I Dare*, pp. 164–5.

80 'If he could smile': *My Life and Times*, Octave Three, p. 238.

6 THE SEARCH FOR SELF-EXPRESSION

Information concerning Faith's side of the marriage comes from *As Much As I Dare*; letters to her husband, her mother-in-law (Virginia Compton) and her father (Edward Stone). Mackenzie's side is revealed in letters to his wife and his mother. His ambitions for the future are referred to in letters to his parents; in correspondence with Pearsall Smith and John Mavrogordato, and in four notebooks containing partially completed plays and melodramas, gardening notes with particular emphasis on the bulbous iris, manuscript versions of some Cornish poems and three sermons. Information about the Stone family comes from the author's conversations with Janet Stone and Anthea Secker. Edward Compton's fortunes are treated in *The Mackenzies Called Compton* and *Death of a Theatre* (Northampton: privately published, 1960), both by Lou Warwick. The family troubles are referred to especially in Faith's letters to her father, and Frank's subsequent career is contained in the author's correspondence with his family. In Cornwall Faith began to keep a diary, at first patchily but with growing regularity, which she was to continue until the 1950s. Mackenzie also developed the habit of writing regularly to his mother, usually about his debts, but also concerning his ambitions and achievements; this correspondence continued until his mother's death. Wason and Walke refer to his Cornish period. Faith's pregnancy was the subject of letters from her sister Margaret and friends, and of her own diary entries. Her unhappiness is referred to in correspondence between herself, Mackenzie and his mother.

89 'It was no doubt gratifying': quoted in Bernard Walke, *Twenty Years at St Hilary*.

94 'I suppose': *My Life and Times*, Octave Four, p. 52.

94 'I would be half listening': *My Life and Times*, Octave Four, p. 56.

96 'A sword': Faith Compton Mackenzie, *As Much As I Dare*, p. 208.

96 'In my case': *My Life and Times*, Octave Four, p. 62.

7 WRITING THE PERFECT PERFORMANCE

Secker's notes for an autobiography were published in *Blackwood's Magazine* October and November 1962; further information about his life, character and career was provided by his widow, Mrs Sylvia Secker, and son and daughter-in-law, Adrian and Anthea Secker. His correspondence with Mackenzie was considerable except during the period in 1912 when the Mackenzies were living in North Street. Mackenzie's relationship with Chrissie Maude (the stage name of Christine Humphreys) is the basis for *Carnival*; it is also alluded to in Faith's private papers. Further information about her attitude to the affair was provided by Colin Summerford in conversation with the author. The triangular relationship with Harry Pelissier was the subject of letters within the Stone family, and from Edward Stone to Mackenzie. Faith's admiration for him and his growing attachment to Fay Compton were the subjects of diary entries and letters from her to Virginia Compton. Fay Compton provides a bland picture in her autobiography *Rosemary* (London: Alston Rivers, 1926). Bernard Walke described their life at Rivière. The correspondence between Faith and her mother-in-law was frequent during this period.

103 'it betrayed no feature': Leo Robertson, *Compton Mackenzie: An Appraisal of his Literary Work*.

104 'I remember': *My Life and Times*, Octave Three, p. 294.

106 'I sat down': *My Life and Times*, Octave Four, p. 123.

8 CARNIVAL IN LONDON AND NEW YORK

The critical reputation of *Carnival* is taken from a variety of periodicals: *Punch* (25 January 1912), *Manchester Guardian* (29 January 1912) and the *Illustrated London News* (21 March 1912) provide a reasonable sample of middle-brow opinion. *As Much As I Dare* carries a vivid picture of the Mackenzies' social success, and Faith's letters to her father are primarily concerned with their financial problems. Virginia Woolf's *Mr Bennett and Mrs Brown* (London: L. & V. Woolf, 1924) provides a picture of London's intellectual climate before the war. Incidents from Mackenzie's travels in the United States appeared in *Sylvia Scarlett* and *The West Wind of Love*. His absence made for a copious exchange of letters between himself and Faith, and after her arrival in New York between herself and Virginia Compton.

9 THE GREATEST TALENT OF HIS GENERATION

Descriptions of Capri are taken from Norman Douglas's *Materials for a Description of Capri* (MS notes in the British Library); from Jessica Brett-Young's *Francis Brett-Young* (London: Heinemann, 1962); from *The Story of San Michele* by Axel Munthe (London: John Murray, 1929); from *As Much As I Dare* and from *Vestal Fire* and *Extraordinary Women*. The best portrait of J. Ellingham Brooks appears in Faith Compton Mackenzie's *Always Afternoon*, although there are also references to him in E. F. Benson's and Somerset Maugham's memoirs. Among many contemporary reviews of *Sinister Street* the two most significant were Henry James's famous article 'The Younger Generation' in the *Times Literary Supplement* of 2 April 1914 and John Mavrogordato's rebuttal in the *Bookman* of October 1915 of the suspicion, voiced most openly in the *Daily Mail*, that Mackenzie 'just wrote and wrote everything that he had experienced since the age of three or thereabouts'. The quarrel with Hugh Walpole is derived from Rupert Hart-Davis's *Hugh Walpole* (London: Macmillan, 1952); from Frank Swinnerton's *Figures in the Foreground* and

Swinnerton: an autobiography; and from the author's conversation with Swinnerton. The relationship with Henry James is based on his and Virginia Compton's letters to Mackenzie; the latter's account of his meeting with James appears in four of his books of reminiscence. The picture of Casa Solitaria and the description of the writing of *Guy and Pauline* come from Faith's private papers and *As Much As I Dare*.

122 'Wherever we looked': *My Life and Times*, Octave Four, p. 182.

132 'There is no book': S. N. Behrman, *Conversation with Max*, London: Hamish Hamilton, 1960.

134 'It is lavish': Frank Swinnerton, *The Georgian Literary Scene*.

135 'Compton Mackenzie came': Max Beerbohm, *Letters to Reggie Turner*, London: Hart-Davis, 1964.

136 'not a conversion': *My Life and Times*, Octave Four, p. 214.

139 'the gift of belonging': Faith Compton Mackenzie, *More Than I Should*.

143 'I could not honestly claim': *My Life and Times*, Octave Four, p. 243.

144 'I never did see': Faith Compton Mackenzie, *As Much As I Dare*, p. 261.

10 Z IS FOR SPY

Other than Mackenzie's wartime memoirs and personal papers, the sources for his military service are those documents in the Public Records Office which refer to the Secret Service in the eastern Mediterranean, principally in WO 106 5128–31, and partly in PRO ADM 137–2172; FO 372/845 contains the Foreign Office instructions for setting up the Athens visa office on which Britain's overseas espionage was modelled for a generation. Published sources include Wilfred Macartney's *Zig-Zag* (London: Gollancz, 1938); *My Silent War* by Kim Philby (London: MacGibbon & Kee, 1968); *25* by Beverley Nichols (London: Jonathan Cape, 1926); *Tales of Aegean Intrigue* by J. C. Lawson (London: Chatto & Windus, 1920); G. F. Abbott's *Greece and the Allies, 1914–1922* (London: Methuen, 1922); the *Political Memoirs* of Prince Nicholas of Greece (London: Hutchinson, 1928); *The Allied Secret Service in Greece* by Basil Thomson (London: Hutchinson, 1931); and *The Unification of Greece* by Douglas Dakin (London: Benn, 1972). Faith Compton Mackenzie's life during the war is drawn from her autobiographies and personal papers, supplemented by the author's conversation with Colin Summerford.

151 'No one is better aware': *Athenian Memories*.

153 'He offered me': *Athenian Memories*.

154 'So from that practical': *My Life and Times*, Octave Five, p. 44.

155 'from the first moment': *Athenian Memories*.

155 'The quickness of his mind': Frank Swinnerton, *Figures in the Foreground*.

159 'An absurd creature': *Athenian Memories*.

162 'The selflessness': *Greek Memories*.

171 'The only thing': *The South Wind of Love*.

11 LOSS OF FAITH

In addition to the sources for pre-war Capri, information comes from *Pinorman* by Richard Aldington (London: Heinemann, 1954); *Francis Brett Young* by Jessica Brett Young (Heinemann, 1962); *The Letters of D. H. Lawrence* (Cambridge: CUP, 1981); *D. H. Lawrence: The Man and the Work* by Emile Delavenay (London: Heinemann, 1972); *D. H. Lawrence: A Composite Biography* by Edward Nehls (Milwaukee: University of Wisconsin Press, 1957–9). For Faith Compton Mackenzie's affair with Nini Caracciolo, the sources are her private papers and the recollections of Colin Summerford. For the shift in Mackenzie's critical reputation, see especially Schofield Thayer in *The Dial* (30 November 1918); T. S. Eliot in *The Dial* (23 September 1922); Douglas Goldring's *Reputations: Essays in Criticism*; Katherine Mansfield's *Novels and Novelists*; *The Georgian Literary Scene* by Frank Swinnerton; Arthur Waugh's *Tradition and Change* (London: Chapman & Hall, 1919). Mackenzie's personal life is taken from personal papers, Martin Secker's correspondence and the letters of Christopher Stone.

175 'Why don't you both admit': quoted in *My Life and Times*, Octave Five, p. 131.

185 'How right he was!': *My Life and Times*, Octave Five, p. 155.

192 'innate homosexuality': *The West Wind of Love*.

192 'Don't let us': quoted in *My Life and Times*, Octave Five, p. 170.

192–3 'If you are thinking': quoted in *My Life and Times*, Octave Five, p. 235.

12 THE MAN WHO LOVED ISLANDS

The details of Mackenzie's life in the period between leaving Capri and going to live on Herm come from published sources already cited, supplemented by correspondence with his mother, Martin Secker, Christopher Stone and Faith Compton Mackenzie; and from the author's conversations with Frank Swinnerton and Terence de Vere White. The fortunes of the Compton family and particularly Virginia Compton's experiences with the Nottingham Repertory Company are derived from *The Mackenzies Called Compton*, the correspondence of Mackenzie, his wife and mother, and the author's correspondence with members of Frank Compton's family. Mackenzie's life on Herm and Jethou is derived not only from the autobiographies of his wife and himself, but also from Faith Compton Mackenzie's diaries and D. H. Lawrence's two stories, *Two Bluebirds* and *The Man Who Loved Islands* (*The Dial*, April and July 1928). Eric and Ralph Pinker's correspondence, supplemented by fragmentary correspondence with the Treasury and Inland Revenue, provides the details of Mackenzie's financial and literary affairs. The *Gramophone* story comes from early issues of the magazine, most of Mackenzie's reminiscences, especially *A Musical Chair* and *My Record of Music*, and from *The Fabulous Phonograph* by Roland Gelatt (London: Cassell, 1977), supplemented by a copious correspondence with Christopher Stone. Mackenzie's writing regimen is described in his reminiscences

Reaped and Bound – 'Writing for Money' – and in his unpublished collection of articles, *Pages in Waiting*.

201 'Monty was thirty-eight': Faith Compton Mackenzie, *More Than I Should*, p. 60.

203 'The last thing': quoted in *My Life and Times*, Octave Seven, p. 120.

203 'It is his habit': Frank Swinnerton, *Figures in the Foreground*.

204 'If he had passed': Leo Robertson, *Compton Mackenzie: An Appraisal of his Literary Work*.

209 'I could not help': *My Life and Times*, Octave Six, p. 171.

210 'Next morning': *My Life and Times*, Octave Five, p. 224.

211 'I found him cordial': Andrew Turnbull, ed., *The Letters of F. Scott Fitzgerald*, Harmondsworth: Penguin, 1968.

212 'a witty and unpleasant': *New Statesman*, 12 November 1927.

212 'Having had the enterprise': quoted in *My Life and Times*, Octave Six, p. 149.

219 Oliver St John Gogarty: in *My Life and Times*, Octave Six, pp. 39–40.

220 'I count myself': contribution to *Voices From the Hills*, Glasgow: privately published, 1925.

13 THE JACOBITE BECOMES A LORD RECTOR

The upsurge in Scottish Nationalism and the literary revival known as the Scottish Renaissance are described in *Scottish Nationalism and Cultural Identity in the Twentieth Century* by Gordon Bryan (London: Greenwood, 1985); *Scottish Nationalism* by H. J. Hanham (London: Faber & Faber, 1969); *The Scottish Novel* by F. R. Hart (London: John Murray, 1978); *The Northern Muse* by John Buchan (London: Thomas Nelson, 1924); *Scott and Scotland: The Predicament of the Scottish Writer* by Edwin Muir (London: Routledge, 1936); *The Letters of Hugh MacDiarmid* edited by Alan Bold (London: Hamish Hamilton, 1984); and in Eric Linklater's novel *Magnus Merriman* (London: Jonathan Cape, 1934). *Looking Northward* was included in *Voices From the Hills*, a collection of proto-nationalist articles. *The North Wind of Love* gives a close account of Mackenzie's part in the early days of the National Party. The *Pictish Review* is useful for Mackenzie and MacDiarmid's collaboration. Lady Mackenzie provided useful information about her father and mother, Malcolm and Barabel MacSween, and her sister Chrissie, the second Lady Mackenzie. The main source for his BBC talks is the BBC Written Archives at Caversham near Reading: these contain many of the 500 broadcasts he gave between 1928 and his death, together with the repeated scuffling over fees and his fluctuating popularity with producers. The brief occupation of Eilean Aigas is drawn substantially from Faith Compton Mackenzie's diary and letters to her mother-in-law; from Mackenzie's sparser letters to Christopher Stone and his mother; from conversations with Robin MacEwen and Lord Boothby; and from *More Than I Should*. Pinker's correspondence is the prime source for his financial affairs. Mackenzie's Scottish Nationalist beliefs are summed up in his address as Rector of Glasgow University, printed as Appendix B in *My Life and Times*, Octave Seven, and in John Ogilvie's long testimony in *The North Wind of Love*. They are supplemented by reports in *The Scotsman*, Lewis Grassic Gibbon (James Leslie Mitchell)'s comments in *Scottish Scene* (London: Jarrold's, 1934) and MacDiarmid's in the same volume, and by conversation with Robin Mac-Ewen, Sir Alexander's son, and Frank Swinnerton.

221 'the bottle-green water': *My Life and Times*, Octave Six, p. 89.

222 Trades Union Congress: see Gordon Bryan, *Scottish Nationalism and Cultural Identity in the Twentieth Century*.

224 'We will never': *The Letters of Hugh MacDiarmid*.

224 'Of what we discussed': *The North Wind of Love*.

225 'I would not face': letter to Compton Mackenzie quoted in *My Life and Times*, Octave Six, p. 133.

227 'a Scots Catholic kingdom': Lewis Grassic Gibbon and Hugh MacDiarmid, *Scottish Scene*.

227 'upon the real ground': Lewis Grassic Gibbon and Hugh MacDiarmid, *Scottish Scene*.

228 'He addressed her': *My Life and Times*, Octave Six, p. 152.

230 'So when *Extremes Meet*': *My Life and Times*, Octave Six, p. 171.

14 FROM DOCK TO COCKLE BEACH

Barra was the subject of a BBC talk, 'Living Off the Map', given in 1936; other information about Mackenzie's association with the island comes from correspondence with Dr J. L. Campbell, conversation with Ruairidh Mackay and others who knew Mackenzie there; Faith Compton Mackenzie's diary and her letters to her brother and mother-in-law; Mackenzie's letters to these two and to his wife. The published sources are *I Crossed the Minch* by Louis MacNeice (London: Longmans, 1938); *The Book of Barra* edited by J. L. Campbell (London; Routledge, 1936); *Tales of Barra* told by John MacPherson (the Coddie) with a foreword by Compton Mackenzie (Edinburgh: privately published, 1960); *The Man on My Back* by Eric Linklater (London: Macmillan, 1941); *A Fretful Midge* by Terence de Vere White (London: Routledge & Kegan Paul, 1957). Mackenzie's trial under the Official Secrets Act comes substantially from his own account in his autobiography, supplemented by *The Times* reports and comment. As to its origins, in his foreword to the amended edition of *Greek Memories*, Mackenzie refers to a letter from T. E. Lawrence identifying those responsible for instigating the prosecution, which he planned to lodge in the library of Magdalen College; no such letter can be found there, and the nearest to such a thing – the letter quoted in the text, which is held by the University of Texas – names only Eric Holt-Wilson. However, Lady Lovat's letters make it clear that the Foreign Office and MI6 were also involved. Given the mistrust between MI5 and MI6 (which was to facilitate the latter's penetration by Kim

Philby), Mackenzie's presumption that a vendetta between the two departments was also a factor seems well-founded. Unfortunately the intelligence community's greater distrust of public knowledge makes it impossible to prove or disprove. Virginia Compton's last years are well documented in her correspondence with her son and daughter-in-law, her family reminiscences, and in correspondence concerning the Theatre Girls' Club; published sources are *Always Afternoon* and *The Mackenzies Called Compton*.

244 'The older I get': *The South Wind of Love*.
251 'My first emotion': *My Life and Times*, Octave Seven, pp. 96–8.
253 'Those who moved': *My Life and Times*, Octave Six, p. 105.
254 'My thoughts turned': Kim Philby, *My Silent War*.
260 'like all good houses': Eric Linklater, *The Man on My Back*.
262 'a persistent autogamy': Eric Linklater, *The Man on My Back*.
265 'To see him': Eric Linklater, *The Man on My Back*.

15 THE WINDS OF LOVE

Critical opinions of *The Four Winds of Love* are taken from the *Commonweal* of 28 June 1948; *The Tablet* of 23 November 1940; F. R. Hart's *The Scottish Novel*; and White's *A Fretful Midge*. The circumstances of *The Windsor Tapestry* are based upon the author's conversation with Joyce Weiner and contemporary reports in the *Sunday Pictorial* and *Sunday Despatch*. *Edward VIII* by Frances Donaldson (London: Weidenfeld & Nicolson, 1974) provides a modern account of the Abdication.

275 Intellective Novel: Leo Robertson, *Compton Mackenzie: An Appraisal of his Literary Work*.
276 'When war came': *The South Wind of Love*.
276 'As I see': *The West Wind of Love*.
277 'Your mind sprawls': *The West Wind of Love*.
283 'I saw again': *My Life and Times*, Octave Seven, pp. 272–5.
284 'Faith always began': *My Life and Times*, Octave Eight, p. 111.
285 'After tea': *My Life and Times*, Octave Eight, p. 41.

16 THE BLAST OF WAR

The mental and emotional crisis of the early war years is conveyed in Mackenzie's letters to his mother and the outpoured venom in *Calvary*, a volume which also contains a more sober and moving contribution from Faith Compton Mackenzie. Barra in wartime is taken from Faith Compton Mackenzie's letters to her husband and brother; from Mackenzie's correspondence with Christopher Stone; from Lord Boothby's *Recollections of a Rebel* (London: Hutchinson, 1978) and *My Yesterday, Your Tomorrow* (London: Hutchinson, 1962); and from *The Western Isles of Scotland* by Alasdair Alpin MacGregor (London: Robert Hale, 1949). The renewal of Mackenzie's Greek enthusiasm comes from *Greece in My Life*, his correspondence concerning the League for Democracy in Greece, and the author's correspondence with Diana Pym, the League's present secretary. His life after returning to London comes from his correspondence with his wife, supplemented by the author's conversations with Norah Smallwood, Terence de Vere White, T. E. B. Howarth and Joyce Weiner.

290 'Up in Harris': *My Life and Times*, Octave Eight, p. 101.

293 'Kilwhillie's faded eyes': *The Monarch of the Glen*.

297 'Critics always suggest': *My Life and Times*, Octave Eight, p. 227.

300 'Compton Mackenzie': Michael Davie, ed., *The Diaries of Evelyn Waugh*, Harmondsworth: Penguin, 1979.

300 'I met him': Edmund Wilson, *Letters on Literature and Politics 1912–72*,

301 'He was of course': *Sunday Telegraph*, 3 December 1972.

303 'Barra had been': *My Life and Times*, Octave Eight, p. 245.

17 HIS LAST BOW

Mackenzie's journeys through India, the Middle and Far East are detailed in *All Over the Place*. His literary reputation fluctuated from Angus Wilson's attack on Mackenzie, Cannan, Beresford and Walpole in the *Listener* of 12 April 1951 to John Raymond's praise for his comic inventiveness in the *New Statesman* of 25 December 1954 and the opinion of Edmund Wilson expressed in the *New Yorker* of 2 June 1962 and in his letters that Mackenzie's gifts were underestimated. Mackenzie's post-war life in England is referred to in *A Fretful Midge*, and further information comes from the author's conversations with Norah Smallwood, Terence de Vere White, Joyce Weiner, T. E. B. Howarth and Janet Stone, and from the letters of many friends and acquaintances. After his return to Edinburgh, additional information comes from *Friends, Foes and Foreigners* by Robert Bruce Lockhart (London: Putnam, 1957); *Edinburgh* by Eric Linklater (London: Newnes, 1960); and from conversations with Lady Mackenzie, Marjorie Linklater and Sir Rupert Hart-Davis. His attitude towards Greece and the question of *enosis* with Cyprus is to be found in his 'Sidelight' column for *The Spectator* from March 1954 to February 1955 and his correspondence with the League for Democracy in Greece. The filming of *The Glory that was Greece* is covered by his own account and correspondence in the BBC Written Archives. The identification of Henry Fortescue in *Thin Ice* with Lord Lloyd and Harold Nicolson comes from conversation with Lady Mackenzie and Terence de Vere White. The sources for Faith Compton Mackenzie's last years are her diary and the recollections of Lady Mackenzie, Colin Summerford, Joyce Weiner and Sir Rupert Hart-Davis. An enormous number of newspaper clippings bear testimony to Mackenzie's stature as an Edinburgh celebrity. His obituaries are taken from: Peter Lewis in the *Daily Mail* of 1 December 1972, Lord Boothby on BBC Radio 4 on 1 December 1972, and Eric Linklater in the *Sunday Telegraph* of 3 December 1972.

310 'I asked': *My Life and Times*, Octave Nine, p. 261.

318 'If by God's grace': *My Life and Times*, Octave One, p. 16.

319 'the inspiration': *My Life and Times*, Octave One, p. 15.

List of Compton Mackenzie's works

1907 *Poems* (Basil Blackwell)
1911 *The Passionate Elopement* (Martin Secker)
1912 *Carnival* (Martin Secker)
     Kensington Rhymes (Martin Secker)
1913 *Sinister Street*, Volume One (Martin Secker)
1914 *Sinister Street*, Volume Two (Martin Secker)
1915 *Guy and Pauline* (Martin Secker)
1919 *The Early Life and Adventures of Sylvia Scarlett* (Martin Secker)
     Sylvia and Michael (Martin Secker)
     Poor Relations (Martin Secker)
1920 *The Vanity Girl* (Cassell)
1921 *Rich Relatives* (Martin Secker)
1922 *The Altar Steps* (Cassell)
1923 *The Seven Ages of Woman* (Martin Secker)
     The Parson's Progress (Cassell)
1924 *The Old Men of the Sea* (later *Paradise for Sale*) (Cassell)
     Santa Claus in Summer (Constable)
     The Heavenly Ladder (Cassell)
1925 *Coral* (Cassell)
1926 *Fairy Gold* (Cassell)
1927 *Vestal Fire* (Cassell)
     Rogues and Vagabonds (Cassell)
1928 *Extremes Meet* (Cassell)
     Extraordinary Women (Martin Secker)
1929 *The Three Couriers* (Cassell)
     Gallipoli Memories (Cassell)
1930 *April Fools* (Cassell)
     Told (Basil Blackwell). A collection of children's stories.
1931 *Buttercups and Daisies* (Cassell)
     First Athenian Memories (later *Athenian Memories*) (Cassell)
     Our Street (Cassell)
1932 *Unconsidered Trifles* (Martin Secker). A collection of articles.
     Prince Charlie (Peter Davies)
1933 *Reaped and Bound* (Martin Secker). Collected essays.
     The Lost Cause (Oliver & Boyd). A play.
     Water on the Brain (Cassell)
     Literature in My Time (Rich & Cowan)
1934 *The Darkening Green* (Cassell)

Prince Charlie and his Ladies (Cassell)
Marathon and Salamis (Peter Davies)
1936 *Catholicism and Scotland* (Routledge)
Figure of Eight (Cassell)
1937 *The East Wind of Love* (Rich & Cowan)
Pericles (Hodder & Stoughton)
The South Wind of Love (Rich & Cowan)
1938 *The Windsor Tapestry* (Rich & Cowan)
1939 *A Musical Chair* (Chatto & Windus). *Gramophone* editorials.
Greek Memories (Cassell). Revised edition.
1940 *Aegean Memories* (Chatto & Windus)
The West Wind of Love (Chatto & Windus)
1941 *The Red Tapeworm* (Chatto & Windus)
The Monarch of the Glen (Chatto & Windus)
West to North (Chatto & Windus). Volume Two of *The West Wind of Love*.
1942 *Calvary* (John Lane). With Faith Compton Mackenzie.
1943 *Wind of Freedom* (Chatto & Windus). Greece at war.
Mr Roosevelt (Harrap). A biography.
Keep the Home Guard Turning (Chatto & Windus)
1945 *The North Wind of Love* (Chatto & Windus). In two volumes.
1946 *Dr Beneš* (Harrap). A biography.
1947 *The Vital Flame* (British Gas Council). The gas industry.
Whisky Galore (Chatto & Windus)
1948 *All Over the Place* (Chatto & Windus). Travels in India, etc.
1949 *Hunting the Fairies* (Chatto & Windus)
1951 *The House of Coalport* (Collins). The china firm.
Sublime Tobacco (Chatto & Windus). The tobacco industry.
I Took a Journey (Naldrett Press). A tour of National Trust properties.
Eastern Epic (Chatto & Windus). A history of the Indian Army.
1952 *The Rival Monster* (Chatto & Windus)
1953 *The Savoy of London* (Harrap). The Savoy hotel.
The Queen's House (Hutchinson). A history of Buckingham Palace.
1954 *Ben Nevis Goes East* (Chatto & Windus)
Realms of Silver (Routledge & Kegan Paul). A history of the Chartered Bank.
Echoes (Chatto & Windus). Collected broadcasts.
1955 *My Record of Music* (Hutchinson). Collected music articles.
1956 *Thin Ice* (Chatto & Windus)
1957 *Rockets Galore* (Chatto & Windus)
1959 *The Lunatic Republic* (Chatto & Windus)
1960 *Cat's Company* (Elek Books). Memories of cats.
Greece in My Life (Chatto & Windus). Memories of Greece.

1961 *Catmint* (Barrie & Rockliffe). Captions to photographs of cats.
     Mezzotint (Chatto & Windus)
1962 *On Moral Courage* (Collins). Observations on moral courage.
1963 *My Life and Times*, Octave One (Chatto & Windus)
1964 *My Life and Times*, Octave Two (Chatto & Windus)
     My Life and Times, Octave Three (Chatto & Windus)
1965 *My Life and Times*, Octave Four (Chatto & Windus)
     The Stolen Soprano (Chatto & Windus)
1966 *My Life and Times*, Octave Five (Chatto & Windus)
     Paper Lives (Chatto & Windus)
1967 *My Life and Times*, Octave Six (Chatto & Windus)
1968 *My Life and Times*, Octave Seven (Chatto & Windus)
     Robert Louis Stevenson (Morgan-Grampian). A biography.
     The Strongest Man on Earth (Chatto & Windus)
1969 *My Life and Times*, Octave Eight (Chatto & Windus)
1970 *My Life and Times*, Octave Nine (Chatto & Windus)
1971 *My Life and Times*, Octave Ten (Chatto & Windus)

Bibliography

UNPUBLISHED SOURCES

(Unless otherwise indicated, these are held by the University of Texas at Austin in the Humanities Research Center.)

Notebooks dating from 1895–1909 containing schoolboy notes such as cricket teams, library lists, the manuscript of *Hectoma*, first poems dating from the summer of 1900, university exam questions, ideas for plays dating from 1902–04, poems from the same period; fragments, first acts or almost complete versions of some dozen melodramas and plays including *Tomorrow*; and three sermons.

Manuscripts of 26 collections of short stories.

Manuscripts of 11 broadcasts.

Manuscripts of 21 plays.

Manuscripts of 119 magazine articles (excluding TSS of articles for *Daily Mail* c. 240; *Sunday Despatch* c. 145; and *Gramophone* c. 220).

Compton Mackenzie (CM)'s correspondence with his mother, Virginia Compton dating from 1902–40.

CM's correspondence with his father, Edward Compton, dating from 1904–15.

CM's correspondence with his wife, Faith Compton Mackenzie, dating from 1905–55.

CM's correspondence with his brother-in-law, Christopher Stone, dating from 1920–44.

CM's correspondence with his father-in-law, Edward Stone, dating from 1905–14.

CM's correspondence with Martin Secker, dating from 1910–40.

CM's correspondence with J. B., Eric and Ralph Pinker, dating from 1914–38.

Letters to CM from: Logan Pearsall Smith [held by Adrian and Anthea Secker], John Hope-Johnstone, John Mavrogordato, Orlo Williams, Captain Mansfield Cumming, D. H. Lawrence, Francis Brett-Young, Hugh MacDiarmid, Veronica Fraser, John MacPherson (the Coddie), Desmond Flower, Robert Boothby, Eric Linklater, Norah Smallwood and Ian Parsons.

Miscellaneous correspondence, BBC memoranda, etc. concerning CM's broadcasts for the BBC, dating from 1928–58 [held by BBC Written Archives at Caversham, Reading].

Faith Compton Mackenzie [FCM]'s diaries from 1909–57.

FCM's letters to Virginia Compton, dating from 1906–40.

FCM's letters to Christopher Stone, dating from 1920–45 [held by A. and A. S.].

FCM's letters to Edward Stone dating from 1908–16.

Miscellaneous letters to FCM referring to a premarital affair, the stillbirth of her child, life on Capri, and *Gramophone* business.

Virginia Compton's memoirs of her father, Hezekiah Linthicum Bateman; her mother, Sydney Frances Bateman; her eldest sister, Kate Crowe and her husband, Dr George Crowe, their daughter, Sydney, and granddaughter, Leah; her elder sister, Ellen Greppo and her husband, Claude Greppo, and their family; her brothers, Richmond and Harry; her younger sister, Isabel Bateman; and her own childhood and upbringing.

Christopher Stone's correspondence with Logan Pearsall Smith dating from 1905–15 [held by A. and A. S.].

Miscellaneous letters from Herbert Warren, President of Magdalen College, Oxford, to Edward Compton and CM; to Mrs Bateman from G. F. Watts, Anthony Trollope, James Whistler, etc.; to Virginia Compton from Lilian Baylis.

PUBLISHED SOURCES

Depending on the edition, Mackenzie wrote either 105 or 112 books, and other than the children's stories most have some autobiographical interest. Those directly relevant are:

My Life and Times: Octaves One to Ten. London: Chatto & Windus, 1963–71. Autobiography.

Gallipoli Memories, London: Cassell, 1929. War memoirs.

Athenian Memories, London: Cassell, 1931. War memoirs.

Greek Memories, London: Cassell, 1932 and 1939. War memoirs.

Aegean Memories, London: Chatto & Windus, 1940. War memoirs.

Unconsidered Trifles, London: Martin Secker, 1932. Collected magazine articles, largely reminiscences.

Literature in My Time, London: Rich & Cowan, 1933. Reminiscences of books in CM's life.

Reaped and Bound, London: Martin Secker, 1933. Collected magazine articles, containing a musical autobiography first printed in the *Gramophone*, and other pieces of reminiscence.

A Musical Chair, London: Chatto & Windus, 1939. A musical autobiography.

Echoes, London: Chatto & Windus, 1954. Collected broadcasts, largely reminiscences.

My Record of Music, London: Hutchinson, 1955. Repeated reminiscences from earlier collections.

Greece in My Life, London: Chatto & Windus, 1960. Reminiscences of Greece, frequently repeated from his war memoirs.

Faith Compton Mackenzie wrote three volumes of autobiography:

As Much As I Dare, London: Collins, 1938.
More Than I Should, London: Collins, 1940.

Always Afternoon, London: Collins, 1943.

Criticism of Compton Mackenzie

D. J. Dooley, *Compton Mackenzie*, New York: Twayne, 1974.
Leo Robertson, *Compton Mackenzie: An Appraisal of his Literary Work*, London: Richards Press, 1954.
Kenneth Young, *Compton Mackenzie*, London: Longman/British Council 'Writers and Their Work' series, 1968.

A chronological selection of reviews and analyses of Compton Mackenzie and his books.

Times Literary Supplement 10 February 1911; *The Passionate Elopement*.
Saturday Review 27 September 1913; *Sinister Street*, Volume 1.
Times Literary Supplement 2 April 1914; Henry James, 'The Younger Generation'.
Bookman October 1915; John Mavrogordato on CM and use of memory.
New Statesman 7 September 1918; *Sylvia Scarlett*.
The Dial November 1918; Schofield Thayer on CM as 'a puppetmaster'.
New Statesman 27 October 1919; *Poor Relations*.
Athenaeum 14 May 1920; Katherine Mansfield on *The Vanity Girl*.
The Dial 23 September 1922; T. S. Eliot on CM and post-war style.
Saturday Review 24 November 1923; *The Parson's Progress*.
Times Literary Supplement 7 June 1924; *Extremes Meet*.
The Editor 24 December 1927; 'A great novelist tells about his novels'.
Scottish Educational Journal 21 March 1930; C. M. Grieve on *Gallipoli Memories*.
Bookman July 1930; *April Fools*.
Times Literary Supplement 18 June 1931; *Buttercups and Daisies*.
Everyman 9 June 1932; Philip Jordan on CM as 'entertainer'.
Daily Mail 7 January 1937; Douglas West on *The East Wind of Love*.
The Tablet 23 November 1940; Derek Traversi on *The West Wind of Love*.
Times Literary Supplement 13 December 1941; *The Monarch of the Glen*.
Commonweal 28 June 1948; *The Four Winds of Love*.
Le Monde 4 October 1950; Marcel Brion on CM as 'romantic'.
Listener 12 April 1951; Angus Wilson on CM and 'Broken Promise' of 1914 writers.
The Spectator 14 September 1951; L. A. G. Strong on CM as writer of comedy.
New Statesman 25 December 1954; John Raymond on CM's perpetual youth.
Sunday Times 10 June 1956; Evelyn Waugh on *Thin Ice*.
New Yorker 2 June 1962; Edmund Wilson on CM's 'gift of style'.
Observer 20 January 1963; Angus Wilson on *My Life and Times*, Octave One.
New York Review of Books 12 March 1968; Walter Allen on CM as 'part of history of our time'.

Sunday Telegraph 3 December 1972; Eric Linklater, CM's obituary.

General criticism

A. St. J. Adcock, *Gods of Modern Grub Street*, London: Sampson Low, 1923.
Reginald Auberon, *The Nineteen Hundreds*, London: Allen & Unwin, 1922.
Richard Church, *The Growth of the English Novel*, London: Methuen, 1951.
Cyril Connolly, *Enemies of Promise*, Harmondsworth: Penguin, 1961.
J. W. Cunliffe, *English Literature During the Last Half Century*, New York: Macmillan, 1919.
John Freeman, *English Portraits and Essays*, London: Hodder & Stoughton, 1924.
Katherine F. Gerould, *Modes and Morals*, New York: Scribner's, 1920.
Douglas Goldring, *Reputations: Essays in Criticism*, London: Chapman & Hall, 1920.
Gerald Gould, *The English Novel of Today*, London: John Castle, 1924.
Philip Guedalla, *A Gallery*, London: Constable, 1924.
F. R. Hart, *The Scottish Novel*, London: John Murray, 1978.
P. P. Howe, *Malthus and the Publishing Trade*, London: Martin Secker, 1913.
S. P. Mais, *Books and Their Writers*, London: Grant Richards, 1920.
Katherine Mansfield, *Novels and Novelists*, London: Constable, 1930.
W. H. Marshall, *The World of the Victorian Novel*, London: Thomas Yoseloff, 1967.
James E. Miller jr, *The Fictional Technique of Scott Fitzgerald*, New York: New York University Press, 1964.
Mortimer Proctor, *The English University Novel*, Berkeley: University of California Press, 1957.
Lionel Stevenson, *The English Novel*, London: Constable, 1960.
Frank Swinnerton, *Background with Chorus*, London: Hutchinson, 1956.
Frank Swinnerton, *Figures in the Foreground*, London: Hutchinson, 1963.
Frank Swinnerton, *The Georgian Literary Scene*, London: Heinemann, 1935.
Frank Swinnerton, *Swinnerton: An Autobiography*, London: Hutchinson, 1937.
W. Y. Tindall, *Forces in Modern British Literature*, New York: Vintage Books, 1956.
Ioan Williams, *The Realist Novel in England*, London: Macmillan, 1974.
Edmund Wilson, *The Bit Between My Teeth*, London: W. H. Allen, 1965.
Edmund Wilson, *Letters on Literature and Politics 1912–72*, ed. Elena Wilson, London: Routledge & Kegan Paul, 1977.
Virginia Woolf, *Contemporary Writers*, London: Hogarth Press, 1965.

Index

Abbott, G. F.: *Greece and the Allies 1914–1922*, 241
Abdication crisis, 1936, 273, 279–82
Abercrombie, Lascelles, 146
Adelswaerd-Fersen, Count d' (Count Jack), 123, 140, 173, 182, 208, 211
Aegean Memories (CM), 156, 273, 287
Aickin, Eleanor, 8
Albyn Films, 303
Alexander, King of the Hellenes, 170
All Change Here (revue), 102, 105, 107
Allen, Misses (schoolteachers), 28
All Over the Place (CM), 306
Altar Steps, The (CM), 10, 117, 200
Andrew, Prince of Greece, 157, 253
Anstey, Christopher: *New Bath Guide*, 103
Anstiss, Commander, 40
Any Questions (radio programme), 302, 309
Aphrodite (boat), 201
Appletons (US publishers), 118
April Fools (CM), 214
Arcadians, The (stage musical), 97
Argyll, Niall Diarmid Campbell, 10th Duke of, 228
Arnold, Matthew, 62; *A French Eton*, 31
Arnold, Thomas, 31
Ashbourne, William Gibson, 2nd Baron, 228
Ashmead-Bartlett, Ellis, 149
Asquith, Arthur, 63
Asquith, Herbert Henry, 1st Earl of Oxford and Asquith, 164
Astor, John Jacob, 115
Athenaeum (journal), 195
Athenian Memories (CM), 156, 232–3, 242
Attewell, Captain (of Jethou), 200
Auberon, Reginald: *The Nineteen Hundreds*, 103
Auchinleck, Field-Marshal Sir Claude, 306–7, 309
Auden, W. H.: *The Orators*, 238
Austen, John, 101
Austen, Katie (*née* Compton), 33, 85, 101, 197–8
Avonmore Road, West Kensington, 11–12, 59

Baker, Hilary (Nellie's daughter), 187, 209
Baker, Nellie (*later* Eastwood), 115, 181–2, 187, 209
Baldwin, Stanley, 233, 279, 281

Balfe, Michael William, 312
Balkans: in World War I, 150–1
Ball, Lewis, 8
Baring, Maurice, 235
Barra: CM visits, 245–6, 255, 257, 282; CM builds house on, 259–61; life on, 260–4; in World War II, 289–97, 299; CM's comedies on, 289–97; CM leaves, 303–4; CM buried on, 323–4
Barrie, James Matthew, 115
Barry, Shiel, 102
Barrymore, John, 119
Bartlett, Dr ('Dr Waggett'), 261, 291, 295–6
Bateman, Ellen *see* Greppo, Ellen
Bateman, Frank (died as baby), 20
Bateman, Harry (CM's uncle), 18
Bateman, Hezekiah Linthicum (CM's maternal grandfather), 5–6, 17, 19–20, 217
Bateman, Isabel (CM's aunt), 18–22, 28, 45, 56; death, 256
Bateman, Kate *see* Crowe, Kate
Bateman, Richmond (CM's uncle), 18
Bateman, Sydney Frances (*née* Cowell; CM's maternal grandmother), 17–21
Baylis, Lilian, 257
Beach, Sylvia, 188
Beech Farm, Hampshire, 40–1, 45, 52, 214, 283
Beerbohm, Max, 125, 132, 135, 284
Bellinger, Alfred, 129
Belloc, Hilaire, 300
Beneš, Edvard, 297, 300
Bennett, Arnold, 114, 116, 259
Benson, E. F., 124
Bentwich, Norman, 36
Betjeman, John, 310
Birdwood, General Sir William, 148
Birkenruth, Adolf, 49
Black Hand (Tserna Rouka), 159, 163
Blackwell's (publishers), 88
Blücher, Field-Marshal Gebhart Lebrecht von, Prince, 199
Bode, Milton, 45, 197
Boer War, 52, 55, 62
Bone, Muirhead, 102, 117
Bonham-Carter, Guy, 63, 73, 301
Bonnie Prince Charlie (CM), see *Prince Charlie*
Book Society, 304

343